THE DISCOVERY OF

CW00740198

The Discovery of Islands consists of a series of linked essays in British history, written by one of the world's leading historians of ideas and published at intervals over the past generation. The purpose of the essays is to present British history as the history of several nations interacting with – and sometimes seceding from – association with an imperial state. The American colonies seceded in the eighteenth century; most of Ireland seceded in the twentieth century; in the later part of that century Britain itself secedes from the association of nations it has built up across the globe.

John Pocock presents this history as that of an archipelago, situated in oceans and expanding across them to the Antipodes. Both New Zealand history and ways of seeing history formed in New Zealand enter into the overall vision, and the aim is to present British history as oceanic and global, complementing (and occasionally criticizing) the presentation of that history as European. Professor Pocock's interpretation of British history has been hugely influential in recent years, making *The Discovery of Islands* a resource of immense value for historians of Britain, of the British Empire, and indeed of the world. The title itself is derived from the poetry of Allen Curnow (1911–2001).

J. G. A. POCOCK is Harry C. Black Professor Emeritus at the Johns Hopkins University.

THE DISCOVERY OF ISLANDS

Essays in British History

J. G. A. POCOCK

CAMBRIDGE
UNIVERSITY PRESS

CAMBRIDGE UNIVERSITY PRESS
Cambridge, New York, Melbourne, Madrid, Cape Town, Singapore, São Paulo

CAMBRIDGE UNIVERSITY PRESS
The Edinburgh Building, Cambridge CB2 2RU, UK
Published in the United States of America by Cambridge University Press, New York

www.cambridge.org
Information on this title: www.cambridge.org/9780521616454

First published 2005

Printed in the United Kingdom at the University Press, Cambridge

A catalogue record for this book is available from the British Library

ISBN-13 978-0-521-85095-7 hardback
ISBN-10 0-521-85095-9 hardback
ISBN-13 978-0-521-61645-4 paperback
ISBN-10 0-521-61645-X paperback

How shall I compare the discovery of islands?
History had many instinctive processes,
Past reason's range, green innocence of nerves,
Now all destroyed by self-analysis . . .

Compare, compare, now horrible untruth
Rings true in our obliterating season:
Our islands lost again, all earth one island,
And all our travel circumnavigation.

From Discovery (c. 1941) by Allen Curnow (1911–2001).

Contents

vii

Preface and acknowledgements

This volume presents a selection from the essays on its subject which I have published since 1974, when the first of them – Chapter 2 in this series – appeared in New Zealand. That essay has been credited with a role in initiating a project known as 'the new British history', but since the project is now quite widely practised and understood, I have not used the word 'new' in the title of this book. My intention is to present a reading of British history, and an understanding of what those words may mean, which can stand alongside other readings. There is no history which is not many-sided, and no reading to which there are not alternatives.

The essays selected are later in date than the proposal of 1974, belonging to the 1990s and the opening years of this millennium. Among the reasons for this selection, one is that this has been the decade in which the 'British history', then known as new, began to be written by a number of hands and to be examined, sometimes critically, in a number of collections and monographs. I have selected my own writings in order to present them as part of this literature and its problems. They deal for the most part with the period c. 1500–1800, regarding which I practise historiography; the medieval and modern periods appear marginally, but are by no means unnoticed. The essays are divided into sections suggesting a periodization, each preceded by an introductory chapter written for this volume.

There are two respects, however, in which these essays reflect concerns of my own, and include among other intentions that of furthering them. The first in order of time was delivered as a lecture in New Zealand in 1973, and was occasioned in part by the British decision to seek entry into what is now the European Union. I was, and remain, concerned with the impact of this decision on New Zealand and on the history to which we – the reader is desired to note this currently unfashionable pronoun – knew ourselves as belonging. In presenting 'British history' as archipelagic rather than English, I was seeking to present it as a product of many makers – and some unmakers – in which 'we' had voice and which could not be simply unmade by anyone. As well as reminding the British peoples that they inhabited a history more complex than they could readily terminate, this involved continuing that history past the point where New Zealand history had first appeared as one of its components. At that point it became a history perceived from New Zealand and in part made by that perception. I have included essays on ways in which New Zealand continues the 'British history' I have been recommending, and have added others explaining this history as the product of an antipodean perception that can be presented to readers generally. The title of this volume, and the verse accompanying it, drawn from New Zealand poetry,[1] conveys this perception. There are points at which I have also conveyed it by resorting to autobiography, and I trust the reader to accept that I am presenting myself as a piece of historical evidence.

The second aspect of this volume I should mention is that it contains essays and other passages critical of the idea of 'Europe'. British history of course belongs to the history of that globally expansive civilization, originally formed in the western provinces of the European, or Eurasian, sub-continent, to which its own complex of islands may rightly be seen as belonging. I am critical only – but for many reasons – of the proposition that British, in particular English, interactions with the cultures of the adjacent sub-continent in some way diminish, or even eliminate, the history of interactions and processes within the archipelago, moving outward into the Atlantic and the global oceans, the Americas and the Antipodes. I hold that English and British history can and should be written in both a sub-continental and an oceanic perspective, and I am critical of the proposition that either subverts the other. I am sceptical of the idea of 'Europe' when it appears to advance this proposition; when I suspect it of a design to eliminate distinctive histories and sovereignties; and when I find it incapable of distinguishing between scepticism and hostility. All of these conditions arise too often for comfort.

The 'British history' here presented continues to face the problem of how far it can escape the Anglocentricity it was intended to replace; the problem being that it is inescapably, though partially, the history of an English dominance, which the English saw and conducted as a product of their internal politics, while other peoples responded to it, sought to share it, or in some cases resolved to secede from it altogether. All these reactions – the American and Irish secessions not excluded – form part of 'British

---

[1] Curnow, 1943; 1997, p. 217.

history' as I would like it to be understood; for even a secession is part of the history from which it secedes. I understand an Irish desire to see their history in a context outside the obsessive relation with England and Britain to which it has been so much confined; and such a history might well be written on any terms which do not pretend that this relation and obsession have not existed. While there is a 'British history' to be written around a central Anglo-Scottish polarity, one written around a British-Irish polarity would perhaps penetrate more deeply into the histories of two profoundly different cultures which have been historically inseparable. Methodologically, I am interested in the relation between 'national' and 'extra-national' historiographies; ideologically, I am making the claim that both probably will, and should, continue to exist.

A volume such as this is necessarily indebted to many helpers. The footnote references and Bibliography B extend the record of this indebtedness. I must begin by naming Richard Fisher of Cambridge University Press, who proposed the collection and has endured its successive mutations with good humour and sound advice; and the anonymous readers for that Press who have counselled me on successive drafts. On English history I have learned in special ways from John Morrill and Jonathan Clark; on Scottish from Arthur Williamson, Roger Mason and Colin Kidd; on Irish from Jane Ohlmeyer, Ian McBride and Brendan Bradshaw; on American and the history of empire from Jack P. Greene, Eliga H. Gould and David Armitage; and on the history of political thought, as ever, from my colleagues and friends at the Folger Shakespeare Library. In the New Zealand field, I record a special debt to Andrew Sharp and Paul McHugh; one of another kind to James Belich, Judith Binney and (though this may surprise him) Te Maire Tau; while my contemporary Peter Munz will understand, though he may not approve. This is also the point at which to thank Caleb McDaniel for preparing the original typescript and Katherine Hijar for its revision. Felicity Pocock read it aloud at the proofreading stage. My grateful thanks also go to the editors and publishers of the volumes and periodicals in which most of these essays have already appeared. They are listed in the Bibliography and I take this opportunity of thanking them all. Lastly, my debt to the poems and friendship of the late Allen Curnow runs from beginning to end of this volume and holds it together.

In preparing these essays for republication, I have revised them lightly and sparingly in order to improve clarity, lessen repetition and eliminate material now obsolete. I have not attempted to preserve the footnotes in their original form, but have reduced all to author and date with reference to the two bibliographies, indicating in some cases where reference is made to works appearing since the original essay's publication. A very few *obiter dicta* are contained in the footnotes within square brackets.

Baltimore, Maryland, 2004

Note on bibliographies

I have ventured on a complete listing of my publications in the field in which this volume enters; it appears as Bibliography A. Others I have had occasion to mention are listed in Bibliography B, and are accordingly marked (B) in the footnotes.

PART I

The Field Proposed

CHAPTER I

The antipodean perception*

(1)

This introductory essay must be initially autobiographical; to explain what it is to write history from New Zealand I need to explain how I came to do it, and place myself in context as a transitory figure in the history of historiography. It is relevant to what I have to say in these essays that I am of settler descent in the fourth generation, and relevant also that though I write as a New Zealander, I write as that not uncommon phenomenon, a New Zealand expatriate. It would take a long time to explain why this is one way of being a New Zealander.

My great-grandfather, Lewis Greville Pocock (1823–88), joined his brother John Thomas (1814–76)[1] in the Cape Colony of South Africa in the year 1842, and my father, also Lewis Greville (1890–1975), after wartime service in the Royal Field Artillery, took a degree in classics at University College, London, and was appointed professor at what was then Canterbury University College in New Zealand, to which country we moved at the end of 1927, when I was three years old. I am reciting what Maori term a *whakapapa*, a record of one's ancestors and the voyages by which they arrived, and it is part of this statement that his sister, Mary Agard Pocock (1886–1977), became professor of botany in what was then Rhodes University College in Grahamstown, Cape Province, so that the move from middle-class business to middle-class professional life was made by both genders in the generation before my own. If I am a fourth-generation colonist, I am a second-generation academic.

I studied the classics, my father's subject, since I was of the last generation to learn Latin because that was the way to become educated and had been

---

*[Written for this volume in 2003.]

[1] For him see Ashworth, 1974; Holder and Gee, 1980; and Pocock (Tom), 1996.

for a thousand years;[2] but of history, which was to be my main subject, I learned more than any school was able to teach me from my mother, born Antoinette Le Gros (1889–1976), who continued as a teacher after she moved to New Zealand. It is relevant to the theme of these essays that she was by birth a Channel Islander, the daughter of a French-speaking Methodist minister; how there came to be such people is an episode in 'British history' as I suggest it should be studied. Of settler descent on my father's side, I am on hers descended from an island people on the seas between the Atlantic archipelago and the peninsula of Europe; a fragment of the ancient duchy of Normandy which conquered England in 1066, never fully incorporated in the United Kingdom which it now serves as a tax shelter. I recall visiting St Heliers with my mother and sister in 1950, and seeing engraved on the wall of some public building – perhaps that of the States of Jersey? – a couplet by the Norman chronicler Wace:

> Jeo di et dirai ki jeo sui,
> Wace de l'isle de Gersui.

By that time I knew about islands and the need to proclaim oneself from them. It was a lesson I had learned in the Antipodes.

(II)

The New Zealand in which I grew up, during the 1930s and 1940s, no longer exists, though a little digging will reveal many of its virtues and limitations still operating. Though it has disappeared, it is entitled to the respect and understanding due to the phenomena of history, and I describe it here because it shaped a view of history which I still find valid. It consisted of a small and fairly recent human population and their cultures, occupying an archipelago of two major and many lesser islands situated on the globe at a point nearly but not quite the antipodes of the Atlantic archipelago with which most of these essays deal. The New Zealand archipelago is one of a chain of sharply distinct ecosystems running from Indonesia through Papua-Melanesia and Australia, but oceanic distance, currents and weather systems have meant that it has had very limited contact with any of these. It was colonized from the central Pacific; that is, the first terrestrial mammals, who were members of the human species,

---

[2] I attended Medbury School, a private institution in Christchurch, and recollect arriving there at the age of eight to find the first declension of the Latin noun already written on the blackboard. I was neither astonished nor oppressed by this experience, and found ways of profiting by it.

arrived from that quarter a thousand years ago or less,[3] in ocean-going galleys called *waka*,[4] and found the islands populated by large birds, of whom many species had become flightless in the absence of predators. The humans rapidly exterminated most of these, imposing on themselves changes in economy and culture which archaeology does more than tradition to recapture.[5] These occurred in the course of settlement and colonization, in an environment radically unlike that of the central Pacific's island systems; the major islands contained alpine ranges as well as volcanic peaks, and presented sizeable interior spaces of grassland, forest, and rock, snow and ice above the treeline. With all of these environments the Polynesian settlers had to establish a relationship, imagining and constructing systems of animism and ancestry which permitted them to call themselves *tangata whenua*,[6] or peoples of the land. In this imagery it is noteworthy that *te whenua* – the placenta, the birthplace, the land of the ancestors – is more prominent than *te moana*, the great ocean across which the ancestors came, without as far as we know establishing two-way systems of travel or commerce. *Whakapapa* commonly end by naming the *waka* in which the ancestors arrived, but the *tangata whenua*, though descended from great navigators, seem not to think of themselves as a people of seafarers whose culture is shaped by recurrent voyaging. The migration has happened once, and ended at the *whenua*.[7]

In this – if described correctly – the *tangata whenua* differ from the *pakeha*: a word in their language used to denote the European settlers who began arriving in the early nineteenth century and now greatly outnumber them. In the New Zealand of which I write these were overwhelmingly British and Irish in both birth and conscious identity, though subsequent immigration, European, Asian and Polynesian, has changed that and made the cities multicultural as the rural areas are not, while helping to treble the population of one and a half million that I remember. This population

---

[3] The most recent findings suggest a date between AD 1200 and 1300; Howe, 2003. All such datings depend upon archaeological techniques which change and develop rapidly.

[4] These craft were driven by sail and paddle, and have often been called 'canoes'. This word seems unacceptably primitivist to some, and 'galleys' is offered here as an alternative. The crews were not of course slaves or convicts.

[5] Howe, 2003, pp. 179–82; Belich, 1996, chs. 2 and 3. For further bibliography, see Howe, p. 208, n. 51; Walker, 1990, ch. 2.

[6] In New Zealand typography, Maori words are no longer italicized, in order to avoid making Maori culture seem exotic or inferior. In this volume, italicization is practised, in order to ease acceptance of the terms by readers who will find them unfamiliar. For a glossary, see below, p. 226.

[7] For a modern statement of the Maori world view, see Walker, 1990, ch. 1. For poetic comment on the role of the ocean in Maori imagination, see Williams, n.d., p. 10 ('Stride'); Sullivan, 1999. For *whakapapa* in the city where I grew up, see Tau, 2000 and 2003.

has been arriving since the second quarter of the nineteenth century, and has always been composed of peoples whose sense of history and identity is modern and European, more secular than religious. They know they have arrived as carriers of a history in which they are already involved, and which they must both continue and change. What has been and remains at issue is their capacity, and power, to engage in this process as autonomous agents.

The voyages that brought them to their archipelago committed them, before the voyages were made, to a global system of commerce moving in many directions. Every voyage, therefore, was remembered, repeatable, and might in other circumstances not have been made; identity was optional and in that sense fragile. It has yet to appear whether the voyagers in the *waka* knew that feeling. The *pakeha* were not merely capable of the two-way voyage: they were in New Zealand to engage in a two-way commerce, which did, has done and does much to make them what they are. They have remained the people of a dependent economy, exporting products in exchange for the capital they do not generate themselves; and the markets on which they depend are situated at global distances, and have until very recently indeed been the homelands of a particular culture which the *pakeha* have inherited and imported, while wondering how far they can generate culture of their own. This in brief is the antipodean condition. It has been the product of oceanic and global distance, and the proposition that the world-wide web has abolished distance has yet to be tested against the counter-proposition that a culture formed by distance may be willing to change only at its own speeds.

The *pakeha* are a people of European, mainly British, colonists. There has occurred a remarkable shift in vocabulary, whereby the word 'imperialism', denoting among other things the subjugation of non-Europeans to European empire and culture, has been replaced by the word 'colonialism'; peoples formerly so subjected use this word to denote that state, and the word 'post-colonialism' to denote the state in which they find themselves after the empires have been liquidated. It is probably too late to alter this set of usages, and the case for doing so is not specially strong; but it is worth pointing out that colonists colonize, and are not 'colonized' in the sense appropriate to the vocabulary of (post-)colonialism. The imperial culture they brought with them was not imposed on them by alien rulers; they regarded it as theirs by inheritance, and if they come to wish neither to inherit nor to go on producing it, it is to themselves that they must explain that it is no longer their inheritance – to selves, therefore, who did think themselves native to this culture, with the result that its replacement will probably not be a revolution, certainly not a liberation, but a complex and never complete historical process. They may share with non-Europeans in the post-colonial condition a sense that they have not had a share in power sufficient to make them autonomous actors in this process; but almost certainly, they will have had enough power to make the term 'post-colonial' both metaphoric and questionable. Colonies have a way of becoming politically autonomous while remaining economically dependent and culturally 'colonial'; their history becomes one of tension between these conditions.[8]

Colonists, meaning settlers, are involved in what is now called colonialism to the extent to which they are settled among previous or indigenous populations whom they reduce to political and cultural subjection. The South African English-speakers who are among my forebears settled among both Africans and Afrikaners (a settler people of a very different type) by whom they were outnumbered, and it can be said that they never attained political or perhaps cultural autonomy. British policy in South Africa was made in London, or on the Rand, and not by them. In Australia and New Zealand, colonies were established among, and expropriated, Aboriginals and Maori. These peoples, their responses to colonization, and what it did to them, differed so greatly as to give Australian and New Zealand history radically different characters; but in neither case were relations between settlers and indigenous peoples so dominant or obsessive as to be central to the self-formation of the former. Having seized the land of the *tangata whenua*, they did not need their labour, or think about them very much, but set about the importation of a white working class, relations with whom dominated their subsequent politics and history. The New Zealand in which I grew up was able to construct a historical narrative in which Maori played no independent part after about 1870; that people has spent the last fifty years asserting itself in politics and compelling a new historiography.[9]

The history constructed and written by a settler people under these conditions will therefore be a history of itself: of the foundation of a self out of the relationships and conflicts among its component parts. The history of any political community whose awareness of a collective self requires establishment, is increasing, or has been conventionalized, is liable to be

---

[8] In this paragraph I begin to take issue with a currently dominant paradigm which presents New Zealand history since 1945 as a history of 'decolonization'. For a modified and subtle statement of this thesis, see Belich, 2001. A bibliography of recent New Zealand historical writing is not attempted here; it would be rich, complex and lengthy.

[9] Sharp, 1990, 1997; Sharp and McHugh, 2001. These titles stand for a large bibliography.

a history of self, intended for its members, of limited interest to other communities, and not requiring much attention to their histories. A rigorously critical historian will be inclined to say that this is myth, not history, since narratives intended to build up a self will be resistant to critical investigation. (Is the self also a myth?) I desire to present a more complex picture, in which the myths that form the self are always accompanied – not necessarily happily – by critical scrutiny, because the self being constructed becomes aware of its own contingency, insecurity and (in this case) antipodean remoteness. If this should appear at first sight an over-simple account of the conditions under which a critical history of self may appear, the reply is that under these conditions it is not easy to decide on a narrative in the first place.[10]

There were several narratives of settler history partaking of the character of myth: a Whig narrative of the growth of parliamentary sovereignty, relating how the crown in New Zealand had come to accept embodiment in a representative parliament; a social-democrat narrative, focussed on the growth of social welfare, an economy in which government intervened, and a politics of capital and labour; an imperial narrative, proposing that the formation of nationhood was pursued and achieved through participation in the wars – though not the wars alone – of a global British presence, culture and power. All three of these have lost much of their mythic power with the disappearances of both empire and democratic socialism and the growing alienation of the electorate from its representatives (in New Zealand, the last has led to some interesting constitutional experiments); but none has ceased to be the narrative of a process which did take place in history. They have lost mythic power because it is felt that they have ceased to supply identity; the processes they relate do not provide an imaginatively adequate account of who we are or where we have come from. The question becomes that of what narrative is to take their place, and one immediate danger – on the whole, quite successfully avoided – is that of imprisonment within a facetiously patronizing deconstructive account of these myths and any which offer to take their place. Any narrative of autonomy must instantly be rewritten from the point of view of those it fails to include; it is right to do this, but wrong to suppose that the alienation of the excluded automatically deprives the history of

---

[10] For further theoretical enquiry, see Pocock, 1997d and 1998a. I was concerned in the latter essay with the role of those imperfectly included in, or actively excluded from, the politics of making history, which nevertheless they deeply affect. This is another criticism to which the makers of history must reply, but must retain the capacity to do so.

the included of its substance. By far the most interesting development in New Zealand historiography has been the growth of Maori-centred narratives which relate the history of conflict and interchange between two identities; but as we have already seen, the history of the *pakeha* is not reducible to its repression of the *tangata whenua*. They have done other things beside that; whether Maori have been able to do other things beside responding to the presence of the *pakeha* is a question that takes us closer to the themes of post-colonialism.

A historiography which undermines the traditional narratives providing identity may carry the pseudo-radical implication that identity may be found simply in the rejection of the undermined tradition. But those who are forever emancipating themselves will never be free, and the perpetually reiterated rejection of imperial myths serves to perpetuate them – or rather, to perpetuate the fear of a former identity, and the inability to manage oneself within it, which is at the heart of the culture of resentment.[11] Too much fear of a former colonial identity inhibits one from replacing it, and one of the objects of these essays has been to prompt New Zealanders to rethink, not merely to reject, British history and their role within it as it was (and may perhaps continue being). To manage one's history is to study it, not simply to subvert it, and the post-modern suspicion of all identities is dangerous to former colonial societies, as perpetuating their sense of dependence upon a history they are not making (as perhaps nobody is).

I have begun using the word 'colonial' in the special sense proper to a society of colonists who formerly thought of themselves as 'colonials', meaning that they lived in a culture and history which they had brought with them, not yet one which they were making for themselves, and were uneasily aware of a certain contempt in which they were held by metropolitans. At this point I must revert to the study of history as it was when I was a schoolboy and undergraduate in the 1930s and 1940s. I do not think of the view of history it implied as 'colonial', but others do and it is desirable to see why; part of the story may be that as a fourth-generation colonist but first-generation New Zealander, I was less troubled by the thought of being 'colonial' than those whose fathers and grandfathers were New Zealand born often were. I valued the voyage as well as the land.

It is certainly the case that, in those decades, we studied Western, European and especially British history more than we did that of

---

[11] I develop this term from 'the culture of complaint' (Hughes, 1993). By it I mean the culture of those who cannot live without seeing themselves as insurgents and insist upon others whom they may see as dominators; a world view which is often true, but must not become a necessity.

New Zealand. That is scarcely the issue; there was a good deal more of the former to be studied. The problem was – and was known to be – that we had not yet found ways of rendering New Zealand history interesting to ourselves, or central to our self-formation. The three myths I have mentioned were in place and not without historical substance; but they did not avert a feeling that the formation of a New Zealand society and culture was rather dull as a subject of study; colonial (of course) rather than provincial, and lacking in intellectual excitement. As far as I remember, such were my own feelings at the time; history that excited the intellect and imagination had happened elsewhere. But it is important to stress that this did not prevent – it rather stimulated – a lively concern, often frustrated but now and then satisfied, with finding a home for the imagination in New Zealand and imagining that country in new, challenging and if possible enriching ways. In this process the re-imagination of tradition – of what had come in and with the ships – might stand beside the imagination of place and distance; but the relation between the two would not be an easy one.

(III)

In the early 1940s – as I was beginning my undergraduate studies – a group of poets began publishing their work at the Caxton Press in Christchurch. Charles Brasch (1909–73), Allen Curnow (1911–2001) and Denis Glover (1912–80), who was printer as well as poet, were South Islanders, inhabiting a landscape where mountains and forests immediately confronted farmland and cities, there was an ocean eastward of one's back, and it was known that another sea lay not far west of the formidable ranges.[12] Samuel Butler, nearly a century before, had looked at the Southern Alps and longed for the partly humanized landscape of alpine Switzerland;[13] he was obliged to imagine the descent into the anti-utopia of Erewhon instead.[14] It was the first statement of the problem with which a landscape so recently inhabited by humans confronted an imagination that must hesitate even to conquer it; the high country does not lend itself to the facile pantheism of the environmentalists. The Caxton poets, as they were sometimes known, had

---

[12] Their poems were published in many forms over many years, and the process of collecting them may not yet be completed. There is a valuable bibliography, not limited to its immediate subject, in Ogilvie, 1999. See also Sturm, 1991, and most recently, Jones, 2003.

[13] Butler, 1923, vols. I (*A First Year in the Canterbury Settlement*), II (*Erewhon*).

[14] For an account of the curious route by which Butler's imagination came to affect the narrative in these pages, see Pocock, 1991c.

much to say about the encounter between the human and a land which resisted all attempts to imagine it, and made it their business to present this encounter as itself imaginatively exciting; it is this paradox which we have yet to locate in the imagination of the *tangata whenua*.[15] The *pakeha*, as I have said, remember a voyage before they imagine a land, and the tension between the two is very strong. The poets situated the unimagined land – an essayist of the time called it 'the waiting hills' – in what he also called 'the encircling seas';[16] an island or archipelago, 'not in narrow seas'[17] but in the vastness of the planetary ocean. But the ocean had been traversed, and what came out of it – 'always to islanders', wrote Curnow, 'danger is what comes over the sea'[18] – was not the unknown, but history; a history we already knew, which might overwhelm and smother our attempt to make a history out of the encounter with the land and ourselves, and might present us with problems – there was a world war in progress – that we had not made and might not be able to solve.

It was through the poetry of Allen Curnow that this conjunction of images and problems became in my mind a way of looking at history and living in it, when both had to be done a long sea voyage from anywhere else. He presented an imagination which could never be fully at home where it was, could never fully return to where it might have come from, and had travelled too far to fly off and live anywhere else. The poems written in the first half of his long life developed this theme – 'Whole-hearted he can't move from where he is, nor love whole-hearted that place'[19] – with a crispness and energy of language that made it clear that this was not an unhappy or impotent condition, but one intensely stimulating to the imagination it challenged; and this was Curnow's contribution, in the 1940s and afterwards, to a project it remains inadequate and misleading to call nationalist. It was about nationality, not nationalism. To his readers in that decade it was anything but news that nations were imagined communities; we were saying that ours would not be a nation or a community until it learned to imagine itself; but we were saying also that the antipodean imagination could not create itself out of any unifying myth – if we had known anything about our Maori fellow islanders we might have said to them that there was no *whenua* – but out of knowledge

---

[15] See, however, a summary of the tradition of *waka* settlement in both islands in Walker, 1990, ch. 3.
[16] Holcroft, 1940, 1943, 1946.
[17] Curnow, 1939. It is a theme of this volume that neither England, Britain nor the Atlantic Archipelago is encircled by the narrow seas east and south of them.
[18] Curnow, 'Landfall in Unknown Seas' (Curnow, 1943; 1997, pp. 226–9).
[19] Curnow, 'The Eye is More or Less Satisfied with Seeing' (Curnow, 1962; 1997, p. 184).

of its own historicity and fragility. Since the voyage to Erewhon had carried us beyond the islands of myth, there was no Tír na n'Óg, no being born again, at the end of it; we must learn to live in more places than one and more histories than one. It was not a bad lesson to spend the rest of the twentieth century learning.

This phase of Curnow's poetry came under vehement attack, later in the 1950s, from younger poets, often living in the northern cities: Wellington the political capital and Auckland the commercial, both aspiring – as Christchurch did not – to be the cultural capital as well. Members of urban élites that could believe themselves self-sufficient, these writers took exception to an easily misunderstood line in which Curnow had mentioned 'that great gloom which stands in a land of settlers, with never a soul at home'.[20] I read him as aiming to dispel that gloom and make the condition of never being quite at home a spring to the imagination. The younger poets, however, insisted that they were at home and the voyage was no longer a problem; though a cynic might observe that having proclaimed themselves at home, they lost no time in telling us how satisfactorily alienated, modern and in due course post-modern they were in that condition. Curnow, after a period of silence, moved into a poetic mode sharply different from, though not discontinuous with, his earlier verse, and went on writing poems of great clarity and authority until he died at the age of 90, having outlived nearly all his enemies and not a few of his friends. I am proud to have been one of the latter, but unlike many New Zealand historians, I am not a poet.

I am, however, concerned to show how the poetry of the 1940s interacted with the growth of a New Zealand historiography. The latter encountered a double problem, whose two faces affected one another: how to write a history of the people – perhaps the nation – we were making of ourselves, and how to rewrite the history from which we had come, but which we had brought with us and had not left behind. Given that the latter history was economically, politically, militarily, culturally and historiographically powerful in ways that we were not, it was natural that the effort to create the former should appear a contest for power, a struggle against hegemony; New Zealanders trying not to be 'colonials', in the sense of cultural dependants, might be tempted to accuse the metropolitans of the empire of cultural hegemony and repression, and the discovery that the metropolitans were hardly aware that they existed, still less that they had a history, might appear one more instrument of that repression. A culture of

---

[20] Curnow, 'House and Land' (Curnow, 1941; 1997, p. 234). See Murray, 1998.

resentment – perhaps already built into the modern mindset – might take over; but the question would arise whether resentment was enough. Incessantly to stigmatize a culture as hegemonic may have the effect of perpetuating that hegemony; a culture of resentment needs the objects of resentment so badly that it may never be free of them. If, then, the presence of 'British history' was impeding the growth of 'New Zealand history', the question must arise of what we were to do about the former. There might be ways of re-imagining it and making it our own, so that we were equals in its practice.

The creation of a historiography of New Zealand was necessarily the work of many hands, but no scholar did more to make it a distinctive academic discipline, even an academic industry, than Keith Sinclair (1922–93) of the University of Auckland.[21] As a poet, he was among Curnow's critics; as a historian, he was a leading spirit. Together with his colleagues, his pupils and his peers, he created or anticipated most of the lines of enquiry into New Zealand history which have been pursued since, and was a founding father of the historical culture which continues to pursue them. I emphasize this the more because, during one period (1959–66) when Sinclair's activity was at its peak, I was associated with the history department of the University of Canterbury, where other things were going on. N. C. Phillips, J. B. Owen, and later Marie Peters and J. E. Cookson, were following a post-Namierite path into the history of eighteenth-century England,[22] and my own work had already led me into the history of English (and British) political (and historical) thought. Auckland and Canterbury worked together in several ways, and there was a legend that Keith Sinclair had declared that the latter was the only department beside his own for whose work he felt respect. If not true, the tale is *ben trovato*, for it was more widely believed that he regarded with suspicion the study of any history but New Zealand's, on the grounds that to study it was to submit to it. There was a report that at Auckland 'British history' was defined as 'imperial history', as if that were the only relationship that mattered. Certainly, the *New Zealand Journal of History*, which carries on Sinclair's legacy at Auckland, is really a journal of New Zealand history and publishes very little else.[23] This is highly defensible, but it would be well if the country had room for a second and complementary journal.

---

[21] A bibliography of his writings to 1987 may be found in Binney and Sorrenson, 1987.
[22] Phillips, 1961; Owen, 1957; Peters, 1980; Cookson, 1982, 1997.
[23] I am happy to report an essay on fitting New Zealand into the discipline of world history (Gibbons, 2003).

On the one occasion when Keith Sinclair invited me to comment on a work of his,[24] I was moved to make two suggestions. One was that New Zealand should be thought to possess two totemic birds: the kiwi, flightless, nocturnal and inhabiting the forest floor, and the godwit, a migratory species whose flocks traverse the Pacific between New Zealand and Siberia or Alaska. 'The godwits vanish towards another summer' was one of Charles Brasch's images of the New Zealand condition.[25] It was implicit that they were capable of the two-way voyage, though Robin Hyde (1906–39)[26] had written a novel, *The Godwits Fly* (1938), on the theme that they could never make it back, and had later died in London by her own hand. The godwit stands for both the travellers who return and the expatriates who do not, but live in the pattern. I wished to say that if the kiwi knew what was happening at the fernroots, the godwit knew what was happening in the upper winds of the world, and that, even if each was tempted by its own kind of arrogance, there was little it would be worth their while for them to quarrel about. I suggested also, however, that there were in Sinclair's writings traces of the confusion – its origins fairly evident – between independence of mind and resentment of English upper-class practices. These often deserved resentment, but there was the danger of obsession; those who cannot cease attacking the 'cultural cringe' or the 'colonial cringe' are not free from it and may be perpetuating it. I was also troubled, in Sinclair's last writings, when he seemed to find signs of national independence when working-class New Zealanders expressed dislike or contempt for working-class British;[27] this was no time, I thought, to perpetuate the premiss that the Self can only exist through its enmity for an Other. Here were the faults of the kiwi, which might be corrected by the world view of the godwit. When Sinclair entitled his autobiography *Halfway Round the Harbour*,[28] in allusion to his residence on the Waitemata harbour which urban Auckland now surrounds, I was aware of a preference for situating myself halfway round the planet. I was by then an expatriate, but had not ceased to be a godwit; it is part of the pattern that this can be so.

---

[24] Pocock, 1983b.
[25] Brasch, 'In These Islands', 1948; partly reprinted in Bornholdt, O'Brien and Williams, 1997, p. 372. A line from this poem gave its title to Sinclair, 1961.
[26] There is a considerable recent literature concerning her (for a recent assessment see Jones, 2003, passim) in which she is accorded an importance I don't recall she had for me. She has, and may then have had, it for others.
[27] Sinclair, 1986, pp. 104–8, 159–62, 245–6.   [28] Sinclair, 1993.

The imagery of voyage, distance and historic ambivalence was already apparent in the historiography. J. C. Beaglehole (1901–71), the premier historian of the age-group preceding mine, had published several works – including a history of the University of New Zealand[29] – written throughout on a high level of derisive and indignant eloquence; but though the author of a memorable lecture on *The New Zealand Scholar*,[30] he never wrote the detailed history of the country that might have come from him. Instead, he became a world authority on the exploration of the Pacific, and ended his life of James Cook with the following:

Such things; Geography and Navigation; if we wish for more, an ocean is enough, where the waves fall on innumerable reefs, and a great wind blows from the south-east with the revolving world.[31]

This is not romantic language; it states that oceanic and planetary space must be part of a way of seeing the world, and may be all that lies at the end of certain lines of enquiry. There remains the question of the history which is carried across such space and is the product of crossing it, and here it is proper to quote the very recent language of W. H. Oliver, a contemporary of Sinclair's and mine, probably the premier historian of New Zealand now living. His pre-eminence has more to do with biography than with narrative, and in a recent autobiography, after considering the life of his father, a working-class emigrant from Cornwall, he has this to say:

The two worlds we inhabited were, however, rich enough. We were untroubled, too, by any thought of disjunction between the inherited world across the seas and the acquired world near at hand. It was simply a matter of looking at the immediate world through the eyes of the encompassing world and at that world through the eyes of the one close to hand. I still cannot believe that absorbing some of the great inheritance our origins offered us was in any way servile, colonialist or a distraction from the local 'reality'. Nor can I avoid the conclusion that it is better not to feel too wholeheartedly at home wherever you might be . . .

Surely people from the warmer and more abundant islands of the Pacific felt the shock of an alien land as keenly as other immigrants? I have come to think of that trauma as an integral element in the ancestral heritage of all the peoples who live in this country, and one which we forget or ignore to our loss and at our peril. For to eliminate the experience of being a stranger is also to preclude a sense of belonging that stretches across oceans to places both as distant as the other hemisphere and as close as breathing. That sense is, for me, the source of the looking about and setting down which ends as history in the many forms of the written word.[32]

[29] Beaglehole, 1937.   [30] Beaglehole, 1954.   [31] Beaglehole, 1974, p. 714.
[32] Oliver, 2002, pp. 54–5.

Oliver says here what I want to say; it should be remembered, however, that we are both the sons of immigrants, and that *pakeha* in the third or fourth generation may feel differently. I might also raise a notch or two higher the possibility that the two worlds may challenge and discomfort one another. I should want historical intelligence to begin on the far side of some lines of Allen Curnow's, already quoted in part:

> Whole-hearted he can't move
> From where he is, nor love
>
> Whole-hearted that place . . .
>
> Does true or false sun rise?
> Do both half eyes tell lies?
>
> Cradle or grave, which view's
> The actual of the two? . . .
>
> Snap open! He's all eyes, wary,
> Darting both ways one query . . . [33]

I turn at last towards the birth of these essays at a time when the two histories came into sharp and complex opposition.

(IV)

The New Zealand of the 1940s had been involved in the Second World War and had suffered considerable loss of men, though not on the scale of the First. The era of New Zealand participation in wars elsewhere coincided (Vietnam excepted) with that of its location on what a recent historian has termed the 'protein bridge',[34] the sea routes along which its pastoral produce – wool, mutton and butter – passed to feed and clothe the urban populations of the United Kingdom, its principal market. The bridge actually consisted of three routes: Panama, Suez and Cape Town; and it was along all three, in the era before air travel, that New Zealanders travelled by steamship, in the endeavour of many of them to discover and explore the history they belonged to. In the wars of the twentieth century New Zealanders fought at points along the sea routes, or at their European abutments: the Transvaal, Gallipoli and Passchendaele, Alamein and Cassino; and it is helpful to visualize the 'protein bridge' as defining that area of the oceanic world and its politics to which the New Zealand I am

---

[33] Curnow, 'The Eye is More or Less Satisfied with Seeing', 1962; 1997, pp. 184–5.
[34] Belich, 2001, makes extensive use of this concept. Butter is not of course a protein.

describing belonged. Of the three routes, that through Suez and the Mediterranean was doubly significant: it was the theatre of wars, and the theatre of empire – though the deep commitment New Zealanders used to have to the image of British empire had more to do with their own relation with Britain than with rule over Egyptians, Africans and Indians; with the empire of colonization than with that of 'colonialism'. The wars in which New Zealanders died had to do with maintaining both a global system and a certain idea of themselves, though it is true that by 1939–45 the latter had undergone change. I recall a testy exchange with a brisk young intellectual in the 1990s, who wanted me to agree that the Second World War had been another war for King and Country; I reminded him that ours had been a social-democratic culture, and that the war against Hitler could not have been fought without the widely accepted myth of democratic socialism that survived even the Nazi–Soviet pact. This was as much part of the New Zealand ethos as it was of that of the British, and the changes in historical outlook I shall be describing had to do with the death of socialism as well as the death of empire.

After the American and British naval disasters of December 1941, John Curtin, the Australian prime minister, issued a stirring New Year's Eve broadcast to his people, summoning them to what would soon be a very serious war in New Guinea and the seas around it. The Australian infantry divisions were recalled from the Middle East – replacing the division lost at Singapore – and committed to the campaigns in the islands between Australia and Indonesia, in which they served for the remainder of the global conflict. New Zealand did not follow this strategy; after garrisoning Fiji for a while, reinforcements continued to go to the division then fighting in Egypt and Libya, and New Zealand remained committed to the war in Europe, not the Pacific. I find it valuable to reflect on this difference between the two national histories. It might be argued that the New Zealand I knew was not yet ideologically situated in the Pacific Ocean, but rather in the world-girdling Southern Ocean into which the Pacific opens out, or – for material and ideological reasons of greater solidity – on the tracts of ocean defined by the 'protein bridge', which, it could be argued, we were still fighting to maintain. Unlike the Australians – who had very pressing reasons for acting as they did – we sustained in arms a relationship with both Britain and Europe; and the New Zealand military decision belongs with the American and Allied decision to give priority to the defeat of Germany over that of Japan.

There is now a conventional wisdom which seems to hold that New Zealand ought to have followed the Australian decision of 1941–2, largely on the grounds that it would have been less 'colonial' to do so.[35] This makes little sense to my historical memory. Curtin's New Year's Eve broadcast informed the Australians that they were no longer protected by the British navy, but by that of the United States instead; a courageous thing to say three weeks after Pearl Harbor, but an odd way of proclaiming national self-reliance. In the event, one might argue, the United States did not much want allies in the Pacific war, and the formidable Australian infantry ended it conducting subsidiary operations in Sulawesi while Douglas MacArthur went on to the Philippines. The New Zealand Division, in comparison, after heavy losses at Cassino, ended the war helping to keep the city of Trieste Italian when Jugoslav partisans hoped to take it over; an intervention in history of a certain significance. And it is always to be remembered that the Third Reich (and later the Soviet Union) were acting in ways we understood, in terms of a history and philosophy European, American and global. However mind-defyingly appalling their actions (and ours), we knew them as inhabitants of our world; that was the depth of our quarrel with them; whereas the Japanese, in the understandings available to us then, might as well have been Martians from outer space. This should be, and is being, changed; but it is not yet clear that an Asian, or a post-colonial, understanding of history has replaced an Anglo-European or Anglo-American scheme as a means of making sense of the history of the South Pacific or the Southern Ocean. It is much easier to quarrel with the Americans than with the Indonesians or Chinese.

Between the end of the Second World War and the delivery of the lecture printed next in this volume, more than a quarter-century went by, and it would be absurd to attribute the mentality of 1945 to audiences in 1973. It might be tedious, on the other hand, and perhaps it is still not possible, to offer a detailed history of the changing circumstances and mentalities of both New Zealand and Britain during that period.[36] It is the case, however, that the relationship between the two, in the era of the 'protein bridge' and the British Commonwealth of Nations, was intimate and dynamic as well as stable, and that a history of ideologies since 1945 is largely concerned with the dissolution of that relationship and its causes. It is surely a commonplace that what befell the British in the second half of the twentieth century was the failure of empire, the failure of socialism and the failure of industrialism, occurring concurrently rather than

[35] Belich, 2001, pp. 284–7, concludes that this decision was the product of a 'recolonial' mentality. The use of this adjective serves more to relegate than to illuminate.
[36] Belich, 2001, pp. 325–45 and 391–465, should be read on this period.

successively; and that it remains a question – I do not say one that cannot be answered – whether a coherent or autonomous history of the British peoples can be written in consequence of these catastrophes. There have been negative answers of which I wish to speak negatively. One is the claim that 'Britain' and 'the British' existed only in consequence of the attainment of empire, and have now ceased to exist in consequence of empire's disappearance. Another – superficially at variance with the first – is the claim that the same history has never been that of an imperial, oceanic or global people (or peoples) and has existed only within a 'European' history which is the past of a future relationship. The New Zealand equivalent of these has been the claim that its history cannot be written – and since it has been, must now be forgotten – in terms of a 'British' identity or relationship, and must now be rewritten in terms more populist, Pacific and postmodern. There is much to be said for this – it is Keith Sinclair's reading of history carried on by a succeeding generation – but the danger is that it may fail to understand, and may dismiss as 'colonial', the history of a New Zealand when things were otherwise.

My own career in these decades – it will be recalled that this essay must be in part autobiographical – continued to be a story of voyagings between histories. I spent several years in England (I use that word advisedly) beginning a study – later completed in New Zealand – of how the English had once constructed their history in terms verging on the autochthonous, and had then challenged it with an alternative that made it a consequence of the European invasion of 1066.[37] I subsequently moved more than once between England and New Zealand, but in 1966 departed from that pattern by accepting an offer from Washington University in St Louis – thus moving from the distance between antipodean archipelagos to the junction of two rivers in the heartland of a continent. Since then, I have continued to live in the forty-eight contiguous states, but still regard the world as an archipelago of histories rather than a tectonic of continents. I see histories as both transplanted by voyagings and generated by settlements and contacts, and consequently as never quite at home. In this I claim to have anticipated and accommodated some part at least of the post-modern stress on fictiveness and momentariness (just as the 'linguistic turn' was not altogether astonishing to one who had studied texts and their contexts with Butterfield and Laslett in Cambridge before and after 1950).

[37] Pocock, 1957 and 1987 (B).

(v)

The first lecture here reprinted was delivered in Christchurch in 1973 (the centennial year of the University of Canterbury) as the first in a series honouring the memory of J. C. Beaglehole, who had died two years earlier. It may be thought of as continuing that Canterbury counterpoint to history as studied at Auckland, described earlier in this introduction; but it is also, and more widely, a proposal to refigure the history of Britain, put forward in the context of the ongoing British negotiation for entry into 'Europe', successively defined as market, community and union. That negotiation lasted for many years; indeed, it is not over yet; and the same may be said of New Zealand's responses to it, including the revaluation of our own history and identity it necessitated. I recall some moments in this historical process more vividly than others; for example, the grim amusement, appropriate to a family quarrel, with which we received the news of President de Gaulle's temporary veto of British entry in 1963. As our own vernacular might have put it, the old man's mistress had thrown him out of the pub, and it served the bastard right; at the same time, we knew that de Gaulle's hostility – it was mixed with respect – was aimed in part at Britain's association with nations like ours, and that he was our enemy just as he was Canada's. At issue was the continued existence of a global Britishness, an association within which – I differ here from younger historians who can see it only as involving a dependency – we held ourselves entitled to certain kinds of equality. To this the French might be indifferent, if they knew of it at all; but it was the British of the United Kingdom who seemed bent on dissolving it, on the grounds that they had no longer the power to sustain it and it was inconvenient to them to pay any further attention to us. There were moments, in the British debate with themselves over 'Europe', which revealed all too clearly a perception of New Zealanders as faithful servants no longer needed, who might now be pensioned off and forgotten; an insult deeper than any de Gaulle could have intended, to which there must be reply.

Speaking at Auckland, there would have been no need to outline ways in which New Zealand history might be re-assessed; these were already in place and in practice. Speaking in Canterbury, I chose to consider ways in which New Zealanders certainly, but at the same time anyone else concerned, might re-assess British history as a shared possession. In the Second Book of Samuel, it is written how:

the men of Israel answered the men of Judah, and said, 'We have ten parts in the king, and we have also more right in David than ye: why then did ye despise us, that our advice should not be first had in bringing back our king?'[38] And the words of the men of Judah were fiercer than the words of the men of Israel.[39]

And there happened to be there a man of Belial . . . and he blew a trumpet and said, 'We have no part in David, neither have we inheritance in the son of Jesse: every man to his tents, O Israel'.[40]

'David the king' in this story might be the name not of a sovereign, but of a *taonga*, a Maori term for a cultural inheritance; in this case a history we had supposed ourselves to share. Maori know, however, that *taonga* bring *mana*, a cultural power and self-respect which continues the being of the ancestors. The 'man of Belial' – Keith Sinclair might have enjoyed the ascription – being denied his inheritance, denies that he ever had one, and goes out in search of *mana* of his own making; in the Hebrew narrative he comes to a bad end.[41] He need not do so; but in the analogy I am applying, he sees himself as under David's hegemony, and his inheritance a badge of inferiority. The men of Israel (later to be the lost ten tribes) affirm that they are the equals of the men of Judah, and in a real sense of David himself. The New Zealand response to the British denial of community could therefore be a denial of *taonga*, a denial that they were or had been part of a history that could only be a means of hegemony, a reduction to colonial status. It might on the other hand be an affirmation of equality, a declaration that New Zealanders had their own part in British history, and their own right to continue writing it and – unless we are all owls of Minerva to whom history becomes intelligible only as it ends – to continue making it, by interpretation as a form of action. This equality would have existed in the past as well as in the deeply shadowed present and future.

The version of British history here put forward was proposed in the antipodes and is pervaded by the antipodean sense of distance and ambivalence. To claim equality, however, is to address oneself to one's equals, and the 'British history' that now began taking shape was proposed to British historians, and any who might be interested in British history, as a narrative and scenario that might make sense as a way of viewing it. Though distinctively antipodean and designed to serve antipodean interests, it did not attempt the absurdity of imposing an antipodean framework on the history of the British kingdoms. It did, however, invite their inhabitants to see themselves as an association of insular and emigrant peoples, who had set going a diversity of histories in settings archipelagic, Atlantic and oceanic, might have to continue

---

[38] This text was chosen by the minister appointed to preach before King Charles I when the latter placed himself in the hands of the Scottish army in 1646.

[39] II Samuel, 19, 43.   [40] II Samuel, 20, 1.   [41] II Samuel, 20, 22.

living in those histories, and must recognize that others were still living in them in ways to which they must pay attention.

This is the point at which 'British history' comes into collision with the ideology of 'Europe', and may perhaps be the product of that collision (how far this was the case in 1973 I am not sure I remember). It is now affirmed – loudly, dogmatically, and often without much corroborative detail – that the British states and peoples must henceforth be and, as far as this can be asserted, must always have been, part of a history exclusively 'European', perhaps better defined by what it excludes than by what it narrates. 'Europe' is an association of former empires which claim to exercise sovereignty better if they share it among themselves; latent in this, however, is a strong impulse to assert the obsolescence of the sovereign community without replacing it by any other community capable of governing itself. It therefore negates the history of any former 'nation state' such as Britain – the term 'nation state' is used dismissively or as condemnation – but does not replace it by any other history in which peoples can be defined and seen as governing themselves. It therefore operates negatively, denying histories more energetically than it seeks to rewrite them; and the impact of 'Europe' upon Britain is to deny it any past of cultural autonomy, political sovereignty, empire beyond the European peninsula, and – of course – any historical association with Anglophone North America. The antipodean neo-Britains recognize that among the aims of this exercise is the denial or marginalization of their own histories but are tempted to take part in this marginalization by constructing autochthonous narratives which know nothing of any history but that they have made for themselves. There are, in consequence, two claims that may be made for the 'new history' I began proposing in 1973. To peoples like the New Zealanders – there are several – it offers a history in which they have taken part, which may help explain them to themselves, and to which they may lay claim, as equals, in the art of renarrating and interpreting it. To the British peoples – I use the plural deliberately – it offers a history which is not simply one of unity and empire, but a complex enterprise in which they have been involved and have acted in various ways. This history is not complacent or hegemonic, but deeply problematic; it may not be over yet, in the sense that they are still in search of ways in which it may be continued. It challenges the apparent alternative – that of abandoning all history of their own, and repeating the word 'Europe' as a mantra signifying that history is at an end and we have arrived at the world of Nietzsche's and Fukuyama's Last Men – by suggesting that a narrative of how they have interacted with one another, and spread into the oceans, may exist and interact with one of how they have interacted with adjacent peoples of the European peninsula. There is everything to be said for writing a history of 'Britain' as 'European', until it becomes paradigmatic and hegemonic. If it is proposed for no other purpose than to exclude other histories, it will never have much to say for itself.

This history owes something to the antipodean perspective. It sees peoples in motion, histories traversing distance, and 'identities' (the word is overworked) as never quite at home. Formed partly in an archipelago of the Southern Ocean, it presents the islands including Britain as another archipelago (hence the title of this book), not the promontory of a continent; it presupposes histories 'not in narrow seas'. It questions identities, but waits to hear answers. In this, I believe, it is indebted to the culture, and the moment in history, in which it was formed; but its test, needless to say, must be its success in explaining, and enlarging, the histories to which it has been applied. It is exposed to that test in the essays now to be reprinted.

CHAPTER 2

British history: a plea for a new subject

It seems all wrong to be delivering a memorial lecture for John Beaglehole.[1] In the first place, he ought to be here himself; and in the second, though he wrote a style entirely capable of building monuments more lasting than bronze, it never disguised a Chaplinesque delight in whisking away the veil before too white and glistening a perfection could conceal the veins in the marble. He was not a marmoreal figure himself and one should not attempt to make him one; he was a man one should not commemorate so much as enjoy. In giving a lecture to his memory, then, one should seek to do something which one enjoys oneself and which JCB might have enjoyed too; and in this way, as he would certainly have pointed out, one may give one's colleagues about as much prospect of enjoying the occasion as they can reasonably expect. Something exploratory, something reflective and something not unduly reverent seems to be what is called for, and I shall do my best to comply with those specifications.

A. J. P. Taylor's volume of the *Oxford History of England* opens – in a way which may or may not have escaped the attention of Scottish reviewers – with a flat and express denial that the term 'Britain' has any meaning. It is, he says, the name of a Roman province, which never included the whole of modern Scotland, and was foisted upon the English by the inhabitants of the northern kingdom as part of the parliamentary union of 1707. Moreover, he continues, the term 'Great Britain' – which properly denotes no more than the Anglo-Scottish union – is non-identical with the term 'United Kingdom', since the latter's scope included the whole of Ireland from 1801 and the dark and bloody rump of that island from 1922.[2] There could be a Plaid Cymru comment on all this, I suppose, and one might also

---

[1] This paper was presented as the J. C. Beaglehole Memorial Lecture to the meeting of the New Zealand Historical Association at the University of Canterbury in May 1973. It is printed here as it appeared in the *New Zealand Journal of History* (Pocock, 1974). It was reprinted, with commentaries by several hands, in the *Journal of Modern History* (Pocock, 1975).

[2] Taylor, 1965, p. v and n.

like to hear the views of Orkney and Shetland regionalists who may
consider themselves a Norse fragment unsatisfactorily subject to an alien
Scots culture. But Taylor's remarks conclude with an announcement that
when he has occasion to mention people and things emanating from
Scotland – which he clearly implies will be no more often than the
exigencies of a history of England compel – he intends to use the adjective
'Scotch', not 'Scots' or 'Scottish', on the grounds that the former is the
English word and the latter, though used by Scots to denote themselves, no
part of his native vocabulary. Now, as Taylor knows very well, there are
parts of the world in which men are killed for less; he is deliberately
dabbling in the politics of language and the politics of identity, which
are among the more murderous and aggressive pursuits of our murderous
and aggressive world, but he clearly expects to get away with it. One finds
the same insistence on using 'Scotch' instead of 'Scottish', on grounds
which are unmistakably arrogant rather than merely pedantic, in the pre-
face to C. S. Lewis's volume of the *Oxford History of English Literature*,
though Lewis redeemed himself by devoting separate and serious chapters
to the history of sixteenth-century Scottish literature, which he saw to be
written in an autonomous if disappearing variant of the Inglis tongue.[3]
Lewis, after all, was an Ulsterman; but on this occasion he claimed the right
to call himself English and to speak of the Scots only in a language which
was English, not Scottish, and by a name which Scotsmen do not employ
in speaking of themselves. Again, this can easily be a killing matter; but – as
with the use of the macron vowel in Maori[4] – things have not in fact gone
so far. But we all were – were we not? – brought up to understand that it
was polite to say 'Scots' and not 'Scotch', since Scotsmen so preferred; just
as it used to be polite to call Black Americans 'Negroes' – with a capital N –
until the rules of this game were somewhat suddenly changed.[5] One hopes
that the word 'Maori' will continue to give satisfaction.

The politics of language, however, are less my theme than some interesting implications that may be drawn, and lessons that I think may be learned,
from Taylor's characteristic exercise in coat-trailing. It is informative to hear
an eminent English historian – once distinguished for his understanding of
the difference between *kleindeutsch* and *grossdeutsch* ideologies[6] – declare
frankly that the term 'Britain' has no meaning to him, and none in history

---

[3] Lewis, 1954, pp. v, 66–119.
[4] There has been vehement debate as to whether long vowels should be spelt with a macron – e.g. Māori –
or doubled – e.g. Maaori. Both spellings remain in usage, but I have not ventured to determine between
them.
[5] An episode of the late 1960s.   [6] Taylor, 1946, passim.

either, and that he has no more than an obligatory sense of identity with any
of the peoples of his island group other than his own. Within the memory of
everyone here, the English have been increasingly willing to declare that
neither empire nor commonwealth ever meant much in their consciousness,
and that they were at heart Europeans all the time. The obvious absurdity of
the second part of the claim is no bar either to the partial truth of the
first part, or to the ideological assertion of the claim as a whole; and if it
has been psychologically possible for them to annihilate the idea of the
Commonwealth – white as well as non-white – it is not altogether beyond
the bounds of possibility that 'United Kingdom' and even 'Britain' may
some day become similarly inconvenient and be annihilated, or annihilate
themselves, in their turn. With communal war resumed in Ireland and
a daily cost in lives being paid for the desire of one of the 'British' peoples
to remain 'British' as they understand the term, it is not inconceivable that
future historians may find themselves writing of a 'Unionist' or even
a 'British' period in the history of the peoples inhabiting the Atlantic
archipelago, and locating it between a date in the thirteenth, the seventeenth
or the nineteenth centuries and a date in the twentieth or the twenty-first.[7]

   These are of course dismal imaginations; we all at least claim to dislike
balkanization, and I doubt if the most resolutely nationalist among us
could say that the disappearance of all meaning from the term 'Britain'
would do nothing at all to his sense of identity. I am going to advance the
claim that there is a need for us to revive the term 'British history', and
re-invest it with meaning, for reasons relative to the maintenance of a number
of historically based identities. But in order to make this claim intelligible,
I must first establish the truth of a proposition which did not become fully
clear to me until I read and reflected on Taylor's dictum that the term
'Britain' is without historical meaning. He was after all contributing to
a History of England, and there is at least this much truth in his claim: no
true history of Britain has ever been composed. Geoffrey of Monmouth in
the twelfth century, William Camden in the sixteenth, Robert Henry in the
eighteenth, made the attempt according to the standards of their times, and
even today there are some distinguished and even brilliant partial exceptions to the rule I am enunciating. But when one considers what 'Britain'
means – that it is the name of a realm inhabited by two, and more than two,
nations, whose history has been expansive to the extent of planting settlements and founding derivative cultures beyond the Four Seas – it is evident
that the history of this complex expression has never been seriously

---

[7] [Whether these speculations were predictions or prophecies I cannot now tell.]

attempted. Francis Bacon, on the occasion of the union of the crowns in 1603, proposed to James VI and I the construction of a history which would make that of England and that of Scotland as simultaneously visible as had been the histories of Israel and Judah in the Books of Kings and Chronicles; but one has only to walk through the relevant section of any library and glance at the shelves to see that his advice has not been taken. Instead of histories of Britain, we have, first of all, histories of England, in which Welsh, Scots, Irish, and in the reign of George III Americans, appear as peripheral peoples when, and only when, their doings assume power to disturb the tenor of English politics; second, and read by limited and fragmented publics, histories of Wales, Scotland, Ireland and so forth, written as separate enterprises in the effort, sustained to various degrees, to constitute separate historiographical traditions. Of this state of affairs it may be said – if it may be said of any state of affairs – that A. J. P. Taylor is its logical culmination.

I can best begin sketching what a history of Britain might be like by describing one or two of the exceptions to my rule – works which have done something to whet my appetite for more of the same. David Mathew's *The Celtic Peoples and Renaissance Europe*,[8] though marred by the author's extraordinary *pointilliste* technique in writing history, did at least achieve a real imaginative sweep. Starting with the appearance of some Anglo-Welsh dependants of the house of Devereux in the Earl of Essex's rebellion in 1600, Mathew worked his way out along the military route to Ireland through South Wales and Milford Haven, and then made a *tour d'horizon* of the whole Celtic frontier and trans-frontier world, from Cornwall through Wales, and through Ireland, the Western Isles and the Scottish Highlands, to the Gordon country and Aberdeen; at the end of which the reader was left with the excited sensation of having been introduced to a new realm of historical experience and convinced that it was really there. Though Mathew wrote of the world of the Hebridean gallowglasses – known also to Shakespeare – in terms which indicated that they were so very Gaelic that even the Irish found them a little incomprehensible, and he himself was forced to write of them in Kiltartan English, the effect of his book was strictly non-Ossianic. One found oneself convinced of the existence of a world outside manorial Western Europe, on which the settled societies of the English, Scotto-Anglians and Anglo-Irish steadily encroached; and I found this impression reinforced when I read a then little-known Jacobean work, Sir John Davies's *Discoverie of the True*

---

[8] Mathew, 1933.

Causes why Ireland was never thoroughly subdued until His Majesty's Happy Reign.[9] Davies, James I's Attorney-General for Ireland, one of whose aims was the conversion of brehon conceptions of inheritance into common-law land tenures, was moved by this experience to write an early classic of colonial history and administrative literature, its theme being that only the anglicization of tenure could bring settled conditions to Irish society, and that earlier failures to do this had left Norman and Old English ruling groups stranded in an Old Irish world with no alternative but to become *Hibernicis ipsis Hiberniores.* Davies, with imperialist intentions, wrote an intercultural history, concerned with conflict and cross-breeding between societies differently based, and it is my contention that this is, with other intentions, how 'British history' will have to be written.[10]

Reverting to modern historiography, J. C. Beckett's *The Making of Modern Ireland* performs the service of recounting the whole period which we know as that of the First Civil War, 1642 to 1646, from the standpoint of the Marquis of Ormond, the greatest Anglo-Irishman of his day and the greatest of the king's servants in Ireland; and in order to do this properly, Beckett was driven to rebaptize the whole conflict and call it by the name of the War of the Three Kingdoms.[11] As soon as one looks at it in that way, a revolution in perspectives takes place; one sees that 'the First Civil War' is a purely English term, appropriate only to English conditions – since in Scotland there was never a civil war, even Montrose succeeding in launching no more than a Highland raid of a desperately unusual character, and since Ireland had not attained the degree of political integration necessary if the term 'civil war' is to have any meaning. The War of the Three Kingdoms was in fact three wars, originating independently if interconnectedly, and differing in political character – a national rebellion in Scotland south and east of the Highlands, a frontier rebellion (perhaps aiming to be more) in the multicultural conflict-zone of Ireland, and a civil war in the highly integrated political society of England – and flowing together to form a single series but not a single phenomenon. Charles I would not have summoned the English parliament but for the war in Scotland, or been challenged by it for control of the militia but for the war in Ireland; and though the outcome was such as to increase the ascendancy

---

[9] Published in 1612. For further analysis, Pocock, 1957, 1987 (B), pp. 59–62.

[10] [Irish historians assure us – no doubt rightly – that Davies was a nasty little man and his policies a failure. This does not diminish the intellectual muscle of his book. See Pawlisch, 1985, Flanagan, 1999 and Canny, 2001.]

[11] Beckett, 1966, ch. 4. [I did not enquire here whether Beckett originated the term I learned from him.]

of England over Scotland and of England and Scotland over Ireland, it is evident that we are studying three, and in some ways more than three, interacting histories.

I am using 'British history' – for lack, an Irishman might add, of a better term – to denote the plural history of a group of cultures situated along an Anglo-Celtic frontier and marked by an increasing English political and cultural domination.[12] The last work I should like to mention as offering the kind of pluralist treatment I am advocating is J. R. Pole's *Political Representation in England and the Origins of the American Republic.*[13] Concerned with a highly specific historical problem – the American Revolution and the birth of federalism that followed – Pole conducts a survey of political structures and electoral systems which moves from England through Massachusetts, Pennsylvania and Virginia, with glances at other sub-cultures on the way, and returns to the deliberations of the Philadelphia Convention in 1789. The effect is to convince the reader that there once existed, as a single system, a diversity of political cultures grouped around the northern Atlantic – an English, two Scottish, three Irish and an uncertain number of American – increasingly dominated by the English language and by veneration for, if diverse modes of interpreting, English political norms and institutions; and that these were disrupted in the great civil war of the American Revolution, which can be interpreted either in terms of one group of these cultures making a radical choice from among the alternatives before it, or in terms of the geopolitically pre-ordained emergence of an American nation qualitatively distinct from the Anglo-Atlantic culture which gave it birth. To this the response was the authoritarian consolidation of the eastern group of cultures at their weakest point, in the Irish Union of 1801, so that one may look ahead from the second to the third of the major civil wars which have convulsed British history – the Irish Revolution of 1911–22, the first terrorist war of modern times, a marginal campaign of which is still [1973] being fought.

The nature of the subject which might be designated 'British history' ought by this time to be emerging, though its complete outline cannot be traced within the confines of a single lecture. We should start with what I have called the Atlantic archipelago – since the term 'British Isles' is one which Irishmen reject and Englishmen decline to take quite seriously. This is a large – dare I say a sub-continental? – island group lying off the north-west coasts of geographic Europe, partly within and partly without the oceanic limits of the Roman empire and of what is usually called 'Europe'

---

[12] [A paragraph of the original is omitted here.] [13] Pole, 1966.

in the sense of the latter's successor states; in which respect it somewhat resembles Scandinavia. Historical geographers supply us with accounts of the configuration of the islands composing it, notably its divisions into lowland and highland zones and the diversity of its littorals as these face towards quasi-inland seas on the European side and an oceanic water-region on the Atlantic; I could imagine analogies between the relation of this archipelago to Roman-Germanic Europe and the relation of the Japanese archipelago to China and East Asia – the main difference being that the Atlantic contains only one archipelagic group[14] instead of the Eastern two or three. Historical geographers, prehistorians and archae-ologists – the only specialists so far to have accepted the perspective I am proposing as a norm – further supply us with keys to the ethnic and cultural patterns of human settlement in the archipelago: the establishment in its various geographical zones of different kinds of maritime, stock-rearing and agricultural economies, and its linguistic divisions into communities speaking different kinds of Celtic, Anglo-Saxon and Norse. The incorpora-tion of a large part of the major island as a province of the Roman empire raises the problem of the archipelago's involvement in the history of complex literate and political cultures organizing power on the adjacent continent – in other words the problem of whether 'Britain' is part of 'Europe' – but the Roman empire, like Latin-German Christendom after it, does not effectively penetrate to all the oceanic or Atlantic regions of the archipelago, and the second-largest island is not directly affected by Roman government. The period of provincial organization is succeeded by one of resettlement, during which the techniques of the human geographer and archaeologist – dominant in periods which have left little documentary deposit – have once again most to tell us. For the first time we become aware of the distinction between history as the recorded and perennially re-evaluated memory of literate societies, and history as the past recovered, by whatever means appropriate, where it has not been consciously remem-bered and preserved, or at points where written and restated memory does not yield whatever results we are looking for. This distinction presents us with what will become the greatest single methodological difficulty in the construction of British history – a difficulty largely co-terminous with the problem of nationality.

'English history' certainly, and 'Scottish history' probably, begin with the consolidation of kingdoms which later become states – *loci* of

---

[14] [This might be challenged by mentioning the Canaries and the Faroes. It also sets the Caribbean Sea apart from the ocean of which it is a branch.]

government, law enforcement and service to a king, which begin to preserve archival deposits and concerning the doings of whose leaders chronicles begin to be written. One of these *loci* – to be called 'England' – is
formed by the consolidation of the Wessex–Mercia kingdom, of which the
Norman Conquest of the eleventh century was a takeover; the other – to be
called 'Scotland' – is formed because a local kingdom in a northern lowland zone is separated from the southern consolidation by the highland
area called 'Northumbria', which for a variety of reasons, including Danish
settlement, Norman devastation and the formation of marcher lordships, is
for a long time not fully absorbed by either kingdom. These two monarchies are differentiated from earlier petty kingdoms by the Anglo-
Norman capacity to maintain contact with the clerical and post-Roman
traditions of church, law and administration, and because they are *loci* of
centralized military and governmental power, they come to maintain
marches, or quasi-militarized border zones; first against one another, in
the debatable lands of the Northumbrian highland region, and second,
each against its unincorporated neighbouring Celtic area: Wales in the
south, the Gaelic Highlands and Islands in the north-west. The latter area
merges oceanically into that of the Irish peoples of the second great island,
but it is not here that the impact of Norman power upon Ireland – to use
that geographical expression – significantly takes place. The southern
kingdom is after the mid-eleventh century involved in a series of continental European power systems, and in Anglo-Romance cultural
exchanges; and in the twelfth century there takes place that momentous
occurrence in archipelagic history, the establishment of Anglo-Norman or
Norman-Welsh penetration into Ireland, which in due course takes on
some of the characteristics of a march. The governmental and cultural
focus to be called England now begins fully to straddle between a French
and continental world on the east, a Celtic, oceanic and extra-European
world to the west, and to engage in contacts upon both sides which
historiographical tradition will tend to minimize. The northern kingdom,
involved in a parallel duality but less self-contained in its culture because
less efficient in its government, develops a consciousness casting far greater
emphasis on the Highland Line on the one hand and the Auld Alliance on
the other.

With the beginnings of Anglo-Norman power in Ireland, the history of
the Three Kingdoms has in a sense begun; or at least we have the makings
of a set of themes common to the north and south of the largest island and
to both large islands together. 'British history' – if the term may be retained –
now becomes the history of contacts and penetrations between three *loci*

of Anglo-Norman power – one might use the term 'Scotto-Anglian' for distinction's sake – a variety of predominantly Celtic societies based on kinship rather than administration, and a diversity of marcher and marginal societies brought into being by these interactions. Among the latter are powers like the great Norman-Irish lordships, the western and northern marcher lordships in relation to the English monarchy, the Lordship of the Isles and the Earldom of Orkney on the periphery of Scottish power; and, as happens in penumbral systems of authority, some of these sometimes maximize their influence with respect to the settled and administrative zones behind them. Welsh nationalists today like to point out that had the conspiracy of Glendower, Percy and Douglas against the English king Henry IV succeeded – which does not seem so absurd to them as it did to the English poet Shakespeare[15] – a belt of marcher principalities, running from Wales through Northumbria to south-west Scotland, might have fragmented the advance of both centralized kingdoms; and the modern historian S. T. Bindoff dates the final absorption of the Northumbrian marches into 'England' no earlier than the repression of the Northern Rising of 1569.[16] Our historical perspective, it is worth remembering, is not merely Anglocentric: it takes as predetermined the triumph of that Wessex–Mercian–East Anglian combination which has been called 'political England'.

It is not only the marcher lordships of the expanding governed societies which create the political and cultural pluralism of the early and middle phases of 'British history': there is also the creation of a diversity of intermediate and counter-reactive societies all along the line which links, rather than separates, the conflicting and interacting cultures. There are Normanized Irish and Hibernicized Normans; there are bilingual Anglo-Welsh, as well as monoglot Welsh and English; there are Lowland Scots assimilated to the clan world of the Highlands, as well as clans which expand at the expense of others by methods of litigation rather than war; there are Celts who enter a Norse world and Norsemen assimilated to the Celtic pattern. Culture conflicts, the language barriers, the phenomena of the marches, the distinction between lowland and highland zones; these all join to make 'British history' – the expansion of government at the expense of kinship – a history of the constant creation, accompanied by the much less constant absorption, of new sub-cultures and even sub-nations. The *locus classicus* of this sort of process is of course Ireland, where by the end of the seventeenth century one sub-nation, the Catholic Old English, has

---

[15] *Henry IV, Part I*, Act III, scene I, lines 69–90.   [16] Bindoff, 1950, pp. 107–8, 208–10.

been partly extinguished and there have emerged three sub-nations in a single island: the Protestant Anglo-Irish or New English, a garrison land-holding class who generate a high culture without becoming a nation; the Scots-Irish, who survive into our own times as the classic example, along with the Afrikaners of South Africa, of the settler nation which is at the same time an anti-nation; and the Catholic and Gaelic 'native' Irish, undergoing a social transformation as violent as any in the history of colonization and for that reason evolving towards the presentation in the nineteenth and twentieth centuries of a revolutionary nationalism of an East European or Third World type, situated however within the confines of the history of the Atlantic archipelago.

The pluralist approach which I have been outlining has somehow to be reconciled with the evident fact that the pattern of 'British history' entails the steadily increasing dominance of England as a political and cultural entity. Even the nationalisms of the twentieth century do not reverse this generalization; it can be shown without much difficulty that Ireland became more nationalist and more revolutionary as it was increasingly assimilated to English-derived political and cultural norms, and that, in this case as in many others, revolutionary nationalism is less a means of resisting acculturation than a method of asserting one's own power over the process. But the Irish case is a partial exception – to be considered at a later point – to the generalization I want to put forward. This is that the history of an increasing English domination is remarkably difficult to write in other than English terms. The conqueror, after all, sets the rules of the game; he determines, in proportion to the extent to which his domination becomes effective, what people shall do, how they shall think and what they shall remember. And the conquering culture may be – and was in the case we are considering – the culture which maintains rules, speaks a language and preserves a history so powerfully effective that it obliges others to act in the same way and submit to, if they do not acquire, its consciousness. This was, by the way, pretty much Sir John Davies's explanation of the Hibernicization of Anglo-Norman settlers; but the problem it sets for the modern historian is best exemplified by the history of Scottish participation in the English theatre of the War of the Three Kingdoms. English politics, it is perfectly evident, took the Scots captive; they did not understand the behaviour of their allies, who were – partly for this very reason – stronger than they were; and consequently they were manipulated by events which they had no means of controlling and to which they were never admitted with the status of equal agents. Much against their will, they played the role of the dog's tail.

Now the relative weakness of the seventeenth-century Scots as political and historical actors cannot be separated from the relative dearth of Scottish means of expression. They were then, as they are now, a formidably articulate people; the distant drone of their sermons can still be heard; and we have at least two collections of personal papers, those of Robert Baillie and Johnston of Wariston,[17] in which an excruciating verbal sensitivity to the political and religious scene is amply documented. But these have to be set against the records of the Tower of London, the journals and unofficial diaries of the House of Commons, the many thousand pamphlets of the Thomason Collection; English administrative, legal, religious and political consciousness was already and long had been in mass production, and this fact was both an index to, and a means of, England's superior power. The English monarchy, largest, wealthiest and most expansive of the British political cultures, had for centuries been depositing official records and had recently undergone an uncontrollable explosion of the means of unofficial expression; and this was both cause and consequence of its being the strongest power, as well as of its being currently in a state of revolution. The English were both making and writing their history; it was a cause as well as a consequence of the Scottish inability to make theirs that they were ill-placed to write it either. And should it be objected that Cromwell carried off many of the records of medieval Scotland and that a ship bringing them back was wrecked on a sandbar in 1660, this misfortune – like the loss of the Irish records in the Four Courts explosion of 1922 – may be considered an illustration of the parable of the talents. The guardianship of one's past is power; the court of record is the kernel of English government; and from the political culture which has not enough self-determined and self-preserved history shall be taken away even that which it hath.

What I am arguing can be put in this way. A highly governed society is a highly literate society; in a multitude of forms from court records to history books, it puts forth articulations, linguistic and mental structures, which are – along a scale varying from official to unofficial, public to private, conscious to unconscious – highly paradigmatic, in the sense that they authoritatively determine the patterns in which men think and that the authority they exercise can be replaced only when there are found alternatives to it. Among these paradigmatic structures will be found a style of narrating, studying and criticizing history, with the result that a highly governed and literate society's consciousness of its own history will be of

[17] Laing, 1841–2; Paul, 1896–1911.

a different order – both more authoritative and, quite possibly, more self-critical – from that possessed by a society less centrally and bureaucratically organized. When a society of the first kind expands at the expense of societies of the second, the paradigmatic command of self which is one source of its power becomes means by which it exerts power over others. In obliging others to play the game according to its rules, it in some degree obliges them to accept its structuring of history and the past, and from this there will develop conflicts and problems both for the subordinated societies and for historians like ourselves. In the first place, there will appear the characteristic ambivalences of empire: the conquerors' uncertainty whether to impose their consciousness of the world upon the conquered or exclude them altogether from it; the uncertainty of the conquered whether to accept the dominant consciousness unequivocally, to accept it in order to modify it, or to reject it altogether and construct a new ordering of historical consciousness out of their awareness of the dilemma in which they are involved. The problems of the conquered produce a greater diversity of responses, but by no means all of these are valid modes of historical criticism.

These are problems of men living in history, and given the assumption that consciousness is paradigmatic, they are problems of the modes of exercising power. When the historian like ourselves appears, having – let us assume – no immediate commitment to the maintenance or reversal of any particular exercise of power, he finds himself involved in a related series of problems. The history he is trained to write consists in the inspection and criticism, the restatement and replacement, of paradigms which must be already existent, if for no other reason than that thinking starts with making assumptions, and communication with sharing assumptions, made by other people. But in a situation of cultural pluralism and partial domination like that we are considering, the history which he is invited to re-assess is not only history as seen by the dominant culture; it is actually the history of the dominant culture itself, somewhat to the exclusion of others, since the data, the traditions of scholarship and the currently operative paradigms he is to criticize are all preponderantly the product of that culture – which is one important reason it is dominant. As a major obstacle to all that I have said about the need for British history, we have to acknowledge that there are extremely powerful and valid professional and historical reasons pressing us towards the continuation of the Anglocentric perspective.

I practise English history a good deal, and I have no great anxiety to see that subject radically transformed; but I am arguing that 'British history'

needs to be re-invested with meaning, both because it contains areas of
human experience which it would be beneficial to study, and because I have
come to believe that we are doing harm to our understanding of ourselves
by not studying it. But I have called it a 'new subject', and it should be clear
from what I have said that I envisage it as existing alongside English history
as an old one. The point next to be explored is that we are now involved in
the problems which arise when we turn from the pursuit of one mode of
historical understanding to another, of a structurally different order. There
is a great difference between studying the history of a people who have
diligently studied it themselves – notably if you are yourself one of that
people, or if your understanding of history has the same sort of structure as
theirs – and studying the history of a people which has never been studied
by anybody at all. In the former case the conceptual field is already thickly
populated with paradigms – authoritative formulations which order the
understanding of history and form part of the history they order – and in
the latter case it is not. One is tempted to say that a historical *tabula rasa*
would have the charm of untrodden snow, but in practice we have all been
trained overwhelmingly in the reformulation of paradigms and the attraction of the thickly populated field usually proves irresistible. And a meth-
odology heavily reliant on the notion of paradigms[18] impels one to say that
two such fields as I have described certainly cannot be studied simultaneously, as if doing so formed a single historiographical operation, because
the mental actions involved where paradigms are numerous and crowd
upon your attention are too far removed from those required where you
have constantly to be providing them for yourself.

   The Irish historiographical tradition seems to have reached, in the works
of Conor Cruise O'Brien, Owen Dudley Edwards and a great many
others, a point of maturity where it may be emancipated from, by recognizing, its own compulsions. Irish historiography has to deal with a theme
common in the annals of romantic and revolutionary nationalism: how
a collection of pre-modern cultures were violently transformed – I am
anxious to avoid the word 'modernization' wherever possible – by an alien
power acting on them from without, and how the emerging collectivity
discovered the conceptual, political and social means to take charge of the
process of its own transformation. That seems to comply with the modern
definition of 'revolution', and the fact that it issued in the foundation of
a stolid petty-bourgeois society need not deter us; many revolutions end
that way. The history of this process is now highly available, and Irish

---

[18] [So it was then; I might not make the claim now.]

scholarship has passed, with characteristic delight, from the making of myths to the study of the making of myths and (God help us) the men who made them. But it remains true, of course, that Irish history is to an inordinate degree the history of responses to England, while English historians writing of Ireland maintain – as I suppose they always will – the traditional tone of mild wonder that such things should be going on in their otherwise orderly universe. The obvious first step, pedagogically speaking, in passing from 'English' to 'British' history would be to make sure that the student read as much of Irish as he did of English historiography, and read them concurrently. A twofold consciousness is part of the equipment we all need; less in order to repent of the sins of our ethnic ancestors than to recognize that things happen in different places at the same time.

The Scottish mode of historical consciousness is of a less concentrated complexity, but for that reason harder to describe. Scottish universities usually maintain departments of Scottish history alongside departments of history in some more general sense, and I understand that this has on the whole proved counter-productive;[19] the emphasis has fallen too much on the prevention of poaching and too little on the development of one's own preserves. Behind this dichotomy, a sharp distinction between Unionism and nationalism has also been at work; but what is of more concern to our theme, behind this again can be discerned a Scottish opinion, visible at least as far back as the beginnings of sixteenth-century Protestantism, that the future of the northern kingdom lay less in independence and any closer relation with the Celtic or the European world, than in a closer integration with the Anglian chain of societies, for which the term 'Britain' even then seemed appropriate. It is true, then, as English writers exasperatedly maintain, that 'Britain' is a Scots invention, a piece of pluralist semantics designed to assure that the integration of 'England' and 'Scotland' should be an *Ausgleich* and not an *Anschluss*. David Hume and other great men of eighteenth-century Edinburgh, who insisted on describing themselves as 'North Britons', meant by that term to assert that they were not Englishmen, and that even Englishmen were now British. It is the case, however, that Scottish culture, even at the peak it reached in their time, was not fully able to maintain its autonomy.[20]

But to compare these instances is to realize that Scottish national and historical consciousness remains one in which the choices of identity are open, probably because they cannot be resolved. Irish history presents the

---

[19] [These reproaches have long been obsolete.]   [20] Daiches, 1964. [See now Kidd, 1993.]

case of an agony, a classic identity crisis capable of solution only by the death of the divided self and its rebirth in a new, exclusive and revolutionary form. By comparison, Scottish history has been, and may remain, a mere matter of choice, in which the acceptance of anglicization, the insistence on the concept of Britain, Lowlands localism and Gaelic romanticism, remain equally viable options, and the problem is to reconcile one's sense of identity with one's awareness of so open-ended a structure of choice. I offer this distinction less in order to predict that a revolutionary nationalist solution is improbable – though one senses that there is some deep level on which Yeats was not spurious and MacDiarmid is[21] – than in order to establish a hypothesis of some importance to my theme. This is that there is an important difference – important certainly to ourselves – between a romantic and a tangential identity. In the first of these the subject's crisis is so profound that he must resolve it by re-creating his self; in the second, where irony suffices and need not become tragedy, the subject moves eclectically between avenues of possible self-determination and counts it his freedom that he can, since he must, continue to do so. He is given several roles to play and sets out to play them; and he defines the culture, even the nation, to which he belongs as possessing the same tangential identity as himself, and as solving the same problems in the same way. To say this, of course, is not to command success, but it is to exert the freedom to set one's own goals.

The second point we have reached is that one possible presentation of 'British history' would emphasize its consisting of the three modes of historical consciousness I have defined. I will assume for simplicity's sake, what may not in fact be true, that there are no more than these three, and that Welshmen, Orangemen and Orkneymen have not developed complex historiographical traditions of their own. One highly sensible way of beginning to learn some 'British history' would be to familiarize oneself with all three; by which is not meant that anyone can achieve an equal degree of empathy with all of them, or that there might exist some ideal synthesis of them all, through which 'British history' might be perceived and experienced as a whole. To desire such a synthesis would mean that one had become a 'British' nationalist, which I think no one ever has, ever will or ever should. The fact is that these three traditions, if I have described them correctly, make different demands, and arise out of the making of different demands, on the subject's sense of identity, so that no

---

[21] [A claim which may still cause fury. Yet when I read MacDiarmid I am aware that I do not believe him; when I read Yeats, that it does not matter whether I do.]

one individual can immediately share the experiences which have called all three into being. English historiography down to the present – though we may be at the beginnings of change here – rests upon a sense of identity so secure as to be unreflective and almost unconscious; Irish historiography affirms and records a romantic crisis of identity, and Scottish a tangential identity consisting in a continuous movement between alternative roles.

Now this may be the reason why Scottish historiography is on the whole [1973] the least developed of the three, and why Scottish scholars have tended to remove themselves to English universities, leaving the study of Scottish history to those who have happened to be interested.[22] But it must be clear that, in endeavouring to articulate the case for a pluralist and multicultural perception of British history, I have been outlining an attitude which one would virtually need a tangential sense of identity to adopt, since both ethnocentrism and nationalism entail a high degree of commitment to a single and unitary point of view. Where the Scots have failed – after a glorious start in the eighteenth century – it may seem that I am arguing that other tangential cultures must take up the challenge; and though I would be suspicious of myself if I thought I were sounding any kind of patriotic trumpet, the thought has something to do with the location of today's audience and today's speakers within the context of another phase of 'British history', about which I will say something in conclusion.

The expansion of Anglo-Norman – now English – control to nearly all parts of the Atlantic archipelago was completed by the first half of the eighteenth century. Scottish Gaelic society was effectively subdued, though it was not to be physically threatened until the Highland Clearances of a hundred years later; and Ireland, ceasing to be a mere Anglo-Celtic frontier zone, was in an early phase of that social transformation which was to produce a revolutionary politics after two hundred years. The dominant English society was now embarking on two related enterprises beyond the confines of the archipelago, the successful combination of which was to break up only in our own times. These two were the exertion of a real, if limited, military dominance in the power relations of the continent of Europe, and a related commercial expansion beyond the oceans into North America and Southern Asia. The Union of the Kingdoms in 1707 – the creation of 'Britain' as a political entity – came about, it was and is generally agreed, because these were the only terms on which the

---

[22] For the record of complaints on this point see Hanham, 1969. [This too may be dismissed as no longer valid.]

Scottish kingdom could secure even a secondary role in the two enterprises, and because the English were prepared to let the Scots inscribe 'Britain' at the head of the deed of partnership if they really wanted to. The third of the Three Kingdoms obtained no such partnership – to the discontent, be it said, of that natural imperialist Arthur Griffith in the twentieth century.

Transatlantic expansion leads to the establishment of a number of colonies of settlement. As a rule one thinks of these, as they appear to have thought of themselves, as 'English', but there is a Scots-Irish emigration and a Highland Scottish emigration, and one may speculate on the exact ethnic and cultural makeup of the eighteenth-century Americans and wonder what both coasts of the North Atlantic world might have looked like had African labour not been readily available for the American plantations. But the predominance of English political and cultural forms creates that loose circle of Anglo-Atlantic societies of which I spoke in connection with the work of J. R. Pole. This we saw as disrupted by the civil war which led to American independence, with the beginnings of Anglo-Canadian history as a secondary consequence; while the history of other segments reaches a linked series of culminations with the Scottish Enlightenment – clearly a major event in the history of social consciousness – the upheavals in Irish history from the Volunteer movement of 1780, through the Rebellion of 1798 and the Union of 1801, and in England the beginnings of a political transformation half-furthered and half-frustrated by the resumption, on a really massive scale, of British involvement in the wars of Europe and the pursuit of maritime power in Asia.

From about this time – perhaps the British decision to abandon claims to the Ohio country in 1783 would do as a date[23] – one has to begin ceasing to regard the history of the United States as part of 'British history', to the extent to which that culture passes out of the archipelagic and Atlantic world into a continental orbit of its own. The imperial crown, one remembers, did not like frontiers of settlement. Nevertheless, among the diversity of peoples whose history makes up 'British history', a place must be kept for the vanished people – those million or so Britons from the larger island who emigrated to the United States rather than the British colonies and were effortlessly absorbed, leaving scarcely a hyphen to mark their passage.[24] The complex of colonies known as Canada, however, remained, to involve the crown in relationships with settler communities and so to provide 'British history' with a continuing *outremer* in which the

---

[23] For the Canadian perspective on this see McNaught, 1969, pp. 55–6, 68–9.
[24] Berthoff, 1953; Thornton, 1966, pp. 157–9.

conflict of cultures and the creation of new sub-cultures went on as it had been shaped in the archipelago proper. I have quite recent memories – too recent, it might very well be said – of the intellectual excitement of reading some Canadian history and realizing that, in addition to the major theme of *l'histoire québecoise*, I was studying both a North American society which had taken a turn of its own – having been settled partly by American Loyalists excluded by the War of the Revolution, partly by immigrant groups, some of whom cared little which side of the 49th parallel they were on – and a British society in which the pluralisms of the archipelago are still vividly reflected, so that even today [1973] it may be desirable in parts of Ontario to know who is Loyalist, who is Orange, who is Catholic and who is Highland.

From Canada one instinctively turns – though it is unclear how far this is a natural transition – to those other nineteenth-century colonies of settlement which were established outside the zone of archipelagic-Atlantic expansion, for the most part in the Southern Hemisphere. Of these, two have become established as viable national societies; a third and a fourth seem doomed to absorption, one way or another, by the revolutionary nationalisms of Africa – of which Afrikanerdom is one; and a fifth, that of the Kenya highlands, seems to be disappearing altogether. 'British history' now takes on a global dimension, constituted by the establishment of the societies I have mentioned, by the partial anglicization of non-European societies in the Caribbean, Africa, Southern Asia and Oceania, and by a third phenomenon which our projection must include: the catastrophic Irish *diaspora* of the mid-nineteenth century, which changed the character of the archipelago, the United States, most overseas British societies and, last but not least, the Catholic Church in many of the areas of nineteenth-century settlement. The Irish now became a people visible on a world stage, and Arthur Griffith, employing the Central European distinction between 'historical' and 'non-historical' peoples, contended that they were entitled to share empire with the British as the Hungarians shared it with the Austro-Germans.[25] His thought was less nonsensical than it was malignant.

On the global as on the archipelagic and Atlantic stages, then, we may continue our projection of 'British history' as the conflict between, and creation of, societies and cultures which it has been since the beginning. I have just been speaking of societies most of which were episodically linked by what has been called *The Commonwealth Experience.*[26] This remains one important determinant of their history; but we know that

---

[25] Griffith, 1904.   [26] Mansergh, 1969.

this term denotes only a part of their shared inheritance, and does comparatively little to explain the internal development of each one of them. That is to say, it is possible to write the history of New Zealand or Australia, as it is that of England, with a minimum of reference to 'the Commonwealth experience' and with none at all to the internal development of any other 'British' society, as it is remembered and re-assessed by the society whose history it is. These are societies which, by and large, do not study one another's history; each of them studies its own, after which it studies English history, Western European history, American history and the history of such other civilizations as it may be persuaded matter to it – and the study of Irish history is a purely sectarian phenomenon. The same pattern, I was once told by a Puerto Rican historian, obtains among the Hispanic societies of the Caribbean and Central America; each studies its own history and Spanish history, but not the history of its neighbours. It is easy to see how a derivative society may fall into this highly insular mode of treating its own derivation; I have heard it complained that there are those at the University of Singapore who rely for an understanding of both Chinese and Malay civilization on a somewhat excessive concentration upon Singaporean history.[27] We are back at the problem that history is both a mode of understanding oneself and a mode of understanding others. We can all agree that a society must constantly re-evaluate its own history, as part of its own self-image, and that it must study the history of others, partly as a means of understanding its own place in the world. The problem is that of the best strategy for reversing the perspective.[28]

This presentation has room in it for the development of several types of historical consciousness, and I have stressed this because I believe it to be peculiarly suited to the historiographical needs of societies possessing what I described as the tangential sense of identity. That is, it is not a task for those concerned to continue the main traditions of English or Irish historiography, but the rest of us – and I am thinking from the banks of the Mississippi as well as those of the Waimakariri[29] – are, I believe, involved in the perspective I have been trying to focus. The British cultural star-cluster is at present in a highly dispersed condition, various parts of it feeling the attraction of adjacent galaxies; the central giant has cooled, shrunk and moved away, and the inhabitants of its crust seem more than

[27] [I do not recall where I heard this, or whether it was – still less, is – well founded.]

[28] [A paragraph commenting adversely on Louis Hartz's *Founding of New Societies*, 1964, is here omitted.]

[29] [I then held an appointment at Washington University in St Louis. The Waimakariri is that one of the major rivers of Canterbury whose course lies closest to Christchurch.]

ever disposed to deny that the rest of us ever existed. Since it no longer emits those radiations we felt bound to convert into paradigms, we are free and indeed necessitated to construct cosmologies of our own. But the presentation of history I have been advocating, while post-Commonwealth and extra-European, is also highly anti-nationalist: I do not propose that each star should consider itself the centre even of its own universe – though this is within limits a legitimate perspective – so much as that it should seek new and interesting ways of defining its tangential identity by remapping the various systems within which it moves, of which I have tried to define one. There are others. John Beaglehole was a historian of cartography, which he knew as a singularly full human experience, and I have tried to salute him by an exercise in mapping the historical consciousness.

PART II

The Three Kingdoms and the English Problem

CHAPTER 3

*The field enlarged: an introduction** *

(1)

An essay pursuing the themes proposed in 1974 appeared eight years later.[1] It tentatively explored the relations between a kingdom and its marches, since British history was to entail the expansion of medieval and early modern states into lands where human society had been otherwise organized. It is not reprinted here, since this volume aims to present essays written after the 'new British history' had been taken up by other hands – a process belonging on the whole to the 1990s and after. The previous decade appears in retrospect a time of profound change in both Britain and New Zealand, as globalized economies and their politics replaced industrial social democracy, accompanied by the administrations of Margaret Thatcher in Britain and David Lange and Roger Douglas in New Zealand.[2] In Britain, it produced a literature of disorientation, in which both a known history and its implied future were said to have been lost, and the turn towards Europe was enjoined on terms which left it unclear whether this implied the acquisition of a new history or the abandonment of any history distinctively British or English. Among professional historians, however, it was a time of exciting revisions, in which the pasts of state and church, nation and empire, were better understood when seen as precarious and exposed to multiple contingencies. This volume intends neither criticism nor apology for what has been going on in the academy, whatever may be said of public intellectuals.

It is now possible to supply a selective and certainly not exhaustive bibliography of works published in the last decade and a half, which explicitly or implicitly pursue the objectives recommended in this

---

*[Written for this volume in 2004.]

[1] Originally printed as Pocock, 1982.
[2] Pocock, 1992d, not reprinted here, was an attempt to view the historiographies of both cultures in this setting.

volume.[3] To this may be added one (edited by a New Zealand expatriate) which specifically addresses the 'new British history' as both a programme and a problematic[4] – as indeed do most of those listed and others that may have escaped my notice. The present volume aims no higher than at taking its place among them, but some generalizations may assist in defining that place. The works listed review history from medieval to modern, whereas the essays presented here focus on the early modern period, c. 1500 – c. 1800. The medieval literature isolates a set of crucial themes, which continue to govern the history here reviewed. These include, first and predominantly, the exceptional strength and durability of the pre-Conquest English kingdom,[5] which may almost (but never incontestably) be said to have assimilated its Norman and Angevin inheritors, so that they claimed to be its continuators – thus founding the constitutional mythology of which English historiography so long consisted.[6] The Anglo-Norman kingdom, always aggressive, became expansive in the thirteenth century, and attempted what we should term an empire of the entire archipelago.[7] By this time, however, there had come to exist a differently structured but equally persistent monarchy defining 'Scotland', which successfully resisted absorption into the English kingdom – thus leaving open the question whether the English myth is not one of self-sufficiency even before empire, the Scottish myth one of independence of England. We encounter here what these essays will term the 'English problem', which is also the problem of how far 'British history' can negate the Anglocentricity it is designed to combat.

Edward I's kingdom carried out a successful conquest of Wales, which however remained a land of marcher lordships not fully incorporated into England until the sixteenth century. In the large island of Ireland, where Anglo-Norman lordships had been established in the preceding century, the organization of state was less successful, and the same may be said of the Scottish kingdom's dealings with the Gaelic and Scandinavian far north of the long island of Britain and the lesser island groups beyond it. In Ireland especially, we encounter the problem of 'British history' as it expands beyond those islands it has succeeded in defining as 'British' – a problem which is also that of 'Europe' and British history's place within or without it. The term 'Europe' can be defined in so many ways that one must always ask – but

[3] Tompson, 1986; Robbins, 1988 and 1998; Kearny, 1989; Helgerson, 1992; Ellis and Barber, 1995; Grant and Stringer, 1995; Bradshaw and Morrill, 1996; Brockliss and Eastwood, 1997; Claydon and McBride, 1998; Murdoch, 1998; Bradshaw and Roberts, 1998; Connolly, 1999; Smyth, 2001; Powell, 2002.
[4] Burgess, 1999.   [5] Campbell, 1995, with bibliography; Davies, R. R., 2000, pp. 54 –5.
[6] Pocock, 1957, 1987 (B); Greenberg, 2001.   [7] Davies, 2000.

not always hope to be told – in what sense it is being used at the moment. One is that it defines a civilization taking shape in the far western, Latin-speaking provinces of the former Roman empire, that of 'Britain' having included most of the larger island of the Atlantic archipelago but not the rest of that complex. In the high medieval period this civilization expanded in three directions, redefining 'Europe' as it did so:[8] east, by settlement and conquest, through Germany into Slavonic and Lithuanian lands higher up the peninsula between the Baltic and Mediterranean seas; north, through adoption more than conquest, into the non-Roman peninsula of Scandinavia; and west, through processes of Norman and English conquest, into the Celtic-speaking parts of the Atlantic archipelago. In this sense, 'British history' – defined as the establishment, the expansion, and the responses to the expansion, of the post-Norman English and Scottish kingdoms – is rightly defined as part of the history of 'Europe'; and between 1066 and 1453 there are many occasions on which French-speaking kings of England are deeply involved in the warlike politics of Normandy, Aquitaine, Gascony and the kingdom of France, which they try but ultimately fail to take over. A point has unhappily been reached, however, at which the ideology of European union demands, or commands, that this kingdom's involvement in France be recognized as more important, because more truly 'European', than its involvement in the maritime frontier of the Atlantic archipelago. Whatever may be meant by the proposition that one historical process is 'more important' than another, we are clearly confronted by the further proposition that some 'Europeans' are more 'European' than others, and that the history of the sub-continental peninsula is more 'European' than that of the islands prolonging it. Of all the post-imperial states now joining to constitute 'Europe', Great Britain is the only one to be assailed by these confused dichotomies and their curiously bullying tone. The issue is less that of whether Britain is or is not part of 'Europe' than of how the word 'Europe' is being used. The assumption throughout this volume is that the history of interacting political formations in the archipelago is a story worth telling in its own terms, as is that of the same structures interacting with those of the sub-continent. Neither can be denied meaning.

(11)

Medieval British history therefore studies the history of the islands as attentively, and in as much detail, as that of the interactions of France,

---

[8] Bartlett, 1993.

Flanders and England. It notes, however, that in the former field the collisions between organized states and cultures resistant to these structures reached a point where the intellect of the former was tempted to define the latter as 'barbarian';[9] a point where 'Europe' crosses a cultural frontier and begins to expand into cultures marginal to or beyond it. The modern words 'imperialism' and 'colonialism' are foreshadowed. The essays in this volume, however, focus on an early modern period between 1500 and 1800, during most of which the word 'empire' bore a different meaning. They take their departure from after the year 1453, taken to mark the final expulsion of the English monarchy from the kingdom of France; and it might be held that they make too little of the significance of this in the history they seek to define. The emphasis now falls on the history of states within the islands of Britain and Ireland, and on a period of two and a half centuries during which the English monarchy played a militarily limited role in the politics of sub-continental Europe.

The Lancastrian dynasty gives way to the marginally Welsh Tudors,[10] and Henry VIII appears as a revolutionary if catastrophic actor in both British history and English. The emphasis falls on a series of parliamentary statutes[11] by which Wales is incorporated within the English kingdom, the English crown's lordship in Ireland is converted into a kingship, and – perhaps most momentously of all – England is declared to be and have been an 'empire', a term denoting less its exercise of sovereignty over subject realms than its exercise of unshared sovereignty over itself. This 'empire' is as much ecclesiastical as political; the king exercises a jurisdiction over the church in England which he does not share with the pope; but this statement transforms the character of state as well as church in the kingdom now an empire. This empire is proclaimed in parliament, as the most solemn and sovereign mode of declaring and exercising the authority of the crown, and though its consequences are, over time, necessarily Protestant, the Anglican Reformation has characteristics not shared with the Lutheran or Calvinist. The problems of empire are now those of the relation between crown, church and parliament; and since England exercises 'empire' over subordinate realms as well as itself,[12] the solution to problems self-imposed upon England will have to be imposed upon those realms if it cannot be shared with them.

---

[9] Gillingham, 1995; Davies, 2000, ch. 5.

[10] I have often wondered whether the audiences attending Shakespeare's *Henry V* knew that after Henry's death Catherine of France married Owen Tudor. If they did, the King's conversations with Captain Fluellen would take on a special meaning.

[11] Below, pp. 136–7, 164–5.

[12] For a detailed study of the emergence of this duality, see Armitage, 2000.

Henry VIII's policies then act within Latin Christendom in its dividing crisis as well as within the history or histories of the Atlantic archipelago. There is a dynastic marriage which opens up the prospect of an English claim to the Scottish succession, and in the War of the Rough Wooing a brutal, if inconclusive, attempt at annexing that kingdom by conquest. The history is complicated first by the different ways in which papal authority was extinguished in the two kingdoms, and second by the series of accidents which flung both the Tudor and Stuart dynasties into crises not only of succession but of gender. There are periods of female rule – the 'monstrous regiment of women' – whose effects on both kingdoms are durable and still being analysed.[13] The 'age of the monstrous regiment', as it is a temptation to call the second half of the sixteenth century, is finally terminated in 1603, when James VI of Scotland becomes James I of England. Here begin the periodizations of British history with which this volume is chiefly concerned. An 'Age of the Three Kingdoms' leads to the sequence of the First and Second British Empires. The meanings of these terms, particularly of the last, will require elucidation.

King James was that rare if not unique phenomenon, a crowned king who was also an articulate political theorist. This has rendered him of peculiar interest to historians of discourse, notably to the Folger Institute Center for the History of British Political Thought, under whose auspices several of the ensuing chapters were first written. His thinking about kingship and kingdoms has much to tell us about the kingdoms he ruled, the problems they presented and the ways in which he and his various subjects responded to these problems; not in the light of the old controversy as to whether he was an 'absolutist' or a 'constitutionalist', but in that of his widely accepted understanding of how a king was related to his kingdom, as a head to its body or a husband to his wife – the political theology, as it has been called, of the King's Two Bodies.[14] But James VI and I was the head of a multiple monarchy of Three Kingdoms, and if he was not to be emperor – a style he may briefly have considered – but a king, he must either be three heads, which would be monstrous, or the head of a single body. His third kingdom was so far anomalous that he (and we) might be tempted to dismiss it; what he had in Ireland was kingship – for so the law said – but hardly a kingdom, since there was no body politic to which he stood as head. 'I am the husband', James once said, 'and the whole isle my wife', but the use of the singular tells us he meant Ynys Pridein but not Inis Fail. There was an Irish parliament and a Church of

[13] Wormald, 1988; McLaren, 1999; Guy, 2004.   [14] Kantorowicz, 1957.

Ireland; it would be possible, though it is little documented, for his New English Protestant subjects to hope for the status of a kingdom in the full sense of two-bodies political theology; otherwise Ireland must be a subordinate kingdom annexed to the English crown by conquest, not a wife but a captive concubine. It is significant that Irish Catholics – Old English, perhaps, rather than Irish-speaking – offered a Stuart king the undivided loyalty they could not offer a Tudor conqueror and heretic; but James could never be head of a Catholic kingdom in the sense in which English 'empire' made him head of the Church of England (or Ireland).

Here we meet James as a European sovereign, pursuing ecumenical policies which he hoped would reconcile him with Spain and promote peace in Christendom.[15] There is a strong presence in these schemes of a 'Gallican' theory of monarchy , in which a king might remain in communion or at least relation with Rome while exercising virtually all jurisdiction over the church within his realm; and Irish Catholics must hope for something of the kind if they wished to be James's subjects in a Catholic kingdom. But the possibility was seldom if ever mooted. In England the Royal Supremacy was law in a sense that came close to defining the papal supremacy as Antichrist, while in Scotland it was doubtful whether James were head of the Kirk at all – a role reserved for Christ – and he was working at a reinforcement of the powers of bishops as his sole means of ecclesiastical authority. James knew very well what headship of the church meant, and did not think he could govern without it. A Christian monarchy of the Three Kingdoms appeared an impossible triplicity; it was imaginable only in Protestant terms,[16] hence the cult of Constantine that took shape around James; and even in Britain proper the reconciliation of the two Protestant churches was no simple matter. If Stuart multiple monarchy faced the problem of Church and Kirk, it inherited from the Tudors the greatest of its failures, the inability to Anglicanize Irish Catholicism (as it had Welsh) by any means other than Protestant colonization.[17] British history is so much the history of a Protestant monarchy that there is an Irish Catholic history with which it finds hard to deal.

(III)

King James's most conspicuous failure as head of a multiple British monarchy – this does not mean that he was a failure as king of either England or Scotland – was the frustration of his attempt to bring about

---

[15] Patterson, 1997.   [16] Williamson, 1979.   [17] Bradshaw, 1998; Canny, 2001.

a union of his two kingdoms into one.[18] As husband of two wives, he was unable to reduce two wives to one wife, and the irreducible individualities this metaphor implies can be explained in more than one way. A union of England and Scotland would have been a union of two churches, and we have begun to see reasons why this would have been difficult. It would also have been a union of two laws, and the reasons why a majority pronounced this impossible almost from the start tell us much about the problems of writing a British history. The voices making this pronunciation were English. The legally educated gentry and professionals of that nation were acquainted with Sir John Fortescue's fifteenth-century dictum[19] that the customs of a people made them what they were, furnishing them with a 'second nature' that could not be abandoned without abandoning their distinctive existence – the medieval version of 'identity'. It was for this reason that Thomas Hedley told the House of Commons that they might make changes in the common law, but could not abolish it without abolishing themselves.[20] The proposal for a union seemed to entail this prospect, and may well have intensified, if not occasioned, the English belief that they possessed an 'ancient constitution' produced by their own immemorial self-creation. They could imagine the Scots accepting English law as theirs – as they believed the Welsh were doing and as might yet be done in Ireland – but if Scots might become English, the English had no intention of becoming Scots. Did they think of Scotland as possessing an alien law, or no law at all? What did the Scots themselves think? We know more of the English response to union than we do of the Scottish; but Scottish histories traditionally depict their thinking as sophisticated, historicist, and able to accept their own historical contingency, and this indeed was the response of Sir Thomas Craig when he described English and Scottish law as two stems from a common feudal origin.[21]

The English long resisted this thesis, and it is one of the points at which we encounter, at the heart of 'British history', what may be termed 'the English problem'. British history must be, in large measure though never in totality, a history of the encounter of peoples not (or no longer) English with an expanding English state and (in more senses than one) empire; it sets itself the objective of viewing this encounter in the setting provided by

[18] Galloway, 1986; Levack, 1987; Mason, 1994; Wormald, 1996.
[19] Chrimes, 1949, p. 17.
[20] Pocock, 1957, 1987, pp. 270–1 (1987 text) (B); Burgess, 1992, pp. 25–6.
[21] For Craig's *Jus Feudale* (1603), Pocock, 1957, 1987, pp. 79–90 (B); for his *De Unione* (1604), Mason, 1994, pp. 185–6.

Scottish, Irish, American or indigenous histories as these have shaped themselves. The story of the Jacobean union and its failure informs us that the English already possessed, and deeply believed, a history of their own self-formation, to which we do not yet know that Scots or Welsh possessed an equivalent, and that they were interested in either extending, or denying, this history to other peoples of the British monarchy, as a means of refusing to admit those peoples to a share in making English history. This, over the centuries, has not meant that the history the English relate of themselves is serene, secure, or unproblematic; it has on the contrary been replete with problems; but these problems have been seen as self-generated, arising within English history and resolved, however violently and disturbingly, within its continuity. The English have, in short, claimed to make their own history, even when it has included – or failed to include – the history of others; so that the history of empire, meaning the expansion of the English state beyond England, has been regarded as an aspect of the history of England's 'empire' over itself. 'British history' is therefore obliged to revise, where it should not aspire to abolish, a large part of the history the English have constructed of themselves. It cannot do this by becoming a history with the English left out, but a British history of the English will be difficult to achieve.

The debate over the Jacobean union introduces us to this problem, but it first appears in its full complexity when we study the historiography of the War, or Wars, of the Three Kingdoms.[22] The history of that historiography centres on the reduction of those wars to the English Civil War. This war was no fiction; it was the central trauma of early modern English (and British) history; but the English were so horrified at finding themselves at war with one another that they assumed the causes of this disaster must lie within English politics, and have written many works of genius to discover what they were. We need not (though we may) assume this enterprise to have been mistaken in order to point out that the wars broke out in Scotland and Ireland, and that there are presumably Scottish and Irish histories within which their genesis is to be found. It is a paradoxical consequence, however, that while most histories of these wars are Anglocentric, we do possess histories of the War of the Three Kingdoms written from an English point of view, whereas it is easier to find histories of the Scottish or Irish role and experience in this conflict than histories embracing the whole course of the War of the Three Kingdoms written from a Scottish or Irish point of view

---

[22] Chapter 5, below.

and presenting Three Kingdoms history as they see it.[23] Nationalism is not a complete response to imperialism.

(IV)

England is not an island, and the island of Britain is neither small nor simple. In the twenty-first century, it is still possible to pursue 'the discovery of islands' by travelling north, out of the arable lowlands of southern England with the 'narrow seas' of the English Channel behind one, into the pastoral and industrial North, historic Lowland Scotland, Argyll and Skye, ending in a terrain as much Norse as Gaelic, with the Hebrides to westward and Orkney and Shetland in an oceanic north. At the end of such a journey I found the title of a volume of haiku by a seventeenth-century Japanese poet, *The Narrow Road to the Deep North*,[24] evocative of the road I had been taking; and as a South Islander, I remembered travelling, quite late in life, to a northern New Zealand where history was more Maori than I had recognized: from the wide maquis of the Urewera, where Tuhoe and Ringatu fought the crown and its Ngatiporou allies,[25] to the ultimate promontory of Cape Te Reinga, where one may stand and feel both islands as giant *waka* at one's back. Both were historical as well as spatial experiences; journeys through many histories and their landscapes, of which one knew some and others had been left out of one's reading; and an island is not small if one can live at one end of it and know nothing of the history going on at the other. (Ireland is the contrary example; it is not small because one knows only too well what is happening at the other extremity.) Britain, I saw, is an extraordinary island; and islands and archipelagos can contain more histories than can be easily seen together, or explained away. It is a continental snobbery to suppose that they are necessarily small.

Islands are in oceans, not in narrow seas; and from the English south-west, the Gaelic west, and the Norse far north of the Stuart monarchies, the seas of Europe open out into the Atlantic and the global or world-girdling ocean.

---

[23] There are military histories (Gentles, 1992; Bennett, 1997; Kenyon and Ohlmeyer, 1998) of the conflict as a whole that are necessarily political histories as well. For a proposed 'holistic' history of the Three Kingdoms crisis, see Morrill, 1993, pp. 91–117, 245–72, and 1996. For a study of an individual actor in a multiplicity of contexts, Ohlmeyer, 1993. None of these is quite the Scottocentric or Hibernocentric history of the whole, which I identify as lacking above. See, however, Ohlmeyer, 1995.

[24] Basho, 1966. His 'deep north' was that of his own island of Honshu, not the culturally distinctive Hokkaido, which he did not visit.

[25] Binney, 1995.

The English, and less successful Scottish, footholds on the North American continent and in the Caribbean, established during James I's reign, begin the creation of an Atlantic space and emporium – extended to the African coast and the trade in slaves – into which English empire is extended and British history acquires a new dimension. There is a certain continuity between these colonizing activities and those in Ireland; but the latter are part of the establishment – questionable though it always was – of a kingdom in, or of, Ireland, whereas the colonies in America were not thought of, now or until it was too late, as subordinate realms within an empire (the sense of that word changes). They were not vice-regal kingdoms (the Spanish formula) or counties palatine (the nearest there was to an English formula);[26] they were nearer to being trading posts than realms, commonwealths or civil societies. As they evolved towards the latter condition, their legal definition lagged behind; it was the first, momentous, and ultimately disastrous instance of that Seeleyan 'absence of mind' by which the English acquired an empire without engaging their intellect in its definition. How far this is true of empire within the archipelago is another question.

(v)

Two of the following essays, and much more of the perspective of this book, are shaped by the work of the Folger Institute Center for the History of British Political Thought. At the conclusion of a series of seminars between 1984 and 1987, surveying the field as we then knew it,[27] we realized that we had been operating almost wholly within the rich history of English political thought, and set about further enquiries into the political discourse of Scotland, Ireland and pre-federal America.[28] At this point our history of 'British political thought' may be said to begin; it entails, of course, an enquiry into the meaning – even the meaningfulness – of the term itself. The Center is now investigating interactions and exchanges, in the field of political discourse, between the kingdoms of the archipelago and the states, churches, academies and presses of the adjacent parts of Europe; there are shared histories here.

The focus of study is less on political theory and philosophy than on the organization of thinking about what was happening in the politics and

---

[26] Koebner, 1961; Greene, 1986, 1990; Palumbo, 2001.   [27] Pocock, Schochet and Schwoerer 1993 (B).
[28] Mason, 1994; Robertson, 1995; Morgan, 1999; Ohlmeyer, 2000; Connolly, 2000. Other volumes arising from the Center's activities are Peck, 1991; Burgess, 1996; Smith, 1998; Mendle, 2001.

history of the peoples concerned. There is a 'British problem' in the sense that it must be asked, then and now, whether their experience could be brought together in the framework imposed by a 'British' kingdom and empires; it is here that the problem of an English hegemony is at its most recalcitrant. The emphasis in such a history of discourse, however, must fall upon the communities of discourse within which history went on; and the following essays enquire in what ways it was possible for the consciously literate among the Irish, the Scots, the Americans and – left to the last because they placed themselves first – the English to identify themselves and discuss their politics. The Age of the Three Kingdoms was upon them and concerns us.

CHAPTER 4

Two kingdoms and three histories?
Political thought in British contexts

Dr Mason has edited, and powerfully helped in writing, a series of essays[1] which in the first place examine the political discourse concerned with a 'matter of Scotland'. The period is the sixteenth century and the medium of discourse is print. We are therefore looking at an age in which historians once conventionally located the emergence of 'national monarchies', and indeed 'nation' and 'monarchy' are organizing concepts in the discourse before us. In such an age it would be reasonable also to look for the emergence of canons of authoritative literature, invented either by contemporaries or in retrospect by subsequent authors and authorities. Canons are to be mistrusted, lest they come to control our minds as they may have controlled those of others; nevertheless, in organizing a new field of study – and we are still exploring 'the unknown subject'[2] – it can be of experimental value to construct a canon and then enquire if it needs to be deconstructed. Let it be suggested, then, that scholars are now in a position to organize (should they decide to do so) a 'history of Scottish political thought' around a canon or succession of prominent authors, minimally consisting of John Mair, Hector Boece, John Knox, George Buchanan, James VI (and I), Sir Thomas Craig and (if we reach as far as the covenanting period) Samuel Rutherford. There are figures who might be added – Arthur Williamson speaks strongly for David Hume of Godscroft, Robert Pont and John Napier[3] – and absences that may be felt: it is an inconvenience that neither Andrew Melville nor any of his colleagues is known to have expounded in full folio his view of kirk and kingship. But we have a canon; it sets paradigms which endure until, and even after, they are challenged – Craig's statement of Scottish law's historic distinctiveness lasts into the age of Stair and the age of Kames, George Buchanan's mythic

---

[1] Mason, 1994, in which this essay – the opening paragraphs now abbreviated – originally appeared (Pocock, 1994b).

[2] Pocock, 1982.   [3] Williamson, 1994 [also McGinnis and Williamson, 2002].

history endures until it is deconstructed after 1707[4] – and it would be possible to construct a history around these major figures and then to look critically at our own construction. However organized, a history of Scottish political thought would be a valuable addition to our resources, and Dr Mason and his collaborators have taken long strides towards providing us with one.

Faced with a canon, and in consequence a tradition, which we have invented – that is, which we have both constructed and discovered – we ask with what image of the political culture surrounding it we are now furnished. There appears a 'Scotland' and a 'kingdom' – in Buchanan's phrase a *jus regni apud Scotos* – constituting a nation, a monarchy and a 'European' cultural province: one, that is to say (since 'Europe', too, is a construct and not a given), built out of interacting Latin, Roman-British, Gaelic, Norman, Norse and Anglian (since we had better not say English) cultural components in an archipelagic province of the expanding Latin West. The connotations of 'province' are cultural and not political; the *rex Scottorum* is not a *subregulus* but wears a closed imperial crown, though he has had to fight for it against the endeavours of his powerful southern neighbour to reduce it and him to vassal or tributary status. He can be the contested focus of loyalties and images of community capable of stating themselves in national terms, and histories of kingdom and nation can be written in ways which affirm their autonomy. At the same time, however, our canon arrestingly begins with an affirmation that Scottish history can only be written within the context of a *Historia Maioris Britanniae.*[5]

This is an Anglo-oriented if not an Anglocentric proposition, but at the same time it is to be observed that 'Scotland', nearly if not quite alone among the kingdoms of Latin 'Europe', believes itself to possess a cultural and even a barbarian frontier. John Mair's 'wild Scots', speaking a Gaelic or Irish tongue from which the very name they share with their civilized neighbours may be derived, form part of the cumulative European image of 'savage' or feral man, and Lowlanders entertain an image of them as ethnically 'other' no less vivid than that which the English entertain of Scots in general. In this volume, aside from Edward Cowan's brief exploration of the possible Gaelic roots of the marquis of Argyll's political ideas,[6] we do not hear much of any political discourse which the *Gaidhealtacht* may have practised or possessed, and it is a question whether any such existed in scribal or typographic form. Gaeldom was not an illiterate

[4] Kidd, 1993.   [5] Constable, 1892, pp. 48–50.
[6] Cowan, 1994 [also MacCraith, 1995; Macinnes, 1995; Dawson, 1998].

culture, and the idea that its discourse must have been oral and bardic in character is part of an Anglo-Scottish stereotype which perhaps ought to be challenged; but while there may be no reason in principle why an ecclesiastic or humanist Latin-Gaelic discourse should not have existed, the reader of this volume is left ignorant whether one in fact did. Is it an unfair assumption that Gaelic units of government were not of a size or a sort to have been held together by systems of practising law both written and unwritten, or by courtly centres where lay as well as sacerdotal clerisies might form themselves? Ecclesiastics, lawyers and humanists furnish the three professions which originate the literate and literary discourse helping to hold together the monarchies and commonwealths of early modern Europe and generating their 'political thought'; in this respect Anglian-speaking 'Scotland' is not an exception, and we are left asking whether Gaelic-speaking 'Scotland' is. Both 'wild' and 'civilized' Scots are 'Scots' to John Mair.

England – we enter here on the dangerous but useful course of defining Scotland by the non-presence of English characteristics – was a highly if imperfectly unified *communitas regni* or *corpus misticum* held together by (*inter alia*) a common law or common custom of the realm, administered by a hierarchy of courts in all of which the crown was mystically present (*coram rege*), and by a polity of counsel which humanists were engaged in partially transforming into a literary and rhetorical culture. A discourse of common law, common lawyers and law students therefore entered into a series of complex interactions with a discourse of courtly humanism, proliferating in increasingly sophisticated poetical forms, and an increasingly populous print culture with its centre at Paul's Churchyard, to develop and disseminate an image of the realm as mystical body with the crown as its mystical head, the law as its nerves or ligaments and counsel as its spirit or intelligence.[7] The great discourse of 'the king's two bodies' was certainly not unknown in Edinburgh; James VI was its accomplished exponent before he became James I; but it does seem possible to say that it was not supported and disseminated by so thick and widespread an integument of institutions and language as can be detected in England. There was no Scottish institution closely resembling the English common law or the political culture of the shires; the marriage of court and country was not the intimate and ubiquitous love-hate relationship to be found in England; there was less of a parliamentary or court-seeking gentry; and for all these reasons Scottish humanism had less to lay hold on in its incessant

---

[7] For all this see, among many monographs: Ferguson, 1965 and 1979; Pocock, 1987; Kantorowicz, 1957; Helgerson, 1992; Fideler, 1992.

struggle to convert baronial counsel into a counsel of rhetoric, and the baron into God's and the king's good servant in a culture at once courtly and civic. Consequently the practice and the discourse of Scottish politics remained conspicuously baronial. The greatest of Scottish civic humanists, George Buchanan,[8] developed a historical myth in which noble rebellion and regicide formed the ultimate check on royal misgovernment, and even his sophisticated and scholarly pupil and enemy, James VI, liked to affect a rough and genial informality when chatting with his nobles – though one wonders how well he did it, and he lost no time in re-educating some of them at the English court when he had the chance.

Behind the baron stood a more ancient figure, the chief of a clan or kindred. Blood ties and the honour of the name formed part of the image of the 'wild Scot' or Gaelic barbarian, but could not be excluded from even the revered and legitimate values of the Lowland kingdom. The 'kindly Scot' practised the 'lovable' ('allowable', 'laudable') customs of obligation to his kindred, not exclusive of manrent and deadly feud; and it is possible to see that French- or English-trained humanists and jurists were less than happy about this. We must not be tempted – even though contemporaries were sometimes tempted – into dismissing the kin culture as backward by civilized standards. Jenny Wormald has argued strongly that manrent and deadly feud formed a workable and self-moderating system,[9] and it can also be argued that if the level of private violence was high in Scotland, that of public violence, dynastic and civil war was low. There were feuds and forays, Rizzio murders and Gowrie conspiracies, but no Scottish Towson Moor or Tewkesbury, Marston Moor or Naseby. But humanists propounding the religion of counsel found Scottish blood and name[10] even harder to deal with than English hunting and hawking, and some areas of Scots political discourse are haunted by a sense of backwardness. Their attitudes towards the Auld Enemy and the Auld Ally are marked by ambivalence, and the union of kingdoms which came to be known as 'Britain' was more a Scottish invention and agendum than an English.

We have next to ask a question whose premises are partly, but by no means wholly, counterfactual. Blessed or cursed with hindsight, we know that an autonomous Scottish discourse did not develop over the next two centuries; there was not, that is to say, a continuum of publication and debate concerned with the character of an autonomous Scottish polity.

---

[8] [See further McGinnis and Williamson, 1995.]   [9] Wormald, 1980.
[10] For studies of how far this ethos was overcome in English northern and highland regions, see James, 1974 and 1986.

The union of the crowns diverted Scottish self-fashioning into a British context; it became engrossed with establishing the character of a 'Britain', with maintaining Scottish autonomy as that of a province or partner in that 'empire', and with resisting the incapacity of an intensely self-centred English discourse to conceive of 'Britain' as anything but an enlargement of 'England'. Yet throughout the reigns of Mary Stuart and James VI (until his metamorphosis into James VI and I became a certainty) there was such a discourse centred on 'Scotland', its character and its problems;[11] and we can ask, factually, what its character and parameters were, and counter-factually, how they might have developed had they continued to do so in autonomy (never, of course, in isolation).

We can isolate major figures as dominating the last phase of Scottish historical discourse before it became part of the discourse of Britain. There is George Buchanan, enemy of Mary and tutor of James; there is James himself, developing a theoretical intelligence rare among kings in rebellion against his detested preceptor; there is Andrew Melville, James's second and perhaps principal opponent, from whom unfortunately we have no major text, so that we are obliged to reconstruct the Melvillian challenge of kirk to crown from a variety of sources, including James's by no means always direct rebuttals. The king's response to the challenge of Melvillian Presbyterianism is of vast consequence in Scottish, English and British history all three; but it is often subordinated or disguised. Catholics as well as Calvinists employed populist arguments, and royalist attacks on Genevan or Melvillian claims to the independence of Presbyterial authority are often concealed within attacks on Catholic and Jesuit claims that the pope may depose kings because the people has elected them. Rightly or wrongly, we do not think these claims as great a practical danger to kings as contemporaries did; our hindsight urges us to bring the danger from Presbyterian claims to the foreground, reversing the monarchical strategy of situating them within the paradigm formed by the popish menace. This is not necessarily how James VI, or Thomas Hobbes, perceived matters.

In the second place, James's response to what was assuredly a Melvillian challenge was often directed against George Buchanan, both because he lacked a Melvillian opponent text and because he was obsessed by Buchanan's role and personality; yet when we look at Buchanan we may discern less a classic Genevan or Knoxian Calvinist than a Protestant-Stoic humanist of the same stamp as François Hotman or Duplessis-Mornay – with whom Buchanan was grouped by the circle of Sir Philip Sidney in

11 Burns, 1996; Mason, 1998.

England[12] and of whom, it has recently been argued, Algernon Sidney may have been a late and eccentric descendant.[13] There was a west European international of Protestant noblemen and theorists, and Buchanan is a figure European enough to rank among them – just as his principal Scottish opponents, other than James himself, were Catholics living abroad, in France, Lorraine and Germany.[14] To characterize Scottish debate as that between Buchanan at one pole and James at the other may be to depict it as one between monarchomachs and monarchists of a classic if confusing European pattern; yet to do so may be to ignore problems about the specific character of Scottish history which refuse to go away.

To our eyes it may seem evident that both the king and the baronial nobility of Lowland Scotland were in large measure products of Norman expansion; in search of a unifying model for 'British history' we may orchestrate the diversities of Norman organizing power in England, Wales, Ireland and, more independently, Scotland. However, neither Buchanan nor James takes an exclusively Norman route; both focus on the kingdom of Dalriada and the Irish origins of the 'Scots' themselves, and the debate comes to turn on the question whether 'Scotland' is a monarchy ruled by the descendants of Fergus the Conqueror, or an aristocracy ruled by the noble and baronial heirs of his companions. For Buchanan it is the one tempered by the other. Malcolm Canmore, his English queen and the incoming Normans after him are brought in by various writers to mitigate the unalterable Anglo-Scottish conviction that Gaelic forms of rule, whether Irish, Hebridean or Highland, were less baronial than barbaric, and the argument turns back towards the European themes of the association between kingly power and the noble commonwealth – the *jus regni apud Scotos*. A cultural frontier ran through the kingdoms of *Britannia major* and the seas which linked and divided them; it inhibits us in reducing – but never in relating – Scottish debate to the Franco-Burgundian model which is meant by 'Europe' in this context.

The Scottish monarchy faced a turbulent, partly Protestant nobility, as did other princely rulers from Languedoc to Transylvania; but if we state – or stage – the opposition between the views of Buchanan and James on the character of Fergusian kingship, we perceive them as debating a Scottish prehistory in terms Gaelic and archipelagic enough to have included some vision of Ireland. What effect the Dalriadic thesis had on Scottish perceptions of pre-Norman (or pre-Norse) Ireland may be a question worth asking; the debate over the Irish origins of the *Scoti* re-emerged in the

[12] See Phillips, 1948–9.   [13] Scott, 1989.   [14] Burns, 1993.

late eighteenth century.[15] So much for the Gaelic and archipelagic – it would be inappropriate to call them 'British' – aspects of the matter of Scotland. As James VI moved towards – when did he begin? – perceiving himself as James I, his thought and writings began to move into the dominating (perhaps we should say domineering) contexts provided by English self-fashioning, and his Scottish concerns began to incur the perils (*traduttore traditore*) of translation into English. It used to be a common-place that James I understood little of the people he had come to rule; it needs to be added that he can hardly be blamed for that – the English were an idiosyncratic people – and perhaps further, that he possessed his own means of understanding them and they did not always like it.

We may make it a point of first instance that in England he did not meet with a dangerous baronage claiming descent, and inheriting rusty swords, from the companions of some conqueror. Historians are rightly re-emphasizing the power of the peerage in English politics, and the extent to which their notions of counsel were still as much baronial as humanist;[16] but their actions were conducted within an intensely articulated corporate unity or community of the realm as body with the crown as head, conducted through the intimate associations of king with counsel and court with country. This was not simply a union of king and nobility; when all is said and done, there existed in England a parliament and a house of commons, serving alongside the court to associate, in the mechanisms of counsel, the king with the communities of shire gentry, as well placed to assimilate the boroughs as to be assimilated to them. The Scottish realm in council may or may not have consisted of the 'thrie estaits' of Sir David Lindsay's *Satyre* (1552); but two houses differ from three estates. This parliament already possessed a discourse of its own, which was increasingly becoming a discourse of the common law. We no longer believe as unhesitatingly as we once did that to depict James as ignorant of his new subjects means that in his bookish ignorance he did not know that the English were inveterate ancient-constitutionalists and long had been; the proposition that they were has not been falsified so much as joined by others, providing a context in which it must be read.[17] What was perhaps new to him was that he was coming to rule a kingdom in which head and body were so tightly bound in one by ties of law, counsel and religion that the body had its own voice and could accuse the head of breaking away from it. James understood the vocabulary of the Two Bodies

---

[15] [Kidd, 1999, ch. 6.]   [16] Guy, 1993.
[17] See the revisionary material added to Pocock, 1957, 1987 (B).

very well, and could deal not unacceptably with the great ambivalences of a prince both above the law and subject to it. His English subjects were in no imaginable circumstances likely to tell him that his kingship was elective or conditioned by the principle that all power originated in the people. What could not be anticipated was that they would find themselves telling his son that he was laying claim to his divinely sanctioned monarchy in ways that were fatal to it, with the result that the unimaginable happened and they were compelled to enunciate principles in which they fundamentally did not believe. This was not the predicament of the Scots, who spoke other languages to other ends.

It is now a commonplace that to understand this process we do better to begin with church than with constitution. The proposition that James's English kingdom affirmed its unity of head and body with a more passionate and dangerous intensity than did his Scottish, now rests less on its supposedly ancient unification by a common law, and its more recent unification by a discourse of counsel, than on an exegesis of the sovereignty proclaimed in the preamble to the Act in Restraint of Appeals (1533). Here a parliamentary statute declared and enacted, but denied that it was inventing in the sense of creating, the crown's imperial headship of a body both political and ecclesiastical, so that its duality of person became a duality of spiritual and temporal, and a king's failure to accept counsel in his realm might come to seem its betrayal as a church of Christ. Such – vastly complicated by contingencies – was the fate of Charles I as king of England, but not as king of Scotland. In the latter kingdom there was no such statute, no such imperial duality-in-unity, and James VI's perception of his Two Bodies and his role as a vice-regent to God must have been shaped less directly. Here we must look for the origins of his Scottish conviction that Buchanan and Melville together threatened him with a populist Presbyterianism, which grew into his more English (and Anglican) conviction that his crown was menaced by Jesuits and puritans in an unholy alliance.

If it is uncertain how far George Buchanan shaped his political thought as a Calvinist, let alone as a Melvillian, it is less certain still that he envisaged his baronial populism as conducive to the independence of Christ's people, under their presbyters, from 'God's sillie vassal'. Similarly, it is uncertain how far Andrew Melville relied on Buchanan's histories of justified baronial rebellion; he may have shared the strong convictions of Geneva and Sedan on the subject of civil order. What is clear is that the two themes came powerfully together in the mind of James VI, and doubtless in the minds of many others; a further question which may be asked is how far this convergence contributed to shaping the mind of James I, and on the contrary to shaping a Buchananite and covenanting synthesis which would be the Scottish equivalent of English parliamentary Protestantism. By the time he wrote the *Trew lawe of free monarchies* (1598), King James was conscious of the difference between the English Reformation as an act of state, king and parliament, and the Scottish as unfortunately achieved by noble and popular rebellion.[18] It seems safe to infer that he was thinking about his succession to the crown of England, directly challenged by Catholic assertions of the illegitimacy of both Elizabeth's rule and his own, and less directly, but more far-reachingly, by Jesuit and Dominican theses of the popular origins of power. No doubt his counter-theses of the indefeasible and absolute authority of kings, proof by divine right against popes, presbyters and peoples all together, could have taken shape around his fury at Melvillian impudences; but once he found, or as soon as he imagined, himself king of England and supreme governor or head of its church, he possessed a kingship, and a sacred, royal and imperial self, which must be asserted by means of richer and more potent discourse against dangers more universal and far reaching. The Gowrie conspiracy might have threatened James VI, but the Gunpowder Plot which threatened James I was of incomparably greater symbolic significance. The better stabilized the polity, the more terrible the threat to it.

The political thought of James VI therefore reached full flowering as the political thought of James I, wearer of one sacred and two imperial crowns and in every way but the papist, lawful inheritor of Henry VIII and Elizabeth I. In a great many ways he understood his English subjects very well and was telling them exactly what they wanted to hear. If he lectured them too much, and said things which made them uncomfortable, about his relation to the privileges, customs and laws of parliament, we now see these matters as capable of being handled and James himself as quite capable of handling them. But this image of a not unsuccessful or unconsensual reign applies least well to its closing years, overshadowed by a mighty favourite and bedevilled by the calamitous wars touched off by James's son-in-law on the continent, and to its opening, if characterized by the great abortive act of state with which so much of this book has been concerned: his attempt to make the union of the crowns a union of Great Britain.

---

[18] Mason, 1994, ch. 5.

This enterprise placed the 'matter of Britain' on the agenda of both kingdoms. Foreshadowed by John Mair and others, it used 'Britain' as a term denoting a Scottish initiative aimed at a union of the poorer with the richer kingdom, and in choosing the name of the Roman province for its planned merger, it annexed Arthurian and Galfridian traditions to Scottish uses, much to the indignation of the by now partly anglicized Welsh, who declared that they and not the upstart descendants of Irish freebooters were entitled to glory in the name of 'Britons'. So saying, they enlisted on the side of the English in the dispute over the priority of the title to the imperial crown, and any full study of the discourse of 'Britain' must allow the Welsh their voice. Since King James inaugurated the union debate, however, it has normally been the Scots who have insisted on using and clarifying the term, and the English who have refused to pay attention to it beyond employing it as a simple extension of 'England'. Such was James's achievement and the measure of his failure.

It helps in understanding the character – if not necessarily the causation – of the union enterprise and its failure if we think of it as originating in the king's clear and vivid perception of the demands of his Two Bodies. He was the husband, he said, and the whole island was his wife; he could not be the husband of two wives, or the head of two bodies. (It was George III, a century and two-thirds later, who found himself briefly faced with the demand that he keep a harem of twenty or more independent legislatures; this role as a British Solomon was rejected even before it was clearly expressed.)[19] But James was not to escape the beast with two backs; he rightly understood that to wear a single crown he must make his two kingdoms a single corporate body, but he underrated the challenge of the few means then existing of uniting head and body to make a corporation. If in England he wore a closed imperial crown, that of Scotland had been closed and imperial since the reign of James III, though there was no Act in Restraint of Appeals to give Scottish empire the terrible specificity the term possessed in England. James united his crowns by a single proclamation, but by so doing incurred the obligation of making two bodies one body, two wives one wife; and it was not clear that there existed anywhere the power to do that.

The Nimrodic or conquering king ruling *regaliter tantum* could give his subjects laws, but this was not to form them into a single corporate body; Fortescue's king ruling *politice* owes his being as head of a mystical body to an act of self-incorporation in which the *populus* appears to have

[19] For this see Koebner, 1961; Greene, 1986, 1990; Robertson, 1995.

played some part.[20] The aetiology of the body politic, however, matters less than its ontology; when it exists, head and body are unified by a network of law and counsel, and the laws are multiple in their origin so that it is needless to decide which lawgiver came first. 'Kings were the authors and makers of the laws, and not the laws of the kings', James had declared, alluding not improperly to Fergus and William the conquerors; but to say that the king made laws was not quite to say that his laws made his kingdom (or in consequence that the laws he had made he could unmake at will). To make the king author, begetter or creator of the body of which he was head was to make him more divine even than godlike; to say that he could abolish or unmake his own kingdom and merge it in another was to make his *patria potestas* a *potestas vitae et necis*. James claimed no such power; his proclamation did not abolish and unify his kingdoms, but directed them to set about abolishing and unifying themselves by counsel and consent. It did not, and James could not, furnish them with the means of doing so.

The judgement in the case of the *post-nati* resolved that allegiance was due the king in his natural, not his political person; a conclusion dangerous in Fortescuean terms, since it ascribed an indefinite power to command obedience to the Nimrodic ruler *regaliter tantum*, and might threaten to separate the king as conqueror from the king as head of his people – the charge to be brought against Roger Manwaring by Pym's impeachment in 1628.[21] The unsuccessful argument in the same case, however, pointed to dreadful difficulties when it seemed to argue that allegiance being due to the political person, Scotsmen and Englishmen could never be subjects of one another's crowns:

Scotland is of itself an absolute kingdom, an absolute government, and hath absolute laws whereunto they are subjects, and are not subject to the crown, government and laws of England . . . The politic body of a kingdom consisteth of a head, which is the king, of a body, which are the subjects, of a life [? lief], which is the laws, of a soul, which is the execution of them.[22]

The central assertion was that only laws united a head and body and formed them into a *corpus politicum*; consequently two such bodies could become one only if their laws were homogenized. Yet neither kingdom contained the authority to annul the whole body of its laws, which would be to abolish itself, and any such authority if it existed must be extra-legal

[20] Chrimes, 1949, pp. 30–3.
[21] Johnson *et al.*, 1977–78, vol. III, pp. 261–2; Burgess, 1992, pp. 173–8.
[22] Quoted in Wormald, 1992, p. 183, n. 16. Spelling and punctuation here modernized.

and extra-regnal. To effect his more perfect union, James must not only rule both his kingdoms by an authority derived from conquest; he would have to reconquer them both, and there was a sense in which his original proclamation could be read as an attempt to do just that. But James disclaimed any such authority, and sought to persuade his two political persons to become one, in virtue of their union in his natural person. As king of England and as king of Scotland, unhappily, he was not merely the husband of two wives; he was two husbands.

The premiss that law was the essence of union between a political head and body was insuperable, both because in England there existed a common law, or common custom of the realm, which defined the realm and was held to be coeval with it, and because James's long and successful reign in Scotland had witnessed an expansion of the practice, the concept and the profession of the law to the point where the expression 'common law' could form part of Scottish discourse. Sir Thomas Craig, James's active supporter in promoting the union, figures in our canonical history of Scottish political thought as the first great Scottish jurist. He was far removed from what we used to miscall the 'insularity' of the English 'common-law mind'; he had studied the interactions of Roman law, *droit coutumier* and feudal law, and emerged with a sophisticated grasp of their complex history which he was as prepared to apply to English law as to Scottish.[23] The opponents of the *post-nati* in England might observe that the more 'absolutely' Scotsmen possessed their own laws, government and kingdom, the more 'absolute' became the authority of these over them, and the less were they capable of escaping, renouncing or abolishing the second nature and political personality which was now of their essence. But Craig's understanding of law and nationality was both Roman and feudal, imperial and provincial; he saw Scotland as one province of a Roman and feudal cosmopolis in which the interactions of the historical patterns of law had worked out in one way as in other nations they had worked out in others. He therefore saw Scottish political personality less as 'absolute' than as historically contingent, and was unafraid of the task of adapting it to the new contingencies of a 'British' history.

In *Jus Feudale*, he told the English that the same was true of them, but could by no means get them to listen. We reach the point at which historians customarily observe that Scottish culture was highly cosmopolitan, but English provincial to the point of 'insularity'. King James's phrase 'the

---

[23] Pocock, 1957, 1987 (B), pp. 79–90. For this capacity re-emerging in eighteenth-century Scottish jurisprudence, see Lieberman, 1990.

whole island' should be enough to warn us that 'insular' is the wrong adjective; his English subjects were engaged in denying that their part of the island had anything in common with the part he had ruled, while Lowland Scots were little less resolute in denying kinship with the Highlands and Islands north of them in the archipelago. Even the term 'provincial' may prove two-edged. Scots were more 'cosmopolitan', more willing to admit that Roman and French (if not Gaelic and Irish) components had gone to make them what they were, precisely because their kingdom was more 'provincial' in the sense of less autonomous. Englishmen were more 'insular', more 'ethnocentric', more 'provincial' in their refusal to admit 'cosmopolitan' components in their national life and history, because they could and did assert that they possessed 'sovereign' and 'absolute' power over themselves in the two vital respects of law and ecclesiastical structure. It was this passionately – one could add desperately – preserved sense of sovereign autonomy, traceable back to the Act in Restraint of Appeals by one route, to Fortescue's *De laudibus legum Angliae* by another, and to time whereof the memory of man runneth not to the contrary by a third, which James VI and I's proclamation of union had seemed to threaten; one of the first in a long series of steps by which the Stuart monarchy came to be perceived as a menace to the unity of its English realm; probably the first which we may ascribe to the exigencies of 'multiple monarchy' and the 'British problem', and which ended in the imposition of English upon 'British' history.

The immediate problem was that there existed two political bodies (and persons), defined by two apparently incommensurable systems of royal and national law. Craig was prepared to set about the long task of assimilating Scots and English law by means of precedent, judgements and legal reason in Scottish courts, and in this foreshadows such figures as Kames and Mansfield late in the next century. Among English jurists, Francis Bacon could entertain philosophically exciting visions of a codification which should reduce both systems to one, and in this (if in little else) he resembles Jeremy Bentham two hundred years after him. But the mind of Lord Ellesmere did not reach quite so far, and the alarmingly powerful intelligence of Sir Edward Coke was trained in quite other directions. Dr Wormald provides reason to suppose that the effect of the union debate was to intensify, not mitigate, the English sense of the autonomy and uniqueness of both their law and their sovereignty.[24] The Virgilian tag *divisos ab orbe Britannos*, once used to enjoin the union of Scots and

---

[24] Wormald, in Mason, 1994, pp. 17–40.

English under a common name, was by 1628 employed by Coke in declaring that English law was autochthonous, self-sustaining and admitted no law within the realm that it had not itself approved.[25] *Divisos ab orbe Britannos; divisos ab insulis Anglos.* In a sense which could well be termed anti-historical, English history was to be written in exclusively English terms – 'like a silkworm which formeth all her web out of her self only'[26] – and could acknowledge no 'British history' which was not its own. It was a reaction as much defensive as expansive; a question of maintaining sovereignty over one's own laws and customs, one's own identity and history.

The union of head and body, which constituted a political kingdom, was thus formed by laws which were nationally and culturally specific; the more 'absolute' (and less relative or contingent) each kingdom's laws, the harder it was to merge its personality with another's. The same union could also be conceptualized in religious and ecclesiological terms; the sovereign must be head of his realm in its spiritual capacity, and the way in which he was so was another determinant of its personality. In England this had been written into law in 1533, to a point where it was definitive of the Two Bodies and the political person. The king's headship of his temporal realm was inseparable from his headship of the church coextensive with it. In Scotland, as James was uneasily aware, the separation of the realm from Rome had not been effected by unalloyed royal authority, and those who had effected it might claim ecclesiastical independence of him. Hence 'no bishop, no king'; once he found himself supreme head of the Church of England, James would be far from unwilling to assimilate Scotland to the English model. Even after his defeat and elimination of Melville, however, James acted cautiously; but the English must decide how much responsibility they wanted for the recalcitrant Presbyterians of the north. It was hard enough work accustoming the Scots to the authority of bishops *jure humano*; the disasters of the next reign followed when a section of the English clergy began insisting on them *jure divino*. Ecclesiology was less salient than law in the debates which derailed James's union policy, but the two differences in structure have together ensured that Britain has never been the single political culture which James desired, but lacked the means, to make it. Brian Levack's title, *The Formation of the British State*,[27] therefore contains an ambiguity: is there a single state, or is 'state' distinct from 'civil society'?

---

[25] Johnson *et al.*, 1977–78, vol. II, pp. 101, 550, 555.   [26] Pocock, 1957, 1987 (B) p. 34.
[27] Levack, 1987.

It is, in the older language of historiography, instructive as well as amusing to speculate on what might have happened had James carried out two intentions which figure briefly in his inscribed and spoken discourse: those of taking the style of 'Emperor of the whole island of Britain', which appears on a medal struck at his accession to the English throne, and of setting up his seat at York, leaving both his Scottish and his English subjects *procul a numine, procul a fulmine*[28] – to quote the witty and menacing phrase he used to parliament in 1607.[29] There was the well-established, though rather Scottish than English, language of Constantinian empire, which Arthur Williamson has memorably brought to light,[30] and York was a city of late-antique Constantinian associations. If James wished to be the Protestant emperor of reformed apocalyptic, as his son-in-law Frederick so disastrously attempted a decade later, he had the symbolic means of assuming the role at York, more safely than at Prague. But as Williamson has also shown, Constantine was a dangerously ambiguous figure – the founder of the Christian empire, the author of fatal concessions to the papal Antichrist – and apart from the effects on the English hierarchy of such an exaltation of York at the expense of Canterbury, the English already possessed their own image of the 'godly prince', defined in the royal and parliamentary language of the Act in Restraint of Appeals, which made the legend of King Lucius more native to their symbolism than that of the Emperor Constantine.

The reasons why James retained the royal and did not adopt the imperial style are complex, if evanescent, since in fact the move was never debated in detail; but it is possible to render them of some significance. As Adam Blackwood, one of Buchanan's opponents, observed,[31] an emperor was something other (and perhaps less) than a king further magnified; he ruled over many bodies politic and was not necessarily the incarnate head of any one. James might have taken the style of emperor of Great Britain while retaining those of king of Scots and king of England, France and Ireland; but this would have entailed admitting the plurality of his empire and the multiplicity of his political persons. He set out to make Britain a single body politic and reign as its head and king; the style of emperor would have entailed resignation of the duality-in-unity of the Two Bodies, which appears to have been what rendered him kingly and godlike in his own sight. We have already found two reasons why he failed to reach his goal: law and ecclesiastical authority, two principal ligaments uniting the head

---

[28] 'Far from the god, far from his thunderbolt'.   [29] Wormald, 1992, p. 175.
[30] Williamson, 1979.   [31] Mason, 1994, pp. 149–50.

and body of the political person, differentiated England and Scotland to the point where they resembled Judah and Israel – two kingdoms ruled by the same divine law – less than Judaea and Samaria, between whom there were no dealings, and who could not be reduced to one. The phrase *procul a numine, procul a fulmine* provides us with a third, to which the clue may be found in the word *procul.* What united head and body, in this third perspective, was counsel; counsel depended on access, and access depended upon court. When James proposed setting up his seat at York, or becoming peripatetic between Holyrood, York and Westminster, he was making a threat: he was warning his subjects north and south that they might find themselves *procul a numine,* far from the focus of service and counsel, the fount of office and honour (the seats of justice were already fixed). They might be obliged to travel greater distances in search of access to their king, or to take turns in having that access conveniently at hand. It all sounds very reasonable, but in fact the threat was two-edged; kings everywhere, and kings of multiple monarchies in particular, were having to decide between rendering themselves accessible or remote, stationary or peripatetic – the problem confronted by Deioces the Mede in the imaginary history by Herodotus.[32] The Escorial, and later Versailles, were palaces designed to make the subject seek out the king, and hopefully to exploit distance to the latter's advantage. Would the court and palace of a British Constantine at York have proved a British Escorial, a British Byzantium, a British Kyoto? We cannot answer, because the experiment was never made. James in 1607 was threatening the English with something he knew they would not like, but implicitly and surely unconsciously they called his bluff. He remained stationary at Whitehall and went once (though more often than his successors) to Holyrood; that is, he chose to situate himself in a body larger and more richly textured than Scotland, united by a more complex integument in all three modes of counsel, law and religion – though a price to be paid was that the challenges with which the head-and-body union faced a king of England in all three modes were greater in proportion as the union was more intense. Meanwhile, it was a lesser price that Scots (and Irish) notables would have to journey to Whitehall in search of their king, and that the English would have to get used to seeing them there. James kept his promise that he would not rule Scotland through a viceroy (like Naples) or a deputy (like Ireland), though his reported words 'Here I sit and govern it by my pen' indicate that this kingdom had not quite escaped provincial status; and it was the judgement of William Robertson that the

32 Herodotus, *History of the Persian War,* I, pp. 96ff.

departure of a court culture in 1603 had condemned it to be a provincial culture,[33] until Union and Enlightenment had made possible a *translatio studii* to Modern Athens.

With the abandonment of James VI and I's vision of reducing two imperial crowns and two bodies politic to one, the principle of multiple monarchy triumphed; we enter the age of the ambiguities of 'Britain', and at the same time the age of the Three Kingdoms. These consisted of the two bodies politic of England and Scotland – the latter easily imagined as possessing unincorporated barbarian marchlands to the north and west – and the conquered kingdom of Ireland, whose ruler was not the head of a mystical body and which resembled a captive concubine rather than a wife. Wales, which had been conquered, was now incorporated; Ireland was conquered but not incorporated until 1780 (in one sense) or 1801 (in another). The American colonies which now began their existence were neither conquered nor properly incorporated as bodies politic; to declare themselves such, as 'independent states', was to be a revolutionary act in 1776.[34] This political typology at once provides a framework for 'British history' and raises the question whether, or in what sense, there can be said to have been such a thing. Of the two bodies politic properly so called, one – England – claimed to be so tightly and intensely incorporated that it contained its own history (which was principally that of the ancient constitution) and could recognize 'British history' only as contained within, or a simple extension of, the history of England – a propensity which has survived so stubbornly that it is not even yet eliminated. The other – Scotland – contained authors capable of seeing its history as that of a province of western European culture, whose autonomy consisted in the recognition and management of its own marginality – a history of Scottish interdependence with Roman and French jurisprudence, Norman and English feudalism, Pictish and Gaelic kin systems, Scandinavian settlement and Flemish commerce. In Craig we are entitled to see foreshadowed the capacity of Scottish Enlightened historians to present both Scottish and English – and therefore 'British' – history as that of provinces locally manifesting the principles of a general 'history of mankind', convinced that they were writing English history better than the English could write it themselves.[35]

But there was another side to the medal. The Scottish capacity to see their history as marginal and contingent was the product of their

---

[33] Robertson, 1824, vol. XXII, pp. 245–8.   [34] Pocock, 1995a (ch. 9, below).
[35] Hume, 1754–62; Robertson, 1759; Henry, 1771–93; Millar, 1787–1803.

conviction that their body politic was not (as the English believed theirs was) so intensely unified as to contain its own history; and consequently what George Buchanan supplied was the history, not of an 'ancient constitution' in the English sense,[36] but of a turbulent baronial polity in which monarchical misgovernment was tempered by noble rebellion. It took major collapses of government, such as those occurring on either side of the year 1649, to force the English to admit that their history had once been baronial in this sense; and even this they contained within the paradigm of an 'ancient constitution' in every way they could imagine. Buchanan depicted a primeval politics in sophisticated language; perhaps there is room for regarding him as a Gaelic-Latin humanist after all;[37] and his image of the Scottish past had to be overthrown before the philosophical history of the Scottish Enlightenment could be developed.[38] Scottish sophistication and a Scottish sense of backwardness went together, as they had for John Mair himself. Scots might write English history better than the English wrote it, but when the English wrote history they seldom admitted the Scots to it.

It follows that there was, and still is, no 'British history' in the sense of the self-authenticated history of a self-perpetuating polity or culture. The term must be used to denote a multiplicity of histories, written by or (more probably) written about a multiplicity of kingdoms and other provinces, which have interacted to produce intelligible narratives, or the need and capacity to write intelligible narratives, of their interactions to produce 'Britain' and 'British history'. In more recent work, such as Linda Colley's,[39] the possibility has re-emerged that there may have been produced a 'British' culture, politics and nationality more durable than it has been fashionable to suppose; but it does not seem likely that this culture will provide itself, as the English once did, with a unified and monostructural history. More probably there will continue to be written a multiple history of what was once (and perhaps still is) a multiple monarchy, whose unity is contingent upon its multiplicity and may not persist, though equally it may.

This should be good news for historians, since it enables them to write 'British history' with the sophisticated attention to the shifting balance between provincial and universal perspectives that characterized their great Scottish and English predecessors. In the history of political discourse, however, it is particularly evident that 'British history' can be written only

[36] Trevor-Roper, 1966.   [37] Buchanan, 1827, vol. I, p. 9.   [38] Kidd, 1993.
[39] Colley, 1992.

when there is dialogue between the several national discourses, when there can be found a perspective in which they can be viewed as coexisting, or when there is a history of a discourse 'of Britain' – one concerning the possibility that such an entity can be created, invented, said to exist or to have existed. In such a history Anglo-Irish, Old English and Old Irish discourses must play their part, and one might look beyond it to a history which would reconstitute the patterns of Irish political discourse as the present work has reconstituted those of Scottish. This history would move both in and out of British history, finding its turning point in the fateful third union of 1801.

CHAPTER 5

The Atlantic archipelago and the War
of the Three Kingdoms

This paper[1] will seek to develop a position on the history of the Atlantic archipelago in early modern times, originally stated in articles published up to eighteen years ago. Since those times a good deal has happened, and we have all gone on thinking about what is no longer 'the unknown subject'[2] – though it would not be true to say that we have a governing paradigm for treating it. In developing these earlier positions, I wish to select, however tendentiously, a few positions away from which I think there has been some movement, and see if I can employ that pattern in an attempt to define where we are now.

In the first place, there is the phrase 'Atlantic archipelago' itself. One book has been published with that title, by an American scholar, Richard S. Tompson of Utah;[3] on the other hand, Hugh Kearney's book is entitled *The British Isles: a History of Four Nations.*[4] I offer the term in an attempt to get away from inappropriate pan-national language. The problem lies less with the term 'British Isles' than with the term 'British history', a concept to which there are or might be objections on various nationalist grounds, but which we have been employing speculatively and aggressively in the attempt to overcome a writing of history so Anglocentric that 'British history' itself has in the past denoted nothing much more than 'English history' with occasional transitory additions. I will cautiously defend the new use of 'British history' to denote archipelagic history in general on the following grounds. This history in the early modern and modern periods has been dominated by the attempt to construct a 'British' kingdom, state and nation embracing the archipelago as a whole, and even the great antithesis furnished by the largely successful secession of the Irish Republic is part of 'British history' to the extent (real if not absolute) that Irish history is dominated by the struggle to escape from British. That

---

[1] Originally printed as Pocock, 1996b.   [2] Pocock, 1982.   [3] Tompson, 1986.
[4] Kearney, 1989.

struggle, in turn, is not the whole of 'Irish history', which must be and is being written within parameters of its own, but means that 'Irish history' can be viewed as part of 'British history' in the larger sense: the fortunes and vicissitudes of the attempt, and the reactions against the attempt, to create a multinational 'Britain' which has a past and may have a future. Similarly – extending the term 'Atlantic archipelago' to include piedmont and tidewater North America – one can include 'American' within 'British history' through the War of Independence, until the formation of the federal republic, when it becomes 'United States history', and a field of study self-affirmed in its own terms.

'British history', then, is located within 'the Atlantic archipelago', an expression partly geographically and partly politically defined, so that it includes the Shetland but not the Faroe Islands, the Channel Islands but not the adjacent coasts of Normandy and Brittany. An archipelago is a group or collection of islands, and the effect aimed at in using this term is to remind ourselves and our readers that we are writing a history pelagic, maritime and oceanic, into which an extraordinary diversity of cultural and other movements has penetrated deeply after making their way from the adjacent extremities of the Eurasian landmass. Here we reach the point of employing the tendentious and aggressive term 'Europe', an expression once again both geographic and cultural; it denotes in the first place a peninsula (or strictly speaking two, one Europe proper and the other Scandinavia) extending from the landmass into the inland seas and the ocean, and in the second place a civilization, Latin in its origins and exceptional in its expansiveness, which made its way into the Scandinavian peninsula, the Atlantic archipelago and many other parts of the planet. This combination of meanings renders 'Europe' a term dynamic, indeterminable and hegemonic; it can be used to include human societies or to exclude them, depending on how it is employed by those who have appropriated the power to define it, and as I have found myself both included and excluded by those who use it to instruct me as to who I am, I look on its employment with a certain critical concern. In using the term 'Atlantic archipelago', therefore, we encounter the term 'Europe': and we affirm that the history of 'Europe' can either be confined to that of a continental peninsula, or include a history of islands and mountains and a waste of seas, in which case it is a different history from that which it would be if it did not.

The notion of an archipelago invites us to let our mental vision travel out into a diffusion of pelagic cultures lying beyond the frontiers of 'Europe' and 'civilization' as conventionally imagined. This is of course a way of thinking full of dangers, which have to be resisted if they cannot be evaded, and one has to challenge it as soon as one has embarked upon it. But there are senses in which one cannot avoid embarking on it; a real sense, for instance, in which the archipelago takes us beyond the territories of the Roman empire and the papal, feudal and royal monarchies which succeeded it. The expansion of this barbaro-Latin civilization is what creates 'Europe' as we know the term, and it expanded west as well as east, into the further islands of the archipelago and Scandinavia, as well as into the Saxon, Lithuanian and Slavonic lands at the heart of the European peninsula. This expansion was still going on in early modern times, when it took the form of the consolidation of the English and British monarchies in control of the Atlantic archipelago; and very complex and intricate interactions developed over centuries between governments based on the control of land tenure defined as 'property' through written redactions of customary, statute and punitive law, and cultures where similar ends were attained through the obligations of kinship backed by various forms of partly ritualized violence. This is one of the more important frontiers in Atlantic, European and indeed world history, because mutual incomprehension between the two systems reached a height where each regarded the other as altogether alien and barbaric, and the writ-governed culture set out to establish its control of the kin-governed culture by means of conquest. We are expected to deplore this state of affairs, but we have to study it; and it is a circumstance to which we must constantly return that the English and Scottish monarchies in the archipelago were distinguished among those in the west of Europe by their conviction that they existed on a barbarian frontier, and by the existence of a frontier on either side of which peoples did regard one another as barbaric.

It was this chain of considerations that led me, in those articles that I mentioned earlier, to make much of the distinction between kingdom and march, between the zone of government, in which the written law operates normally and minimizes its resorts to violence, and the zone of war, in which the writ has to impose its authority on the kindred by a more frequently visible employment of the sword. A good deal has been written about the extent to which these two zones penetrate one another and are hard to tell apart, and this has been a theme of Anglo-Irish historiography, for instance, since there began to be such a thing. There is Hiram Morgan's monograph on the outbreak of Tyrone's rebellion,[5] in which the queen's men and the chiefs, the men of law and the men of the sword, behave in ways between which there is singularly little to choose; but let me recall

---

[5] Morgan, 1993.

Sir John Davies's Jacobean apologia for conquest, in which the point is repeatedly made that this is precisely the problem which the rule of the kingdom needs to overcome – even though the problem might not exist if the kingdom were not there. We should also consider the point made by several Scottish historians, Jenny Wormald among them,[6] that in blood-feud societies the level of private violence is high but containable, whereas in societies governed by king and law the level of public violence is occasionally explosive and devastating. It is in the latter that we find armies fighting pitched battles in pursuit of dynastic and civil war; and the *Problematik* of what constitutes civil war should now receive the attention of historians.

Nevertheless, it may still be useful for some purposes to retain the model of kingdom and march, and keep in mind the extent to which Mountjoy, Cromwell and Ginkel, and Wade and Cumberland far into the eighteenth century, were engaged in the ancient imperial pursuit of reducing provinces to obedience. Eliga Gould has written a most persuasive doctoral dissertation,[7] in which 1745 and 1759 emerge as significant moments in the re-organization of Anglo-Hanoverian empire between the Elbe and the Ohio, not without bearing on the American Revolution. But to say this is to pass from the model of kingdom and march to the model of multiple monarchy, and perhaps the ascent of the latter model to its present authority is the most important change in the construction of 'British history' since the time when I began proposing the latter subject in those early articles.

It was J. C. Beckett who seems first to have used the phrase 'the War of the Three Kingdoms' – or was it 'the Wars'? – but the phrase has gone on growing since it first became known, and we are now in a position where we must borrow a term from our Chinese peers and speak of an 'Age of the Three Kingdoms' in British history and the history of the Atlantic archipelago, lasting from 1534 or 1603 to 1707 or 1801. Within it might be located a sub-period of the 'Wars of the Three Kingdoms', datable from 1637 to 1691, in which the concepts of wars of conquest, social wars and civil wars skirmish to command our attention. The 'Age of the Three Kingdoms', in the larger sense, is that in which sovereign or imperial kingdoms in England and Scotland, and a subject kingdom established by conquest and legislation in Ireland, come first under a single dynasty, constituting a multiple monarchy, and then under a common parliamentary sovereignty, constituting or never quite constituting a unified parliamentary state.

---

[6] Wormald, 1980.   [7] Gould, 1992. [See now Gould, 2000.]

It is succeeded by an 'Age of Union' lasting from 1801 to 1921, and beyond that the enterprise of periodization by nomenclature had perhaps better not go. The attention of scholars has been focussed predominantly on the problems of multiple monarchy, and perhaps on the Wars of the Three Kingdoms in particular; but it is possible to carry on beyond the seventeenth century, and in conjunction with Scottish, American, and now and then English colleagues, I have found myself discussing the American Revolution as growing out of the problems of multiple monarchy,[8] while J. C. D. Clark is prepared to go further and examine it as the last (or not the last?) of the British wars of religion.[9]

The model of kingdom and march presents an image of sovereignty and its spatial limitations, but that of multiple monarchy presents that of the relations between modes of sovereignty when several are exercised by the same crown or person. But this is tricky language; James VI and I once complained that he could not be the husband of two wives, and the head of a plural monarchy has several mystical or political persons met together in one natural body. And if the king of Scots who became king of England could not merge his three bodies in that of an emperor of Great Britain, what person had he as king of Ireland, where his sovereignty was acquired by conquest and Ireland was perhaps not a body politic incorporate at all? From these abstract and symbolic, but not for that reason insignificant considerations, we move to consider the problems of plural majesty: that is to say of *The Causes of the English Civil War* and *The Fall of the British Monarchies*.[10]

There is a historiographical, linguistic and political problem here. Are we substituting the War, or Wars, of the Three Kingdoms for the English Civil War, in spite of Russell's choice of a title for his Ford Lectures? If so, why and with what effect? Let me generalize his argument by saying that its thrust is to deny that there was anything wrong enough with the English kingdom as a whole to break its structure apart, to divide its ruling élites into opposing camps, to furnish them with opposed and irreconcilable patterns of religion and political belief, or to need explanation in terms of the long-range operations of social change. What happened was rather that the strains imposed on the monarchy by the need to govern three kingdoms led to its breakdown, and that the English, like the other, ruling élites fell apart in consequence of this failure of leadership. The British problem caused the dissolution of government, and – to quote James Harrington – the dissolution of government caused the war.

---

[8] Below, ch. 9.   [9] Clark, 1993.   [10] Russell, 1990, 1991a and b.

This is a simplistic account of Russell's complex narrative, but I have no difficulty in accepting his argument in this simplified form. I accept all that is said about the need to escape from Whig constitutionalist or Marxist socialist explanations, though when we have escaped from them I want to go back and look at both, and see what may be left of them. What does trouble me is a current conviction that we live in a time of the breaking of nations and the unmaking of states, which impels many opinion-makers and not a few academics to deny that English history makes any kind of sense, or contains within itself any of the motors of its own dynamic or the causes of its own crises. With these intentions some of our contemporaries inject the Civil War of 1642 into a British context or the Revolution of 1688 into a European context; not because we learn more about English history when we realize that it was not the whole of the story, or because there are other stories needing to be told, but because they want to deny that the English were ever the makers of their own history in any degree whatever. It was not with intentions like these that I broached the idea of a 'British history' in a lecture to the New Zealand Historical Association in 1973. I hasten to add that the revisionist debate, of which the British reading of seventeenth-century history has been part, has not had these insanitary effects; rather, it has rendered the national sovereignty and the national history tougher because more fragile, because more exposed to external and internal contingencies than we used to realize.[11] But in this perspective, the result of absorbing the English Civil War into the War of the Three Kingdoms should be to illuminate the former, not to make it disappear.

Let me ask two questions: was there an English Civil War, and was there a War of the Three Kingdoms? I have already suggested my answer to the second question, and I want now to put forward for consideration the still rather abstract proposition that there was a confluence of several wars, which arose separately but had to be fought together for the reason that they could not be pursued, much less brought to a conclusion, separately. This proposition opens up a problem. Can we construct a holistic explanation of the War of the Three Kingdoms, or must we concede that a multiple monarchy cannot have a single or holistic history?[12] The issue turns on the extent to which the single dynasty ruling several realms had created a single polity, or a complex of polities centred on itself, which had its own life and within which a series of things could go wrong; an entity which engendered or suffered its own crisis, in short, and – above all – which had its own history. There is, as we have seen, a sense in which

[11] Pocock, 1992d.   [12] Morrill, 1993, 1996.

Conrad Russell is denying that English history engendered the English Civil War, and John Morrill can be seen accepting this, but asserting that Russell's explanation is still insufficiently 'British' or 'Britannic' in the sense that Scottish and Irish history figure in it only as the external forces which impelled the unwilling but still central English into a civil war they did not want. Russell has characterized the English role in this crisis as that of 'the pig in the middle'; the victim of external forces, but still in the middle. It is a temptation to see in this a reflection of the British self-image in the 1980s and 1990s.

If a 'holistic' account of the crisis could be put forward, it would be because the multiple monarchy had created a unity of structure some-where, within which a crisis could develop and a breakdown could take place. This unity would have a history of its own, and we should have found *a* 'British' or 'Britannic' history within which we could situate *a* War of the Three Kingdoms. But what would be the architecture of the structure of which this was the history? Of what institutions or conventions or relationships would it consist? In one projection intelligible to seventeenth-century minds, it would consist solely in the natural person of the king who was head of all Three Kingdoms, and there is much latitude for explaining the crisis as the effect of the natural personality of Charles I – even when, with Russell, one thinks he did not do badly all the time. But it was equally well understood that a king's natural person could not be finally separated from his political person, which he enjoyed or endured as the head of a body politic; and it was of the essence of multiple monarchy that one natural person might find himself, or herself, endued with two or three political persons – the predicament so accurately expounded by James VI and I. In the historicist language I am deliberately, and I hope not blindly, employing, this might mean that such a king found himself acting in two or three histories at once – each political body having its own history, the effect of whatever social or cultural forces it had mobilized by existing as a political structure – and he might find his government, his court and his person the focal point at which all these histories converged, whether in confluence or in collision.

But to say only this leaves open the question of whether or not such a king, and any predecessors he might have as head of a multiple monarchy, had about him some set of institutions or conventions or usages for dealing with this convergence, or whether it was dealt with only by the king's natural person dealing with problems as they came along; was there a *jurisdictio* or was there only a *gubernaculum*? In the former case there would be a locus of politics complex, stable and unstable enough to have a history of its own; there would be a 'Britannic' history along with the English,

Scottish and Irish histories, one in which the latter converged so as to form a whole, which must exist if a 'holistic' explanation is to be offered. But we shall not find ourselves pursuing this hypothesis to the point where the whole has absorbed the parts; it is simply *ex hypothesi* that there did not exist a 'Britannic' state or empire, or consequently a 'Britannic' history, in which the Three Kingdoms and their several histories were absorbed and swallowed up. We need not go so far as to say that there never has existed such an entity, and that consequently the search for a 'British history' is a search in vain. There is a British history in so far as its several components have converged in a shared political culture, and in so far as the attempt to make them do so has a continuous history. In that 'matter of Britain' which is the problem of the War or Wars of the Three Kingdoms, we appear to be faced with an opposition of extremes which are not absolutes. At one – let us call it Russellian – extreme, the central locus or focus is simply the place where the accidents go to happen, where the decisions of *gubernaculum* (the 'high politics') are made, wrongly made or not made at all. At the other – let us call it Morrillian – the central place has a structure and a history of its own, and may in some measure have reshaped the Three Kingdoms by drawing them to itself. There is clearly plenty of room – the more so as we are dealing with a breakdown of government, both central and local – for both readings to be right and to exist together; we do not even have to synthesize them.

I am moving towards the re-opening of the first of the two questions I proposed earlier, by setting up the implication that in a history of the Three Kingdoms each kingdom has its own history, no matter how much it converges, or interacts by refusing to converge and instead colliding, with the histories of others; particular histories do not cease to exist when it is seen that they cannot be written in isolation. Before I turn to the particular case of the English, however, I ought to emphasize that one did not have to be a kingdom in order to have a history, and that we must avoid falling into some Central European error of distinguishing between peoples that have histories and peoples that have none; though it seems not unreasonable to add that for an entity to have a place in political history, it needs a political structure of some kind with which to receive and respond to the actions of others. There is the case of Wales, which was never a kingdom and was no longer a principality or a collection of marcher lordships but had been shired and incorporated within the kingdom of England, while retaining a cultural and social distinctiveness with a capacity for response;[13] there is

---

[13] Thomas, 1988, suggests that Wales divided in the Civil War along lines not unlike those dividing England.

even the case of Cornwall, for a long time no more than an English county but possessing a certain cultural personality of its own.

There would not have been an English civil war – I show my hand by saying this – if the King had not found an army willing to fight for him, and it is my understanding that initially he found it at Shrewsbury rather than at Nottingham, and that it consisted in significant measure of men from Wales and the Welsh Marches. At a somewhat later date there were the Cornish regiments, who for a while fought with a determination that suggests they may have had something on their minds. This is a war in which it is possible to know something about the common soldier's point of view, and one could wish to know more about what these Welsh and Cornish regiments thought they were doing and who they thought they were.[14] I am not over-impressed by the tendency of historians of the left to ascribe a merely 'traditional' consciousness – whatever that is – to the royalist rank and file, as opposed to the enhanced religious and political awareness of godly Londoners and East Anglians; any more than I am overwhelmed by the perfectly true contention that most soldiers in most wars are too much preoccupied by thoughts of pay, food, loot, sanitation and survival to have much time for significant discourse. The remarkable thing about this among the early modern wars is that some of the soldiers did develop their own political awareness, and one would like to know more about how far it went and what forms it took.

If the King had found no Englishmen willing to fight for him in 1642, the pig in the middle would never have fought a civil war; but he did, and we are no longer pursuing the suggestion – fruitful though it was – that England was a collocation of county communities, who acted out of their own local considerations and not as members of an English realm at all.[15] The reason it cannot be pressed further is that the county communities did not wish to fight one another, still less to fight within themselves, but nevertheless did because they found they had to; from which one may conclude that the English realm possessed such unity that even in its breakdown it could oblige its subjects to engage in the public quarrel against their wills and against their strenuous opposition, and that this was not a relapse into some Hobbesian anarchy – though often it looked very like that – but a public quarrel or civil war. The bitter unwillingness of the English to fight one another – which of course increased the bitterness with which they did so – is used, as we all know, to demonstrate that it was

---

[14] Stoyle, 1994, 1996, 1998, has written interestingly on the Cornish experience.
[15] For the rise and perhaps the fall of this interpretation, see Morrill, 1993, chs. 8–11.

a civil war they found themselves engaged in. It is not exactly news, after all, that the war in England was a conflict between people who had thought themselves, and to that extent had been, in a condition of profound consensus. Harrington and Clarendon both premised this in the seventeenth century, and David Hume thought so in the eighteenth. Harrington and Hume both went in search of profound changes, occurring in the historical world, which had converted consensus into conflict. At present we do not want to follow that line of enquiry – it may be revealing to ask why not – but we do not have to follow it in order to perceive that the English war was fought between people who supposed themselves to belong to the same political culture, and that this may be the definition of what a civil war is. To say this may be to turn Russell's interpretation on its head, and at the same time to endorse Harrington's dictum that the dissolution of the government caused the war, not the war the dissolution of the government.[16]

That famous dictum, however, can always be turned around once more: Russell's British war causes the dissolution of the English as well as the British government, Harrington's dissolution of the government causes the English Civil War. I am revealing my answer to both the questions I posed. There was a War of the Three Kingdoms but it was several wars going on together. There was an English Civil War, but where Harrington and nearly all his successors thought its origins lay deep in English history, Russell invites us to consider it a product of the War of the Three Kingdoms; that is to say, of a rebellion in Scotland followed by a rebellion in Ireland, with which Charles I's headship of a multiple monarchy was so far unable to cope that it broke down as a government of each of the Three Kingdoms, so that war followed both among the three of them and within each of them severally.

Russell further invites us to suppose that there was nothing going on in English history which necessitated this process, so that it should not be considered as an English-generated civil war, but as something else. Be it so; but I have two further questions. Does it follow that there was nothing going on in Scottish or in Irish history either, so that the origins of the conflict must be located in the history of another entity, which might be called 'Britain', 'the British monarchies', 'the Three Kingdoms', or whatever? I have already considered this possibility, and I am fairly certain that Russell is not proposing it; in which case it must follow, I think, that under any one

---

[16] [Pocock, 1999e, studies 'dissolution' as a governing notion in Thomas May's underrated history of the Civil War.]

of these names we are looking at a field of action in which at least three histories – there may have been more – impinged upon one another, and the task in which Stuart government failed was that of managing their interactions. The Three Kingdoms acted in one another's history, we begin to say; from which it follows that each had a history which others could act in, but which could also react against those interventions.

I am beginning to ask – this is still an extension of the first of my two questions – how the word 'history' is being used in the discourse before us; and one implication my question rather disturbingly bears is that history may still be, among other things, the memory of the state. A body politic conducting its own affairs will have institutions, discourse and memory; it may discover for itself, or leave for historians to discover, complex processes defined by its structure and modifying it. This is what we mean by speaking of 'English', 'Scottish' or 'Irish' history – terminology which is certainly contingent and contestable; but if we abandon this way of putting it altogether, we will end by abandoning the concept of Three Kingdoms in its turn, and the problem is that these entities, and their capacity to act and suffer, may have existed as *verità effettuali* in early modern history, and may refuse to disappear when we try to exorcize them. There may therefore have been an English history, a Scottish history, an Irish history, at other levels a Welsh or a Cornish, an Argyll or an Ulster history, a history of England divided into cities, counties and regions, in all of which the War of the Three Kingdoms happened and became different wars, or from which it arose as well as arising from the interactions between them; it depends on where people have history and what sorts of history they have. My second question bears on the problem of how many of these *verità effettuali* we are compelled to discover.

I have been insisting that the English experience in the Wars of the Three Kingdoms was an experience of civil war. I do so from the standpoint of a historian of discourse, who studies what people said was happening around them and how they tried to affect what was happening by what they said. The English of the period we are debating possessed an enormously articulate print culture, in which an enormously complex discussion occurred; and what this tells us is indeed that they did not wish to fight one another – they insisted with one voice that the war in which they were engaged was 'unnatural' – and that it was a new idea to them, though one which they were compelled to explore, that there might be deep-seated fissures and processes within their culture which had got them where they were. We might say, as they might, that these issues had not obliged them to fight each other, but once they were so obliged they had to give them their attention; the great debate over political and religious issues had not caused the dissolution of government or the war, but once dissolution and war had happened the great debate had to occur, because the war could not be comprehended or resolved without it. We may say that the crisis was not resolved in 1660 because the issues had been resolved, but because 1660 was an imperfect resolution the debate had to continue; and what I am seeking to say is that these are the characteristics of an intensely integrated and articulate society, in which violence when it occurred did not mean the disappearance of these characteristics, but would be conducted between people who had a great deal, including a capacity for complex discussion, in common. This is the profile of conflict within consensus, which is to say of civil war.

I propose therefore that the impact on England of the War of the Three Kingdoms was such as to produce the English Civil War, which was as it was because England was the culture it was. By the civil war I mean that the English found themselves fighting each other over the nature of the English polity. Their disagreements about its nature may have been the effect rather than the cause of their civil war; I suspect that this is the case; but this may be a problem of chicken and egg. The breakdown in their government may have been thrust upon them by actions originating among Scots and Irish; but once they realized that this was so, they went out and eliminated these interferences at source by such actions as Drogheda and Dunbar; some pig, we might say with Winston Churchill, and some middle. War within England could not be other than civil war, because of the intensity of English ecclesiastical and governmental integration; and the difficult question which I shall now raise is that of whether civil war, in this sense, can be said to have occurred in the other kingdoms of the Atlantic archipelago, and if not, what other kinds of war can be said to have been going on within the concept of the War of the Three Kingdoms.

The Scots, it appears to me, did not fight each other very much, and if this is correct the concept of a Scottish civil war is out of place. The most obvious exception, perhaps, is Montrose's war of 1644–6, in which Montrose could contend that he and Argyll were fighting out a conflict over the meaning of a Covenant both had subscribed to, and were therefore engaged in a civil war within the Scottish polity. But in so far as his following consisted not of dissident Covenanters but of men of the house of Gordon, these were fighting out the politics (partly religious) of the north-east Highlands, while the men of clan Donald – some of whom came from Antrim – were fighting out those of an archipelagic marchland extending from Argyll to Antrim, on the maritime borders of two of the

Three Kingdoms.[17] Did Montrose perhaps not succeed in converting his war of the frontiers into the civil war within the Scottish polity he desired to make it? There were armed clashes between Engagers and non-Engagers at the time of the Second English Civil War; but were they enough to constitute a Scottish Civil War?

The crucial war in which that polity was engaged was not a war with itself, but an attempt to maintain the British character of the War of the Three Kingdoms by containing the English Civil War within it and ensuring that the latter could have only a British solution. In this the Scots failed; the English, engrossed in their civil war, regarded the Scottish intervention as essentially an interference, and ended by conquering Scotland itself, less to annex it than to eliminate it as an actor in events. But what character shall we assign to the Scottish war in England? It was only at moments in 1648 a civil war among Scotsmen, and in so far as the English made it marginal to a civil war among Englishmen they repudiated the thesis that it was a civil war among inhabitants of any single polity. It was a war among (not between) the kingdoms composing a multiple monarchy, and to find an appropriate label we should turn, I suggest, to the ancient Roman distinction between *bellum civile* and *bellum sociale*; I retain the Latin because the English term 'social war' suggests a war between members of the same social system, which is not the relevant issue. A *bellum civile* was a war between *cives*, citizens of the same polity; a *bellum sociale* was a war between *socii*, polities associated in a system comprising a multiplicity of states. The great *bellum sociale* of antiquity turned on the eligibility of Italian *socii* to be treated as *cives Romani*; it has a formal similarity with the Scottish endeavour to establish by military means that English and Scots should be members of a uniform ecclesiastical polity. Something converse yet similar may be said of the next great war between polities subject to a British monarchy, the War of the American Revolution; the concept of a *bellum sociale* appears to have its uses to historians of multiple monarchies and confederations. At the risk of inadvertently hoisting a Confederate flag, I will say that a War between the States is not the same thing as a Civil War, and that a war may be fought to determine what kind of war it is. Are we trying to reverse a military decision which subjected the War of the Three Kingdoms to the English Civil War?

There remains the third kingdom of Ireland, of which I know least and am therefore at greatest risk of speaking imperceptively. There is a

[17] [I did not consider here the possibility – for which I am indebted to Jane Ohlmeyer – that Montrose's Irish contingent were pursuing objectives of the Confederation of Kilkenny.]

suggestive essay by Hiram Morgan,[18] in which he challenges what he calls a 'colonialist' model of Irish history. In this model Ireland is treated as extra-European, as an alien and what would be called (as Ireland was called) a barbarous culture, on which history is inflicted by way of conquest and colonization and which does not share a history with its invaders. Repudiation of this model can, of course, take place in situations till recently more unqualifiedly termed colonial: Amerindians, Africans and Polynesians are learning to mobilize a history of their own, out of which they acted and reacted before and after colonization took place. But the argument in the case of Ireland goes further: non-Roman Ireland became Christian just as soon as did the ex-Roman provinces which were its neighbours, and can be said to have shared their Christian or European history – though there is the recent work by Robert Bartlett,[19] in which 'Europe' is shown as an explosion of Latin and Frankish aggression against Christians in the archipelagic west, Muslims in the Mediterranean south, Slavs and pagans in the continental east. Is the model I have begun to elaborate to be applied to the third of the Three Kingdoms?

Readers will have observed that my taxonomy of wars so far has made no use of the conceptual category of 'wars of religion', so energetically developed by John Morrill.[20] This is not because I reject or even modify it; on the contrary, I take it as self-evident that all of the wars with which we have to do were wars of religion, and that these continued in the archipelago after the year 1648, when they are conventionally held to have ended in the Franco-Netherlandish-German region. I tend therefore to suspect that the archipelagic Wars of Religion differed somewhat in character from the continental. I adopt, however, a perspective on all such wars extremely common among participants and observers in the sixteenth and seventeenth centuries – though adopting it does hold out the temptation to exaggerate the secularity of their thought. According to such commentators, the predominant character of a war of religion was its appalling capacity to disrupt government and civil order, so that humans found themselves fighting for religious reasons within a structure of government it was their first desire to maintain. We are in the world depicted in the frontispiece to Hobbes's *Leviathan* – though as that work remains Anglican to the extent that it is directed against Catholicism and Calvinism with equal vigour, it reinforces the belief that it was the 'dissolution of government', the disruption of the Tudor unity of church and kingdom, which was at the centre of the stories we are re-telling. 'War of religion', in short,

---

[18] Morgan, 1991, pp. 50–5.   [19] Bartlett, 1993.   [20] Most recently in Morrill, 1993, Part One.

is a category which interacts with others that have been used in attempting to establish a taxonomy of those wars which together made up the War of the Three Kingdoms. The English Civil War was fought within the Church of England, within the unitary monarchy or 'empire' in church and state established by the Tudors. The Scottish *bellum sociale* was fought within the multiple monarchy over several churches and kingdoms established since 1603, which the Scots were trying to bring to greater homogeneity if not unity. How may this complex taxonomy best be applied in the history of Ireland, or of three kingdoms of which Ireland was one?

That there was an Irish *bellum sociale* seems established beyond much doubt. The Old English and Old Irish aristocrats involved in the rebellion of 1641, the leaders of the Confederation which some of them became, possessed a clear image of their role in the structure of a multiple monarchy, and of Ireland as one of the kingdoms constituting that monarchy; and they resorted to the sword as a means of re-asserting and re-defining that role. Even if there were those who reached the point of demanding an independent Catholic monarchy in Ireland – and this one understands to be doubtful – they would not compel us to abandon the notions of multiple monarchy and *bellum sociale*, since it would be from that system that they desired to secede; and there appears no anticipation of the startling success enjoyed by the American rebels of 1776 in transforming a *bellum sociale* into a war between unconnected states. The programme of placing the Irish kingdom under Spanish or French protection aimed no higher than involving foreign kingdoms in the affairs of the Stuart monarchy, and I am not quite able to accept Jane Ohlmeyer's contention that French and Spanish subventions, aimed largely at the recruitment of Gaelic mercenaries, transformed a War of Three Kingdoms into a War of Five.[21] Ormonde and his Old and New English following, Inchiquin (that Protestant Gael) and his New English, were engaged in the Irish *bellum sociale* as champions of the authority of the English king and parliament respectively, over what was to remain a subject kingdom; though one might at the same time regard both, and Monro's Scottish army as well, as establishing an Irish theatre for the English Civil War and the Scots attempt to Britannicize it, at which point the concept of a War of the Three Kingdoms approaches completeness of meaning. Montrose's campaign now begins to appear a re-exportation of the War of the Three Kingdoms to Scotland, but not to England.

We are not yet forced out of the paradigm of *bellum sociale* in accounting for the wars in Ireland, but phenomena may be found which will produce

---

[21] Ohlmeyer, 1993, ch. 7.

that effect. The paradigm in question depends upon that of multiple monarchy, and to a large degree on the concept of Ireland as a kingdom subject to that of England. If there were Irish who resorted to war to make Ireland a sovereign kingdom under the Stuart or any other crown, and Irish or English or Scots who fought to keep it subject, still that would be *bellum sociale* as the term is being used here. *Bellum civile* – an Irish civil war categorically identified with the civil war going on among the English – could exist only if there were Irish who agreed that Ireland was or should be a sovereign civil polity, but fought each other to determine what kind of laws and polity there should be. The present writer confines himself to asking whether such a war among Irishmen can be found.

An alternative model – which need not exclude the foregoing but might exist side by side with it – would be stated by supposing Ireland at this period to have been not only a kingdom subjected by conquest, but a zone of settlement and resistance in which wars of conquest were still going on; and a war of conquest is generically distinct from a *bellum* either *sociale* or *civile*. This is to re-institute the 'colonial model' to which Hiram Morgan takes exception; but it may be one thing to deny that Irish history as a whole should be subjected to this model, another to deny that the model has some place in the interpretation of Irish history. If we think of Ormonde as a royalist leader of (mainly) the Old English, Inchiquin or Jones or in the end Cromwell as parliamentary leaders of the New, we can go on to credit the latter with an agenda of conquest and settlement of which Cromwell made use in pursuing the English objective of eliminating Ireland, along with the rest of Britain, as an actor in the English Civil Wars; while the English and Scottish adventurers in Ireland retained their agenda of conquest.

There remains, not unrelated to this question but at a distance from its main theatre, the war carried on by Clan Donald in Ulster, the islands and Kintyre, of which Montrose's war was in some ways an extension; and there remain the recent studies of the Marquis of Antrim by Jane Ohlmeyer and of Alasdair MacColla, the most famous of his captains, by David Stevenson.[22] The latter's Alasdair is exactly what the writers of empire meant by a barbarian; he appears out of the world of another culture and momentarily imposes its military superiority. The 'Highland charge' intrudes the antique tactics of sword and buckler on those of pike and musket, with startling if occasional success until both are superseded by those of the ring bayonet. I have observed Ohlmeyer's assertion that many

---

[22] Stevenson, 1980.

of Antrim's men were veterans of pike and musket, schooled by mercenary service in the armies of Spain; and I do not know if the Highland charge figured in the battles in Leinster and Cork, where MacColla and most of his men ultimately perished. Yet I am not ready to give up the image of them as actors in a war along the borders of empire, which was among other things a clash between cultures alien to one another. This image, though it may smack of colonialism, is reinforced rather than weakened by Jane Ohlmeyer's portrait of Antrim as a genuinely hybrid figure, who had real reason for uncertainty whether he was a lord of the isles or a great Caroline courtier, and was consequently none too successful in either role. There were others like him in Anglian-Gaelic history; and if I am focussing my attention on Clan Donald, where I could and perhaps should be focussing it on the Catholic Confederation which Antrim briefly led, it is because I want to keep open, alongside the image of multiple monarchy and war among three kingdoms, that of empire and march in the Atlantic archipelago.

At the centre of my argument there remains the War of the Three Kingdoms as a great *bellum sociale*; but at one wing stands the English Civil War, so engrossing and agonizing an experience that it was all that the English knew was going on, and at the other those aspects of war in Ireland – though not at this time in the Scottish Highlands – which were wars of empire and its frontiers, of conquest and colonization, not without the accompanying phenomena of ethnic war and ethnic cleansing; though it is to be remembered that ethnic groups and their wars are not the simple product of cultural diversity, but arise out of the pressures of conquest on populations which find themselves on its frontiers.[23] In the year of Bosnia, it is important to get this right. The war by which Cromwell terminated the First War of the Three Kingdoms (1637–51) was, in Ireland, as it was not in Scotland, a war of conquest and colonization; and there was to be one more such conquest as part of the Second War of the Three Kingdoms (1688–91), which was both the opening of a major war within the European states-system[24] and, in a strange invisible way, the last of the English Civil Wars brought about by disjunction within the headship of the Tudor Church and state.[25] There is no circumscribing these wars within a single dominant paradigm.

---

[23] [Here attention might be directed to the reading of the New Zealand wars of the 1860s as including wars between Maori *iwi* and religious movements differing as to ways of accommodating themselves to *pakeha* pressure. See Head, 2001, and Pocock, 1997e.]

[24] Israel, 1991.   [25] Pocock, 1988b, 1991a, 1996a.

CHAPTER 6

The Third Kingdom in its history

The essays in this volume[1] were delivered to a seminar sponsored by the Folger Institute Center for the History of British Political Thought, and to that extent belong in the context currently termed 'the new British history'. This is a problematic term, since it denotes a problematic history, and among its problems is the question whether it does so misleadingly. On the one hand, Scottish and Irish historians rightly query whether the term subjects their national histories to a paradigmatic structure still centred upon England;[2] though it is still unclear whether they look to the autonomy of those histories or their partial submergence in a regionalist Europe, which will either generate a history of its own or insist on the irrelevance of history to its enterprise. Their mistrust of 'British history' is partly based on a mistrust of the geopolitical term 'British Isles', which has been shared by those responsible for mounting the former programme to the point where they have proposed replacing the latter term by 'the Atlantic archipelago'.[3] From another wing of this debate, however, has come a sternly English denunciation of this term of art, as entailing a defeatist willingness to abandon the familiar 'British Isles';[4] a reaction on the whole to be welcomed, as a reminder that 'British history' cannot be merely a history of those not English, and that a 'British history' of England and the English must recognize both their recurrently dominant role and the fact that this role is not the whole of their history.

'British history' is multinational: a history of nations forming and deforming one another and themselves. It implies the proposition that no

---

[1] Ohlmeyer, 2000. This essay appeared as an Afterword, pp. 271–80 (Pocock, 2000a).
[2] See Brown, 1993; Asch, 1993.
[3] I may have been the first to propose this term in my article of 1974–5. See also Tompson, 1986, p. 1, n. 1.
[4] Nicholls, 1999, p. 321. Dr Nicholls appears to write on the Eltonian premise that the history of the state is what matters and explains itself; Ireland is therefore a 'shadow kingdom', and its history marginal to that of Scotland and England.

nation's history can be understood without that of its interaction with other histories; that national histories have been shaped in the process of shaping other histories and in interaction with the self-shaping of others; and that the identities thus shaped have been so far interactive that there is a high degree of indeterminacy about them and their shaping in a process which never attains finality. We are all left wondering about the identities – in this case national – that have been shaped for us; and this is as it should be. But 'British history' does not lead to the fashionable if under-examined proposition that national history has no meaning and is now to be written out of existence, replaced by a history that recognizes only transgressive experiences annihilating the frontiers between identities which they cross. The very concept of transgression implies that there are frontiers to be crossed, and that crossing them both affirms, and subjects to scrutiny, the identities they demarcate. That every identity is contestable, interactive and negotiable means neither that it does not exist nor that it has not a history. If it is not the whole of the story, it has been part of the shaping of the story.

It follows that any political, national or other community which has generated an image of its own identity as existing over time requires two kinds of history: the one autocentric, a record of how its inhabitants have dealt with one another over time, and the experiences they have undergone in establishing the bases of their existing community; the other heterocentric, a record of how encounters with others, some of whom they have ruled or been ruled by, have contributed to the shaping and present character of both the 'self' community and the 'others', autonomous or not, now contiguous with it. These two histories can never be separated, but can never be identical; their *dramatis personae* and their plots must overlap, but are organized into distinct narratives. As historians we need the double tongue able to tell both concurrently, but we cannot afford to believe that either annuls the other. In the present case, it is evident that Irish history is not part of British history, because Irish people read it, quite correctly, as resisting inclusion in a British community and ending in independence of it; but that it is part of British history for essentially the same reason, namely that neither Irish nor British history – and the same may be said of English and Scottish – is intelligible without the constant presence of all these peoples to one another.[5] In the same way, though within a different pattern of pressures, the history of England – that is, of

[5] This is the point at which one is regularly instructed – often in peremptory tones – that English history is to be studied in its 'European' context; that is, in the setting of its relations with its peninsular rather than its insular neighbours. There seems little point in bowing down to this idol.

how 'England' came to be and continued being – is formed both by the dealings those now accounted English have had with one another, and by the dealings they have had with other peoples, some of them included within the narratives constituting 'British history'. This last can be considered, first the history of a series of encounters between Janus-headed beings, each regardant of both self and other; secondly, the history of a problematic, that of whether the encounter between these beings shall assume or retain the form of a lasting association. By calling this a problematic, we provide that any answer to the question may be kept in view, since the end is not yet. 'British history' is neither a concealed imperial enterprise, nor the blueprint of a new confederation, nor the prelude to a 'breakup' or 'unravelling' of Britain;[6] it is the history of how all these possibilities have from time to time come to exist.

In the present volume, the image of an Ireland altogether outside the structures of authority existing in the larger archipelago is present but evanescent, existing in the writings of Conor O'Mahony in Portugal or the visions of the 'Gaelic Maccabees' in the Spanish service.[7] The dominant theme is the obstinate loyalism of the Catholic 'Old English' towards the Stuart but not the Tudor occupants of the English throne, and it is here that we are entitled to make, and at the same time to question, the claim that in this part of the story 'Irish history' was part of 'British history'[8] – the term 'British' being at all points contestable and self-contestatory. The central assertion of the Old English was that Ireland was organically connected with the English crown but that the management of this connection lay with Irish counsellors and councils of that crown. The English crown could be thought of as 'British' from the moment of its dynastic but not juridical union with the crown of Scotland, and James VI's Scottishness seems to have made it easier for his Irish subjects to accept him. Nevertheless, the crown of Scone played no part in the Irish rhetoric reported here, and what they accepted was the crown of England, remaining so even after it had become the crown of 'Great Britain' – an early case of that practice of saying 'Britain' and meaning 'England' with which we are so persistently concerned. Scots settled in Ireland and behaved as Scots after doing so, but brought no flowers of the Scottish crown with them.

The 'British problem' was archipelagic in character; Spanish, French and Dutch actors intervened in it for good reasons, but it was not produced by their reason of state. The archipelago is neither more nor less 'European' than the sub-continent known by that name.

[6] Nairn, 1977; Samuel, 1998. These two publicists were not pursuing the same objectives.

[7] Ohlmeyer, 2000, chs. 7 and 8.   [8] [See now Canny, 2001.]

How far the older English populations of Ireland referred to themselves as 'British' or 'Britons' is not very clear. This is not surprising, given the rapid changes which 'British' and 'Britain' were undergoing; from being words used by Welsh authors to assert their autochthony within the English kingdom in which they had been incorporated in 1536, these terms were being switched towards denoting the new and limited unity between England and Scotland, forming that *Magna Britannia* to which John Major had punningly alluded in his *Historia Majoris Britanniae* two generations before.[9] The Irish claim was that their polity constituted a third kingdom, autonomous though subject to the crown of England now linked with that of Scotland to form the metaphorical rather than juristic entity known by the name of 'Great Britain'. Rather than allow the contestable validity of the term 'British history' to dominate our thinking, it may be better to concede that the Irish claim and the manner of English response to it situate Irish history in the period we have come to term that of the 'Three Kingdoms' – a term as applicable and contestable when applied to Hiram Morgan's volume as to Jane Ohlmeyer's.

The term is contestable, as we learn from the sub-titles of the first two volumes of a new *History of the Modern British Isles*, respectively 'The Two Kingdoms', ending in 1603, and 'The Double Crown', ending in 1707.[10] The language is correct; this was what existed in law, since there was no crown of Ireland. Yet on the presumption that 'British history' is a history of contestation rather than decision, the contention that Ireland was a kingdom was often enough made, recognized and resisted, to give heuristic value to the concept of an 'Age of the Three Kingdoms', beginning either in 1534, when the Lordship of Ireland was erected into a kingdom, or in 1603, when the dynastic union faced a single monarch with the problems of exercising kingship in both major islands of the archipelago. This 'Age', including the 'Wars of the Three Kingdoms' from 1637 to 1652 and from 1688 to 1691, may be held to last until 1707, when a 'First Age of Union' begins, followed by a 'Second' lasting from 1800 to 1921. What name to give the succeeding age it would be premature to determine, since once again the end is not yet; but a working periodization of 'British history' is emerging. To accept 'Three Kingdoms' rather than 'Double Crown' has the advantage of conceding that there is an Irish history made in part by Irish actors; but it enters on the question, energetically contested among Irish historians, whether Stuart Ireland is to be thought of as a distinct kingdom or an English colony. The answer may be that both readings had

[9] Constable, 1892. [10] Nicholls, 1999; Smith, 1998.

validity in the seventeenth century, and therefore for us today; and that there was a complex interplay between them, so that neither excludes the other.

The persistent loyalism of the Old English appears to have two faces and is not merely quixotic (indeed, its windmills were often real giants whose fierceness could not be denied). On its religious face, Irish loyalism was Catholic and made the king an offer he must find it necessary to resist. It invited him to act as the protector of the Catholic majority in his third kingdom, but did so in the knowledge that as king of England he was supreme head and governor of the church in that kingdom, and was committed to the support of a Protestant and episcopal Church of Ireland of which he was head in the same way. There could be no question, therefore, that James or Charles might become a monster of ecclesiastical triplicity: an Anglican head of state and church in England, a Presbyterian head of state if not church in Scotland (where he was the only king of a Calvinist kingdom in Europe) and a Catholic head in Ireland. Not even Leviathan might be equal to this triplicity, and the giant of English political philosophy was English enough to pay little attention to the nature of multiple monarchy. Irish loyalism offered allegiance in return for protection; but could the kingdom so defined be more than a protectorate?

Leviathan was a figure born of civil war. Four decades previously, James VI and I might have found his third and Catholic kingdom easier to rule had his ecumenical ambitions for a reconciliation of Christendom borne any fruit at all; we have recently been reminded of what these were and on what presuppositions they must rest.[11] They entailed the vision that every Catholic kingdom might approximate the Gallican position in which the pope received spiritual obedience but exercised no civil authority, and the authority of a general council outweighed his. There is a counter-Tridentine vision of the early seventeenth century, helping account for the reception accorded in England to Paolo Sarpi; and to understand James's overtures we have to think ourselves back into a world in which lay Catholics and regally minded clergy might be prepared to downplay the papal power in every way possible. Not only, however, was there the claim to a deposing power; there was the resilient ultramontanism whose triumph at Trent Sarpi had recounted; and it is easy for the British historian to tell the story in terms of two immovable objects – papal supremacy and English royal supremacy – brought, however unwillingly, into collision, in such a way that any offer to mitigate the latter produced

[11] Patterson, 1997.

the paradox of rebellion against it by those so bent on maintaining it that they saw mitigation as a surrender to the former. On their side of the looking-glass world of British politics, the Irish Confederates went into rebellion against the crown because they feared it was about to lose authority, and found their chief enemies to be those determined to restore the crown's authority by parliamentary action independent of it. The logic of rebellion was always more complicated than even Hobbes understood.

Once we introduce the Supremacy, however, the story becomes inescapably English-dominated. The War of the Three Kingdoms was long known as 'the English Civil War' for the reason that there was an English civil war, which the English were resolved to settle among themselves, admitting no interference from the associated kingdoms; a war over the location and definition of sovereignty in church and state. They were less determined to maintain English sovereignty over Scotland or even Ireland than to deny Scots and Irish any role in determining the future of the English kingdom. Allan MacInnes[12] traces the history of the Scottish Covenanting attempt to impose a settlement 'British' in the sense of a Presbyterianism of both church-states in the larger island. Though it failed, it was not unthinkable, since the Church of England could be thought of in Protestant Calvinist terms; and its intellectual symbol was James Ussher, Church of Ireland Archbishop of Armagh.[13] The Irish Confederacy, being Catholic, had no 'British' or 'Three Kingdoms' solution open to it. Short of an *ecclesia hibernica* Catholic without being papal, it must be either an independent kingdom guaranteed by a foreign prince – it is here that Conor O'Mahony appears the realist who demands the impossible – or a protectorate and subordinate kingdom in which Catholics enjoyed the protection of an Anglican sovereign.

To pursue a re-defined subordination by the means of armed rebellion appears in hindsight obviously foredoomed, the measure of a colonial status in which even the Catholic Old English found themselves. The formula helps us, however, to pursue the complexities and even confusions of the Confederacy's war as one of the Wars – the plural re-asserts itself – of the Three Kingdoms: a war both social, in the sense of one fought among a group of kingdoms in disagreement over the terms of their association, and perhaps civil, in the sense of one fought within the Irish kingdom to determine the relations among its inhabitants. The Irish war, furthermore, became entangled in both the English and the Scottish wars it had helped precipitate. Alasdair MacColla's campaigns in Argyll and east of the North

[12] MacInnes, 2000.   [13] Ford, 1998, 1999.

Channel can be seen in three ways: as part of Montrose's Anglo-Scottish strategy of creating civil war in Scotland, as pursuing in that kingdom the strategic aims (whatever they were) of the Confederacy, and as conducting a strictly ethnic war of Clan Donald against Clan Campbell. MacColla cannot be relegated to a clan world exterior to the state, but there was a clan dimension to what he did.

Within the multiple perspectives of British history, there is an Irish history in which the Confederacy is, or is not, a blind alley, part of the larger failure of the Old English to secure a status for a Catholic Ireland within the multiple monarchy of an otherwise Protestant Stuart dynasty: an enterprise repeatedly wrecked by the English, not only necessitated to maintain control over Ireland but bound to fear any multi-state or multi-church solution as threatening the unity in sovereignty of king and parliament which they had fought civil wars among themselves to maintain. Given Ireland, and given the union of the crowns, the empire of the English over themselves was inseparable from their empire in the archipelago and beyond it in the Atlantic and the American seaboard. The Second War of the Three Kingdoms – which Dr Ohlmeyer prefers to call the War of the Three Kings – was not a Fall of the British Monarchies, a dissolution of government, or a general collapse into wars of religion, but the archipelagic face of a European conflict, in which England, Scotland and Ireland became involved in William III's struggle against Louis XIV for supremacy in the Low Countries and lower Germany. At the same time, however, it transformed that conflict, by bringing about the construction of the British fiscal, military and parliamentary state capable of acting as a power in Europe and at the same time exercising empire in Britain, the archipelago and beyond Europe in America, India and the global oceans.[14] The problems of empire in the Tudor sense persisted, but their context was enlarged. We enter the First Age of Union, with its climaxes and crises in 1776, 1798 and 1801.

In the cycle of wars from 1688 to 1691 – bloodless in England, civil rather than ethnic in Scotland, wars of renewed conquest in Ireland – the distinctively Catholic enterprise of the Old English is held to have ended at Limerick and in its aftermath. It might seem, then, that the history of Catholic loyalism to a Protestant dynasty had met the giant behind the windmill; but Irish history is more complex even than that. In the history of word and discourse, to which volumes originating with a Center for the History of Political Thought are necessarily committed, the Old English

---

[14] Pocock, 1991a, 1996a.

and the Confederates are seen as leaving something behind them, to be used by others than themselves in history, Irish, British and American: the claim, originating in the circumstances of the Kingdom of Ireland set up in 1534, that this kingdom and its parliament were subject to the crown but not the parliament of England, so that the crown's authority in Ireland was to be exercised with Irish consent in an Irish parliament. One head and many bodies, or as many heads as there were bodies? Could Leviathan be a hydra, or was this a Pufendorfian *monstrum informe, ingens, horrendum?*[15] King James had not needed a Hobbes to give him his answer; but the claim was to be pressed again, even while the increasing incorporation of English crown in English parliament – as much a remedy as a cause of civil war – made it seem increasingly monstrous to English understandings. The practical impact of William Molyneux may well have been small, but in retrospect his symbolic importance must appear great; in 1698, a year when Andrew Fletcher was active in Scotland and the English parliament was reacting against the demands of the state being created by King William's wars, he shows us a claim originally Old English passing into the hands and pens of Protestant settlers discontented with the status of a kingdom now their own. In 1707 the Scots were to surrender the opportunity to make such a claim, failing to insist that their union with England should be 'federative' rather than 'incorporating'; and when the claim resurfaced in Ireland about 1780, it was to be in a context where American colonial assemblies had claimed that they too were connected with the crown but not the parliament of England, throwing off the crown only when it would not separate itself from that parliament[16] and inaugurating a third cycle of wars, and this time secessions, within the empire – an empire, be it noted, far more than colonial.

The Irish and American crises are not to be separated in the 'British history' of the late eighteenth century; but that era brings to an end the 'First Age of Union', and it has not been the business of Ohlmeyer's volume to travel beyond 1707 and the beginnings of that age, which in Irish history is also the Age of the Ascendancy. A further volume[17] is to carry us through that age, towards the maelstrom of 1776–1801; but the purpose of this one has been to effect a transition from the Wars of the Three Kingdoms to the War of the Three Kings and the brink of the age succeeding it. To make it a fully 'British' history, there might perhaps have been a sequel to Allan MacInnes's chapter, exploring in depth the politics of post-Covenanting Scotland from the Cromwellian occupation to the

---

[15] [See now Armitage, 2000.] [16] The thesis of ch. 9, below. [17] Connolly, 2000.

Williamite Revolution and the Union which followed; and this might have been in part an Irish history, if the Scots in Ulster were shown responding to what they saw happening in their kingdom of origin. In the next age, again, there can be seen a Dublin Enlightenment visibly English and Whig, an Ulster Enlightenment visibly Scottish but not Moderate, both with their affiliations in America.[18] The focus of this volume, however, has been on Irish history in so far as it was in British history; that is to say, on the history of the Third Kingdom.

Each of the peoples, or nations, of whom 'British history' is made up exists, it is here argued, in two overlapping but distinguishable histories. One is the history of its 'self', as that self has been fashioned both in the relations between those who have come to be its component members and, concurrently, in relations with 'others' who have not. The second is a history of the relations between selves and others of which its self-fashioning may be seen as a part, but which is not to be written from the standpoint of any 'self' at all, whether individual or comprehensive. In the period with which this volume has been concerned, it might be said that the Third Kingdom – a.k.a. 'Ireland' – had not fashioned a coherent self or yet come to exist in a history of its own; both because of the presence of distinct and bitterly contending cultures – this has been a history of Gaelic, Latin and English language, and of Catholic and both forms of British Protestant religion – and because of powerful exterior forces, represented by the English, which was increasingly a British, crown, insisting that the Kingdom of Ireland was a dependent, even a conquered, kingdom and to that extent not the author of its own history. From Captain MacMorris to Stephen Dedalus, there are voices in the literature of Ireland expressing the uncertainties of colonial and postcolonial identity. Yet there is a kingdom and the opportunity to fashion it, and this volume contains evidence of vigorous and lasting efforts in that direction.

Leaving aside – perhaps unwisely – the problems of defining a Catholicism which could be neither royal nor fully papal, there has been a history of settler nationalisms able to claim that what indigenous nationalism there was could be comprehended within them. A fully Gaelic nationalism drawing on pre-Norman memories being elusive and little encouraged by the structure of the Kingdom of 1534, we have been left with the claim of the Old English to be the true 'Irish nation', founded on the acceptance of the crown by both Norman and Irish consentients as far

---

[18] Molyneux and Viscount Molesworth might be held to stand for the former, Francis Hutcheson for the latter.

back as the twelfth century. Whatever the O'Neills, O'Donnells and O'Mahonys may have thought of it, this was a settler nationalism, though the Old English had been in Ireland long enough to be thought, and think themselves, *Hibernicis ipsis Hiberniores*. It issued in the most characteristic of settler nationalist claims, that to the independence of their own parliament in conducting their relations with a multinational Crown of the Three Kingdoms. Here it collided with the central Anglocentricity of British history: the Royal Supremacy and the Civil War producing a compulsive unity and incorporation of English crown with English parliament, meaning that no Irish, Scottish or American legislature could claim a separate relationship with the crown without seeming to threaten the integrity of the English, as well as the United, Kingdom. This is a problem from which in the year 2000 the British have by no means escaped, though they are seeking to redraw it.

By the year 1698 the theses of settler nationalism were beginning to pass – not without vigorous counter-moves – into the discourse of a 'Protestant nation' claiming to be at the point of absorbing what remained of its Old Irish and Old English predecessors, so that all Irish could be said to be English. This was no less a nationalism than a colonialism; colonists as well as colonized have their quarrels with the authority that sent them out and seeks to pursue them, and may base claims to autonomy on their wars and treaties with the indigenous peoples preceding them. Thus Peruvian creoles claimed to be the heirs of the Inca, and an Irish Protestant nationalism sought to base itself in a Catholic, Norman and Milesian past. This, however, was a phenomenon little seen before 1780 or thereabouts.[19] Molyneux may hint to us how it came to be achieved, but if we take the theme of Dr Ohlmeyer's volume to be the assertion and defeat of the Catholic Old English attempt to speak in the name of the Kingdom of Ireland, it must be the task of Dr Connolly's volume[20] to pursue Protestant, including Presbyterian, settler nationalisms towards the American and Irish crisis of the last quarter of the eighteenth century. In the second half of the seventeenth century and the First Age of Union, we listen to a diversity of voices fashioning a diversity of selves; a clamour, not a consensus or even a debate.

---

[19] [It might be argued that the re-modelling of New Zealand history around the Treaty of Waitangi is yet another instance.]
[20] See n. 17.

PART III

Empire and Rebellion in the First Age of Union

CHAPTER 7

*Archipelago, Europe and Atlantic after 1688**

(1)

The period of the Three Kingdoms is broken but not ended by the archi-pelagic war-cycle of 1637–51 and the interregnum of 1649–60: as we have seen, a sequence of crises and restorations in the relations of state, church and civil society in the multiple monarchy and the several histories of the Three Kingdoms. This sequence is connected with the European war-cycle of 1618–48, but the connection is rendered indirect by the peculiar structure of the English monarchy and its church – so much in the War of the Three Kingdoms having been occasioned by the crisis in that system as it inter-sected with the other British kingdoms. To study that war in its connections with the Thirty Years War is legitimate and valuable,[1] but the former cannot be reduced to an aspect of the latter. The Three Kingdoms period is brought to an end by a second war-cycle, that of 1688–91 in British history, where it might be known as the Second War of the Three Kingdoms; but this sequence bears a different relation to the history of Europe, being the opening phase and in some ways the product of the war-cycle of 1688–1714, directed against the predominance of the French monarchy and, later, the danger that it might absorb the monarchy of Spain. This crisis may be said to have begun with the French invasion of Holland in 1672; that, and William of Orange's expedition in the Irish war of 1690–1 which concluded it, were undertaken for Dutch and Orangist reasons and form episodes in Dutch history[2] as well as in that of the European states system.

It is proper to emphasize this, in modification of an English historio-graphy which has sometimes treated the 'Revolution of 1688' excessively or exclusively in the context of English parliamentary and constitutional history. That context does not disappear, however, when English history

*[Written for this volume in 2003.]

[1] Scott, 2000.   [2] Israel, 1991 and 1995, chs. 32 and 36.

is viewed in the context of British, nor do English and British history disappear when viewed in the context of European.[3] William III came to England, and made himself king of England, Scotland and Ireland, for Dutch and European reasons; but he was invited to come by a group of English magnates for reasons inherent in the complex history of church, crown and parliament in England.[4] That history developed in two directions. In one, the consolidation of crown with parliament was bought at the price of a continuing uncertainty in both dynastic and ecclesiastical history which left the Revolution and the Hanoverian regime imperfectly legitimized far into the eighteenth century. In another, the continual if never actualized danger of civil war this entailed became an aspect of the wars of Europe down to perhaps 1760, so that the British kingdoms were obliged to take part in those wars for their own dynastic, religious and constitutional reasons, among others. The events of 1688–9 are important in British history as drawing it more closely into the states-system of Europe, and as compelling the Anglo-British state to re-organize itself so as to participate in European wars. This was noted, if more often resented than welcomed, by contemporary observers.

If this revolution entailed a potential civil war and foreign invasion upon England – for reasons including the dissatisfaction of the Church of England[5] – the drastic eviction of the episcopal clergy by Scottish Presbyterians was more 'revolutionary' than anything that happened in England, and entailed a potential civil war that became actual in 1715 and 1745. This conflict had its bearings on the politics of Lowland and Highland, and culminated after 1745 in something like a colonial policy of repressing, transforming and sometimes expelling Gaelic society in the far north of Britain and its islands. In the relations between the two historic British kingdoms, however, the crucial transformation occurred in 1707, when the reconstruction of England as a fiscal-military state based on commerce – undertaken as a necessary consequence of the Revolutionary involvement of England in European wars – was seen as having set processes in motion with which the Scottish state and society could not cope as independent entities.[6] The Union of 1707 was a union of parliaments as well as crowns – though not of churches or of laws – and this, undertaken for reasons European as well as commercial, was to have drastic consequences in the

---

[3] Israel, 1991; Hoak and Feingold, 1996.
[4] Beddard, 1991; also Jones, 1972; Speck, 1988; and for the continuing validity of English constitutional history, Schwoerer, 1981 and 1992.
[5] Clark, 1985 and 2000.   [6] Robertson, 1995.

history of Britain, Europe and empire. The creation of a kingdom of Great Britain led directly to the question whether there was to be a British nation or a history of that nation: the question to which this book is aimed at providing answers.

In Irish history, the revolutionary end of the Three Kingdoms period has consequences perhaps more strictly archipelagic than those it has in the history of the British kingdoms proper. In order to consolidate his hold upon England as a resource in the wars of Europe, King William was obliged to complete the conquest of Ireland; which by that time meant the victory of New English and Scottish Protestant settlers over the Catholic Old English and Gaelic Irish – the last playing a role not utterly unlike that of a *tangata whenua*. The Treaty of Limerick symbolically marks the beginning of the period of Irish history known as the Ascendancy:[7] the hegemony of an Anglo-Protestant landlord and middle class over a Catholic majority, with Scottish Presbyterians – known by the English name of 'Dissenters' – as a third force. This Ascendancy was secure enough to permit Irish, or Irish-settled, Protestants, to develop their own discontents and their own kind of nationalism, which was to play a complex part in the cycle of wars and rebellions that terminates the First Age of Union, whose origins we trace before 1707, to the Williamite wars that ended the Age of the Three Kingdoms.

(11)

The Kingdom of Great Britain, established by the Union of 1707, that emerged from the war-cycle ending in 1714, was an imperfect multiple monarchy, with a single parliamentary sovereignty but a diversity of national churches and legal systems; the subordinate kingdom of Ireland was not united with it. Perhaps more significantly, it was a powerful military-fiscal state,[8] equipped to take part in constructing a Europe of sovereign states, capable of wars and treaties, linked by a shared commerce and (it was thought) a shared culture of manners and civility. This Europe was engaged in oceanic expansion beyond its geographic limits; it was not based on a common retreat from empire. Before the end of the European war-cycle – indeed helping to end it – there was reason to fear that the British kingdom was excessively engaged in re-drawing the map of Europe, and a Tory government engineered a withdrawal from wars and alliances of which the greatest of Whig historians seems to have approved.[9] There

---

[7] Connolly, 1992; Claydon and McBride, 1998.   [8] Brewer, 1989.   [9] Pocock, 1985, p. 303.

ensued a rhetoric which contrasted European engagement, bringing about increases in national debt, standing armies and 'the influence of the crown', with a blue-water strategy of commerce and colonies that enabled Britain to influence European politics without being drawn into them.

The Europe including Britain that emerged by the time of the Treaty of Utrecht (1713) aimed at the termination of wars of religion as well as the threat of French universal monarchy. It therefore enables us to define Enlightenment – while remembering that other definitions are possible and useful – as a programme for bringing both war and religion into a system of civil society, based on sovereign government and international commerce.[10] The British kingdoms now united took part in this pro-gramme, and encountered the problem of reconciling it with the spiritual autonomy and ecclesiastical government of Christian churches. In both Anglican England and Moderate Scotland it became a question how far a church of Christ could be drawn into the empire of civil society without provoking either a loss of faith or a variety of responses ranging from intolerant theology through evangelical revival to outright disbelief. In this problematic, dissenters from established religion played their part, and it became evident that Tudor 'empire' in church and state had not been extended from England to Britain. Queen Anne was not head of the church in Scotland as she was in England. In Ireland the Protestant communities, English and Scottish, encountered the problems of Enlightenment against the background of a silent majority disabled by the lack of sovereignty from dealing with those problems when Enlightenment was Catholic.

In the second half of the First Age of Union (1707–1801) the great figures of Scottish Enlightenment were expanding the moral philosophy, political economy and civil history appropriate to a universe of commerce – an enterprise in which no major English thinker was comparably engaged – but were doing so in a context of radical criticism and incipient rebellion in the outer provinces of the Hanoverian system. 'Europe' and oceanic 'empire' were as we have seen so closely linked that choices between them were questions of priority; Britain's European role was largely based on supremacy in the maritime empire of trade, slavery and American produce. The system set up or imagined by the Treaty of Utrecht was ended, in part, by the increasing rivalry between Britain and France for control of North America, the Caribbean and India, which in the war of 1756–63 increased the debt of both states to a point which was to have revolutionary con-sequences. This 'first crisis of the *ancien régime*,' as it has been challengingly

---

[10] Pocock, 1999 (B), I, pp. 109–14.

called,[11] culminated in the War of the American Revolution, which now demands its place in the patterns of British history.

Commercial 'empire' – it is well to remember that this use of the word is a metaphor – led to the increase of population in the English (and Iberian) colonies in America to the point where these become civil societies with politics, histories and cultures of their own. 'British history' thus acquired a further dimension – for simplicity's sake we say a fourth – which became a problem of 'empire' in the Tudor sense of the term. The problem of 'America' became the question of whether these new, vital and expansive societies could be included in the system whereby the crown in parliament governed the English state which had expanded to include Scotland and Ireland. There was a religious dimension to this, since the colonies tended to be multi-church congregational polities, and established churches where they existed were not immediately supported by the crown;[12] but the narrative of American revolution is commonly related as a process whereby these colonies claimed to be autonomous societies, demanding first a voice in the decisions of government, then to govern themselves under the crown, and finally to be independent states with no allegiance to it. This revolution may be traced to an original failure to define colonies as kingdoms, vice-royalties, palatinates or any other species of political society within the 'empire' of the crown. It was a consequence of global importance that the independent states of Anglophone America defined their new relationship in a political language which placed them outside the terms in which British history had been and continued being conducted.

The Declaration of Independence severed the American states from the British with such finality as to lessen its impact on the internal politics of the latter. In England, the politics of George III had produced a state of dissatisfaction whose language had much in common with that of the colonists, but this must be seen as a process whereby England moved away from the actual and potential civil wars of the seventeenth century, and what had been a language of division became no more than a rhetoric of principle. In the post-Revolutionary era of 'the rage of party'[13] English politics had been a continuation of civil war by other means – a second 'dissolution of government' was at all costs to be avoided – but in the 'present discontents' of George III's reign the language of revolution

---

[11] Venturi, 1979 and 1984; Litchfield, 1989 and 1991.
[12] For a challenging statement of the case for viewing the Revolution as a war of religion, see Clark, 1993.
[13] Holmes, 1967; Gunn, 1971.

became theatrical, a means of taking stands, close to the striking of attitudes.[14] The claim that the king and his ministers had achieved a complete corruption of government was made more often than it was acted on – other than by Thomas Paine, who went to America to engage in revolution against the English régime, and found there the reality of civil war, which he helped to promote.[15]

This is an English story. In Scotland, an oligarchy that came close to a vice-royalty encountered violent anti-popery rather than political radicalism, and something similar may indeed be said of England and the Gordon riots.[16] In Scottish Ulster – which may be thought of as Scotland without the Moderate Enlightenment[17] – it was another matter; but we enter here upon the Irish dimension of the crisis which ended the First Age of Union. Here we return to the politics of empire, still in a Tudor sense of the term. Protestant settlers – who now called themselves Irish – shared the discontents of American colonists to the point of making demands like theirs for parliamentary sovereignty under the crown; demands less radical to the extent to which Ireland was a kingdom rather than a colony, as no North American state had been. The mixed success and failure of the Patriots and Volunteers led to the formation of the United Irishmen, in which Protestant settler nationalists close to Americans in their politics looked for support from Presbyterians in the North and Catholics both urban and peasant, thus raising the question of what Irish nationality was to become. If we carry this narrative into the 1790s, we may think of the American Revolution as the first of a chain of crises and rebellions which terminate the First Age of Union as the war-cycle of 1688–91 terminated the Age of the Three Kingdoms. The union of Great Britain and Ireland in 1800–1 ends the First Age of Union and inaugurates the Second.

These processes, however, occur within the history of empire in the Tudor sense: the problem of how the self-government of the English state is to be reconciled with its incorporation of other realms. That history does not end with the independence of the United States, an event whose huge importance is rather global than structural; America did not liquidate 'empire' by departing from it. In a later chapter it will be argued that even Irish independence – the second revolutionary secession from British history – does not terminate the problem of empire within the Atlantic

---

[14] Sainsbury, 1987.   [15] Claeys, 1989; Fruchtman, 1994.
[16] The Edinburgh riots of 1779 are held to have ended the political career of William Robertson (Brown, 1997, p. 31). For the Gordon riots still see Butterfield, 1949.
[17] McBride, 1998.

archipelago; and if this is accepted, it will follow that the so-called 'First British Empire' is not liquidated by either the independence of America or the acquisition in India of 'empire' in the new and modern sense in which we use the word. Meanwhile, the chain of crises that terminates the First Age of Union is to be seen, like its predecessors in 1637 and 1688, in the context of a European war-cycle: that of 1793–1815, in which British maritime and extra-European supremacy was deployed in a European struggle against universal monarchy in a new, because revolutionary, form.

CHAPTER 8

The significance of 1688: some reflections on Whig history

(1)

'Well, doctor,' William of Orange is said to have remarked to Gilbert Burnet, as they stood on Brixham beach on 5 November 1688, 'what do you think of predestination now?' The jest, if it was one, might be taken as referring to the extraordinary series of physical events which had brought them where they were – to the multiple changes of the Protestant wind, blowing them east, west and east again; or it might refer to the no less extraordinary series of contingencies in church, state and dynasty which had led to William's being invited to England and had made it worth his while to set out thither; or finally, it might be taken as indicating that neither William nor Burnet at that moment could have had the least idea what was about to happen. With the benefit of hindsight, we know; and we know also that William had done his best to ensure that some things should happen which did in fact happen. We are therefore tempted to see the outcome of William's expedition as a foregone conclusion, which is to know more about predestination than William or Burnet did. A warning against 'Whig history' in a very crude sense may therefore be uttered at the outset of this essay.[1] William was a careful planner, but careful planners in military and political affairs are at the same time very daring gamblers, and he was engaged on a gamble of a quite breathtaking nature.

He was in Tor Bay at the head of a powerful military expedition, involving a number of the regiments which he commanded as captain-general of the United Provinces. He was there because a group of powerful English magnates had asked him to come;[2] he was there in pursuit of his wife's dynastic interests and his own; and he was there in pursuit of reason

---

[1] Originally printed as Pocock, 1991a.

[2] [It is possible that they would not have asked him if he had not asked them to ask him (Hoak and Feingold, 1996, p. 24). This does not mean that they did not have reasons of their own for asking him.]

of state, as this declared the interests of the House of Orange and the Republic of the Netherlands – which might be, but were not necessarily regarded as, identical. In this last respect, the descent upon England was, or turned out to be, an enormously dangerous but successful fling in the political and military struggle against the king of France: the Sicilian expedition of the wars of the Grand Alliance, which transformed their nature by extending their scope and succeeded where its analogue had failed. But the first and second sets of reasons for William's presence in Tor Bay might well have moved a French statesman, on hearing that the Prince of Orange intended to set out for England, to the thought that if the prince meant to involve himself in the affairs of the wild and unmanageable kingdoms beyond the Channel and the North Sea, he should by no means be prevented from doing so. These reasons were such as to create a strong probability that William would involve himself in an English civil war, swelling into another war of the three kingdoms of Britain and Ireland, which would absorb and destroy his resources and from which he might never return.

England in 1688 had not emerged from the conditions which had produced one such series of civil wars between forty and fifty years previously, and had nearly renewed them on two occasions in the most recent decade. These conditions arose from instabilities within the ruling structure of the Established Church, which compromised the role of the monarchy and the lay and clerical governing élites. Some of these problems were constitutional in character, recognized as problems in the location of sovereignty, and had come to pass in the grim realities of civil war in 1642 and temporary dissolution of the historical structure of government in 1649 – two memories which did more than anything else to determine the political consciousness of the governing classes (to look no further) in 1688. All knew that there had been a civil war which nobody had desired; all were determined that it should not happen again, but were at the same time aware that such a determination might not be enough to prevent it recurring; and in 1688 matters were in such a state that civil war was being risked again.

The restoration of the monarchy in 1660 had been followed by a restoration of the royal and episcopal church in 1662, but the relation between the two had not been stabilized. As well as a small Catholic minority in England, a rather larger one in the Highlands of Scotland, and a partly subjugated Catholic majority in Ireland, there was in England a significant group of semi-organized Dissent; and though this last was far from militant in its politics, the sons of Charles the Martyr – who were not reliable witnesses to the church for which their father was said to have died – were tempted to exploit the opportunities which they saw in this degree of ecclesiastical fragmentation. Alliances between clergy and parliamentary gentry had on occasion been formed to pull the monarchy back into its necessary alliance with the church; but these had forced groups active in politics to choose between their visceral Anglicanism, which presented church and king as the sole guarantors of the ruling order, and the equally visceral Erastianism which impelled them to reject the clergy as arbiters in matters of state.[3] Some had carried mistrust of both monarchy and clergy so far as to attack the alliance between the two, and this tension had been vastly exacerbated by the prospect that the successor to the crown and its headship of the church might himself be a Catholic. Though the attempt to force the crown to review its relationship with the church was known to be a recipe for civil war, the prospect of a popish successor had carried England within recognizable distance of such a war in 1679–81 and had led to an actual attempt to renew it in 1685. Each time, however, the prospect of civil war had brought about renewed support of church and king even under a popish successor, and this had been reinforced by the assurance that the succession to James II was guaranteed to his Protestant daughters and their consorts. Threatening as the actions of James appeared, therefore, they were endurable until a major breach between the king and the bishops coincided with the birth of a male heir to the throne. The public causes professed in the invitation to William to present himself in England, and in his printed Declarations on doing so, were therefore dynastic, in the sense that the heir (being intolerable) was supposed to be spurious and the interest of William's wife in the succession at risk; ecclesiastical, in the sense that the monarchy was seen to be engaged in an attack on the church of which it was head; and political, in the sense that William was calling for the meeting of a free parliament to settle these and other issues, including James's attempts to pack parliaments so that they would obey him.[4] Any one of these problems might have to be resolved by the sword in civil war, and here were sufficient reasons why William should bring an army with him; but his mind was engaged, so far as we know it, by thoughts of European, not English, war, and the exact calculations of his reason of state are a fascinating enigma. Perhaps he was placing his reliance on predestination; which would be to say, in other words current at the time, that he was making an appeal to heaven.

[3] I draw near here to the arguments of both Scott, 2000, and Clark, 1985 and 2000.
[4] For these see Jones, 1972 and 1978.

John Locke had written the scenario of such an appeal a few years before, and it had been a scenario of civil war. The concluding chapters of his *Treatises of Government*, written when desperate associates of Shaftesbury were turning to thoughts of violence after their defeat in parliament, envisage a people determining that their government is in a state of war against them, decreeing that government to be dissolved, making their appeal to heaven, and resuming the power to place the government in new hands or continue it in old, as they see fit. Every one of these phrases – dissolution of government, appeal to heaven, reversion of power to the people – carried as its normal connotation the kind of thing that had happened in 1642, when the subjects had been obliged to draw swords against one another, and in 1649, when they had been obliged by the collapse of the main structures of government to face the dreadful necessity of constituting a new régime by deciding where to yield their submission and give their allegiance. Locke was exposing himself like Sidney to the penalties of treason, by imagining and compassing a civil war that had not happened yet; and this aside, he was inhabiting the world of Thomas Hobbes – of the frontispiece to *Leviathan*, in which dissent over the location of authority in church and state can plunge a kingdom into civil war, and this condition can be ended only by replacing the appeal to heaven by the yielding up of the subject's sword to a sovereign who can exercise it for him. But it took more than the free gift of the sword to constitute a sovereign who could keep it in his hands. The English had attempted the Hobbesian solution in 1660, when they solemnly declared that power over the militia was forever vested in the king; Charles I had posthumously triumphed in one of the things he had chiefly fought for in 1642; but a Leviathan who fumbled with the crozier he held in his left hand might press back upon his unwilling subjects the sword he should have retained in his right. That was the menace of a popish successor, and it was nearer happening in 1688 than when Locke was writing in the early 1680s. And Hobbes's readers in 1651, when *Leviathan* was presented to Charles II after the defeat of his army at Worcester, may have seen that Hobbes offered no advice on what was to be done when two rivals for the role of Leviathan were claiming the subject's allegiance with their swords drawn. That too was the condition of England from 5 November 1688, when William of Orange landed his army, to the second flight of James II at the end of December.

The success of William's expedition must be measured by the proposition either that what happened between those dates was not an English civil war; or that if it was one, as Edmund Burke contended a hundred and one

years later, it ended without battle on English soil and without the disintegration of the ruling élites into groups compelled to draw sword against
one another, as had happened in the well-remembered catastrophe of 1642.
I have tried in another place to emphasize how very narrowly we must see
civil war as having been averted;[5] how very easily James II, by fighting one
inconclusive battle, might have rendered the military issue uncertain and
compelled his subjects to take decisions about an armed contest for
sovereignty. When his father left London and Westminster for York in
1642, when he exposed his person in battle at Edgehill, when he left Oxford
for Newcastle in 1646, when he left Hampton Court for Carisbrooke in
1647, he was on every occasion dramatizing the fact of civil war; he was
dramatizing his own indispensability to legitimate government and finding
men willing to hazard war in his support. The tactic had proved disastrous
but in the end effective; the monarchy had won the civil wars. But when
James abandoned his capital in 1688, he did not throw himself into the
heart of his own kingdoms or yield himself with conscious dignity into the
hands of his adversaries. He took refuge at the court of the king of France,
thus going far towards converting a civil war into a foreign one; and by such
actions as the jettisoning of the Great Seal, he did much to declare that he
had tried but failed to dissolve a government capable, since he compelled it
to the necessity, of functioning without him and replacing him.

What may be Whiggishly asserted about these events is that they
expelled the reality, though not by any means the threat, of civil war
from English experience, and in so doing went far to constitutionalize
English perceptions of drastic political change. Civil wars are fought
among those who know what civil sovereignty is, but are in conflict over
where it is located and how it is to be exercised; they may find that they
have destroyed it and are in disagreement over how it is to be restored. The
English of the 1640s had faced themselves with these terrible questions, and
John Locke was envisaging that they might confront them again. When
James II fled to France he kept the location of sovereignty an open
question; he retained a very good case for claiming that he was lawful
king and his son his lawful heir, and that the dispossession of both was
deeply fraudulent.

We used to hold that his case was so good that it could be answered only
by a revolutionary restatement of the nature of kingship, though the great
Whig writers Burke and Macaulay were at pains to point out that no
such restatement was ever promulgated. But James abandoned, or never

[5] Pocock, 1988b.

exercised, the weapon of civil war; by not waging war within the kingdom he lost the power to oblige his subjects to choose between two claimants to sovereignty, each with his own definition of what it was and each at the subject's door to demand his allegiance. In consequence the English of 1688 did not re-enter, and as things turned out they had forever left, the world of politics as Hobbes and Locke had known it.

In 1642 the powerful sovereignty built up by the Tudors had split apart but retained the strength to force subjects into civil war against their wills. In the new year of 1689 the English found the edifice of sovereignty deserted by its king, but themselves possessed of most of the resources for continuing it in existence. There had been a desertion but not a dissolution; the people had neither declared nor discovered the government to be dissolved, and if they had done anything it had been to frustrate the king's ineffective attempts to dissolve it. 'Government' could therefore be defined less as 'sovereignty' than as 'constitution', and those few who took immediate notice of the *Treatises of Government* which Locke now anonymously published could respond that there had been no dissolution of government because the constitution retained its ancient form and force, so that all which had been done was authorized by the necessity of preserving it. This view of the significance of 1688 was that retained by aristocratic Whigs and Revolution Tories thereafter; the only question contested by a few was whether the constitution reserved to the people or their representatives a power, not to dissolve the government, but to divest of power those guilty of seeking to dissolve it.

We have reached a point where it is necessary to walk carefully; paths lead from it in a number of directions, and we may construct either Whiggish or narrowly revisionist histories if we follow one of them to the exclusion of the rest, or presume that one of them is the main road and the others mere by-paths. The flight of James reinforced constitutionalism, in the sense that it left the parliamentary and legal fabric in a position to remedy its own predicament; and for this reason it came to be held that the Revolution of 1688, precisely because it was not a dissolution, was a victory for the ancient constitution, that James's misdeeds could be defined as transgressions against it; and English history before and after 1688 could be written in terms of the constitution's persistence in the teeth of Stuart and Cromwellian attempts to overthrow it. The Whig need to distance 1688 from 1649 produced a historiography of the civil wars which vindicated the parliamentary cause while condemning the regicide; and republican, and much of what we call 'Whig', history came to be written in these terms from Rapin de Thoyras to Macaulay, with some notable dissents from

David Hume and Catharine Macaulay. But though there came, rather momentously, to be a reading of English politics which was both constitutionalist and consensualist, to say this is not to say that there came to be a consensus about either the workings of the constitution or the claim that the problems of the kingdom had been solved in constitutionalist terms. There is plenty of evidence to the contrary, and all I am claiming here is that the non-recurrence of civil war and armed conflict over sovereignty made it massively more possible than it had been before to interpret English politics and history in these terms.

There continued to be a radical Whig reading of the events of 1688, though if we are to say so we shall have to decide what significance to attribute to its survival. Few (though a few) argued that the Revolution had constituted a Lockean dissolution of government and reversion of power to the people; this scenario of revolution, though invented in England, has never been practised there – except in the deeply counter-revolutionary cases of 1649,[6] or perhaps 1659 – and this is one reason it is difficult to put forward a populist theory of British as opposed to American democracy. But we can find those – and Locke may have been one of them – who thought that such a dissolution ought to have occurred in 1688 or 1689, and regretted the lost opportunity to conduct one. There were the originals of the eighteenth-century commonwealthmen, who thought the opportunity should have been seized to institute frequently summoned parliaments and lessen the patronage powers of the crown. Locke does not seem to have been among these, but he did publish the *Treatises* to promote the view that William III (he does not here mention Mary) owed his crown to the choice of the people, the only foundation of all lawful government. This may or may not make the monarchy as elective or conditional as it sounds; it need not entail a dissolution by the people of the entire fabric of government (which is what the text of the *Second Treatise* necessarily envisages) but merely a power reserved to the people to 'cashier' (as Richard Price was to put it) a monarch guilty of misgovernment and choose another in his place; so that any monarch ruling with the support of his people may be said to rule with their consent and by their approbation and election. What is paradoxical about this assertion – voiced recurrently by a minority

---

[6] [A challenging statement: regicide and abolition of the monarchy were revolutionary acts, but led only to the establishment of a *de facto* régime over a polity unable to dissolve itself and hold a constitutional convention. Sovereignty remained lodged in the surviving hands of those who had held it. Dissolution resulted in the decision that there should be no dissolution; in 1659 it led to a restoration. The statement in the text is paradoxical to the point of being self-annihilating; this is why it was put forward.]

throughout the century beginning with the publication of Locke's *Treatises* – is that it rests on an implicit denial that there had been civil war in 1688. The flight of James had irretrievably constitutionalized the English perception of revolution itself; the deposition of a king and the substitution of his successors, the dissolution of a régime if not of a constituted form of government, could now be seen as taking place bloodlessly, within the fabric of an ancient constitution, and without imposing on the people the savage choices about allegiance and sovereignty, violence and submission, under which they had suffered in 1642 and 1649. It now became by degrees open to the English to believe that they could have revolution but have it painlessly; a belief so remote from their experience in the seventeenth century that it took another hundred years to form it after 1689.

There is a posturing theatricality about Wilkes and even Paine reminding George III of the fate of his predecessors, and Burke poured out his wrath on Richard Price because he could see that revolution had become, as it has remained, a spectator sport for middle-class intellectuals, tempted to believe that they can proclaim governments illegitimate without anyone getting hurt in the process. It took a long time for this sort of left to take shape in British political culture, but 1688 is among its preconditions.

From the existence of a commonwealth left, populist and quasi-republican, operating on the flank of a rather complacent constitutionalism, we now move right, into areas where there was nothing to be complacent about, because the legitimacy of the régime traceable to 1688 was far from being clearly accepted. Much emphasis is now very rightly given by historians to two persistent instabilities in post-Revolution England: the inability of a great many churchmen to accept that the secular power could change the supreme governor of the Church of England even when that governor was an aggressively popish successor; and the consequent survival of a Jacobitism which held at the least (and it sometimes held a good deal more) that the Williamite and Hanoverian régimes were a government *de facto* and that authority *de jure* resided with the exiled family, against the day when it should please that family to return to the church of which they were lawfully the head.

Let us accept, then, that the tensions and cleavages left behind by the Revolution were extraordinarily deep; that they included a succession of rulers insecure on their throne and a church unsure about its establishment; that what has been called 'the rage of party', persisting through the Hanoverian accession and beyond it, can quite rightly be described as the continuation of civil war by other means. Civil war did not break out again, in the sense that Englishmen did not again draw swords against one another in a dissolution of effectively sovereign government; to use Roman language in an Anglocentric perspective, the wars in Ireland and Scotland down to 1745 were not civil but social wars, taking place in associated but inferior provinces of the English imperium. It is of course true, as Thomas Hobbes pointed out, that the state of war is not identical with the day of battle, but consists in 'a known disposition thereto', present all the time 'in the nature of weather';[7] and in that sense a disposition to civil war existed in England as long as there was a potentially active Jacobitism, which we now know was longer than we used to think. But Hobbes's formula does not go to the heart of the seventeenth-century experience of civil war, which was that men fight each other not merely because there is no sovereign to stop them, but because an existing sovereignty has disintegrated and they must fight each other in the effort to reconstruct it. Englishmen had fought each other in this setting in 1642 and 1648; they had not had to do so in 1688.

One reason widely recognized why they had not had to do so was the rise of what was known as the standing army, consisting of permanently embodied regiments financed and controlled by a state. The first English civil war had been fought the way it was because no such army then existed in England, and the relations between king and parliament had reached a point where each set out to mobilize the county militias against the other; Leviathan could not draw the sword without returning it into the hands of the subject. But in 1688 William landed at the head of a force of professional regiments and James advanced to meet him at the head of another. Because they did not come to battle, the warlike activity of the southern élites was limited to giving political support to one army rather than the other. In the Midlands and the North the earls of Devonshire and Danby were in rebellion, but there too the sword was not drawn in civil war. In the frontier kingdoms of Scotland and Ireland the sword was drawn and battles were fought; but with our eye on the structure of the English state – which held together in 1688 as it had not done in 1642, and so determined much of what happened elsewhere – we may be tempted to suppose that the advent of the professional army had rendered impossible a recrudescence of the initially amateur civil war the militias had fought in 1642. The matter was not put to the test. What actually happened is that because James fled without fighting there was no civil war in England, and William was called to exercise the sword of Leviathan. What he did with it was to proceed, once the campaigns in Ireland were over, to re-organize a force of English and Scottish regiments capable of assisting him in his wars in the

---

[7] Hobbes, *Leviathan*, ch. 13.

Netherlands. Perhaps it was with this aim and no other that he had come to England, though how he thought he was going to achieve it when he went on board ship in 1688 defies our imagining.

There followed during the Nine Years War – or War of the League of Augsburg, or War of the English Succession – that re-organization of the fiscal and military structures of the English state which would transform it into Britain and render it capable of a major role in the wars in Europe and the European presence in America and India. If there is a revolutionary change in the course of early modern British history it is to be found here; at least, this was the point at which observant contemporary intelligences became capable of saying that such a transformation was going on. They identified the re-organization of politics as consisting of two innovations: the institution of a standing army, and the institution of a system of public credit capable of maintaining such an army, both during long campaigns in the field and during periods of peace – which was what made it a standing army – without beggaring the state in the process. A few years later, Marlborough could march from Flanders to Bavaria and back again, fighting a major battle on the way, without seeing his army dissolve into plundering hordes, because he paid his way with letters of credit on Dutch and English bankers, a feat which would have been beyond the capacity of Wallenstein or Turenne. England was leaving the world of civil and social war and entering that of European reason of state; was passing out of the age of Wars of Religion and entering that of Enlightenment, in which states were capable of controlling their armies and their own fissiparous tendencies towards religious and civil war. It was the end of Hobbesian politics; or rather, it was the victory of Leviathan.[8]

Because there was no more civil war in England, England became capable of imperial power; of fighting major wars in Europe and beyond. Figurative language such as I have just been using is the necessary consequence of our speaking of long-term processes in structural history; but it comes to be justified when we think there are such processes to describe, or when we are dealing with the emergence of a discourse in which they are supposed and depicted. Within a decade of 1688, observing intelligences – whose existence and activity are a part of history if they are not the key to it – thought that they were in a process of long-term yet rapid structural change. They held it to be one involving the rise of the standing army and the preconditions of its existence, and they were aware of it precisely because the conditions making civil war a possibility had by no means

---

[8] Pocock, 1996a.

disappeared. The standing army and public credit had been instituted in England both to confirm the Revolution régime and to make it capable of defending itself by extending its power abroad; and whenever in the next half-century country politicians and republican ideologues sought to reduce the standing army and lessen the public dependence on credit, they were suspected – sometimes with reason – of a design to weaken the régime and facilitate a restoration of the exiled family. One such moment occurred in 1698, when the wars in Europe had ended and the English parliament set about compelling William to reduce his armies. In the printed discourse of the time, we find an interesting debate between the Scot Andrew Fletcher, the Anglo-Irishman John Trenchard and the Londoner Daniel Defoe about the history of standing armies.[9] All three are writing Whig history in one of the accepted senses of the term; that is, they agree on the existence of a process of change in the structure of society, to which the political structure cannot refuse to respond; they differ on the extent and character of the response required. It is common ground between them that a growth in commerce and culture has made it possible, desirable and perhaps unavoidable that the subject shall cease to be the proprietor of the sword, letting it pass out of his hands into those of a professional paid by a state in which the subject is active, and controls the sword, only through his representatives. Fletcher (writing from a point of view both Scottish and British) wants the militia preserved as a remedial device, in order to institutionalize and preserve the subject's control of his own sword and his own liberty. Defoe (whose stance is English, but at the same time British) thinks it pays the subject to let the process go all the way, retaining only parliamentary control over the taxes which pay the soldiers.

Here are the makings of a Whig interpretation of history, in the sense of a perceived long-term process which was to make sense to both Hume and Macaulay in providing the civil wars with a history; but it was not the product of any sudden slide into complacent ancient-constitutionalist consensus. The debate over the role of arms in history was to continue down to the Scottish Enlightenment and the American Revolution, and it was formed by a period during which the continued existence of the Jacobite possibility determined the character of the militia debate which lay at its core. The turning point I have detected in 1688 continued to hold significance.

The debaters of 1698 had been supplying a social-change explanation of the conditions under which a final transfer of the sword from the

---

[9] Pocock, 1975, 2003 (B), ch. 12; Robertson, 1986.

individual's hands into those of Leviathan had become possible. As long as he retained the property of his sword, the individual could not yield it up to Leviathan without the risk that Leviathan would thrust it back into his hands; no mere act of will would get him out of the state of nature. But once he ceased to be merely the proprietor of his own land, his own sword, and his own right and duty to use it, and became instead the generator of wealth and credit which could be used to pay soldiers and to multiply culture, the sword might be borne by an agent other than himself, whom he could pay Leviathan to pay for him. There was resistance to this process; the classical rhetoric of the militia as necessary to the security of a free state is found in Jacobite mouths as well as republican, and there were many Whigs who feared for the consequences to the individual; but by the time of the Seven Years War, the Hanoverian line felt strong enough to mobilize a national militia, and to keep it under canvas for two years as a standing army for home defence, to guard against a landing of French troops and any pretender (if there still was one) they might have brought with them. It was service in this militia, wrote the historian Edward Gibbon, combined with 'the accession of a British prince' brought up in the Church of England, which finally reconciled Jacobite families like his own to the Hanoverian Succession and the Septennial Act.[10] Opposition to that prince's policies, expressed in a medley of commonwealth and Scottophobic language, began in a very few years; but Leviathan retained his grip on the crozier as well as the sword, and it became apparent that the urban factions and the great men who might promote them were no longer parties capable of pushing the realm into civil war. The Sacheverell riots had threatened a régime; the Gordon riots threatened only the public peace.

A process of structural change, in the character of property, the technology of warfare, and the production of wealth – it was now possible for those interested in the history of justice, police, revenue and arms to say – had done in history what Hobbesian man could not do for himself in the emergence from the state of nature. The perceived macro-process was an enlargement of a micro-process by which civil war was becoming less probable in England. Hobbesian politics, and the Hobbesian solution from which Locke had not much departed in his writings before 1688, had been rendered less immediate by the events of that year and the next; and the rapid-seeming transition from the state perpetually lapsing into civil war to a state capable by its new military and financial structure of

---

[10] Bonnard, 1969, pp. 109–11.

evading civil war and exercising imperial power, could be and was envisaged in terms of an historical process. Neither Hobbes nor even Locke had done much to describe the process, and there is no need to invoke it in order to explain the events of 1688 – or indeed the actions of those in high politics at any moment thereafter. Long-term processes, it is worth remarking, seldom explain what political actors do; they only explain what they turn out to have done. The significance of 1688 which we are here considering was not immediately operative, but took time to become apparent. That is a statement in Whig history; it exercises hindsight and renders the event significant in terms of its consequences. It is also a statement about Whig historiography; it begins to show how the event generated its own history, and became significant in terms of both constitutional persistence and structural change. We can choose for ourselves whether to accept such historiographies as providing explanations of the event or as rendering it significant; we cannot deny the historical fact that they were generated by the event and by those reflecting on its consequences, or that the event was an agent in producing its own significance. Whig historiography, to that extent, is a product of Whig history.

(11)

There is a sense in which the processes just described can be characterized as belonging to what we call Enlightenment. That is, it is useful to say that Enlightenment denotes a series of occurrences whereby England, Scotland and other states of western Europe passed out of a period of religious and civil war, in which sovereigns could not adequately control their churches or their armed men and were consequently threatened with dissolution, and entered a period of more settled government and interactions between states, which lasted until the French Revolution and was partially renewed after it. There are historians who prefer to call this the period of the *ancien régime*, but there seems no reason why the two terms should not be used interchangeably. The process involved a certain dissociation of the individual from activity in political and religious conflicts, which he was encouraged to allow the sovereign to manage for him; he was encouraged to think these conflicts less urgently important than he had, and to think that he had other ends and values to pursue. The individual described by both Fletcher and Defoe, interested in commerce and culture to the point where he is content to let the sword which protects his liberties be managed for him, is a type of what I am here calling the individual of Enlightenment; and we have seen that he was encouraged to see himself as produced by a process of

historical change, which rendered him modern as distinct from his predecessors. His 'modern' characteristics, both cause and effect of his transfer
of the sword into the hand of Leviathan, were defined by theorists following Defoe as 'manners', 'politeness', 'taste' and other terms denoting an
increased capacity for civilized intercourse in a society increasingly commercial, urban and reliant on the exchange of goods, ideas and cultural
traits. This was to be a major theme of Enlightenment historiography.

A not dissimilar development can be detected in the religious field.
Leviathan, we know, wielded a crozier as well as a sword, and his left hand
might impair the strength of his right. The most delicate area we have to
treat, in assessing the significances of 1688, is the Revolution's impact on
the church; even today [1988] when Anglicans probe the foundations of
authority in their communion, terrible things can still happen. Since the
Restoration and even before it, the Anglican clergy had been propounding
a doctrine in which the Word and the Spirit acted in the world without
departing from the forms of civil society, of which the authority of the
magistrate was necessarily one. This made it difficult – though for many it
also made it necessary – to submit to the replacement of the church's
supreme governor by a civil process which the clergy found understandably
questionable. We may emphasize both the continuing restiveness and
Jacobitism to which this gave rise, and the thoroughness with which the
majority of clergy who took the oaths to William and Mary succeeded in
transferring their doctrines of divine and apostolic authority into the new
framework of allegiance; though to emphasize both with equal rigour
points towards a revisionist posture of affirming that authority persisted
without consensus.

But it is also important that the church's problem of allegiance be seen as
part of an enterprise in which the clergy had been engaged ever since the
disintegration of the Commonwealth's godly rule: that of exorcizing
rebellious enthusiasm and antinomianism by insisting that the Spirit
never rebelled against the Law and teaching a civil piety which was by no
means the same as a civil religion. If the Spirit was to be mediated to
humanity through the forms of civil order, with which the church was to be
congruent, it was necessary to dismiss all claims that the Spirit's presence
might be recognized by those acting outside those forms – whether a
priesthood claiming the authority of Christ really present in the sacra-
ments, or an anarchy of sects claiming the authority of the Spirit immediately present in the congregation or the prophetically illuminated
individual. Ecclesiastics inclined to this way of thinking might not be ill-
disposed towards John Locke's argument that the mind knew not things

but the ideas which it had of things, not God but the reasons which it had for believing in his existence. As a polemic against enthusiasm, the *Essay Concerning Human Understanding* is part of an enterprise in which the church had been long engaged, and it may have been by publishing this work (and owning it as his) in 1690 that Locke began moving away from the subversiveness of the writings which he published anonymously in the same year.

It was the aim of much that we call Enlightenment to increase the powers of reason by limiting its range; by redirecting it from metaphysics towards experiment. This enterprise was highly congruent with the endeavours of both states and established churches to reduce the danger of religious civil war by combating the various forms of fanaticism which had claimed authority from the certainty of spiritual knowledge.

There arose – I am compressing the story here – an Anglican probabilism which tended to replace theology by the history of theology; by the discussion of beliefs which had been held and of the grounds there had been for holding them. It was both an Anglican and an Enlightenment belief that the human mind did what it was capable of doing; this could be used to suppress doctrinal challenges to the authority of the magistrate as well as to deter the magistrate from imposing restraints on the freedom of enquiry.

There could thus be a history of religion written as a history of opinions held, or (by more sceptical and scientific intellects) as a history of the belief systems which the human mind was capable of generating. It could coexist with a history of social and governmental systems written as a history of manners, by which was meant not only codes of behaviour but the intellectual, aesthetic and ethical systems generated by human minds in interaction with one another, often on the foundation of property systems increasingly geared to exchange. Both historiographies depicted humans as moving from ancient to modern: from ancient metaphysics to modern experimentality, from ancient virtue to modern politeness, from ancient autonomy to modern sociability; and each was explicitly connected with the emergence of sovereign government over settled societies free from the dangers of religious civil war. Enlightenment grew under the sword and crozier of Leviathan.[11] The first history of England written entirely in the enlightened mode is that completed by David Hume between 1754 and 1762; it ends in 1688 because Hume considered the Revolution to have ended the civil wars of the seventeenth century and did not wish to enter on

---

[11] See further, Pocock, 1985, 1995 (both B).

the turbulent history of the régime which had succeeded them. His history is in our eyes deeply revisionist in its refusal to see constitutional rights and wrongs at issue in the civil wars, and at the same time deeply Whig in its willingness to see both political and religious fanaticism as the products of a process of social change – a 'revolution in manners' at work in both England and Europe with changes in the character of property as its infrastructure.

Hume can be seen as taking English historiography in an altogether new direction, but it is as well to remember that he was a Scot, and that his *History* was a companion to his friend William Robertson's *History of Scotland*, published as he began work, and was in some sense a precursor of the great conjectural histories of the progress of society which the Edinburgh literati began producing during the 1760s and 1770s.[12] The Scots were writing enlightened history: their works were histories of manners and modernity, in which the redistribution of arms and the changing nature of property played a large part, and the supposed progress of mankind from fanaticism to politeness allied the Moderate Robertson with the irreligious Hume – though the latter's deeper pessimism foresaw the replacement of religious fanaticism by political. They were writing in this way because, though their strong emphasis on military virtue is a response to the Highland incursion of 1745,[13] they believed that Scotland – merged with England in the extensive monarchy of Britain – was now living under strong and settled government and free from religious civil war. The modernity of Leviathan was upon both nations.

Belatedly in this essay, I have reached a point where we may consider the significance of 1688 for British realms and dominions other than England. I have a better than ethnocentric reason for postponing it so long. Between 1638 and 1642, rebellions in Scotland and Ireland imposed strains upon the English polity it was in no condition to bear, and precipitated its disintegration in civil war. In 1688 – though we might do well to ask how far the invitation to William of Orange was a product of what was happening in Ireland – there was no civil war in England, the English polity did not disintegrate, and as re-organized by William for his wars was able to impose solutions immediately on Ireland and after twenty years on Scotland. The wars fought in both associated kingdoms as a result of 1688 were not civil wars in the English sense. The Highland war from Killiecrankie to Glencoe was momentous in the history of British intercommunal conflict, but was not a civil war to those many Scotsmen who did not consider Highlanders

---

[12] See further Pocock, 1999, vol. II (B), chs. 11–19.   [13] Robertson, 1986; Sher, 1985.

members of a shared civil polity, but in Roman terms rebellious barbarian *federati* who might be subjugated or exterminated if the means were at hand.

Nevertheless, Leviathan, that very English figure, is at his least imposing in his outer realms and marches, where he must wield his sword over those who are not incorporated in his body and may have little respect for his crozier. Even in Scotland, where incorporation was carried out and has endured, it was no light matter to create a unified realm with two national churches; and outside the island of Britain there were two frontiers of conquest where it is reasonable to ask whether Leviathan obtained the victory or wrote a new history. If in England 1688 was the year of the civil war that did not happen and the end of a cycle of such wars, in Ireland it marked the last of a series of wars which were less civil wars than wars of conquest: a series that had begun in the reign of Elizabeth I and consisted in collisions between older Irish and English communities and new patterns of English and Scottish settlement and sovereignty. William's Irish war ended at Limerick, and the harshness of its settlement marked the beginning of the longest period of peace in modern Irish history. During this hundred and more years various forms of settler nationalism took shape; these are ideologies in which settler communities appropriate to themselves the authority by which settlement has been carried out, and seek to use it in governing themselves and determining their own identity. In Ireland this move was prematurely made by William Molyneux in 1698, claiming that the right to rule Ireland by conquest belonged not to the English Crown and parliament, but to the Anglo-Irish settlers as a community of conquerors.[14] The claim, made in Lockean language, was repudiated by Locke and little heard of again until the Volunteer movement of 1780; but the events of the Irish war following 1688 also provided heroic myths which were to be used in furnishing the Protestants of Ulster with their own militant identity. That formidable people, however, remained for a century radical, emigrant and rebellious, and did not till after 1798 become the loyalist sub-nation which, to the discomfiture of British and Irish alike, they remain. But where Leviathan was thus imperfectly corporate, it was understandable that there should not develop a Whig history of Ireland. From the Scottish parallel we know that one could have been written; it would have traced a passage from pastoral, warrior and monastic antiquity to commercial and Protestant modernity. It may very well be that histories pointing in this direction were attempted, and the phrase 'an Irish

---

[14] Simms, 1982.

Enlightenment' has been applied to intellectual developments in Dublin and Belfast; but there did not take shape, as there did in Edinburgh and Glasgow, an authoritative élite promoting Whig history in furtherance of their image of national identity and the British state. Scottish enlightened history contributed powerfully to form the Whig historiography of Macaulay.

The colonies established by the English crown and its grants to proprietors beyond the Atlantic constituted a further border area: a frontier of conquest and settlement, which was described as an 'empire', but only in part juridically organized as one. Leviathan, being English and invented in the struggle to avert civil war, knew better how to be king than Caesar; his sword and crozier did not extend readily to the creation of provinces beyond his realm. Ireland was defined as a subordinate kingdom, conquered and ruled by the crown of England in its parliament, but this concept was not systematically extended to the settlements in America. It is tempting to suggest that the significance of 1688 in American history lies in the abandonment of whatever attempts James II had been making to re-organize Virginia and New England into dominions ruled directly by the crown.[15] This enterprise was imperial; had the colonies become subordinate states within an empire, they would not have found it necessary to begin a revolution by declaring themselves states, which is what they did in 1776. The American secession of that year may be considered as a response to the incoherence of empire, which had left room for the growth, in the course of human events, of a settler nationalism in which the colonists took the authority of empire to themselves and claimed the right to wage war, to conquer others and to conduct their own government. What is remarkable is that they drew in doing so upon arguments which had put forward an alternative interpretation of 1688 and criticisms of the régime founded upon it: a Lockean doctrine of emigration and dissolution, which they employed first to declare the relations between crown and colonies a confederation between states and then to declare that confederation dissolved;[16] a republican doctrine of the relations between the powers composing a government and between the state and the arms borne by its citizens; and a sectarian, and increasingly Unitarian, doctrine of the separation of the state from the church. They were about the creation of a congregational polity in which the crozier would have little place, though before Leviathan could lay it down the authority of his sword must be established.[17] They made no attempt to promote a British revolution or

[15] I have ventured to do so: Pocock, 1987 (A) and 1988 (B).
[16] Ohmori, 1988.   [17] Pocock, 1988 (B).

dissolve the authority of George III over his kingdoms; they separated themselves from the state of Great Britain by declaring their ties with it dissolved; but their perception of themselves and the governments they would have was shaped in the first instance by the radical Whig critique of the Revolution, which was as old as the Revolution itself and was now being revitalized by the English enemies of George III and the aristocratic and Anglican régime.

On both sides of the Atlantic an anti-Georgian Whig historiography took shape, which tended towards both a radical reading of 1688 as a deposition – the better to threaten George III with the fate of his predecessor – and a radical critique of 1689 as an insufficient remedy for political abuses. The commonwealth and republican rhetoric on which it drew offered means of criticizing the enlightened moves towards modernity which I have considered in this essay; but at the same time it appropriated many elements of that progressive programme, presenting both aristocracy and established clergy as medieval and archaic, instead of the powerful modernizing forces which the English and Scottish Enlightenments had shown them to be. The Enlightenment of the *ancien régime* had been a direction of modernizing processes by the established élites; the democratization which followed was both an annexation and a criticism of progress. It is against a secularizing and democratizing pro-gressivism, still very much part of our thinking, that the contemporary polemic against Whig history is for the most part directed; with the effect that a democratized and secularized society, which certainly exists today, is being commanded to do without a history that guarantees it.

Starting with a deliberately non-Whiggish reading of the events of 1688, I have tried to show how they can be situated in the context of continuing historical processes which can still be used to invest them with significance, and at the same time to show that they acquired the kind of significance which goes with the construction of Whig interpretations of history. That is, it has been my aim to show how Whig histories – I use the plural because there have been several – have been themselves the product of English, British and American history, ways of investing it with significances which it has itself generated.

It is therefore a problem that the demolition of Whig history is a programme for asking the present to live without a past that justifies it. To do so vastly enriches our understanding of both the past and the present; but we need to know whether this is other than a programme for the owl of Minerva, for mood being the more as our might lessens. Historiography has been so much a matter of the construction of usable pasts that it is desirable for the historian engaged in denying the past usability to ask himself what demands he is making on the present. Given the world-wide failures of revolutionary dialectic, it should seem that the deconstruction of history as a process for justifying the present is a programme for emphasizing irony and contingency, for inviting the inhabitants of the present to conduct their affairs in the knowledge of how very easily things might have been otherwise, and of how complex and contradictory were the processes that have made them what they are. David Hume, the first truly great historian of England, clearly thought it good for people to learn to live in the ironies of history; but he also thought the English too self-centred, philistine and faction-ridden a mob to sustain such an awareness very long, and he was not sanguine about their political future. Two hundred and more years later, here we are. 'Well, doctor,' a modern William might say, 'what do you think of demystification now?'

CHAPTER 9

Empire, state and confederation: the War of American Independence as a crisis in multiple monarchy

(1)

There is taking shape a pattern for the writing of British history,[1] of particular utility to those historians whose attention is focussed on the history of political discourse. Those of the societies component of what we call 'Britain', 'the Three Kingdoms' or 'the Atlantic archipelago', whose political cohesion reached the point of generating several self-centred political discourses,[2] can be studied in both an 'internal' and an 'external' perspective. In the former case, we examine the political discourse concerned with the structure of the polity and the problems to which it gave rise; and we examine events and crises in the history of each polity as taking place in the history depicted by discourse concerning that structure. During the sixteenth and seventeenth centuries, we note, the kingdom of England acquired characteristic patterns of discourse which shaped its history: the papal aggression, the ancient constitution, the balance of government, the balance of property; and these constructs retained paradigmatic status in English historiography so far into the modern period that, now they no longer possess that status, they have to be considered factors in shaping English history. During the same period, the kingdom of Scotland acquired similar patterns of historic self-shaping, but among the effects of the Union studied in John Robertson's volume, these had in large

---

[1] Robertson, 1995. This volume arose from a seminar, conducted for the Folger Institute Centre for the History of British Political Thought, designed to illuminate the history of Scottish political thought within that setting. The three concluding essays, of which this is one (Pocock, 1995a), and those contributed by Jacqueline Hill and Ned Landsman the others, pointed towards subsequent seminars on the Irish and American dimensions of the same history.

[2] The stress on the shaping of a political self owes much to recent critical and historical writing, and in particular to Helgerson, 1992. The assumption behind the present essay is that a public, political and national 'self' may be created by many actors and authors, and legitimated by their and others' consent.

part to be given up and replaced by others. This process too had long-term consequences in the history of Scottish historiography.

In the second or 'external' perspective, we examine the history of each polity as shaped by its interactions with neighbouring entities, which may or may not have been polities or states shaped like itself. We enquire how these interactions figured in, and helped shape, the discourse of each polity about itself, and further, whether they generated a discourse of their own, inventing and shaping the construct of a society of states. In the particular case of 'British history', we note that from at latest the early sixteenth century, there existed a discourse which spoke of 'Scotland' and 'England' as together composing an entity named 'Britain', which might possess a history of its own (the *historia majoris Britanniae*) and might be organized into a larger polity or association between polities.[3] We enquire whether there existed a discourse concerned with this 'matter of Britain', to which the term 'British political thought' might be applied with precision, instead of being employed loosely to denote the aggregate of political discourses arising in England, Scotland and elsewhere. It is now clear that we have found that such a 'discourse of Britain' did indeed take shape, but had to compete on terms often unequal with an English political discourse so intensely centred on the English political structure and its troubles that it could do no more (or less) than annex Scotland to itself and consider it part of English history, and with a Scottish discourse shaped in large measure by the need to respond to this English self-centredness. We are therefore faced with a treble structure: there is an English discourse, there is a Scottish, and there is a discourse of Britain which sometimes posits 'Britain' as a political entity, and sometimes treats it merely as a field in which political (the term includes confessional and ecclesiastical) entities interact. We deal with this problem by proposing that the history of 'Britain', or 'the Three Kingdoms', is that of a 'multiple monarchy', whose political structure is indeterminate for the reason that it is multiplex; with the consequence that such terms as 'empire' and 'confederation' have both been found applicable in discoursing of its character, and that from time to time choices have had to be made between implications arising from these terms.

It has further to be kept in mind that the 'external' perspective does not stop with the field of relationships constituting 'Britain'. The kingdoms and other entities constituting archipelagic 'Europe' interact with the kingdoms, confederations and empires constituting adjacent continental 'Europe'; they affect one another's history and create a history which they

---

[3] Mason, 1994.

have in common. In the case we are considering, the kingdom and empire of 'Great Britain' are shaped largely by the intervention of, and by inter-action with, the imperial and maritime wars of continental 'Europe'; but they respond vigorously enough to impose themselves on the history of this entity (or society) and help to shape it. We are also concerned with a period in which these multiple histories, 'British' and 'European', extend them-selves across the Atlantic[4] and play a part in involving the English and French colonies on the American seaboard in an imperial struggle for control of the interior of that continent. The relations between archipelagic and continental 'Europe' do much to remodel those between maritime, piedmont, Laurentian and Mississippian 'America'. Only in the period of the American Revolution is it determined that certain colonies will become 'states' and organize themselves as an 'empire' – which is at the same time a 'republic' and a new species of 'confederation' – and that an entity named 'America' will henceforth create a history (United States and Canadian) of its own making.[5]

(11)

The obstacle which had prevented the Union of the Crowns being more than a personal union – neither a confederation nor an incorporation of the two kingdoms – was in the first place the intensity of the internal union of the kingdom of England. The Act in Restraint of Appeals (1533) had proclaimed and enacted that this kingdom was an 'empire' in the sense that it contained within itself absolute sovereignty over itself, so that its king (in parliament or out of it) was absolute and sovereign head of all jurisdiction both spiritual and temporal, and therefore head of the English Church as inseparable from the English body politic. 'Empire' in this sense could not be shared with another prince, at peril of mitigating the absolute separation from Rome on which Englishmen's hopes of salvation were seen to depend; and if the king of England could not conceivably share his *imperium* with the pope, he could not share it with himself as king of Scots. The two crowns, the two realms and the two churches should therefore become one; but the English showed themselves incapable of imagining this union as other than an annexation of the Scottish dimension, in each case, to the English. As we shall see, they were responding as much out of

---

[4] The *Annual Register* in the years of the American revolution regularly treated events in the colonies in a section headed 'History of Europe'.
[5] See Pocock, 1957, 1987 (B), 1988a.

insecurity as out of arrogance; but they were able to claim that head and body were bound together in the English body politic by municipal laws and an ecclesiastical structure generated by that body itself, which could not be given up without terminating that body's existence. The Scots were necessitated to reply that their king wore a crown as imperial as the English one, and that they had created laws and a church polity as much their own as were those of the English. If they were on the whole more willing than were the English to contemplate assimilation of these structures to those of their neighbours, they drew the line at being annexed and swallowed up, and at being assimilated in the sense of digested by the unmodified church-state of the English monarchy. The Stuart dynasty therefore found itself ruling a multiple monarchy, or more precisely a multiplicity of kingdoms, wearing at the same time the imperial crown of Scotland, the imperial crown of England and the presumptive crown of Ireland created by conquest alone and inseparably annexed to the second but not the first person of this far from perfect trinity. The age of the Three Kingdoms had begun, and it is a key problem in 'British history' to determine its character and duration.

It is possible to speak of the Three Kingdoms as constituting 'a monarchy', as we speak of the Spanish or the Austrian 'Monarchy' as a co-incidence of many crowns upon one head.[6] Since 'empire' in the Roman sense denoted a 'universal monarchy', it is also possible to describe any one of these monarchies as an 'empire', and James VI and I toyed briefly (as did the Lord Protector Oliver Cromwell after him) with the thought of assuming the title of 'Emperor of Great Britain'. But there was the difficulty that as king of England, France and Ireland (to give that title in its partly fictional fullness) he possessed a sovereignty more 'imperial', in the sense given it by the Act in Restraint of Appeals, than any he could possess as 'emperor', and by no means capable of being shared with the latter sovereignty, had that ever come to be invented (which is why it was not). We may see that the entity called 'England' was obliged to assume 'empire' in the sense of hegemony over two other kingdoms, precisely for the reason that it possessed an 'empire' in the sense of sovereignty over itself which it could not afford to share with them in a union of equals. Whether anything similar may be said of Castile in the case of the Spanish 'Monarchy' or of the Hapsburg lands in the case of the Austrian, is not a question to be considered here.

[6] Pagden, 1990.

The sovereignty or 'empire' claimed for the English crown by the Act in Restraint of Appeals is therefore the key to English history in the age of the Three Kingdoms,[7] and in the longer period of early modern history now extended through the 'long eighteenth century' to 1832. It was a sovereignty as well ecclesiastical as civil; and to make it a 'key' to history does not mean that it was a rock-solid and unshakable consolidation of national power which of itself rendered England capable of 'empire' over the other kingdoms. On the contrary, from a date within the reign of Charles I to the end of the seventeenth century, it was shaken and very nearly shattered by a series of violent internal and external crises which became known by the name of 'dissolutions of government'. These did not weaken it, so much as render the exercise of its formidable power deeply unstable; and it was this instability, coupled with the need to restore and consolidate it by any means necessary – regicide, restoration and revolution among them – which rendered impossible any sharing of English sovereignty within a wider system of multiple monarchy. The English were at times obliged to exercise 'empire' over others because they were unsure of their 'empire' over themselves.

It does not diminish the force of these statements if we suppose that the English civil wars and their long aftermath came about, not through deep-seated weaknesses in the English structure, but through the strains imposed by the task of ruling a number of monarchies.[8] However the disasters of 1642 originated, once they had come about they were cleavages between crown and parliament, between the king as head of the church and that church as many subjects perceived it; and the desperate need to restore these unities at all costs was a main cause of the revolutionary changes attempted in their nature. For this reason the English dimension of the War of the Three Kingdoms (1637–52) had the character of a civil war, in which Englishmen fought each other, bitterly because unwillingly,[9] to determine the structure of a civil and ecclesiastical polity which they had thought they shared in common; whereas Scotsmen did not fight each other very much, and never to determine the character of such a polity, and the diverse religious and ethnic groups inhabiting (but not yet constituting) Ireland fought each other in the absence of any shared polity at all. What we misname the Third Civil War of 1650–2 was in part a war of England against an invading king of Scots whose title the English did not challenge,

---

[7] In proposing the concept of this age, I find convenient the limiting dates of 1533 and 1707. Others could be proposed, and preferred; none can be cast in bronze.
[8] Russell, 1991a.   [9] Best displayed in Fletcher, 1981.

even when they conquered Scotland in order to dethrone him; in part a war of religion between the saints of a British Israel and Judah, fought over the reading of a Covenant which had bound them together.

Any analysis of the great mass of printed discourse produced by the experience and memory of civil war, regicide and interregnum must lead to the conclusion that the crucial English experience in the War(s) of the Three Kingdoms was that of 'the dissolution of government', and that it was remembered as the worst political experience through which England had ever passed. To say this is to pass over the brief but intense revolutionary moment of 1647–50, when there were those who saw dissolution as opening a window of opportunity to make all things new; it is to pass over the no less intense and short-lived visions of rule by liberated soldiers, visionary parliamentarians, saints in arms or out of them, and a newly imagined republican citizenry, which were offered as forms of 'government' alternative to that of the historic institutions of sovereignty.[10] The discourse we have, it could be said, is that of governing élites deeply shaken but ultimately restored. But the loss it agonizedly describes is not that of the opportunity to govern so much as the security of being governed according to law. The 'government dissolved' is primarily the Tudor sovereignty of 'empire' in church and state, exercised by king and parliament in a relationship variously described; secondly, the 'ancient constitution' held to underpin it and provide it with a history; thirdly, the condition of civil government itself, which delivers humans from the appalling responsibility to choose between forms of legitimate rule, or to choose a form of government where none exists and legitimate it out of no resources other than their own unaided natures.[11] 'The dissolution of government' was recalled as so dreadful an experience that it remains amazing that John Locke, a powerful and cautious thinker, should, even in a moment of radical aberration, have recommended it in print as a right and prerogative vested in a people who might exercise it of their own choice. The printed discourse of 1689 loses no time in denying that it has occurred.[12]

The failure even to attempt revolutionary experiment in England during the 1650s – which includes the failure to attempt creating a 'Britain' out of the conquests of Ireland and Scotland – led to the successive restorations of the English and Tudor institutions of government between 1659 and 1662.[13]

[10] See Lamont, 'The Puritan revolution', and Pocock and Schochet, 'The Interregnum', in Pocock, 1993 (B).
[11] Zagorin, 1954; Wallace, 1968; Judson, 1980.   [12] Kenyon, 1977.   [13] See Hutton, 1985.

In English terms, we can see that these amounted to a programme of restoring unity between crown and parliament, and (as a precondition rather than a consequence) between crown and national church; and we have a wealth of literature on the complex reasons why this programme failed and had to be re-attempted in 1688–9. There is not so much literature, either contemporary or modern, on Restoration and its failure in Scotland, and we are uncertain how far to regard it as a provincial variation on an otherwise English theme. It seems to have consisted largely of an experiment in episcopacy, with some support from a nobility weary of clerical and Covenanter rule.[14]

Viewed in English terms, the Revolution of 1688–9 takes on the character of a 'second Restoration'; a reconstruction, but at the same time re-stabilization, of the conditions under which crown, parliament and national church could co-exist.[15] There were some significant concessions on points of prerogative,[16] and of parliamentary authority in determining the succession to the crown; the Anglican clergy and squirearchy made significant changes in their position on both authority and dissent.[17] But the crown defined by the Act of Succession was stronger in its relations with parliament than the crown before 1688, and the Act of Toleration did so much to confirm as well as to mitigate the Anglican monopoly of office that it came to stand beside the Test and Corporation Acts as pillars of the Hanoverian régime.[18] So far we can go in maintaining an 'English' and 'internal' perspective, in considering the Revolution as produced by and giving answers to the problems of a peculiarly English history. How it might appear in the context of a Scottish, or an Irish, history 'internally' viewed is another story, or more correctly two stories. But recent historiography has forcefully reminded us that no 'internal' perspective is sufficient. The event could not have happened at all if it had not happened in a 'European' context, and it was very largely its character as an event in that context which obliged its enlargement into an event occurring in a 'British' context, which (in turn) it deeply changed and helped create.

(III)

The problems of English politics can be made to explain the invitation to William of Orange in 1688, but do not explain his motives for accepting it, or for having a powerful armada already in readiness. These must be

---

[14] [See now Jackson, 2003.] [15] This is vigorously argued by Scott, 1988. [16] Schwoerer, 1981.
[17] Spurr, 1992; Rupp, 1986. [18] This perspective seems to emerge forcibly from Clark, 1985.

explained in terms of continental power politics, not excluding William's ambitions dynastic and otherwise; though we must avoid making the inane assumption that because English history cannot fully explain these events, it has therefore no autonomous existence or internal logic of its own. Nevertheless, its problems in this period were external and dynastic as well as internal and structural; the multiple monarchy of the restored Stuart brothers was so weak in the face of French power – perceived as aiming at a 'universal monarchy' – that French intervention in court and parliamentary politics was omnipresent, easier to resent than to evade. William set sail with his armada intending to bring the Three Kingdoms into his anti-French alliance, and not unmindful of his wife's expectations as heir to their crowns. But it is among the many extraordinary ironies of the series of events he unchained that the Three Kingdoms were weak and distracted at the time he annexed them to his ambitions, so much so that they seemed doomed to satellite status under French or Dutch hegemony; yet he mobilized in them a military, fiscal and political power which changed them profoundly and proved formidable, not only in furthering his objectives in continental politics, but in making possible, but at the same time problematic, an English and British involvement in the pursuit of those same objectives.

There is an English history driven by the need to maintain the system of sovereignty laid down by the Act in Restraint of Appeals, and to avoid at all costs the disaster of renewed civil war and dissolution of government. In this context the Revolution of 1688–9 looks like a 'second Restoration', a consolidation of that sovereignty by the removal of a king who was subjecting it to too much strain. Yet the removal of a king was a desperate action, entailing the worst risks in the English historical memory, and the English were moved to run these risks only by a dynastic occurrence. William could never have sailed but for the birth of the infant prince James Francis Edward, and the chance to safeguard his wife's inheritance by proclaiming that birth spurious; and it was in the hope of maintaining the infant's rights that James II fled from his rebellious daughter, his rebellious or uncooperative subjects and the overwhelming power of the prince who had appeared in their support, and placed himself and his son under French protection. By so doing he ensured that civil war in England would not be an aspect of the second war of the Three Kingdoms, which lasted until Glencoe and Limerick; but he left England exposed to a threat, which lasted for six decades and longer, of foreign invasion in exploitation of a contested dynastic succession. Not William alone, but his subjects and his successors, were obliged to engage the British kingdoms in European war to protect the Revolution Settlements; the European conflict of 1688–97 includes among its names that of 'the War of the English Succession'. War abroad to protect the Protestant Succession at home was necessary in order to impose stability upon the recurrent problems of English government; but James achieved a further measure of destabilization since, by withdrawing his son and himself to France, he left the church of England a further reminder of the paradox that the Protestant Succession was being maintained by means the church could not wholeheartedly accept. It was a recurrent problem of English history that the church could not quite trust its own supreme head, and the problem was not yet solved.

In Scotland, a Presbyterian seizure of ecclesiastical power set up problems in the history of that church and state.[19] In Ireland, the last war of Protestant conquest occurred in a multi-ethnic history shaped along other lines. We return to the Revolution in Anglo-British and British-European history. If the Revolution looks like a second Restoration in the enduring context, the *moyenne durée*, of Tudor political and ecclesiastical structures, there are other contexts in which it looks like a revolution in several meanings of the term: like a *peripeteia* in the last months of 1688, like a *ridurre ai principi* in the first months of 1689, and like a *novus ordo seculorum* in a perception taking shape over the decade of the 1690s. Of these terms in the vocabulary of revolution, the two first are ancient and early modern, while the third draws closer to the modern meaning of the term (perhaps growing obsolete under post-modern conditions). The needs of war on the continent obliged William and his commanders to complete the reconquest of the archipelago – Dutch and French generals campaigned in Ireland in a shared distaste for their surroundings – and then to that massive reconstruction of the English capacity to make and finance war which became known by the linked terms of 'standing army' and 'public credit', and was perceived as altering the political structure of the community and the historical conditions which connected men with their political societies. By 1698, English, Scottish and Anglo-Irish publicists were embarked upon a debate which explicitly premised that war and politics had become modern and commercial,[20] and that the European societies conducting them were structurally unlike what they had been

---

[19] For 1688 in Scottish history, and Scotland in the history of 1688, see among other treatments Cowan, 1991; Lenman, 1992; and for its setting in British history, Harris, 1997; Murdoch, 1998, ch. 3, pp. 33–47.
[20] Pocock, 1975, ch. 13; Hont, 1990.

under ancient (Greek and Roman) or medieval (Gothic and feudal) conditions. These writers further debated how far this great historical change was to be welcomed and how far dreaded, or what mixture of the two responses was appropriate and prudent.

The government of England was being transformed by the same processes that obliged it to assume a newly powerful role in the British archipelago, the European continent, the oceans beyond and the American, Indian and African regions then becoming provinces of the world system. There were many, in city as well as country, who resented the ways in which these British and particularly European involvements were incrementally altering the character of political life, and turned their resentment against the Revolution of 1688–9, which they correctly saw as the take-off point of all these developments. The war against French universal monarchy, whose necessity they need not deny, was being conducted in such a way as involved England both in the creation of an 'enormous' or 'extensive' monarchy[21] in the archipelago, and in membership of a European confederacy, swayed by Dutch, Hapsburg and later Hanoverian interests, little less dangerous than Bourbon universal monarchy itself. These involvements were subjecting Englishmen to a new oligarchy made up of patronage-mongers, dissenters, stockjobbers and a military machine and national debt which fed upon one another. This polemic was shared by Old Whigs who thought the Revolution had not gone far enough, and Tories who resented the fact that it had occurred at all. Defenders of the régime, to 1789 and beyond, noted this overlap between 'commonwealth', 'patriot' and 'Jacobite' rhetoric, and drew the conclusion that republicans and absolutists were united against parliamentary monarchy, just as puritans and papists (they said) had been united in the seventeenth century. This was the point at which tensions arising from the newness and modernity of the British and European power structure which England was now obliged to maintain joined and interacted with the older tensions existing within the edifice of Tudor sovereignty in church and state; tensions which dynastic uncertainty and unhealed fissures between crown, clergy and dissent kept alive into the reign of George III.

(IV)

These tensions underlay the union of parliaments which created the Kingdom of Great Britain, and helped determine the character of both.

---

[21] The former adjective is more than once employed by David Hume, the latter by Edward Gibbon.

Just as in 1603, 'Britain' was a policy objective which Scots desired on the whole more than Englishmen did, but, for that reason among others, could achieve only on such terms as the English were prepared to concede; it therefore reflected the preponderance of English power over Scottish. The Scots thrust the Union on the English; the English imposed the Union on the Scots, dictating its character for the paradoxical reason that they did not really want it. Ireland remained at a distance, treated as the recently reconquered kingdom it really was; though we note the beginnings of a settler nationalism in which the Anglo-Irish claim equality with the English on the grounds that they are the conquering, not the conquered people.[22]

The more utopian schemes put forward by Andrew Fletcher – who has emerged as a major figure in the canon of Scottish political thinkers[23]– reflect the ambivalence of the Anglo-Scottish relationship. In political practice, Fletcher strove to make the Union a confederation of two kingdoms; in his theoretical discourse, he imagined a Britain, and a Europe, which should have adopted a 'Swiss solution' and become a confederation of cantons. Implicitly, therefore, he challenged the growing presumption that Europe, archipelagic and continental, should emerge from the era of wars of religion – we may count the War of the Three Kingdoms as one such – and the threat of Hapsburg or Bourbon universal monarchy, as a 'confederation' or 'republic' of powerful sovereign states, related to one another by the ties of commerce and enlightenment by the treaties or *foedera*[24] which should form the public law of the post-imperial *confoederatio*. In Fletcher's system the units were not to be sovereign states but cantons ruled by their militias and their *landesgemeinde*. On the one hand, he joined with those who believed that monarchies maintaining armies by mortgaging their futures would prove too powerful and at the same time too unstable to preserve the peace of Europe and the liberty of the individual; on the other, the cantonal image was necessary to ensure that his confederation appeared Swiss rather than Polish, a league of republics in which free men governed one another rather than of turbulent nobles governing only their serfs and themselves. David Hume, the next great thinker in the Scottish canon, busied himself in showing that a stable and peaceable Europe could consist of powerful and wealthy sovereign states, diverse in their political structures;[25] the advice which the Swiss Rousseau tendered to Poles and

---

[22] Molyneux, 1698; Simms, 1982; Hill, 1995.   [23] Mason, 1994; above, p. 58.
[24] It seems no accident that the major archival achievement of Anne's reign was Thomas Rymer's *Foedera* (1704–13), a collection of the external acts of the English Crown preserved among its records. Douglas, 1943, pp. 285–301.
[25] David Hume, 'Of the balance of power', Miller, 1985, pp. 332–41; Robertson, 1993.

Corsicans places him in the company of Andrew Fletcher, of whom he may or may not have heard. It was this confrontation between an ideology of state-building and its alternative in early modern discourse which lent a contemporary poignancy to John Robertson's seminar and its successor,[26] conducted at the Folger Library in the years of debate over Maastricht and ratification.

The English of 1707, it may be said, cared for none of these things, and it was their indifference and introversion, rather than their vaulting ambition, which ensured that the Union would be one of incorporation rather than confederation. They acquired empire, in this case at least, not in the lapidary 'fit of absence of mind', but out of unwillingness to consider their relations with others in any conceptual form, with the result that these could take no other form than that of an extension of the system to which they were accustomed. They had reasons, however – it may further be said – for this extreme and now and then appalling self-centredness. They had recently acquired an imperial capacity to act as a major power by sea and land, and were divided as to whether they were happy with it; if some saw the opportunities of empire and pursued them, others saw the same opportunities and rejected them with fear and loathing; indeed, it is uncommon to find a perceptive author in whom these responses are not mixed. If we probe, and when they probed, the reasons for this powerful ambivalence, it is not long before we come upon the roots of instability within the Tudor system of sovereignty in church and state which had caused so many dissolutions of government in the seventeenth century and were not fully removed in the eighteenth.[27] It took a long time to legitimate the Revolution Settlement, and longer than we used to suppose to legitimate the Hanoverian Succession. If this has been one of the chief lessons taught by recent historiography,[28] a corollary must be that the English response to instability old and new was immediate, instinctive and non-negotiable. The unity of crown and parliament and of both with established church must be maintained at all costs; the problem of 'empire' in the modern sense merged with that of 'empire' in the Tudor and medieval. The unified sovereign legislature which was all that stood between the

---

[26] 'Empire, confederation and republic: from Atlantic dominion to American union', conducted by J. G. A. Pocock, January–April, 1992.

[27] This would be the present writer's way of defending the 'ancien régime' thesis of J. C. D. Clark. It is not enough to point out that the Church of England's hegemony was insecure and imperfectly enforced; it was enforced, by means that included mitigation, because it was insecure.

[28] The reference is to work emphasizing the persistence of English Jacobitism: Cruickshanks, 1982; Colley, 1982; Monod, 1989.

English and the dissolution of government could not possibly be confederated with any other without putting its unity at risk. This was the *arcanum imperii* that determined the course of the Scottish Union; it can be argued that it also determined the course of the American Revolution. Defoe's contention that the Act of Union was fundamental law, and that to break its terms as a *foedus* would plunge both kingdoms into a dissolution of civil society,[29] was as fragile as Locke's theory of revolution, of which it was in part an elaboration. The English were well acquainted with the dissolution of government, and would on no account be threatened with it again. They were indifferent to the emotions of others because they had been too deeply wounded by their own.

(v)

The British single kingdom – with its newly unified crown and parliament, its dual structures of laws and churches, its conquered annex in Ireland, its petty lordships in Man and the Channel Islands not fully incorporated with either crown, its powerful trading corporations and its colonies in the Caribbean and the coasts of continental America – had been created to safeguard its own stability and act as a power in Europe (where it had in Gibraltar its first continental footing since the loss of Calais). But its two *raisons d'être* – internal sovereignty and external dominion – were not quite reconciled and therefore not quite achieved; there were fears, tensions and conflicting images. The great successes of Marlborough's wars and the defeats inflicted on Louis XIV's 'universal monarchy' brought with them the fear of entanglement in a confederacy of European powers no less 'universal' and permanent, and the fear of permanent subjection to a régime of stockjobbers, war-mongers and borough-mongers; fears which could be articulated by Jacobites, commonwealthmen, and Whig or Tory opposition camarillas, with overtones threatening to the Revolution régime and the Hanoverian succession, so that the language of corruption destabilized the dynasty and drew attention to the instability of the churches. The reserve power of the English parliament and the restive counties and boroughs behind it took control, under Tory leadership, of the formidable military and financial machine built by William III and the Junto Whigs,[30] and withdrew it from its continental alliances in the manoeuvres leading to

---

[29] Penovich, 1995, esp. p. 237.
[30] The growth of this war-making and imperial machinery of state throughout the eighteenth century
      has been studied by Brewer, 1989.

the Treaty of Utrecht, an assertion of the autonomy of the islands in the politics of Europe so decisive that it won the approval of the historian Lord Macaulay and could be praised as setting up a 'balance of power' which stabilized the European 'republic'.[31] Yet the high costs of Utrecht were seen in the succession crisis which accompanied the illness and death of Anne, and brought the Hanoverian line to the throne by a party triumph which was ruthlessly imposed on England and resisted by rebels in Scotland, and which left behind it a weakness in legitimation that two reigns could not live down.

There ensued a 'patriot' discourse – sometimes deist and sometimes Anglican in England and Wales, sometimes radically covenanting in Scotland – which defended the 'country' against the corrupting effects of high finance, European diplomacy and Whig oligarchy, and responded in its own way to the growing power of commerce and imperial aggression by speaking out for a 'blue-water' policy which pursued maritime empire without European alliances and standing armies. It scarcely concealed its latent anti-Hanoverianism, and its persistent calls for reliance on the county militias were not unjustly charged with weakening the régime's military power against the Stuart exiles and their French allies, fear of whom kept the spectre of 'universal monarchy' stalking the English map of Europe. It is being shown, particularly by Eliga H. Gould,[32] how in the middle decades of the eighteenth century the incursion and defeat of Prince Charles Edward coincided with the reversal of alliances as between Austria and Prussia – once so central an object of historical study under the name of 'the Diplomatic Revolution' – and very importantly the re-organization of the English[33] militia as a home-defence army, to consolidate the Hanoverian régime in Great Britain and distance it from the power-conflicts of German-speaking Europe, where the anti-French cause was fatefully left in the apparently Protestant and unentangling hands of the king of Prussia.

In the opinion of Edward Gibbon, the re-organization of the militia further coincided with the accession of George III – a 'British prince' born within both the realm and the church of England – to deliver the Tory gentry (to which the Gibbons belonged) from the burden of their lingering Jacobitism and bring to the Hanoverians their support sometimes so

---

[31] The classic statement of Utrecht's historical importance by one of its chief British promoters is Bolingbroke's *Letters on the Study of History* (London, 1752), letters VII and VIII. For Macaulay's verdict (his *History* did not reach 1713), see his review, 'Lord Mahon's War of the Succession in Spain', Macaulay, 1901, II, pp. 181–6.

[32] Gould, 1991.   [33] But not Scottish; see Robertson, 1986.

unwavering as to be an embarrassment to Whigs.[34] In the opinion of David
Hume, however, it coincided with the disastrous policies of the elder Pitt,
that 'wicked madman'[35] who had doubled the national debt in pursuit of a
continental empire in America, brought down on Britain the reproach of
seeking 'universal monarchy' of a new kind and left it without friends in
Europe to support it against a vengeance-seeking France. The Hanoverian
régime in Britain had extricated itself from one European system to make
itself the centre of an Atlantic and American empire whose brief career
dominates the history of the quarter-century following George's accession
in 1760.

In the rapid and deeply confusing developments of that period, a king
who had 'gloried in the name of Britain' – meaning that he was not a 'wee
wee German lairdie' pledged to his Electoral interests – found himself
excoriated as a puppet of villainous 'North Britons', both by aristocratic
Whigs infuriated because he had taken over the cause they considered their
own, and by urban demagogues whose antecedents were as Tory as they
were commonwealth. The rapidity of this transformation of discourse, as
well as of behaviour, indicates that the stability and even the legitimacy of
the dynasty and the régime were not complete even after the extinction of
Jacobitism. The early years of the reign witnessed the rallying of many
English Tories to a Whig régime, and of many Scots to a Union in which
what we call Enlightenment defined their place in philosophical terms;[36] its
later years were to lay many seventeenth-century ghosts as the Church of
England moved into unreserved support of the Georgian monarchy and
the great principle of subordination. But its first quarter-century witnessed
an alienation of Revolution Whigs from the monarchy, an alienation of
urban crowds from monarchic and aristocratic patronage simultaneously,
and an alienation of newly vocal, largely anti-trinitarian dissent (some of it
originating within the church as well as outside it) from the compromise of
Test and Toleration which formed the ecclesiastical substance of the
Revolution Settlement.[37] These were the 'present discontents' of
England; Scotland witnessed less alienation, as did Ireland until the mid-
point of the war of 1774–83; but in the larger field of 'the empire' – as the
various realms, dominions and dependencies of the imperial crown were
collectively known – there arose a new crisis in multiple monarchy, which
took a turn from which the epithet 'revolutionary' need not be withheld.

---

[34] Above, p. 125.
[35] Hume, letter to William Strahan, 26 October 1775, in Greig, 1932, vol. II, p. 301. See Hont, 1993.
[36] Sher, 1985.   [37] Clark, 1985, pp. 207–8, 276, 283.

(VI)

This crisis may be thought of as arising from a change in the character and self-perception of the formerly and still consciously English colonies of the crown on the American seaboard, excluding the Caribbean and the Gulf of St Lawrence.[38] Its crucial and revolutionary step was the declaration of 1776 that what had been termed 'colonies' were now to be considered, of right were, and therefore in some sense always had been, independent 'states'. From this it may be inferred, without too much simplification, that 'colonies' had been defined as something less than 'states', and now claimed that status as a step so radical that it entailed a concomitant claim to 'independence'. What then was the legal status of a 'colony', and had that status been clarified in law? Here we may find ambiguity; a colony's charter, if it had one, might authorize it to act and exist as something in the nature of a trading company, or a civil corporation akin to a borough, or (to look to extremes) a body political, ecclesiastical as well as civil, subject to a crown whose authority ruled it as the same authority ruled the realm of England according to the Act in Restraint of Appeals. But there were no colonial bishops appointed by royal letters, even in episcopalian Virginia; and bishops as spiritual peers could function only within the historical structure of the English realm. The multiplicity of churches and sects in the American colonies viewed as a whole obliges us to think of Anglo-American religious culture as in a loose sense congregational,[39] and there were sectors in which it was becoming increasingly unitarian. The structure of Tudor sovereignty did not in this sense apply.

There was a very strong sense in which colonists felt themselves to be Englishmen (whatever their ethnic origins), subjects of the crown of Great Britain and entitled to the liberties and protection of English law. But once the status of 'colonies' within the 'empire' was called in question, as it was by the policy of which the Stamp Act (1765) was part, its indeterminacy began to raise serious questions.[40] Even under royal governors, the colonies were not vice-royalties, subject kingdoms, realms or dominions, as were the components of the Spanish Monarchy; even under vigorously assertive colonial assemblies, they were not sovereign 'estates' or 'states' like those composing the Dutch republic. If they had enjoyed any such status, the British 'empire' might have acknowledged a *jus publicum* regulating

---

[38] Greene's (1986 and 1990) is the fullest and most illuminating study of this process.
[39] The American Revolution as a war of religion is studied by Clark, 1993.
[40] Greene, 1986, 1990, and Koebner, 1961, chs. 4 and 5.

relations between its component 'states' and the imperial crown which ruled them; and that *jus* might have defined it as a 'confederation' and an 'empire' (though the Swiss and Dutch confederations could not be known by the latter term). But if the colonies lacked any clear legal definition, there could be no *jus publicum*, and George III enjoyed more 'empire' within the realm of Great Britain than he did in the full extent of his dominions. It came indeed to be said that there existed, or had existed, a code or consensus of informal understandings which governed the relations between crown, parliament and colonial governors and assemblies; and there were those – in fact there still are[41] – who claimed that this code enjoyed the immemorial and customary authority of an 'ancient constitution'. But Edmund Burke – who appealed eloquently for its perpetuation in the face of rival theories of empire – seems to have presented it in terms rather of the prudence of *gubernaculum* than of the binding precedents of *jurisdictio*; and the apex of the ancient constitution had long been the sovereignty of the king-in-parliament.

This 'empire', then, differed from other systems of that name in that it was not composed of sovereign or quasi-sovereign 'states' and was not held together by *pacta*, *foedera* or a *jus publicum*, but by the sovereignty of the crown in parliament, coupled with the common law in which the rights of Englishmen were held to be enshrined. It was one of those unwritten, informal arrangements in which the English believe themselves to excel, but sovereignty in this sense had memorably collapsed in the previous century, and had had to be restored in the form of an unbreakable location of the royal authority in parliament (so that, it was commonly said, the crown's 'influence' had increased as its 'prerogative' had been lessened). The informal structure of 'empire' – meaning the relation of the crown to those of its dominions which were colonies but not realms – disintegrated through the 1760s and 1770s, and Edmund Burke was left appealing to the principle that it was precisely its informality which should never have been challenged, and so destroyed, by attempts at definition which he characterized as empty 'theory' for the reason that existing law was incapable of providing the answers. The reasons why a problem arose to which there was no clear answer have next to be considered.

To the extent to which the individual colonist could be considered an Englishman – a definition he might insist on carrying to the fullness of its extent – he could be thought of as appealing to his rights at common law, and making this appeal to the sovereign who protected and acknowledged

---

[41] Greene, 1986, 1990, ch. 7, pp. 144–8; Reid, 1981. Cf. Tucker and Hendrickson, 1982.

these rights; as doing so even when, and because, the sovereign was legislating in a way the colonist considered an infringement of them. The locus of such appeals was in parliament, but not only was the colonist unrepresented in that body, parliament was itself now part of the sovereign – the crown-in-parliament – against whose legislation he was appealing. There next arose a dimension of the problem in which the rights of the colonist were no longer vested simply in his relation as subject to the law and the sovereign, but were located in the new problematic of subordinate legislatures. He was represented, or so he might claim, in the assembly of his colony, and if his right not to be taxed without his own consent was situated there, it followed that he should not, or in a language derived from the law could not, be taxed without the consent of that assembly. But if right and representation, with which the common law unequivocally endowed him, were located in the colonial assembly, it should follow that the same law provided and regulated a process by which taxation was imposed by parliament with the consent of the colonial assemblies. This it did not do, by any process less informal than that in which the issue had become critical before 1763; and it followed that any appeal to rights enshrined in the common law was enough to destroy that law's informal and customary character by asking it to provide guarantees more formal than it possessed the means of formulating. The essence of common law is the written (or formal) expression of unwritten (and informal) understandings.

From this dilemma there flowed two consequences. In the first place, the rights of Englishmen at common law came to be re-codified in American colonial discourse as rights by a higher law of which common law could always be described as a manifestation: a law of nations and/or of nature. It was by this route that Americans came to believe that they enjoyed the rights of Englishmen in a higher and more perfect sense than that in which Englishmen enjoyed them, and were by nature that which Englishmen were merely by history. But a higher and more ideal history was necessary in order to explain how this had come about; and the second consequence with which we have to deal was that the colonists began to provide themselves with a history in which their rights as Englishmen were seen as having been vested from the beginning in their capacity to represent themselves by a law of nature. From the writings of Richard Bland of Virginia, in the middle 1760s, there began to take shape a history which in its completed form may be stated as follows.[42] Colonists emigrating into

---

[42] Greene, 1986, 1990, ch. 5, and Ohmori, 1988.

the wilderness had taken with them the rights of Englishmen, including the rights to property, representation, and the protection of the crown, whose sovereignty they had therefore been necessitated to carry with them. On entering the wilderness, however, they had entered the state of nature, whether as that term was used by theorists of *jus civile*, to denote a condition antecedent to the establishment of civil society, or as it was used by theorists of *jus gentium*, to denote the space in which sovereign entities were related to one another. For if rights were sufficient to generate civil sovereignty, the rights of Englishmen, transformed by the wilderness into rights of nature, had re-generated the sovereignty of the crown of England as that of a sovereign over subjects defined by the law of nature alone.

If it were held – as by a civilian or a scholastic jurist it might not have been – that the rights-bearers negotiated with the sovereign the terms on which they would accept him as such, it followed – as for a line of colonial theorists from Bland to Jefferson it came to follow – that each body of colonists had negotiated with the king of England a *pactum* or *foedus* by which he became their sovereign, but his sovereignty was exercised primarily in the assembly which represented them and their rights. If it were held – as by theorists of *jus gentium* like Grotius, Pufendorf and Vattel it was coming to be held – that between sovereigns in the state of nature there could exist only *foedera*, and that it was a question how far a system of *foedera* might develop into the *jus publicum* of a confederation like the Swiss or the German, or of Europe ideally considered as a republic of states held together by great treaties like those of Westphalia or Utrecht – then the British 'empire' might be considered a series of *pacta* between diverse civil societies and their sovereign the king of Great Britain, and a series of *foedera* which permitted the crown-in-parliament at Westminster to exercise certain powers for the good of the 'empire' as a society of civil societies, all of them 'English' in the sense in which the rights of Englishmen were the rights of nature.

To colonists, this line of argument – here abstracted and ideally expressed – had the advantage that it gave each 'colony' a legal definition and being, beyond any with which the common law had hitherto endowed it, and at the same time demonstrated that rights at that law were rights by the law of nature – a proposition which, in itself, nobody could very well deny. It further supplied 'empire', as that term was used in British context, a legal definition, a common sovereignty, and a *jus publicum* with which it had not hitherto provided itself. But it did so at the price, which to colonists was not a price but an enhancement of status, of re-defining the 'empire' as a confederation; and this was a price which Englishmen, and at this period to all appearances most Scots, were not willing to pay at all. John Robertson's volume (1995) has been concerned with the Union of the Parliaments as a great act of state which entailed the rejection of a 'confederating' in favour of an 'incorporating' union; and we have seen that the primary reason for this decision was that the 'empire' exercised by the English crown in the Westminster parliament could 'incorporate' other bodies politic within itself, but could not 'confederate' or be confederated with them. Therefore the English (and the Scottish Unionist) response to the claims which Americans now began to put forward was, typically, that they could imagine (though they might be unwilling to effect) 'incorporating' colonies within the realms (and its 'empire') by giving them representation in the Westminster parliament, but could never accept, and could hardly even understand, the proposal to reconstitute the 'empire' as a 'confederation'. The American Revolution is not causally a consequence of the Union of England and Scotland, but it is a consequence of a political logic contained within it.

(VII)

This was the logic of 'empire' in the English sense of the term. This had in 1533 meant the sovereignty of the crown in church and state; it had not then been necessary to determine in detail how far this sovereignty was exercised in parliament and how far out of it. There had ensued a series of devastating crises and 'dissolutions of government', which had led to the decision that the unity of crown with parliament and with church must be maintained at all costs, even the cost of concessions by crown to parliament and by crown-in-parliament to English dissent and Scottish distinctiveness; at the cost last named the Scots had been incorporated in 'empire' as the English understood it. There had further been set up a powerful structure of military, naval and civil power, capable of exercising imperial control within the 'extensive monarchy' of the archipelago, in the reason of state of the European 'republic of states', and on the oceans and in the American and Asian continents constituting European 'empire' in the modern sense of the term; but 'empire' in this sense was still perceived as guaranteeing the unity of crown and parliament which constituted 'empire' in the oldest sense, and guaranteed England against a recurrence of seventeenth-century disorder. Dynastic and ecclesiastical instabilities had kept the régime at risk down to a time still recent when the first American crisis began; and the rapidity with which the Jacobite menace of the 1740s had been succeeded by the 'present discontents' of the 1760s showed that the monarchy of George III was even now not perfectly legitimated. The 'growth of political stability'[43] in England (now Britain) since 1660 had been very real, but had not reached finality.

These historical considerations were interestingly synthesized by Thomas Pownall, the successive editions of whose treatise on *The Administration of the Colonies* supply an acute commentary on the growth of the imperial crisis in the years either side of 1770.[44] Casting about for a response to the increasing demand for a definition of the colonies as legal entities within a political system, he examined (as did others) the solution of proposing that they were (or had been) 'palatinates', in which the powers of the crown had been deputed to be exercised by local authorities. Chester, Durham and the Principality of Wales had been dominions of this order until their incorporations within the realm; the Isle of Man and the Channel Islands still were. Ireland as a kingdom by conquest occupied a different category, and Pownall did not stir up the ancient controversy as to whether the crown of Scotland had been subordinate to that of England before the incorporating union. With regard to colonies, however, he insisted that the status of palatinates was obsolete and no longer available. It had existed only under feudal conditions, when the king's personal authority was not fully incorporated with that of his realm, and the dualities of Fortescuean kingship and the King's Two Bodies had been actual and visible. About 1660, however, in a historical process which Pownall significantly associated with the Navigation Acts, these conditions had ceased; the king became incorporated with his realm in the conjoint sovereignty of king, lords and commons, and subjection to his authority had become subjection to his authority in parliament.[45] As subjects to the crown, therefore, colonists were subjects to the realm (so that, he might have argued, when Englishmen infuriated Americans by speaking of 'our colonies' they spoke within their rights). The flaw in this reality was that colonists were unrepresented in parliament, in the exercise of the sovereignty to which they were subject. If they could not be granted such representation, *ad hoc* agreements would have to be worked out with the assemblies in which they were represented, recognizing the system's necessary imperfection and accommodating to it.

---

[43] Plumb, 1967.

[44] Thomas Pownall, *The Administration of the Colonies, wherein their Rights and Constitution are Discussed and Stated* (London, 1764; five editions by 1774). See Bibliography B, *sub* Pownall, 1971.

[45] Pownall, 1971, pp. 138–40, 172–3.

Pownall supplies us with a model which may be set up in opposition to that extractable from colonial argument as it developed between Bland and Jefferson, to show that in the imperial crisis there actually were major issues at stake. It may be doubted how many of the debaters and spectators understood them; the history of the controversy can easily be written as one of incomprehension on both sides. The absence – which Pownall was trying to supply – of a clear legal concept of a colony as a subordinate political society led to the controversy's being conducted as a debate between local varieties of Englishmen, possessing the same rights and appealing to the same law and the same sovereign; and on this perspective it was easy to arrive at the position, upheld by Edmund Burke, that there were no debatable issues and the mistake lay in trying to debate them. This is, rather strangely, the position of many American historians, who contend that the issues could have been resolved and it was only the purblindness of British ministers which prevented this happening. It is curious to see them arguing that the foundation of their republic, and its new birth of freedom, were not inevitable but could (and should?) have been avoided. The advantage of the argument being advanced in this essay is that it provides the American Revolution with a measure of historical logic. The development of the colonies into self-conscious political societies, and the arguments they adopted to declare themselves such, led them to propose, in effect, the conversion of the 'empire' into a 'confederation'. There was nothing illogical about this, since it was possible for an association of states to be both, and Grotius, Pufendorf and Vattel were inscribed as names in the American pantheon because they showed this to be possible. But in addressing such proposals to the British crown-in-parliament, the colonists were dealing with an entity to which the term 'empire' denoted its own sovereignty and its own unity, which must be maintained at all costs as the only guarantee against its own dissolution, as well as the only guarantee of its continuing imperial power. They thus found themselves contending with the ghost of history, with that terrifying 'rhinoceros charging out of the past', of which Jonathan Scott has so wittily and eloquently written.[46]

The colonial argument came to set up the image of a series of quasi-contractual *foedera* or relationships between each colony, considered as a 'people' seated in the state of nature, and the crown of England (later Great Britain); relations with the crown which were not essentially, but at best contingently, subordinate to the authority of parliament. They claimed in short to be subject to the crown but not to the crown-in-parliament; and

[46] Scott, 1991, pp. xiii–xiv, 26–49.

Pownall had much of the authority of English history on his side when he sought to show them that this claim was historically obsolete, since the civil wars, followed by the growth of commerce and modern 'empire', had ensured that crown and parliament were so irrevocably incorporated in one another that colonies were necessarily subordinate to their conjoint sovereignty, and could only aspire (perhaps in vain) to be represented in its exercise. But the unity of crown and parliament was recent: no older than 1660 in Pownall's projection, and perhaps a century younger if we listen to Edward Gibbon; and the extinction of the Jacobite threat did not mean that it had ceased to be fragile. In appealing to the crown but not to parliament, the colonists came to be seen as separating the two; they were unwittingly raising the spectre of Bolingbroke's Patriot King, supposed to have guided, through sinister maternal and Scottish familiars, the unwise steps of George III in separating himself from the natural leaders of his parliament. The radical populism of much American language aligned the colonists with those, in London and elsewhere,[47] who thought the solution lay in an appeal, from monarchy and aristocracy alike, to the people as repository of all patriot virtue; but the Americans were not appealing to the English or British people, so much as they were claiming to be peoples in their own right. In pursuit of this claim, they set up a confederal relation which they supposedly enjoyed with the crown; this was to separate the king's personal from his parliamentary authority, with the result that those to whom it mattered above all to maintain the unity of crown and parliament could, perhaps must, respond that the American argument simultaneously did the work of Tories who would exalt the King above the two houses and of republicans who would reduce him to a mere 'duke of Venice'. It was already a staple of Whig argument that Jacobites and republicans were allied against the sovereignty of crown and parliament, as had been the papists and puritans of old. In the first three decades of George III's reign, all these ghosts were gibbering in the streets (which is not to say that new things in British politics were not appearing at the same time).

(VIII)

This is to present the crisis leading to American independence as a crisis in multiple monarchy: not indeed in the multiple monarchy of the Three Kingdoms, but in the very specific and self-conscious structure of the

---

[47] Sainsbury, 1987; Bonwick, 1977.

English monarchy and its realm and empire, occurring when colonies which had not been legally defined as distinct political societies laid claim to that status and began defining themselves, in their own terms, as what they ended by terming 'states'. If they had been 'states' within a legally defined 'empire' with a *jus publicum*, there might still have been a crisis leading to independence, but it would have been of a different character from the one which in fact occurred. We have seen that they began, but did not complete, shaping a concept of empire as confederation, in which each component contained the seeds of its own sovereignty and enjoyed its own relation with the crown as a sovereign shared by all. This was not so much unacceptable as unintelligible to the politicians and publicists of the king-dom of Great Britain, less because they had an alternative concept of their 'empire' over colonies than because they had none to speak of, and employed the term 'empire' to mean their sovereignty over themselves, of which they had assumed the colonists to form part. This sovereignty was lodged in the king-in-parliament, and the confederal theory of empire looked like a design to separate the two. James VI and I had strenuously objected to finding himself the head of two bodies or the husband of two wives,[48] but the seraglio formed of twenty or more independent legislatures was one from which George III had little need to escape, since he never entered it and scarcely recognized that it was there. The Anglo-British response to the semi-articulated trends in the colonial argument was less rejection than incomprehension. So far was George from aiming at the status of a Patriot King that he instinctively aligned his authority with that of parliament, and resolutely upheld the conjoint sovereignty of both. This increased the fears of those among his subjects, both colonial and metro-politan, who saw him both as a prisoner of the corruption of parliament, and as aiming through his sinister advisers at corrupting it himself. The bogey of the Patriot King returned to haunt him, most of all when – for once in the history of the British monarchy – he acted as a conqueror, and in the Quebec Act[49] used statute to enact a *pactum concessionis* with his newly acquired francophone subjects, guaranteeing to them – to the horror and dismay of Protestants in Britain, Ireland and America – the continued exercise of priestly and feudal authority. The image of monarchical tyranny thus both reinforced and partly concealed the image of absolute parlia-mentary sovereignty which was the true target of American arguments.

The crown, nevertheless, anchored itself in parliament, and therefore in a Tudor and parliamentary conception of 'empire'; it rejected, perhaps

---

[48] Mason, 1994 and Wormald, 1992.   [49] Lawson, 1989.

without ever comprehending, an American conception of 'empire' as confederation, in which every legislative assembly should represent a distinct 'people' or civil society – or, as the term was coming to be used, a 'state' – enjoying its own relationship with the crown. All attempts to negotiate without resolving this conflict having failed – this is not to say that none could have succeeded – the revolutionary breaking-point was reached in the Declaration of Independence, a document which enacts a great many positions, easier for us to understand once we recognize that it operates as much within a discourse of *jus gentium* as within one of *jus civile.* Stating its objective initially as that of announcing the separation of one 'people', the American, from another, the British, it employs a Lockean language framed to ground government in the 'people' in order to assert the equality of all 'peoples' with one another, and therefore the right of any 'people' to withdraw from the ties linking it with another. The implication can only be that there has existed a relationship between as many 'peoples' as there are colonies with delegates at Philadelphia and the 'people' (evidently a single one) of Great Britain; that the ties existing between them have been those provided by the authority of the crown, now about to be declared dissolved; and that each 'people' has possessed and still possesses the authority to generate its own government, and to enter if it chooses into *pacta* and *foedera* with the crown as furnishing it both with civil authority and with ties linking it with the other peoples of a confederate empire; a choice, however, now rejected.

The Declaration proceeds to employ a Lockean language of dissolution of government, with which it indicts the king for misgovernment, pronounces him at war with those of his peoples who are party to the action the Congress is now taking, and declares his government over them dissolved. It is presumed, however, that they existed, and possessed both governments and the capacity to generate them, antecedently of the royal government; and the consequence must be that it is less the civil government of the colonies which is being dissolved, than the authority of the crown as providing a shared government, or 'empire', over a confederation of many 'peoples'. The British 'empire' is being proclaimed a confederation by the same act as proclaims that confederation dissolved. In consequence, the Declaration asserts, 'these united colonies' are now, and of right ought to be, 'independent states'. The phrase 'of right' strongly suggests that they have always been 'states', or at least civil societies possessing the capacity to enter into contracts of government, and into treaties with other societies and peoples equal with themselves. It is the American solution to the English failure to furnish colonies with a clearly defined legal and civil status; very English, both in its use of the term 'right' to appeal to immemorial antiquity and in its adaptation to American purposes of the Act in Restraint of Appeals's claim that the realm is an 'empire, and so hath been reputed in the world', possessing an absolute and sovereign capacity to govern itself.

But since what is being dissolved is not the civil government of a society so much as the ties between a number of civil societies, it is primarily the crown's capacity to constitute and regulate these external relationships which is being declared at an end; the language of Locke is being injected into the language of Grotius, Pufendorf and Vattel. The matter does not quite end there, since through the governors it appoints the crown has been claiming executive authority in the civil government of each colony. In declaring this at an end and enjoining each colony to set about replacing it, Congress is effecting in each colony a limited revolution on the scale of 1688: a partial dissolution of government, or of one component thereof, which does not amount to a dissolution of the authority composing civil society. It goes further than 1688 in declaring the crown itself deposed, and enjoining each colony to embark on the republican road of replacing it; the republican component in American history is activated from this moment; but what is being dissolved is a relation between a number of civil societies, and if 'dissolution of government' leads to a 'state of nature', the latter term denotes not the human condition that precedes civil government, but the 'state of nature' in which civil governments exist with respect to one another. Americans, the Declaration pronounces, henceforth consider the British government and people 'as we hold the rest of mankind, enemies in war and in peace friends'. It is the language of the *jus belli ac pacis*, and for the moment it is a declaration of war. The war may be terminated by a peace treaty or *foedus*, but not by a *confoederatio* or decision to share and obey a common *imperium*; for that is what has just been declared dissolved.

Implicit in all this is an acknowledgement of the position articulated by Pownall, that the crown, parliament and people of Great Britain are so far incorporated with one another that they cannot be considered apart. There is no indictment of George III's government of his kingdom, no suggestion that this is to be dissolved; those English radicals who threatened the king with such language were grievously disappointed by the word reaching them from Philadelphia.[50] The Declaration of Independence set out to separate one 'people' from another, with the result that all its Lockean

[50] Sainsbury, 1987, pp. 127–31.

indictments of royal misgovernment necessarily implied the existence of a royal government so far incorporated with the British 'people' that to cast off one was to cast off the other. At this point the confederate theory of empire collapsed, since it could not be maintained that the English, or by now the Scottish, people recognized the crown only, or primarily, as the link between them and other peoples. (The Irish might be another matter.) The indictment of George III barely conceals an indictment of both parliament and the people represented by it. Deep down in the language of the Declaration may be uncovered an acceptance of both the Fortescuean theory of English kingship and the 'incorporating' rather than 'confederating' character of the Union of 1707. The American 'people' recognized the 'British people' even as it defined itself by defying them.

(IX)

This essay has traced the history of a crisis in multiple monarchy, arising too late in British history to be solved in the terms – themselves very imperfectly formulated – taking shape around that concept. Interestingly, its language was English rather than British; the idioms in which colonial writers from Bland to Jefferson put forward their concept of empire as confederation owed little to Andrew Fletcher[51] or any of the debates of Union in 1603 or 1707, and it is something of a puzzle to tell where (other than in the European classics of *jus gentium*) they laid hold of them. When the concept was put to the English, and by this time to the Scots or North Britons, it encountered quite insuperable obstacles, the reasons for which lie so deep in English history as well as in that of Union that it is fair to speak of the American crisis as one in which the English, to say nothing of the still nascent British,[52] were obliged to defend themselves as they thought their history had shaped them. It was necessary to maintain at all costs the conjoint sovereignty of the crown-in-parliament, the more so as the American crisis came when, and perhaps because, the relations between crown, parliament and people were for domestic reasons quite sharply destabilized. To unite the colonies with parliament by representation was one means of achieving this overriding purpose; to subject the colonies to parliament by imperial and military power was another; to rid

---

[51] Awareness of his argument for a confederating union may be detected in the Scot John Witherspoon; Greene, 1986, 1990, pp. 155, 172. For Witherspoon see further Sher and Smitten, 1990, section I, chs. 1–6; and Landsman, 1995, pp. 314–17.
[52] Colley, 1992.

parliament of the colonies by recognizing their independence was a third, and from the start there were imperial realists, like David Hume and Josiah Tucker,[53] who wanted to take this route. To compromise the unity of crown and parliament by sharing the crown with other parliaments was an alternative not considered, except in a further case which we ourselves have yet to consider.

With the recognition of American independence in 1783, there began to be an American history in which the ambiguities of the Declaration of 1776 had to be confronted. In what sense were the united colonies now united states? Had the thirteen of them merely entered a state of nature in respect to one another, in which what held them together were merely the *foedera* which might constitute an alliance or a confederation, and might or might not constitute a *jus publicum*?[54] What could have been meant by the Declaration's constitution of an 'American people' forming a single entity, and how was it possible for that people to have manifested itself in thirteen distinct states? Was it conceivable that the unitary people enjoyed sovereignty, and that the multiple states existed only as its 'empire' defined them? Out of these linguistic puzzles it was a practical, indeed an imperial, necessity for James Madison to formulate a science of federal government, inclusive of Alexander Hamilton's pronouncement that the United States formed 'an empire perhaps the most interesting in the world'.[55] It may have been in large part Americans' enduring perception of themselves as still Englishmen, enjoying rights at common law which there must be a sovereign to protect and enforce, which led to the blend of states' rights with national government characterizing the federalist synthesis. In this process, however, the thesis that each colony was a state, whose political autonomy was visible in its own separate and distinct history, disappeared from the discourse of federalism as rapidly as it had been invented to form part of the discourse of independence. Once Congress affirmed the authority to create the territories which should become states, it exerted an imperial power of telling each 'people' where and how it might create itself; the empire of liberty was indeed an empire.[56]

As for the kingdoms and dominions which remained in the allegiance of George III, the loss of thirteen colonies was a painful but not a revolutionary experience; it diminished the territorial extent of empire without compelling its relocation in the structure of political authority, and the fashionable analogy with the decline and fall of Rome was false from the

---

[53] Pocock, 1985, chs. 7, 9.   [54] [See now Hendrickson, 2003.]
[55] The second sentence of *The Federalist*, no. 1, in any edition.   [56] Onuf, 1983; Pocock, 1996c.

start. The American war can only be seen as producing a hardening, to the point of ruthlessness, of the sovereign power of crown, parliament and all that they stood for. If some perceived a potentially revolutionary situation in 1780,[57] this must be seen as leading to counter-revolution in 1783–4, when the crown recovered control in parliament and never lost it again. The aristocracy took on more of the character of an imperial military and administrative élite;[58] it faced the challenges of the French Revolution with its mind made up and its dissenters marginalized. Slowly and painfully over the next quarter-century, it recovered the European position it had lost in 1763–83; it took part in another grand alliance against another universal monarchy, and mistrustfully entered into a restoration of the republic of European states in and after the Congress of Vienna. It enlarged its maritime and extra-European hegemonies in ways that gave rise to two new imperial discourses: the Anglo-Indian, which debated whether empire in South Asia was necessarily despotic because exercised over subjects naturally or historically incapable of liberty;[59] the Anglo-Canadian, in which the French-speaking province of Lower Canada and the Loyalist colonies of Upper Canada and the Maritimes entered upon the complex discourses of sovereignty which constitute 'Canadian political thought'.[60] There as elsewhere on the planet, 'crown colonies' of British settlers began exploring non-American routes towards 'responsible' and 'representative' government.[61]

There remained one zone in which the history of the Three Kingdoms continued to shape 'British history'. If the Union of the Parliaments succeeded to the point where the American crisis produced no crisis in Scotland, and something like a 'British' nationality can be seen taking shape, we need to increase the attention we give to the series of developments in which the Anglo-Irish gentry formed themselves into a patriot militia and claimed for their parliament something not unlike what some Americans claimed for their own assemblies: union with an imperial crown of its own, distinct from the crown and parliament of Great Britain. Immediately there were those who declared that the only possible solution was the opposite: the complete incorporation of Ireland within the parliamentary monarchy of the United Kingdom.[62] From this point the historian of 'British political thought' needs to begin tracing the complex history

---

[57] Butterfield, 1949.   [58] Gould, 1992, ch. 5, and 2000, part 6.
[59] Minuti, 1978; Whelan, 1996; Muthu, 2003.
[60] I know no exhaustive history of this body of discourse. For such understanding as I have of it, I cite Tully, 1995, part 5; Webber, 1997; Romney, 2000.
[61] Francis, 1992.   [62] Tucker, 1781, pp. 96–101.

of the various Irish political discourses – patriot, Unionist and United Irish; Protestant, Catholic and Presbyterian; Jacobin, Orange and Nationalist – and to begin conducting them towards a third Union: the fateful Act of 1801, without which the legislation of 1829–32, bringing an end to the Revolution Settlement in Great Britain, could hardly have occurred[63] and the relations of the United Kingdom with Ireland could not have assumed their modern form. Dr Robertson's volume has studied British history largely from a Scottish angle of approach; the present essay has sought to exhibit it in an English and American perspective. Do we not need to return to the archipelago and (following the lead given by Jacqueline Hill)[64] examine its Irish dimension?

[63] Clark, 1985, pp. 383–420; 2000, pp. 501–64.   [64] Hill, 1995; Pocock, 2000b.

CHAPTER 10

The Union in British history

The emphasis of the 'new British history' has so far fallen on the early modern period, preceding the formation of a unitary state and its disruption in the twentieth century. The Union of 1800–1 is of course cardinal to the latter process, and may be placed on the hinge or *Sattelzeit* marking the transition from early modern to modern 'British history'. In this essay[1] I attempt to review and re-periodize the earlier history as leading to the formation of the Union, so as to suggest some ways in which the modern phase of this history may be pursued. The 'new history' has now advanced beyond the seventeenth into the eighteenth century, and is venturing into the nineteenth; the history of the twentieth century awaits perspective. In this sequence the Union must appear a pivotal event, though its claim to that role cannot be exclusive of others.

The 'Age', 'War' or 'Wars' of the 'Three Kingdoms' are concepts that dominate our understanding of the early modern period, in which dynastic and parliamentary unions precede the formation of a comprehensive state. Scotland and England were sovereign kingdoms; Ireland was not, and is in danger of appearing in the narrative only as part of the 'empire' which the English and their British state exerted over realms not included in its structure. In this essay an attempt will be made to recognize a greater autonomy of 'Irish history' within the 'British' pattern and contributing to its shaping; and partly to that end, but also for larger reasons, there is proposed a somewhat different conceptualization of the relations between 'state' and 'empire'.

The two kingdoms may be seen entering on an early modern history if we focus for the moment on the English kingdom and its marcher lordships. There are three crucial statutes enacted at Westminster and Dublin during the fourth decade of the sixteenth century. First must stand the Act

---

[1] Originally printed as Pocock, 2000d; based on a lecture to a conference held by the Royal Historical Society in Belfast, October 1999. The opening paragraphs have been abridged.

in Restraint of Appeals (1533), which defines England as an 'empire', less in the sense that it exercises dominion over others – as of course it does – than in the sense that it exercises sovereignty over itself: that unshared sovereignty both ecclesiastical and civil, which the crown exercises both in parliament and out of it, and which must from now on be agreed upon and exercised if England is to be a sovereign kingdom and define itself as a Christian community. 'Empire' is henceforth a precarious and deeply contested term, to be exercised in dynasty, parliament and church all together if 'England' is to be governed and have meaning. It is exercised by England over England, as well as by England over subordinate realms; but failures of 'empire' in the latter sense may entail failures of 'empire' in the former, and for this reason no separation between internal 'state' and external 'empire' is satisfactory.

The subordinate realms must now be brought into the picture and assert their historic autonomy, if 'British' history is not be collapsed into 'English'. The Statute of Wales in 1536 liquidates the marcher lordships and completes the incorporation of 'Wales' into 'England' – an assimilation of a society still Celtic to an Anglo-Norman model so uniquely successful that Welsh nationalist historiography consists largely in examining the costs of its success. Since there had at no time been a functioning kingdom of Wales, this union does not figure in the sequence of Unions punctuating the history of the 'Three Kingdoms', and the statute of 1536 is therefore antithetical with that enacted at Dublin in 1541, which erected the English king's 'lordship of Ireland' into a 'kingdom'. This inaugurates a history of the Three Kingdoms, and at the same time renders it problematic, for the reason that 'Ireland' is at best a subordinate kingdom and may not be one at all. The English monarch is king in Ireland, but this does not necessarily mean that he has there a kingdom in the sense of a body politic of which he is the head. There are, however, from an early date élite groups in Ireland who desire that status for themselves – these are as likely to be settler as indigenous, loyalist as rebellious – and there is a history, and a historiography, turning on the question whether Ireland is a colony undergoing conquest or a body politic shaping itself within a multiple monarchy.[2]

It is crucial that, whereas the élites within Wales by and large accepted the Anglican church-state brought into being by the Act in Restraint of Appeals – and were in the next century divided by it along lines not unlike those dividing the English – the élites and the governed classes of Ireland did not. There exists a literature which enquires, with respect to both the

---

[2] See, classically, Bradshaw, 1979, and the ensuing debate among Irish historians.

Gaelic Irish and the Old English, why it was that they remained Catholic and what kinds of Catholic they remained.[3] The persistence of a Catholic majority deeply separates the history of the Irish from that of the two other Kingdoms, and is of course inseparable from the continued status of Ireland as a kingdom imperfectly conquered and still undergoing conquest. A crucial process in the history of the 'Two Kingdoms' of the island properly termed 'Britain' is the occurrence in Scotland of a Protestant Reformation more sharply Calvinist and Presbyterian than was the Anglican. This gives the relations of church and monarchy, and therefore the structure of the Scottish kingdom, a distinct and ultimately unassimilable character; but for a hundred years it was not unreasonable to imagine a convergence of the two monarchies along episcopalian-presbyterian lines. This was imaginable to the Protestant churches in Ireland, but not to the Catholic majority. The Old English who so resolutely proclaimed their loyalty to James VI and I at the conclusion of the Nine Years War[4] must either imagine him as their secular protector, or imagine that the Catholic aspects of his Anglican kingship might be extended to a point where they came close to the Gallican formula of empire over the church coupled to communion with Rome. James's ecumenical interests held out hopes which were to prove delusive.[5]

In 1603 a dynastic union replaces the 'Two Kingdoms' with the 'Double Crown',[6] leaving the status of the Third Kingdom more ambiguous than before – but not (it is important to stress) to be excluded on those grounds from 'British history'. The fall of the Gaelic-Tudor earldoms leaves the Old English exposed to competitors from the Protestant New English influx, while promoting that momentous innovation, the colonization of Ulster by Scottish and English Protestants. This is an event in the history of all three kingdoms, and could not have come about but for King James's interest in consolidating his properly British realms. The history of early modern Scotland is imported into that of Ireland, but is so by the authority of the crown of Westminster rather than that of Scone. Taken in conjunction with events in Argyll and the Hebrides, it may properly appear that the colonization of Ulster was part of an attempted Protestantization of the

---

[3] The Welsh and Irish cases are compared by Bradshaw, 1996 and 1998.
[4] The Nine Years War in Irish historiography, not that in Europe a century later (above, pp. 107, 123).
[5] Patterson, 1997; Ohlmeyer, 2000. The nature of Irish Catholic royalism has been explored in a number of studies. The proposition of Fitzpatrick, 1988, that Old English Catholicism was para-Gallican, Gaelic Catholicism Franciscan and ultramontane is suggestive, though his understanding of both Anglicanism and Calvinism is deeply flawed.
[6] Nicholls, 1999; Smith, 1998.

north-west *Gaidhealtacht* which had always bridged the North Channel; but it occurred in the further context of a kingdom of Ireland which was a realm of the English crown, and the Scottish colony in Ulster was not a colony of the Scottish kingdom. Simultaneously, the colonies of settlement which were extending the empire of the crown to the North American seaboard and the West Indian islands were deemed to be English and the Scots had none of their own; it might have been otherwise.

We now enter upon the problems of church and state – of empire as defined by the Act in Restraint of Appeals – in the multiple monarchy of a single dynasty, and may look forward, at the usual risks of foreshortening and telocentricity, to the Fall of the British Monarchies and the Wars of the Three Kingdoms. The coupling of these terms is the most trenchant move which has yet been made towards a 'British history' of the English themselves, since it entails the assertion that their internal dissensions would never have led them to civil war, and that this was a consequence of a breakdown of government and a failure to control the sword first in Scotland and then in Ireland – in each case produced by attempts to impose English modes of 'empire' in church and civil government.[7] While it is intensely salutary that we have ceased using 'the English Civil War' as a term comprising the wars in all three kingdoms, it should not be forgotten that there was such a war, discussed in great intellectual depth precisely because it had been undesired and unexpected and was desperately hard to understand;[8] or that the memory of this conflict, and the operation of institutions designed to prevent its recurrence, governed English history to the end of the eighteenth century. This is a fact of 'British' as well as 'English' history; we have arrived at a point where 'empire' in the sense of governance of realms beyond England is capable of devastating 'empire' in the sense of England's civil sovereignty over itself. The Cromwellian union of 1651–60 was imposed on Scotland and Ireland largely to ensure that these realms should have no power over the settlement of a dispute the English were having with themselves.

No revolutionary settlement being available, the year 1660 sees a partial return to empire in the government of all three kingdoms. In Ireland the defeat of the Confederation underlines the hopeless position of the kind of Catholicism represented by the Old English; to that extent, Protestant rule is on the way. In Scotland, the willingness of the aristocracy to consider episcopacy as a means of controlling the clergy opens a road to Erastianism and Enlightenment. In England, a separate periodization is necessary; we

---

[7] Russell, 1991; Morrill, 1993.   [8] Pocock, 1999e.

embark on 'the long eighteenth century', lasting till 1832 and marked by parliamentary determination to maintain an established church.[9] This is the form in which Tudor 'empire' was maintained through the Hanoverian era; but it took time and a revolution to bring the Stuart monarchy back to support of the church of which it was the head. In 1688–9 a 'glorious revolution' which was also a 'second Restoration'[10] achieved this end at the high cost of expelling James VII and II from all three of his kingdoms. The war-cycle that moved from Tor Bay through Killiecrankie to Limerick was not a Second War of the Three Kingdoms of the same order as the First, since it was not a breakdown or dissolution of government in all three realms as much as a re-ordering of government in the face of a European power struggle threatening to engulf the multiple monarchy. King William landed in Tor Bay and crossed the Boyne in order to enlist the island kingdoms in his war against Louis XIV in Flanders, and the War of the English Succession was the archipelagic face of the War of the League of Augsburg or Nine Years War. On the other hand, the enlistment of the Three Kingdoms transformed British and European power politics by consolidating that parliamentary and military-fiscal state, the Kingdom of Great Britain, capable of exercising empire in the Atlantic archipelago, intervening at times decisively in the power politics of the European peninsula, and pursuing empire in the modern sense on the oceans and in America and India. This was the true revolution achieved in the quarter-century following the Dutch intervention of November 1688.

With the Kingdom of Great Britain we may begin to write 'British history' in more than a conceptual sense, but there remains the difficulty that the state of which it is the history is preponderantly English and activated by English politics in a sense nearly exclusive of all others. The Kingdom was formed by the parliamentary Union of 1707, largely the result of a Scottish decision that their kingdom could no longer maintain a separate political economy and that a merger with the English parliamentary fiscal structure was the only recourse. On the English side, however, there were reasons, some of them religious in character, why the maintenance of empire in the Tudor sense required a union of king and parliament so close that there could be no thought of a federal relationship in which the king would be responsible to more parliaments than one. For the same reasons, however, what had to be an incorporating union of parliaments had to be a federative union of church-states. The year 1689 had seen a presbyterian revolution in Scotland, where the extrusion of the

---

[9] Clark, 1985, 2000.   [10] For 1688 as 'second Restoration', see Scott, 1988, 1991.

Episcopal Church kept the kingdom in a state of latent civil war till 1746; and the Kingdom of Great Britain, in which theoretically the Kingdoms of England and Scotland ceased to exist, remained one in which the sovereign was head of the church in England and something other than that in Scotland. Theoretically again, this entailed a drastic separation of civil and ecclesiastical sovereignty; practically, it entailed no such thing, since the maintenance of established religion continued to be vital in both kingdoms.[11]

The ecclesiastical dimension can never be omitted from the study of early modern history; nor can 'Enlightenment' – defined as the subordination of religion to civil society – be omitted from that section of it denoted by the term *'ancien régime'*.[12] In English history, 'the long eighteenth century' is the period during which an established church, with an apparent monopoly of civil office, must be maintained by king-in-parliament, but the purpose of doing so is to ensure that neither orthodoxy nor dissent can disturb the civil order. This is the late form taken by Tudor 'empire', the national sovereignty in church and state, and its purpose within England is to prevent any recurrence of the disorders of the seventeenth century. In the larger fields of British, archipelagic and (as we shall see) Atlantic history, this objective merges with that of maintaining empire in the sense of sovereignty over the larger system (this is the commonest meaning of 'empire' in eighteenth-century anglophone discourse). It is with 'empire' in all these senses, including the ecclesiastical and Enlightened, that the Scottish kingdom is merged by the Union of 1707, and this is the point at which to introduce a periodization of British history moving from an Age of the Three Kingdoms to a First Age of Union, lasting from 1707 to 1801. The Anglo-Irish Union can be considered in the setting this provides as inaugurating a Second Age of Union from 1801 to 1921; this will be succeeded by an age or ages to which it would be premature to give a name, since the end is not yet and it is not our business to foresee it.

All such periodizations are verbal devices intended to focus our attention in selected ways, and it is not inappropriate to employ a diversity of them in conjunction. In English history, 'the long eighteenth century' overlaps 'the First Age of Union'; in Irish history, an age of 'Protestant Ascendancy' has a beginning and end of its own. There is also imperial history, in which it has been customary to distinguish between a 'First British Empire' and a 'Second', the moment of transition occurring about 1783, when the recognition of American independence coincides with the acquisition of massive

[11] Robertson, 1995.   [12] Venturi, 1979, 1984; Clark, 1985, 2000; Pocock, 1999 (B), 1.

state power in India. The various meanings assigned to the term 'empire' in this essay may suggest some modifications in the last of these, but several periodizations may be employed in interpreting the Union of 1800–1.

The ecclesiastical-Enlightened dimension sketched above is far from explaining everything that happened, but provides a useful key that may be employed in setting the events in order. In the English kingdom it accounts for significant tensions within the Church of England; in so far as the régime needed to rest upon a church universal, that church must be apostolic and maintain the fullness of catholic tradition, but in so far as it was a pillar of civil society it upheld rational and sociable concepts of the Christian life which might move in directions Arian, Socinian or crypto-deist.[13] A current of non-trinitarian thinking persisted within the Church of England, and about 1772 emerged in alliance with a more radical unitarianism of non-conformist origin, to form the peaceable yet subversive movement which we know as Rational Dissent.[14] In its extreme development, conspicuous if not representative, this reduced all worship to freedom of opinion; it called for an actual separation of church and state, a goal attainable only under revolutionary and millennial conditions; and in denying any ecclesiastical character to political authority, it encouraged radically and even democratically Lockean views of the latter. Though it had little revolutionary potential within the kingdom of Great Britain, Rational Dissent was vocally and disturbingly active in its support of both the American and French Revolutions, and joined with other currents of discontent, Whig and Tory in origin, to act as progenitor of that British Left whose language has always been more revolutionary than its practice.[15]

It plays this not insignificant role in a cycle of rebellions, revolutions and reconstructions, datable from 1776 through 1801, which may be compared with the War of the Three Kingdoms and the War of the English Succession for the way in which it brought to a close both the First Age of Union and – if we retain the term – the First British Empire. In this critical period the Irish crisis of 1782–1800 is conspicuous and important, but we should approach it by way of a detour through the other provinces of the Hanoverian multiple monarchy and empire. In Scotland, the last war fought within the Kingdom of Great Britain – the re-conquest of the north-west *Gaidhealtacht* following the Anglo-Lowland victory of 1746 – is to be viewed alongside the relative peace of the Protestant kingdom within the Union of 1707. There is some potential for radical covenanting and perhaps proto-nationalist discontent

[13] For the apostolic, see Clark, 1985, 2000; for the Enlightened, Young, 1998.
[14] Haakonssen, 1996.   [15] Bradley, 2001.

with the abandonment of the militancy of the seventeenth century, but this is checked and pacified (or perhaps repressed) by that combination of lay patronage, Moderate oligarchy and civil philosophy known as the Scottish Enlightenment.[16] The remarkable success of this experiment in containing the ecclesiastical within the civil can be measured by comparing it with the case of the Scottish colony in Ulster, where Moderate control did not take shape and New Light anti-trinitarianism joined with Old Light Calvinism in the rebellious societies of Belfast.[17]

Before turning to the Irish aspects of the story, we must take account of an American dimension, in which the politics of the archipelago are enlarged into those of the Atlantic and the cis-Appalachian seaboard,[18] and there appear new areas in which the problems of empire endanger the stability of the kingdom in church and state. The colonies and conquests in North America and the Caribbean had not been organized into vice-royalties or subordinate kingdoms on either the Spanish or the Irish model. They were largely, and considered themselves to be, English, though their populations contained – additional to large numbers of enslaved Africans – sizeable ethnic minorities including Scots-Irish (as presbyterian emigrants from Ulster were beginning to be known in American historiography). These colonies were of diverse and often ill-defined juridical and political status, and from one point of view their history in the eighteenth century is that of their search for a more clearly defined political character, entailing demands for political autonomy greater than can be met within the existing structures of empire, so that in the end they take the revolutionary step of proclaiming themselves independent states.[19] We may look on these events as phenomena in the history of settler nationalism, if by that term – 'settler' is preferable to 'colonial', though 'nationalism' may not be preferable to 'patriotism' – we denote the processes which occur when settler populations begin to make claims against the state, and sometimes the people, that originally sent them forth: claims to conduct their own relations with the sovereign, claims to be enracinated in the land they have conquered from, or now share with, indigenous cultures from whom they sometimes derive part of their legitimacy. Phenomena of this kind are ancient in Irish history, where Old English, New English and Ulster Scots constitute three settler populations and as many religions; it is a key to medieval history that the Old English and Gaelic populations interacted, a key to early modern history that they remained Catholic and did not fully accept Anglican empire.

---

[16] Sher, 1985.   [17] I am greatly indebted here to McBride, 1998.
[18] Armitage, Ohlmeyer, Landsman, Gould and Pocock, 1999.   [19] Greene, 1986, 1990.

Publicists writing on behalf, first of the Old and then of the New English, had developed the argument that the Irish parliament was or should be subject to the English crown but not the English parliament – a contention increasingly unacceptable in England as the crown increasingly became a crown-in-parliament. It was taken up, during the 1760s and 1770s, on behalf of American colonial assemblies claiming a similar autonomy, and claiming to be representative of bodies politic which they rendered autonomous by representing them. It is a question whether this claim to autonomy and sovereignty constitutes a 'nationalism' or not; but had it been systematically developed, it would have had the effect of converting the empire into a confederation of states held together by autonomy under a single crown. It is one of the keys to 'British history' that English history rendered this impossible.[20] Not only was there an ancient tradition of regarding Ireland as a conquered realm subordinate to the English king in parliament; in order to govern themselves, and resolve the deep tensions inherent in their polity, the English had effected so close a unity between crown and parliament that it could scarcely be shared with any confederate equals. If the king were responsible to any parliament but the English (British), his unity with that parliament would be broken and the twin spectres of absolutism and rebellion would rise again. That unity, furthermore, was never free from threat. No sooner had George III been freed of the challenge from Jacobitism than he had found both aristocratic politics and enemies of aristocratic politics accusing him of delegitimizing his rule in new ways, so vehemently as to challenge his own dynastic legitimacy. The American crisis grew as part of what Edmund Burke called 'the present discontents'. In these circumstances the King was no more likely to listen to American claims to autonomy early in his reign than to Catholic claims to emancipation towards the end of it; he was insufficiently secure in his position at the apex of empire in state and church.

The imperfect legitimacy of the Hanoverian dynasty may help explain the ease with which figures as diverse as George Washington and Theobald Wolfe Tone found themselves patriots in arms against a monarchy and empire they might otherwise have served, though due weight must be allowed to an ideology of universal right to rebellion which had conservative ideologues asking how any government could persist in face of 'the rights of man'. This, however, did not simplify all problems out of existence. The Americans by 1776 were reduced to proclaiming the empire a confederation in order to proclaim that confederation dissolved by reason

---

[20] Pocock, 1988a, 1995a and 1996c .

of the crown's refusal to recognize it. This entailed proclaiming the absolute independence of thirteen states; at the same time, however, the Declaration of Independence announced the purpose of dissolving the ties which had bound 'one people' to 'another'. In a certain sense, both 'the American people' and 'the British people' are American inventions, though it remains possible that processes more complex than invention were bringing both into existence. The former, held to consist of thirteen states and one people, was by the Declaration committed to entering upon a discourse of federalism, precluded by the nature of parliamentary monarchy from forming part of a British discourse. At the same time, however, the completeness of the separation pronounced between American and British history meant that the Declaration had nothing further to say about the latter and uttered no call to revolution within it. However great the shock of American independence to British empire, the first great secession from British history left the latter's politics much as they had been before it. The second great secession, that of the Irish in the twentieth century, is a very different story.

The crisis of empire in the last quarter of the eighteenth century was the crisis of an empire in church as well as state. Since the American colonies had not been organized as subordinate kingdoms, like Ireland in one sense and post-Union Scotland in another, the crown had not been obliged to consider an establishment of religion in them, and the Anglican and even Catholic confessions – where these existed and were sometimes strong – had something of the character of sects in a multicongregational ecclesiastical polity. Though the crown had no sustained intention of erecting American bishoprics, the fear that it might do was remarkably persistent, especially after the Quebec Act of 1774 seemed to have established the Catholic church in newly conquered French Canada. If religion cannot be considered a major cause of the American Revolution, it did much to determine the character of the society that emerged from it.[21] The English-speaking United States were a model of late-Enlightened Protestant culture, unitarian, liberal and deist at one extreme, sectarian, evangelical and millennarian at another;[22] and the separation of church and state, achieved by these forces in combination, seemed to Rational Dissenters in Birmingham and New Light Presbyterians in Belfast the revolutionary fulfilment of a dream. Antitrinitarian enmity to all establishments is a recurrent if not a necessary feature of the revolutionary ferment in the British ecumene.

---

[21] Clark, 1993.   [22] [The duality persists (2004).]

If the wars of America were not wars of religion, those of Ireland notoriously have been and are of that character. The 'new British history', precisely because it views each particular history in the context afforded by some other, leans away from regarding national identities as primordial, while accepting that there are good reasons for their formation where this has successfully occurred. The history of the Irish response to the imperial crisis, the American Revolution and later the French, culminates with the United Irishmen's attempt to put together a national republicanism which, after its failure and the imposition of the Union, became the foundation of a republican nationalism; but the pluralist approach of the new British history tends to treat this story in terms of the convergences and divergences of three ethnic groups confessionally defined. The strongly Whiggish leadership of the Church of Ireland Ascendancy reacted to the ineffective government of the American war by seeking greater autonomy for their own parliament, and by organizing a national Protestant militia for the patriot purpose of demanding it; a programme natural to what we are calling settler nationalism. In proportion as they came close to achieving a confederal status unattainable by the Americans with whom they sympathized, they faced the problems generated by church ascendancy: the denial of many and various rights to those not of the Church of Ireland, first those significantly known by the English term 'Dissenters' (though they were Scottish Presbyterians, 'Covenanters' and 'Secessionists' when they dissented from their own kirk, as some but not all of them did), secondly the Catholic majority no longer distinguishable into 'Old English' and 'Gaelic', and beginning to enter into new forms of middle-class and peasant organization. There was an underlying problem of empire: was the government of Ireland by means including an established church so narrowly based that it would lead to revolutionary resistance, or could it be broadened and legitimized by measures of relief and emancipation? In England and Scotland, Enlightenment was a means of moderating and confirming established religion, but there was also an Enlightenment which attacked it at its root.

There appeared radicals within the Protestantism that was not presbyterian who aimed to break with both established religion and the executive's control of the Dublin parliament – with 'empire', therefore, in both Tudor senses of the term – and were attracted to American and later French revolutionary models. They came to propound an Enlightened republicanism which offered to include, but at the same time to assimilate, all three confessions. The parallel developments within Belfast and Ulster presbyterians appear of a special character once we begin seeing them as produced by a history peculiar to that people – as the pluralism inherent in 'British history' encourages us to do. A history Scottish but not Moderate turns first towards a revolutionary pursuit of religious and civil emancipation – as 'the Scots-Irish' among others in America are doing already – but there remains the alternative of a hard-core or Old Light Calvinism that either rebels against the state or joins in supporting it.[23] To see this as key to the journey of Northern Protestants from rebellion towards loyalism is to say that they have a history of their own, unshared with others; but it has become the aim of republican nationalism to deny them such an autonomy.

The crucial encounter at all levels is that with a re-organized, largely lay, Catholicism; and here we ourselves encounter a problem in historical demarcation. There were levels, British and Canadian as well as Irish, at which relief and recognition of Catholics could be discussed as matters of public policy and the Catholic hierarchy and laity might negotiate with the state. Here the state might be moved to reconsider its own history, as built upon a repudiation of papal sovereignty so strong as to exclude Catholics from civil society and history, condemning them as inherently disloyal to both. Enlightenment very often inherited this condemnatory attitude from Protestantism before it. The state was under strong pressures to continue a rigorous exclusion of Catholics from both state and society, resting on an established church. On the other hand, Enlightenment, the absorption of religion by civil society, might mitigate the rigours of both establishment and its opposites, Catholic and Dissenting; and in the last third of the eighteenth century, that delusive interval between the fall of the Jesuits and the Bonapartist captivity of the papacy, it was possible on both sides of the divide to believe that civil society and Catholic authority could come to terms. The Gallican strategy of separating civil sovereignty from sacramental communion was one which Enlightenment continued and with which the church might perhaps negotiate, and the Protestant empire of the Hanoverians made offers of conciliation and concession to which the hierarchy responded. There was, however, a Catholic history going on, in which such offers were sometimes embraced and sometimes rejected, and neither statesmen in the eighteenth century nor historians in the twentieth have always known that history well enough to respond to it in the ways demanded of them.

The revolutionary response to the same question, when it appeared, was not other than a more radical version of Enlightenment. The offer to divorce the state from all recognition of religion, granting equal civil rights

---

[23] For all of this see McBride, 1998, and Bradley, 2001.

to those of all confessions, carried the implication that all were equally in harmony with civil society; and Catholics, like other Christians, had to decide whether they were content with the status of civil beings with a set of beliefs peculiarly their own. It is notorious that neither hierarchy nor laity, nor both in dialogue with each other, have been of one mind in this matter, and the debate is continuing. In Irish history this meant that the programmes favoured by Wolfe Tone rested on the assumption that Irish like French Catholics would accept the status offered them by the Civil Constitution of the Clergy; it was the Enlightened, not the Catholic, view of Catholicism. In the larger pattern of British history as the history of empire, the debates leading to Union in 1801 and Emancipation in 1829 turned on how the Westminster if not the Dublin parliament was to handle relations with a Catholic majority that must somehow be modified.

At other levels, a Catholic resurgence took the form of peasant organization which was met by responses, escalating towards violence, of two kinds. The first was Protestant counter-organization at the same social levels, which in due course shaped the evolution of the Northern Presbyterians towards a loyalism previously Orange, in which they had not shared; it is of interest that the turn towards loyalism was connected with a great debate resulting in the condemnation of Arianism, though that was many years later.[24] The presence of conditions intermittently anticipatory of ethnic cleansing is a reminder that political development in Ireland had a character of its own, imperfectly controlled by the state which might either co-opt or be co-opted by it. This points to the second quasi-violent response, that of the state, which at one level develops machinery of police and espionage slower to develop in the island of Britain, where conspiracy is less endemic; but at another helps bring about the rebellions of 1798 through responding to Catholic agitation by dragonnades, that is by military repression supported by regular soldiers but carried out by sub-regular forces, militia, yeomanry and fencibles. It recurrently occurs in the nineteenth and twentieth centuries that the state in Ireland is not perfectly in command of its own military responses. This, however, is a phenomenon of the Second Age of Union, when empire is no longer being exercised in senses confined to the early modern.

If American independence – the first revolutionary outcome of the crisis of the late eighteenth century – leaves the structures of empire in church and state much as they had been before it, the Union with Ireland is revolutionary in the sense that it deeply transforms them (as the

---

[24] McBride, 1998, pp. 219–22.

Revolution of 1688–9 had begun doing a century before). The Union has certainly to be seen in the context of other transformations, brought about by war with revolutionary France and the growth of Indian and maritime empire;[25] but from the perspective adopted in this paper, it is desirable to focus on the interval between Union and Emancipation. That the former made little sense without the latter was known to Pitt and Cornwallis, but it was delayed nearly thirty years – setting afoot processes which point to the ultimate failure of the Union – due in some measure to the opposition of George III. It is a useful exercise to take the King's attitude seriously. Would he have had so much difficulty granting Emancipation if it had been unaccompanied by Union? Queen Anne had had fewer problems with her coronation oath over the Union of 1707, but that had been a union of parliaments, not of churches, which left the Church and Kingdom of England intact (since no one believed for a moment that they had disappeared). 1801 was a union of parliaments, not of administrations; but Ireland was being united with the Kingdom of England, of which it had been an appanage, and if the Church of Ireland was being more closely linked with the Church of England, Emancipation meant, as it did in 1829, a major modification of that special position of the church within the kingdom that the king was sworn to uphold.[26] In a real sense 1829 was the end of the Tudor church-state established four centuries before, the 'national apostasy' of the Oxford Tractarians; it is unhistorical to employ the language of Enlightenment to suggest that this is without significance.

The Union, then, foretells what does not happen until 1829–32: the end of 'the long eighteenth century', that *ancien régime* period in which the crown governs through the historic parliament and church, and 'empire' in the English sense of the Act in Restraint of Appeals is modified by the exercise of 'empire' meaning sovereign dominion over realms other than England. As an experiment speedily resolved and carefully planned by practical politicians too busy, as usual, to consider the meaning of what they were doing, the Union entailed Emancipation but not Reform; there was no reason to anticipate the conjunction of repeal of the Test and Corporation Acts with reconstruction of the system of parliamentary representation. Yet what came about in 1800–1 both was and was not a powerful extension of parliamentary, if no longer of ecclesiastical, empire. The Second Age of Union was one in which a post-revolutionary parliamentary state confronted, and helped engender by way of reaction against itself, a modern democratic nationalism (and, by way of reaction against

[25] Bayly, 1989.   [26] Clark, 1985, pp. 383–408; 2000, pp. 514–64.

the latter, a counter-nationalist loyalism in the distinctive history of the North). A romantic republicanism with its roots in 1798 maintained a tradition of political violence, which it succeeded in legitimating after 1916; while this was going on, however, the Union established in Ireland a parliamentarism (the parliamentarism of Parnell) more effective and deeply rooted than any achieved by the parliament of the pre-Union kingdom. Republicanism, which had to contend with the Catholic Church, had also to contend with a parliamentary style of politics; and this is one reason why the revolution of 1916–22 did not result in a fascist revolution like its Italian contemporary – as it might have done – but in a middle-class Catholic democracy. The Union was an extension of parliamentary empire which ended in revolution within that empire and independence from it (complicated by the Protestant North); but there is a history in which we continue to study 'empire' as the distribution of sovereignty shaped by forces operating within the Atlantic archipelago. At the time of writing, there are two sovereign states joining to contain the violent politics of a border province which can no longer be allowed to destabilize either of them.

PART IV

New Zealand in the Strange Multiplicity

CHAPTER 11

The neo-Britains and the three empires*

(1)

The Second Age of Union (1801–1921) was the peak period of British empire. This last phrase, however, is in need of deconstruction. Certainly, it has for many reasons been conventional to date from c. 1783 the advent of a 'Second British Empire',[1] exercised initially over Hindu and Muslim Indians where the 'First' had been exercised over colonists in America. India, however, was not a colony; its peoples lived under other forms of subjection, and the British residents in India were not colonists in the sense of settlers. In consequence, these two 'empires' differed in kind and did not form a sequence. It was predominantly after the loss of the American colonies that British statesmen began debating the altogether new problem of governing larger populations outside the archipelagic-Atlantic region, European in neither their geography nor their culture; a problem never debated before – though there are moments in the literature of empire in Ireland which in some ways anticipate it – raising the philosophical problem of whether the relations of property to liberty in western Europe were or were not unique and non-repeatable. Ireland, however, is part of the history of empire in an older sense. The debate over India, and the massive acquisitions of power in that region which produced it, stand at mid-point in the history of empire in a new sense: that is, of a process by which some European states and their economies acquired seaborne power over a preponderance of the peoples of the planet. This species of empire, which Europeans retained until late in the twentieth century and whose after-effects are still with us, is that to which the terms 'imperialism' and (more confusingly) 'colonialism' have been

---

*[Written for this volume in 2003.]

[1] Harlow, 1952, 1964; Bayly, 1989; Marshall, 1998; Winks, 1999.

and are applied; and it is currently held that the loss of empire in this sense has occasioned a 'British problem' and rendered 'British history' problematic.[2] This volume is intended as an enquiry into this thesis and as a series of attempts to provide it with a past.

Empire in this sense – the British role in the history of European world domination – has become a thesis so central in the interpretation of modern and post-modern British history that it is in need of the kind of critical examination we term deconstruction. This has been set under way by pointing out that the 'first' and 'second' British empires are discontinuous, except in so far as a global British commercial and naval power served to hold each together.[3] The problem of the colonies on the North American seaboard, it has been argued, is part of the problem of 'empire' in a Tudor and Stuart sense: the problem of how and whether the institutions of English sovereign government could be extended to include other realms, first in the Atlantic archipelago and then in the ocean contiguous with it. The colonists first demanded a closer association with the British crown, and then took the revolutionary step of independence when they found they could not have it; they ceased being 'British' when they could not be 'British' as they understood the term. This revolution took them out of British 'empire' in the pre-modern sense, but did not terminate that empire's existence; no more did the acquisition in India of 'empire' in another sense, which we choose to term 'modern'. The American crisis, and the advent in India of 'empire' over peoples not European, coincided and interacted with a series of crises in Ireland, between 1780 and 1801, which plainly belong in the history of 'empire' as we have so far been using the word: the extension to the archipelago (but after 1783 no longer beyond it) of the English state, such as to make it 'British'. The question whether this can be done is a principal, though not the only, key to 'British history' as these essays are seeking to present it.[4]

The Union of 1801 inaugurates a period, lasting till 1921, which is that of the most ambitious attempt in British history to include the archipelago in a single state; there are reasons to say that this could only have coincided with an age of 'empire' in other senses of the word. Nevertheless, we still have to do with 'empire' in the sense that had existed since the English Reformation, and the history of empire beyond Europe interacts with, but cannot annex or be included in, it. There is a narrative that relates how the

[2] Nairn, 1977; Kumar, 2003; and much ephemeral writing.   [3] Bayly, 1989.
[4] For an excellent brief introduction to the Second Union as continuous with the First, see Murdoch, 1998.

Union ultimately failed, through generating in Ireland a species of mainly Catholic nationalism which it could not contain or satisfy, so that the narrative of the Irish secession differs in kind from that of the American (to say nothing of the Indian or those which accompanied or followed it). But the former narrative visibly continues that which had existed since Tudor times at earliest: the narrative of how the Anglo-British state was created by, and how far it proved compatible with, the exercise of governance in the archipelago as a whole. The creation of a sovereign Irish republic in and after 1921 did not terminate the problem of 'empire' in this sense; it merely continued it, in the new form of how two sovereign states were to exercise empire, particularly over a disputed and self-disputing border province in the north of Ireland. Since that problem is still with us, and will at best take some time to solve, it may be said that 'empire' in its oldest sense has outlasted other 'empires' in the making of British history, and may continue it into the future. The Second Age of Union, and the age that follows it – to which these essays decline to give a name – are therefore central and not marginal to the narrative they do much to constitute.

(11)

There are two sides to the history of the Second Union. On the one hand, it appears in retrospect a high-water mark in the achievement of 'Britishness'– that is, the willingness of the diverse peoples of Britain to come together under that name and its adjectival form, as denoting a shared yet multiple identity. On the other hand, there was a signal failure to extend that commonality to Ireland, where Union – perhaps by its very success in consolidating secular identity – provoked a modern nationalism that began replacing the peasant revolts and religious warfare of the early modern era. The enormous disaster of the Famine, to which the Union state and economy had no answers, produced a powerful and global Irish diaspora in North America and the Southern Hemisphere, and furthered the decline of the over-populated peasant economy that had led to the forced emigrations and evictions continuing after the Famine. Similar phenomena on a lesser scale occurred in the highlands and islands of the north-west *Gaidhealtacht*, with the Highland Clearances and a Gaelic emigration to Canada; but the Liberal achievements of tenant rights in Ireland and in the Hebrides had very different results. In the latter, the state asserted its authority in an outlying region where landlords had come close to being a law to themselves; in Ireland, the partial resolution of the agrarian problem was precursor to a middle-class Catholic nationalism prepared to adopt both parliamentary and revolutionary tactics. There is a history of how parliamentary Home Rule was taken over by men and women who preferred a violent solution; it is a British history and a history of empire, since the proposal of Home Rule provoked a Unionist response that called in question, by intending to maintain, the structure of the Anglo-British state. Unionists in 1886 declared that Irish autonomy would mean a failure of empire in both the archipelagic and the oceanic sense; Unionists in 1912–14 were prepared to imagine and compass the dissolution of government, certainly in Ireland and perhaps in the state at large, in order to frustrate that autonomy.

Under the changed conditions following the First World War, Irish revolutionaries did much to invent and perfect the insurgency warfare, or urban terrorism, that has distinguished the world of the twentieth century and its successor; while counter-insurgency, including counter-terror, was developed by the British in reply. Liberals and Unionists, however, joined in deciding that it was better to grant autonomy than to resist it by these means, and there was no repetition of the Unionist threat to parliamentary authority so vocal in 1912–14. By an accompanying paradox, the Union had done more to establish the structure of the parliamentary state in Ireland than had been achieved when that kingdom had its own parliament; the guerrilla war of 1919–21 had been largely a war for the control of local authorities, and the civil war among revolutionaries of 1922 ended in the establishment of an Irish parliamentary authority in the Free State, often by the sternest of means. The Irish revolution was one of only two to occur in western Europe in the wake of 1914–18, but it ended in the legitimation as sovereign of a conservative Catholic democracy; while the parliamentary state of Great Britain, severely threatened with civil war by the Home Rule Bill of 1914, looked on the secession of 1921 as the departure of an alien and incomprehensible element that left its own authority unimpaired. The interactions of British and Irish history form a strange and deep-running story, and it is possible that British history, as this volume seeks to re-conceptualize it, should be built around a history of these two cultures, deeply antagonistic and altogether inseparable. There are more than two actors in this story, however, and the Protestants of Ulster, a people whose Unionism is as much Irish as British but has not been much exported in their diaspora,[5] have to be seen as embarked on a history of their own, with

---

[5] It is counterfactually fascinating to imagine the Ulster Covenant of 1912 being sent over to America and receiving mass subscriptions along the Appalachian chain and into the Deep South. The Protestant Scots-Irish would then have become a force in United States politics equal to those of the Catholic diaspora.

which both the kingdom and the republic find themselves engaged but not identified.

The Treaty of 1921 marked the end of Unionism, in the sense of a party, powerful in British mass politics, professing the belief that the maintenance of the union with Ireland was essential to the future of empire in both the early modern sense (the unity of the kingdom) and the modern (empire in the oceanic world). Though this belief may conceivably have been true – it has its adherents today, most of whom welcome rather than deplore its fulfilment – it ceased to be, if it ever had been, one of the creeds on which British electoral politics were founded; a circumstance which casts doubts on the thesis that British identity exists only in consequence of empire over others. Like the Americans of 1776–83, the Irish of 1921 were – and when had they not been? – looked upon as an alien people, who if they could not be assimilated might be let go without altering the character of the realm to which they did not belong. This returns us to the thesis that the period of the Second Union was a peak period in the attainment of Britishness, defined as the willingness of the peoples of the larger island to accept a common identity without abandoning their several identities as English, Scots or Welsh (a people of whom too little has been said in these essays). The character of 'Britishness' is changing, and its future is much called in doubt by those of whom some seem to welcome the thought of its end. It is therefore important to consider what made it effective, though we must avoid the historiographical fallacy that to study the origins of a phenomenon is to foretell its end.

We know already that Britishness was and is a complex phenomenon: 'a union of multiple identities'.[6] It clearly did not depend upon the Union of 1801; the proposition that the English or the British could only exist in their own eyes if they succeeded in governing the Irish was absurd in all ages, and we face yet again the problem that the English did not trouble to distinguish between 'England' and 'Britain', thus denying themselves any national 'identity' separable from the Anglo-British state that had emerged from their history. The relative success of Britishness in the period we are studying was therefore a matter of the willingness of Scots and Welsh to consider themselves 'British' in an order shaped by the English, who did not distinguish themselves from it; it is a question how far this impeded an English willingness to consider Scots and Welsh their co-Britons rather than their provincials. Two forces are commonly identified as causes for the relative success of Britishness: industrialism and imperialism. The former

---

[6] Brockliss and Eastwood, 1997.

created new population centres in all four nations: south Wales, north England, south Scotland and north Ireland; these encouraged some internal migrations of working populations, and set up a 'Britain-wide' politics of capital and labour, in which class counted for more than nationality without abolishing it. Industrialism, while provoking fierce social antagonisms, endowed state and society with power, projected both into Europe and into the structure of global domination we know as 'empire' and 'imperialism'. Empire in this sense was a democratic phenomenon; it set up images of identity and power to which peoples might commit themselves, and enterprises in which they might be engaged. That the British empire in India was in significant measure a Scottish enterprise has become a historical commonplace, even among those who depict it as a record of crimes and follies.

It is therefore possible to say that the 'British' peoples were held together in a common identity afforded them by a 'British' state and nationality, only so long as they remained partners in an imperial enterprise capable of projecting power upon Europe and the world. This enables theorists to pass easily and rapidly from saying that the British – and as a consequence the English – could exist and believe in themselves only so long as they had Others to fear as enemies, to saying that this was possible only so long as they had Others to rule as their subjects: a set of conclusions satisfactory to a mindset emerging as the enemy of 'identity' in any form that can be attributed to it. The enterprise of these essays and this volume is to enquire whether more can be found in the histories of these peoples, several and interactive, that may inform them who they are and what they have done and suffered; history that may continue into a future which, whatever its political form, may entail political decision and political being. The coincident failures of imperialism, socialism and industrialism, which befell the British peoples in the second half of the twentieth century, were a major crisis in their complex and problematic histories; it is worth enquiring what history preceded these failures and may continue after them. There are those who do not wish these questions to be asked, or think their answers already known.

In considering the Second Age of Union, we have so far been led to use the term 'empire' in two senses: the one archipelagic and pre-modern in its derivation, the other extra-European and constitutive of modernity. There are two other dimensions to the history of this period. One, which there is a strong case for considering paramount, is the history of Britain as a European state and community; meaning, among other things, as a European 'Power', engaged in the conflicts (and, it will also be said, sharing the culture) of a number of other states increasingly industrial and imperial. The wars of Europe, enlarged into world wars in the twentieth century, end in the exhaustion by these states, including Britain, of their capacity for independent power and empire, and their joining in a post-imperial and post-sovereign association, to which the word 'Europe' becomes annexed, in the hope of exercising new forms of power, possibly post-political and even post-historical; so that to continue writing history may itself be a challenge to the premises of the 'European' order. The writing of these essays, certainly, originated and has continued as a response, both British and antipodean, to the processes in which this post-modern order took shape and declared its premises; and for this reason it is now necessary to return to the Second Age of Union and consider the origins of the antipodean perspective in the history of a third species of empire, which is part of the title of this chapter.

(III)

In the late eighteenth century, continuing through the nineteenth, the rate of emigration from (as well as within) Britain and Ireland began, for reasons of demographic, agrarian and industrial change, to be massive. The Scots-Irish, famine-Irish and Highland-clearances diasporas were part of this phenomenon, but a more prominent role was played by the emigration of labourers, artisans and (not to be forgotten) middle-class shopkeepers, speculators and professionals, from England, Scotland and (to a rather lesser degree) Wales. Of these million or more people, most went to the United States, where (Irish-Americans excepted) they were absorbed without becoming hyphenated – a comment on the new nation's cultural character in that century. Others, however, founded colonies in the proper sense of the term, which the discourse of 'colonialism' tends to obscure: that is, colonies of settlement, capable like the American of becoming national states but spared the necessity of revolution in doing so. They are here termed 'neo-Britains', a word of recent New Zealand coinage, but rooted in a tradition of rhetoric as old as they are, indicating not only that they were (and are) British (and Irish) by heritage, but that some of them deliberately attempted the duplication of British nationality, politics and social structure under conditions of settlement. They consequently belong (or have belonged) in the context of 'British history', and will continue to do so even if they leave it. The historiographic enterprise conveyed in this volume of essays was originally proposed in one of them, the New Zealand of the 1970s, and it is worthwhile sketching their history down to that moment.

The colonies of settlement belong in a context of nineteenth-century empire, but were not situated in 'empire' in either of the senses developed in these essays so far. That is to say, they were not situated, as the American colonies had been until their association broke down, within the 'empire' of England over itself and its archipelagic and Atlantic extensions. Nor – with South Africa as the exception – were they more than tangentially concerned with the problem of 'empire' over non-European peoples. New Zealand indeed raised, and caused British ministers to debate with concern, the question of Maori sovereignty, which was never disregarded however it was mishandled. In both this and the Australian colonies, however, politics and history came to be a matter of relations within civil societies of settlers. They were the product of the generations immediately following the American secession, and they did not intend either an American or an Irish trajectory. To escape such dilemmas, indeed, policy-makers were prepared to accept the thought that these colonies would soon, and might painlessly, become independent. To that extent, they were not perceived as necessary to 'empire' in either the old or the new sense, and in what ways they form part of the history of 'imperialism' or 'colonialism' needs to be carefully stated; perhaps they do not belong under these headings, or perhaps they change their meaning. Certainly, their foundation, even their conception, was possible only in consequence of the global extension of British naval and commercial power; but in the southern hemisphere – with Cape Town as a partial exception – they were not strategically necessary to either; in particular, not to the control of India or the China trade, from which the concept of 'empire' was deriving its new meaning. It was always possible to think of the neo-Britains as superfluous to empire, and their retention within it obliges us to give it a third set of meanings; hence the title of this chapter.

There were classically four neo-Britains, later known as the 'dominions' forming the 'Commonwealth' (the latter either a sub-species of empire, or not part of it, depending on the use of the noun). Of these 'Canada' is a special case, since its European settlement originates in the early seventeenth century and its eastern structure is a product of the French and American wars of the eighteenth. No less a product of the American secession than is the United States, it is situated within the North American history into which streams of British emigration flowed, and to enclose it with other Dominions within 'Commonwealth history' is to tell only a part of its story. That story may share in that of westward-expanding settlement of the North American continent; though the founders of Victoria and Vancouver in British Columbia came by sea, like those of New South Wales and New Zealand. The three remaining were and are situated in the southern hemisphere, connected by the southern ocean which linked the Capes before the Canals were dug. Of them one group of British settlements in the Cape Colony and Natal belongs within the complex history – British, Afrikaner, Xhosa, Zulu – of 'South Africa'. It is perhaps the only case where colonies of settlement, by the mere fact of their existence, involved the imperial government in major wars – though it was long feared that the Canadian colonies might do so – and perhaps for this reason, the self-governing colonies of South Africa did not achieve much autonomy in determining whether there should be war or not; Cecil Rhodes was only an apparent exception. Confronted by an African majority and an independent Afrikanerdom, the English South Africans did not become a nation in their own right; and the presence of Bantu and other labouring populations meant that they did not develop a settler working class as the Pacific Dominions did. Since they were engaged in the subjugation of a non-European population which outnumbered them, they took part in the history we term that of 'colonialism'; but in the history of 'colonization' this circumstance sets them apart from others.

The settlements in western Australia, eastern Australia and New Zealand – situated at complex junctures of oceans which, especially in the last case, did as much to separate as to connect – were met by indigenous populations whose land they needed more than they did their labour. They therefore engaged in expropriation rather than domination, and were more inclined to ignore, even to forget and deny, the indigenous presence than to become obsessed by it. The profound differences between the Maori and Aboriginal societies and their responses to colonization gives New Zealand history a character unlike Australian; in New Zealand there are wars, but no genocide, in Australia no wars but micro-genocides in some number. But the two are deeply alike, and at times hard to distinguish, in that they are from an early date marked by the presence of a settler, 'white', working class, whose relations with other classes make both Australian and New Zealand politics for a long time a politics of labour and capital. They develop increasingly sovereign parliamentary governments within which these conflicts are fought out, and it is this, among other things, which makes them nations writing histories of their own. These are, however, British histories in the sense that nearly all their determinants (including the Irish presence) are the product of British expansion, and this is why these national cultures must be considered part of 'British history' and empowered to engage in its interpretation.

During the classic period of their existence as Dominions – a term invented in Canada to denote the status of a realm of the crown, very close to 'empire' in the Tudor sense – the neo-Britains believed very deeply in something called 'the British Empire'. By this they did not primarily mean – even if they should have – domination over large non-European populations, in which they were more indirectly than directly involved. As 'colonists' they had little to do with 'colonialism', and indeed that term had yet to be invented. When they thought of 'the British Empire', they had in mind an association or partnership between Britain and the neo-Britains, held together by a common culture and loyalties – here the Irish were to be heard from, and Québecois and Afrikaner dissent was more vocal still – and by the material ties symbolized in New Zealand retrospect by the image of the 'protein bridge',[7] the ocean shipping routes along which their agrarian and pastoral produce was conveyed to British markets. This global system was protected by British naval power, and Dominion expeditionary forces took part in wars for its maintenance and protection. That these wars were European as well as imperial was understood, perhaps insufficiently but not in ways entailing any lack of self-awareness; the Dominions knew who they were and how they fitted into the system. Until 1941 and in some ways after, threats to this system were European and did not originate on the other face of the planet.

It can be argued that historiography has not yet caught up with this state of affairs. There is a field called 'history of the British Empire', in which the neo-Britains appear parenthetically, as anomalous exceptions – and so they are – to the generalizations governing British relations with its otherwise non-European empire. There is another, at first sight closer to their concerns, called 'Commonwealth history', situated within the history of empire but not assimilated to it.[8] This is the history of the formal and political association between the neo-Britains and Britain, and it enters upon questions which belong to the field of British history. Much of it is Whig history, that of the growth of the neo-Britains towards parliamentary self-government, reaching a point at which the crown is incorporate with each of its parliaments severally (the solution impossible in the 1770s), and the empire (in the sense appropriate to this association) is once more a multiple monarchy, held together by consensus among its members and the powerful material and cultural forces supporting that consensus. What is usually lacking, however, in the literature of 'Commonwealth history' is the national history which each neo-Britain has constructed and is living

---

[7] Belich, 2001.   [8] Classically Mansergh, 1969; there is a vast bibliography.

and recounting for itself. This is not imperial history in the sense that it is concerned with the rule of subject majorities – South Africa is the exception – though it may deal with the presence of unassimilated peoples, Québecois or Maori (Afrikaners were a more complex case). But the history of a neo-Britain is by definition the history of relations among a people of settlers, entitled to be concerned with themselves and their own divisions and resolutions. Each is therefore a 'national' history, told to itself by a people engaged in forming itself within the history it seeks to tell, and not much communicated to others. Canadians, Australians and New Zealanders do not know each other's history,[9] and the British do not seek to know theirs; there are good (as well as bad) reasons why they need to know the history of Britain, which the present enterprise seeks to enlarge into British history.

There are, as a further consequence, a number of histories to be written – forming a field larger than 'Commonwealth history' in the formal sense – of how these several 'national' histories have interacted with the several histories of empire. In these a central reality – especially in the first half of the twentieth century – has been the myth of the Commonwealth; it was what the neo-Britains had in mind when they spoke of 'the British Empire', and it was the dissolution of this connection, revealing the extent to which it had been a myth, that they experienced under the name of 'Europe'. The myth, and its reality, were founded on the idea of consensus, pressed to the point where it was held to entail no need of a formal structure of decision, federal or imperial; the parties were assumed to understand the nature of their association, and this was fundamental to the idea of nationality as the neo-Britains developed it. They were nations because they were equal partners. The 'empire' they formed was therefore conceived as an 'empire of liberty' – to borrow a phrase from Thomas Jefferson – and belonged within the interactions of *imperium* and *libertas* which offer a key to Western political thought.

Two sets of considerations perturbed the neo-British roles in this association and its ideology. One was the continuing cultural dependence which attended the relationship with historic Britain; it was easier to imagine themselves as British than as formed by histories of their own. This gave rise to a sense of being 'colonial', though they had done the

---

[9] I have been told of a Canadian university press which declined a suggestion that it join in distributing Sharp and McHugh, 2001, on the grounds that the book was not about Commonwealth history but about New Zealand, and therefore of no interest to Canadians. It is a history of treaties between the crown and an indigenous people, which could be fruitfully compared with the Canadian experience.

colonizing themselves and no authoritarian structure but their own was imposing 'colonialism' upon them; a verbal confusion, which may be a category mistake, is visible here. When a New Zealand poet, at the height (or depth) of the Depression, wrote of his own culture as 'white shoots under the wet sack of Empire',[10] he was talking of its dominance by a system of global capitalism then in crisis, which prevented it from imagining or making itself; but this did not equate the colonial experience with that imposed upon non-European peoples. The culture that dominated them was one they had brought themselves, and it was from themselves that they needed emancipation.

It is here that one must seek the history of their consciousness: the tensions between the self transplanted and the self generated, voyage and settlement, *waka* and *whenua*. A neglected poet from Rangiora, in Canterbury, writing a century ago, knew that this tension must become a source of vitality and a kind of joy.

> Here's to the home that was never, never ours!
> Toast it full and fair when the winter lowers.
> Speak ye low, my merry men, sitting at your ease,
> Hearken to the homeless drift in the roaring seas! . . .
>
> . . . Here's to the selves we shall never, never be!
> We're the drift of the world and the tangle of the sea.
> It's far beyond the Pleiad and out beyond the sun
> That the rootless shall be rooted when the wander-year is done.[11]

(IV)

The second set of perturbations – so enormous in its human and material costs that it is difficult to bracket it with those just mentioned – arose from Dominion participation in the wars of the twentieth century. The empire of consensus meant that this participation was more voluntary than obligatory, and it enjoyed very massive emotional support because it was perceived as a way of attaining nationality within a free association. The South African war of 1899–1902 was perhaps the only war fought by Britain and the neo-Britains as an independent partnership; it was fought for

---

[10] A. R. D. Fairburn (1904–57), 'Dominion' (Fairburn, 1938, 1966; repr. Bornholdt, O'Brien and Williams, 1997, p. 431).
[11] First and last verses of 'Song of the Drift', by Jessie Mackay (1864–1938); see Mackay, 1909, p. 82. My thanks to Bruce Harding for finding this reference.

reasons intelligible in 'Commonwealth' terms, and marked the momentary height of belief that this partnership of nations might constitute an 'Empire' acting as a single world power. In the continuing presence of Afrikaners and Africans, however, it was of limited success, and did not result in the reconstitution of South Africa as a neo-Britain. The two World Wars which followed were in this perspective, down to 1942, European wars, in which the Dominions took part – Canada to maintain empire in the North Atlantic, Australia and New Zealand to maintain the empire of the 'protein bridges' – when the threat to the imperial system was perceived as European. A Britain defeated by German power, expelled from Europe or invaded and occupied by it, would be unable to maintain this system; but the emotions driving the neo-Britains to sustain the very heavy casualties of these wars were visceral and part of themselves. The connection with crown and empire, Europe and North America, constituted the world as they understood it, and while such a system could still maintain itself, there was nothing false about their consciousness of it.

This world and world-vision lasted at least until 1942–5, when Britain, rapidly using up its resources in face of the German conquest of Europe, was revealed capable of only a secondary role in face of a Japanese assault in south-east Asia and the western Pacific, and suffered huge losses of empire in consequence. It was to this that John Curtin referred when he told Australians that they were now protected by the navy of the United States;[12] why this is seen as a stirring call to national independence is less evident. The New Zealand decision to remain committed to the war in the Mediterranean was taken in the same context; the protection of New Zealand and the war against Japan depended on the survival of the American aircraft-carriers, but in the long run it was evident that the United States was capable of a war in two hemispheres – as the British Commonwealth and Empire was not – and the New Zealand decision was consonant with the American decision to give priority to the defeat of the Third Reich. And, as pointed out earlier, Nazism, and Communism afterwards, were horrors arising within their own civilization and history; whereas, even after the Japanese have ceased to be incomprehensible aliens, nobody is likely to devise a history of Asia and the Pacific which will both include the episode of Japanese military empire and instruct the southern neo-Britains as to what they are and have been.

On the level of reflective generalization on which this essay is being written, it is hard to account for the persistent implication that the

---

[12] Above, pp. 17–18.

Australian decision to move from the European war to the defence of Australia's northern approaches – obviously necessary as it was – is to be applauded as less 'colonial' than the contrasting decision by New Zealand. James Belich, the brilliantly thoughtful New Zealand historian who has developed the concept of a 'neo-Britain' to the level of an organizing category, has described the era of the 'protein bridge' – also a term of his coining – as one of 'recolonization', and the strategic decision of 1942 as the product of a 'recolonial' mentality.[13] But if it can be presented as a deliberate decision it was not an instance of false consciousness, and this may lead to some questioning of Belich's concept of 'recolonization'. He seems to imply that the intensified relation between New Zealand pasturage and the United Kingdom market – brought about by the invention of refrigerated shipping and the British demand for a meat-and-butter diet – which certainly involved New Zealand in an economy from which it was hard to break away, was a relationship of prolonged, even renewed, dependence, psychological as well as economic and strategic; hence the 'recolonial mentality'. To the present writer, a survivor of the generation of 1942, it is a matter of memory that the mentality of the period was ceasing to be 'colonial' – a word we used as one of opprobrium – and that we were increasing our capacity to inhabit our own history, British history and the history of the Second World War – all of which we knew to be problematic – as adults and equals. The myth of the Commonwealth and Empire was a myth of equality; it was gravely flawed and has not endured; but it was not ineffective, and is not to be read simply as masking a continued colonial dependency. When one encounters – as one still does – the barely hidden assumption that any relationship with the metropolis must be a relationship of subordination, one is in the presence of the colonial mentality in continuing form; it is being implied that this is a relationship New Zealanders cannot conduct for themselves, but must escape and deny. The essays in this volume offer one way of affirming this implication to be false.

(v)

To question the thesis of 'recolonization' is also to question that of 'decolonization', used (as it regularly is) to describe the ideological experience of New Zealanders since the end of the Second British Empire. Since they were colonists, they were not colonized; since they brought British culture and its history with them and imposed it on themselves, their need

[13] Belich, 2001, pp. 283–87.

to modify and rewrite it is not to be identified with the experience of post-colonial élites neither British nor European, on whom it was imposed by the imperial policies to which the name of 'colonialism' has so imprecisely been given. It is the argument of this and a preceding chapter that the relationship between Britain and the neo-Britains was one which implied a certain equality in sovereignty, allowing the latter to conceptualize and continue British history in ways of their own. There is no escaping the need to find ways of doing this after the partnership has been dissolved; but the British withdrawal from the Commonwealth species of Empire has been a withdrawal not from hegemony, but from equality. The British withdrew; the Dominions did not escape; what was refused them was the practice of a known relationship, and the ascent, where this was incomplete, towards the capacity to practise it. Allen Curnow, writing comic verse under the persona of 'Whim Wham', expressed this in a song for British entry into the Common Market.[14]

> When we were a little tiny colony of Britain,
>   With a heigh-ho, the winds and the waves,
> Our feckless history began to be written,
>   And the waves break busily night and day.
>
> When first we fought in an Empire's cause,
>   With a heigh-ho, the winds and the waves,
> It wasn't for the loot, nor yet for the applause,
>   And the waves break busily night and day.
>
> Then when we came to Dominion Status,
>   With a heigh-ho, the winds and the waves,
> Nor slump nor squeeze could alienate us,
>   And the waves break busily night and day . . .
>
> Sir, have you thought what it's like to be,
>   With a heigh-ho, the winds and the waves,
> All, all alone on a wide, wide sea?
>   And the waves break busily night and day.
>
> Much can happen in a very short time,
>   With a heigh-ho, the winds and the waves,
> A feckless history, a foolish rhyme!
>   And the waves break busily night and day.

---

[14] 'Take Your Time, History!' ([Curnow], 1967). Two verses omitted.

What these verses reflect is the thing foretold and not foretold in an earlier poem of Curnow's:

> whatever islands may be,
> Over and under the sea,
> It is something different, something
> Nobody counted on.[15]

Nobody had counted on the ideology of 'Europe', now requiring the British to declare that the history they had inhabited was not the history in which they had led the neo-British to believe, but one in which the latter had no place; so that their history, if they had one, explained neither the history of Britain nor that of Europe, and was more than questionable as an explanation of their own. Nor was it at all clear that 'Europe' possessed a history in the sense in which that word had hitherto been used; since it had had a good deal to do – there was a case for saying that it had had too much to do – with the history of states, made by states through the exercise of their sovereignty; and now 'Europe' appeared to intend the abandonment (in some measure) by states of their sovereignty, their separate identities, and their ability to make histories for (and of) themselves. On further enquiry, it appeared to stand for globalization; that is, for a state of affairs in which the conditions of human existence were manufactured only by markets, and over which the conscious decisions of human beings in political associations had neither power nor authority. This might mean that the markets had no need of historical narratives sustained over time, but only of constantly shifting images of commodification and obsolescence. It was no accident – to use the old Marxist language – that there should appear ideologies of the sort called post-modernist, in which there is no reality, but only language, and nothing can happen because it is only invented; an exaggeration, of course, but the kind of exaggeration we have to live with.

Post-imperial (not to say post-political) history, both as lived and as written, has an authentically post-modern flavour; it has been a time of the breaking, making and re-assembling of sovereignties and the histories and identities that accompany them, in combination with a globalization that knows no frontiers and seems controlled by few or no agents, and an information explosion that leaves it doubtful whether we are being

---

[15] Curnow, 'The Unhistoric Story' (1941; 1997, p. 235). The last two lines form a refrain to each verse of the poem.

informed of anything beyond information. In these circumstances, to write history at all – and in particular, histories of relatively stable identities changing and interacting over long periods of time – is a challenge to the *Zeitgeist*, whose political claims must be frankly stated and evaluated. To write British history, especially from a neo-British standpoint, is to claim that it can be done: to claim to possess and act in it; to say that the men of Israel have an inheritance in David the king, at a time when the men of Belial are blowing their trumpets everywhere and Israel has dispersed to its tents, or in search of them. It is to instruct those islanded in time that what comes over the sea invariably brings something nobody counted on, and that exposure to history as ironic narrative makes the self snap open, all eyes wary and alert to what it may unconventionally be. It aims to inform the British peoples that they have unusually complex histories to live in, that a global culture may not deliver them from having to live in these histories, and that they cannot use the word 'Europe' as a means of pretending that these do not exist. It informs – or it should inform – Europeans (who ought to know this already) that they too live in complex histories, and will have to write even more complex histories of 'Europe' each time they wish to include new peoples in their association. It is concerned with imagination and judgement as means to action.

Some of these matters will be further explored in a concluding section. New Zealand, where these essays began to be written, may be said – as in the title of this section – to experience the post-imperial and post-modern condition as the *Strange Multiplicity* chosen by the Canadian philosopher and historian James Tully as the title – significantly – of his Seeley Lectures at Cambridge in 1993.[16] Tully was concerned with the bewildering variety of cultures claiming sovereignty, in order to establish identity, in the post-imperial world, and the corresponding diversity of meanings the word 'sovereignty' must consequently assume. It followed that it must be increasingly difficult for individuals in that world to live under a single sovereignty or assume a single identity; and he chose to illustrate his published lectures the great sculpture of the Haida Gwaai, by the First Nation Canadian Bill Reid. This consists of a *waka* or canoe, crewed entirely by shape-changers and captained – if that is the word – by the towering figure of a shaman, the *kilstlaai*.[17] To the present writer's eye, the question arises whether this figure is that of Leviathan, making decisions

---

[16] Tully, 1995.
[17] Tully, 1995, p. xvii. Originals of this sculpture may be seen at the Canadian Embassy in Washington, DC, and the Vancouver International Airport, Vancouver, BC.

that arrest or alter the flow of change, or whether he is simply the vehicle through which changes flow and effect themselves. The question – no doubt an answerable one – presented itself because Reid and Tully were western Canadians, and Tully sees Canada as a texture of sovereignties, British, French and First Nation, relations between which must remain fluid and historical. The First Nations therefore negotiate a number of treaties with a number of treaty partners. New Zealand, by comparison, a unitary state rather than a federation, has redefined its sovereignty as an ongoing debate over the treaty, between the *tangata whenua* and the Crown, by which that sovereignty was established. The relations between sovereignty and history are therefore different here, and give rise to histories differently written from those to be found or expected in the Canadian case, or perhaps in James Tully's philosophy.

These are narratives of sovereignty, and I have chosen throughout these essays to make sovereignty, *imperium* and 'empire' keys to the diversity of British history, and history itself a product of the political associations which have possessed sovereignty enough to make it. There are many ways of conceiving history, and all should enjoy parity of esteem; I choose this one because it is under threat and there are ways of being that are threatened with it. In the essays making up this section, I try to show how New Zealand history may be written into the context of the kinds of history I know how to write. One shows how Enlightenment history could be and was extended into the nineteenth-century Pacific; the other pursues the politics of sovereignty in the setting indicated by Tully.

CHAPTER 12

Tangata whenua *and*
Enlightenment anthropology

In the ninth chapter of the *Decline and Fall of the Roman Empire*, and the volume published in 1776, Edward Gibbon wrote about the condition of the German forest peoples as they had been described by Tacitus and as they perhaps were two centuries later, when they began invading and settling in the Roman provinces. He employed language and a concept which are not what we mean when we use the term *tangata whenua*,[1] but nevertheless tells us something about a literal meaning which the phrase could bear and the processes by which it has acquired the quite different meanings which it has for us.

There is not anywhere upon the globe a large tract of country which we have discovered destitute of inhabitants, or whose first population can be fixed with any degree of historical certainty. And yet, as the most philosophic minds can seldom refrain from investigating the infancy of great nations, our curiosity consumes itself in toilsome and disappointed efforts. When Tacitus considered the purity of the German blood, and the forbidding aspect of the country, he was disposed to pronounce those barbarians *Indigenae*, or natives of the soil. We may allow with safety, and perhaps with truth, that ancient Germany was not originally peopled by any foreign colonies already formed into a political society; but that the name and nation received their existence from the gradual union of some wandering savages of the Hercynian woods. To assert those savages to have been the spontaneous production of the earth which they inhabited would be a rash inference, condemned by religion and unwarranted by reason.[2]

In the last sentence Gibbon was of course dismissing the idea that any human group could have been spontaneously generated by seeds of life

---

[1] Pocock, 1992b, 2001a; originally delivered to the New Zealand Historical Association, Christchurch, 1991. [Some of its arguments have been valuably refined and developed by Hickford, 1999, and Moloney, 2001. The reader is reminded that Maori words are not usually italicized in New Zealand typography, and that 'tangata whenua' initially bears the meaning of 'people of the land', or 'birth-place'; above, p. 5, n. 6.]

[2] Edward Gibbon, *The History of the Decline and Fall of the Roman Empire*, vol. 1, ch. 9; Womersley, 1994, vol. 1, p. 233.

latent in the earth of the area which they subsequently populated; that they could have been *indigenae, autochthonoi*, earthborn, *gigantes* or giants. Spontaneous generation was an ancient rather than a modern idea, and Gibbon had modern reasons for repudiating it; these reasons were, however, complicated and problematic. Before I consider them, it is desirable to make a philological point. To use the term *tangata whenua* does not commit us to an affirmation of autochthony, which would indeed be ridiculous in the context of an island group in the deep south-west of the Pacific Ocean; but it does, as most sympathetic readers have believed, affirm something important by way of the plurality of meanings conveyed by the word *whenua*, which is understood to mean both land and *placenta*, thus making the land a birthplace and a source of identity. By setting up this verbal association of land and birth, we proceed to say that the term *tangata whenua* does not entail the literal statement that the *tangata* are *autochthonoi* or *gigantes*, but rests upon a metaphor: that is, a poetic, rhetorical or dramatic statement that there exists a close and rich relationship between the meanings of land and birth, and that there can exist between a people and its land a similarly rich relationship, which can serve as a basis for a claim of right. The richness and the relationship are discovered by exploring the ways in which the metaphor operates in language or discourse; but there exists also a politics of language, by some of the norms prevalent in which we are entitled to say that a metaphor is itself entitled to be respected but not to be privileged – that is, that there are boundaries to its authority. The politics really begin once we attempt to establish what these boundaries are, and who has authority to determine them.

This question cannot be absent from our minds while I explore the language context in which Gibbon wrote the paragraph I have quoted, language in which eighteenth-century Europeans discussed the relations between the formation of human groups and the land which they occupied. Why did Gibbon find it necessary to affirm that the German forest dwellers were not *indigenae*, not *tangata whenua* in the literal sense, that they were not physically or biologically generated out of the soil which they were found occupying? The notion of autochthony was Greek or Roman, a blend of mythology and Epicurean naturalism, and he did not need to repudiate it as a belief widely held in his own time. He did need to consider it, however, because, like other Greco-Roman ideas caught up in Peter Gay's 'rebirth of modern paganism', it had become prominent as a possible but unacceptable alternative in the wake of repudiation of a Judeo-Christian paradigm which had hitherto been used to explain the history of the human race. The paradigm repudiated was of course that of the

Mosaic chronology and the Noachic genealogy; but it is important to realize that though it had been repudiated, it had not yet been replaced, so that the philosopher was in danger of adopting other hypotheses, such as that of autochthony, which were equally unsound.

The repudiated paradigm affirmed the descent of the human race from a single human pair; less Adam and Eve, in this case, than Noah and his wife, who with their progeny had survived the universal deluge. In this part of Gibbon's chapter on the Germans he is engaged in deriding and dismissing the mainly Renaissance genealogies which elaborately traced the ancestors of existing people back to the sons of Noah and divided the human race into a Hamitic, Semitic or Japhetic *iwi* ('tribe') and *waka* (literally 'canoe', 'ship'; lineage tracing descent from a given canoe). It is possible to make this paradigm sound ridiculous, and it is an interesting comment on our culture that we still feel some conventional obligation to do so; needless to say, the historian is not concerned to show that belief systems are ridiculous, but to discover why they were not ridiculous once. The Noachic paradigm had had certain characteristics. It had made the human race a genetic unity, descended from an original human pair. It had precluded as un-Christian the possibility of autochthony, the notion that separate human groups might have been independently generated by the workings of local biophysical conditions. With its repudiation such notions might recur; but autochthony, said Gibbon, was a concept 'condemned by religion and unwarranted by reason'. Did it follow that the *philosophes* were intent on maintaining the unity of the human race? Gibbon does not enter upon the question, but on the one hand it is easy to see from his text that he wished to adopt the perspective of Buffon – whom he greatly admired – and consider the human race as one among the many animal species populating the planet.[3] How these species had originated and how they had come to be distributed were questions to be asked. On the other hand, Gibbon was certainly aware of the writings of Voltaire, who in the *Essai sur les Mœurs* had effected a decisive repudiation of the Noachic genealogies, and had proceeded instantly to suggest that the human species was genetically differentiated into sub-species: that the Lapps were a different kind of human animal from their Scandinavian neighbours, that the sensory organs of Chinese were differently formed from those of Europeans, and that their cultural and even intellectual capacities were different in consequence. Gibbon was not immune from this kind of thinking, predictably enough when writing about sub-Saharan Africans;

---

[3] This is a starting point for some of the themes explored in Pocock, 2005 (B).

it was much easier in his and many previous generations to be anti-Hamitic than anti-Semitic, though he continued to despise Jews even after abandoning Christian anti-Judaism. But he mistrusted Voltaire on nearly every subject, and much admired Joseph de Guignes, whose great history of Eurasian nomadism Voltaire had so incessantly derided. De Guignes had seen his *Histoire des Huns, Turcs et Mogols* (1756–8) as uniting Roman, Islamic and Chinese history in a single narrative and so as restoring human history to the unity which Voltaire had sought to destroy. To this end, de Guignes was prepared to uphold the Noachic paradigm and insist that the Chinese were a Hamitic people, an offshoot of Egyptian civilization rather than a stock emigrating direct from the plains of Shinar after the fall of the Tower of Babel. The minor problem of autochthony was now caught up in a larger subject: how to write human history on post-biblical assumptions. It is clear by now, however, that if the history of the human race were to be traced from a single point of origin, whether the Garden of Eden or the Olduvai Gorge, it must be a history of diffusion and migration, in which the concept of a *tangata whenua* must have the status of a metaphor. It is the prehistory of that metaphor which next requires to be studied, and doing so will enable us to understand it much better than will concentration on the rather barren concept of autochthony.

Biblical history supplied a moment from which the history of human diffusion could begin: not so much the departure from the Ark as the dispersion of the peoples from Shinar, following the confusion of tongues at the fall of the tower erected by Nimrod grandson of Ham. This was a third Fall of Man, preceded by the Deluge and the Expulsion from the Garden. Dante depicted Nimrod as a Titan, one of the giants in the earth in those days; and his progeny, divided less by pedigree than by language, wandered away to begin the repeopling of the earth. It was to be their vagrant and migratory history of which Enlightened anthropology (even in its post-biblical form) chose to make most, but their function in the Mosaic scheme was as background to the distinction between the seed of Abraham, Isaac and Jacob, whom the Lord chose to make his people by covenant, and the rest of mankind, the Gentiles, who lived by reason and nature alone. Sacred and natural history were now clearly differentiated, but it was the former which was authoritatively written; as the annals and genealogies of Babylon, Chaldea, Greece and Rome became known – those of Egypt remaining buried in hieroglyphic and hermetic – they were integrated with the biblical narrative in the great Renaissance science of chronology. Voltaire's *Essai* is the major blow struck at this system;[4] he moved the Chinese chronology centre stage to displace that of Moses, after which he had no further need of the Chinese and dismissed them as a biologically alien race. There existed already an alternative scheme for writing the natural history of the Gentiles, one not so much incompatible with Mosaic history as structurally discontinuous with it: that supplied by natural jurisprudence. We move now out of the biblical paradigm into that in which the natural history of society is written as part of the search for its natural law, and the history of any particular society becomes the history of its jurisprudence, its land tenure and its property.

Any nervous agnostics who may be lingering among us may be glad to know that I am getting out of sacred history and the Book of Genesis, and into the strictly secular, theoretical and eventless history of the state of nature and the origins of civil government. Yet the two have some important features in common. In the early seventeenth century, western European theorists of natural law were turning towards theories of natural right,[5] and to that end were constructing the concept of a state of nature, a primeval condition of human existence in which individuals were depicted as without rights, without mechanisms of distributive justice, and without civil government. This condition was individualist and anarchic; solitary humans were imagined moving in an environment defined as the earth's surface as yet unappropriated – as the wanderers from Shinar might have found it in the age following the universal flood – with the effect that the individual preceded property, and any system of institutionalized values must be the effect and consequence of appropriation. From appropriation followed property, from property rights, and from rights government. Appropriation could only be carried out by the solitary individuals (and their nuclear families), imagined roaming in the state of nature; yet the more carefully the individual was defined in terms of his property, his rights and his appropriation, the more clearly it followed that the individual who had not yet appropriated was not yet fully an individual or fully human. We reach the point of origin from which developed all the ideologies which presented various *tangata whenua* as less than human, because their manner of living in the earth did not conform to the extremely individualistic west European model of appropriation from a state of nature.

This is the paradigm of possessive individualism, which I suggest we should not be too hasty to associate with early phases of the development

---

[4] Pocock, 1999, vol. II, ch. 7 (B).   [5] Tuck, 1980; Tully, 1993.

of capitalism, though it is important to know when and how that association occurred. The late C. B. Macpherson[6] caused unnecessary trouble, I believe, by telescoping 'possessive' with 'accumulative' and 'accumulative' with 'bourgeois', by associating these ideas prematurely. If we look at the paradigm of appropriation from the state of nature, the two things we ought first to notice are that it was constructed by jurists and that the technology it presupposes is that of the heavy plough. The latter turns up baulks and headlands; it demarcates tenure in the act of cultivation; it is as phallic as you like to make it; and it means that any primeval law must take the form of social arrangements which cross from one man's furrow into his neighbour's, a step of much magical significance in both primeval law and primeval anthropology. We are concerned here with the myth of the plough, and I will not pause to examine its reality. As for the first half of the imagined paradigm – the image of the jurist seated on his bench with the ploughmen or their exploiters standing before him – the point I want to dwell on is Alan Macfarlane's: that the courtroom was the theatre in which possessive individualism was shaped long before the market was imagined replacing it.[7] Roman and feudal jurisprudence alike took it for granted that the proprietors who came before it to adjust disputes would be individuals, Gaius and Titius, seigneur and vassal, neighbour and neighbour; not the communities or agnatic kin-groups who were imagined and acknowledged by jurisconsults only in the nineteenth century. They arranged these litigant individuals in adversarial relationships, plea and counter-plea, challenge and response, conflict and resolution, on which each and every image of the state of nature, the origins of *jus* meaning right and *jus* meaning authority, and the transition to the state of civil government has quite unmistakably been formed; and they established all these images at the existential centre of the Western sense of what an individual is. I recall thinking a few years ago, when debate about Maori sovereignty was particularly active, that it might be important to remember that all early modern *pakeha* (New Zealander of European descent) political philosophy is about land rights and sovereignty, and that all early modern theory of sovereignty originated in civil war. The debate then beginning with representatives of the *tangata whenua* was a debate as between two modes of occupying land and acquiring rights, and this paper is about the acquisition of hegemony by one of them: about the growth of a *pakeha* discourse and sense of individuality from which the *tangata whenua* were all too easily excluded.

[6] Macpherson, 1967.   [7] Macfarlane, 1979.

I have been arguing that this discourse of possessive individualism is a great deal older than market relationships, and can be found implicit in both feudal and Roman jurisprudence; law, I claim, is one of its principal sources, and this could raise interesting questions about the relatively higher salience of law in Roman-Western than in Confucian-East Asian civilized discourse. But the next step is to trace the discourse of individualism to times before Roman jurisprudence, and discover it in the thought of both *polis* and epic. There is, after all, something anticipating the jurists' state of nature in Aristotle himself; pre-*polis* and pre-Homeric humanity, he tells us, was made up of Cyclopes, wandering giants like Polyphemus in the *Odyssey*, ruling their nuclear families and knowing no law common to themselves. It is the myth of primeval individualism once again, and raises the problem of how these radically autochthonous savages can be imagined into an association which will make them human and supply an origin for the *polis*. But the *polis* did not invent this primeval-individualist myth of its own origins; Polyphemus himself was invented in an epic world more heroic than political, and I wish I knew the ideological history of the Homeric imagination well enough to know why he was invented. If we generalize our perception of epic and look at a set of archetypal myths on which Aegean, Mesopotamian and European imagination is founded, we find them in every case radically individualist. They start with the expulsion from a paradise, the confusion of a language, the fall of a city; and the creative initiatives are taken, very often unwillingly, by exiles like Adam and Nimrod, fugitives from justice like Cain and Orestes, seaborne wanderers like Noah, Odysseus and Aeneas. Even the great covenants with the Lord, on which Israel is founded and ends by including us all, are entered into by a warrior people nomadic on the margins of a river-valley empire which entertains the false belief that heaven and earth are one. Hebraic and Hellenic man sets out from a circle already broken, from a state of nature rather than from any natural oneness with his *whenua*. And of course all this is as masculine as the words I have just used: masculine, heroic, patriarchal and barbaric; there is a 'we' who do not originate in the great archaic civilizations founded on myths of cosmic unity. We have to recognize that this masculine imagery is very deeply ingrained, and that to modify it is not the same as to reverse it. The anti-patriarchalist and anti-classical historian (and Canterbury graduate) Patricia Springborg is trying to put Egypt and Mesopotamia, the Two Lands and the Two Rivers, back at the centre of our historical consciousness;[8] one wants to wish her much

---

[8] Springborg, 1990.

success, but at the same time to ask whether it can – or even should – be more than partial. It was at Canterbury, in 1944 or 1945, that I heard Karl Popper's lectures launch his indictment of Plato for aiming at regression from the Open Society to the Tribe;[9] and the Open Society has not done badly since then (though greatly at New Zealand's expense) in the civil wars of humanity. Beginning at the end of the seventeenth century, the various movements we group together under the name of Enlightenment continued to operate the historical paradigm supplied by natural jurisprudence, but under historical conditions which have been in need of redefinition. There has been, and is still indignantly defended, a historical schema which depicts the uninterrupted march of possessive individualism towards the collision with a socialist antithesis; but – for reasons only loosely connected with the planetary disasters befalling that antithesis – this schema has been challenged by another, which depicts the Enlightened image of the possessive individual as distracted between two models, the one ancient and the other modern. On the ancient or republican side of the diptych stood the virtuous citizen of Greco-Roman antiquity, proprietor of his land and his weapons, supported by the labour of his slaves and household, who supplied him with the leisure in which he might engage in either contemplation or action; acting in a politics of direct encounter with his peers that engaged his personality directly in the practice of the *res publica* or common good; contemplating in a philosophical activity that permitted direct and immediate cognition of things as they were in their ideas or substances. On the modern or commercial side stood the enlightened individual of what was called polite society, proprietor of a fluid wealth as well as of land, which permitted him to exchange money for services which he did not perform himself; at leisure because he paid the state to hire professional soldiers and need no longer bear arms himself, because he might take part in the election of representatives who would do his self-governing for him, and because, whatever his own activity as a producer or more probably a consumer, he was engaged in a multitude of social transactions permitting a multitude of goods to be produced and exchanged by a multitude of specialized skills. Ancient man's leisure gave him the freedom to be himself; modern man's leisure gave him the freedom to diversify his existence. Ancient philosophy meant the contemplation of the universe as essential substance; modern philosophy meant the contemplation of the human mind as its workings produced the infinite diversities of human culture.[10]

---

[9] Popper, 1945.   [10] Pocock, 1975, 1985 (A) and 2003 (B).

Antitheses of this kind led to the appearance of schemes of history in which the progress of mankind was from simplicity and self-sufficiency towards diversity and socialization. In these schemes the concept of self came to be crucial and problematic. On the presumption that humans were social beings it could be argued that the self was not sufficient, that an individual concerned only to support himself could never be fully human nor fully an individual. On the presumption that humans possessed and ought to realize unique personalities, it could be perceived that the progressive diversification and specialization of separate human capacities could lead to the disappearance of individuality, as the self became deconstructed and absorbed by the sum of its social transactions. It did not take the modern long to predict the post-modern; and the great anti-philosopher of the age, Jean Jacques Rousseau, informed his fellow humans that they were trapped between the extremes of savagery and corruption, with little chance of realizing or maintaining a human capacity. The Enlightened scheme of human progress contains ambivalence even when it looks most complacent, and we have to bear this in mind when considering what it did with the image of the *tangata whenua*, the original individual born on the earth and living in it.

What they did with him – him, of course, though there was an increasing volume of writings about the condition of women in the successive worlds he, of course, had made – was to make him into the savage, the *selvaggio*, the wild man of the woods, *orang-utan* or bushman. This figure was arrived at by conflating the primeval individual of classical, biblical and jurisprudential anthropology with the variety of food-gathering and hoe-digging cultures – if we must lump them all together under a single description – which Europeans had encountered since their oceanic permeation of the planet began around 1492. Here of course is the point at which Western anthropology begins to commit injustices towards the peoples we now think of when we hear or use the phrase *tangata whenua*. The function of the term 'savage' was to establish the presupposition that the inhabitants of cultures practising neither heavy-plough agriculture nor monetarized exchange were living in the state of nature: that they were solitary and feral individuals who had not yet reached the point of establishing civil government by consent, and so lived either under no government at all or under that of despots, either primitive or oriental. Nimrod, the mighty hunter before the Lord who had organized labour to build the first *ziggurat*, neatly telescoped the two kinds of despot.

The function of the term 'savage', then, is to establish the premiss of primeval individualism, and the function of the term *tangata whenua* is to undo it. The concept of primeval, and of course possessive, individualism is importantly double-edged; it proclaims that the origins of society lie in individuality, but at the same time that individuality is underdeveloped without society. The first humans, then, were not quite human yet; they were missing links, such as we still search for in primate paleontology. The essential step into humanity was taken with the acceptance of law and government, and it was premised that this step could not be taken without the preceding or accompanying step of appropriation. Without abandoning the doctrine in the least, Enlightened anthropology added the premiss that the step into humanity was taken with the acquisition of capacity for exchange, commerce, specialization and diversification, and that it was this which appropriation through the heavy plough either preceded or accompanied. Theorists of this period were more likely to telescope agriculture and commerce than to separate them. They even telescoped agriculture and urbanization to form a semi-biblical equivalent of what we sometimes term the neolithic revolution – where their still biblical chronology, by the way, allowed them to date it. Archbishop Usher's six thousand years are quite enough for most of us, though a good deal less than we have had.

This is why Gibbon observes that the German tribes were formed 'by the gradual union of some wandering savages of the Hercynian woods'. He wrote this in the context of an abandonment of the Noachic chronology and an acceptance of Buffon's hypothesis that humans were an animal species, but these steps are not centrally important in shaping the sentence quoted. Its essence lies in the affirmation that the originators of any human culture must have been few, must have been savages, and must have been wanderers; its equivalent in New Zealand prehistory would be an accidental-voyage thesis; and means by this time existed of making these affirmations within the biblical and Noachic chronology. The biblical equivalent of the state of nature was, as we have seen, the confusion of tongues, when the human race had suddenly found itself divided into mutually incomprehensible linguistic sub-cultures, which had wandered off in all directions to begin the repeopling of the planet. Since these sub-cultures had been *gentes*, linearly descending groups whose genealogies could be remembered and reconstructed, it was possible for Filmer or Bossuet to argue that they had been households under patriarchal authority, and that the divinely commanded chain of magistracy had not been broken at the confusion of tongues; humans had never been reduced to the pure atomism of the jurists' state of nature. But the argument from patriarchy could easily enough be bypassed. Aristotle's Cyclopes are patriarchs in the sense that each dominant male controls females and young, but they are capable of engaging in thoroughly Hobbesian war between individuals for control of these assets, just like Jane Goodall's chimpanzees at Gombe.[11] The degeneration of Nimrodic man was, as we shall see, towards a Hobbesian condition, but its starting point was a gentilic condition whose most important significance is the premiss of human diffusion. The *gentes* dispersing from Shinar were *hapu* (sub-tribes) and *iwi* re-groupable into *waka*: the three lineages of Ham, Shem and Japhet, survivors of the great accidental voyage which had preserved the human race. 'Such things,' wrote John Beaglehole, 'Geography and Navigation.'[12] The creation of *whenua* might come later.

The crucial premiss here is that of vagrancy: the premiss that a wandering condition dehumanizes or must precede humanization. We learn this best – at least I do – from a work of Enlightened jurisprudence and anthropology, which Gibbon relied upon and used often, though it operates wholly within the Mosaic and Noachic chronology: Antoine-Yves Goguet's *De l'Origine des Loix, des Arts et des Sciences*[13] (the precedence of law is important). As Goguet's gentiles wander away from the confusion of tongues, they forget the arts of tillage and pasture, and vagrancy is the reason why they forget them. As they wander further, they forget the natural laws of society and morality and regress to a miserable and Hobbesian condition; they may forget language itself – it seemed possible in the Enlightenment that orang-utans were degenerate hominids who had lost the use of speech – and when they reach the condition of the apparently impoverished Patagonians, Kalaharians and Tasmanians glimpsed by voyagers at the extremities of the southern continents, they may even reach the point where cannibalism is normal. The belief that cannibalism was the ultimate departure from nature, evidence of the ultimate desocialization and dehumanization, accounts for the shock undergone by the *Endeavour*'s company at encountering it – whatever it was they did encounter – in Queen Charlotte Sound. If the people practising it had been miserable and inarticulate cave-dwellers, it would have been easier to bear; but they were sociable, communicative and friendly – almost like the Tahitians – and anthropophagy among them was a deeply disturbing anomaly to the Enlightened mind, almost like the Lisbon earthquake. It is interesting to read in the journals how Banks and Cook set about inventing hypotheses of protein deficiency and sympathetic magic to account for it.

---

[11] Goodall, 1990.   [12] Above, p. 15.   [13] Goguet, 1758.

Goguet's degenerate hominids finally turn around and set out on the road back to humanity, recovering in its later stages the arts of pasture and tillage in that order. The thesis that early humans had been herdsmen before they were ploughmen, and ploughmen before they were merchants, was in the first place a Greek and Roman speculation; its revival in Enlightened anthropology is important to this story, precisely because pastoral nomads, for whom the whole earth is one long paddock,[14] do not look very much like *tangata whenua*, and in fact serve to keep alive the premisses of vagrancy and primeval individualism. Their Japhetic ancestors in the old chronology, Gog and Magog, had been giants and hunters in the earth like Nimrod. In the eighteenth century they had been restored from myth to history by the Jesuit missions in China, whose translations from the dynastic histories had revealed the global importance of Central Asian nomadism. I have mentioned the role of Joseph de Guignes in shaping the work of Gibbon. This is part of the background to the crucial role which 'the shepherd stage of society' plays for Adam Smith and Adam Ferguson, but there is a problem here which caused much trouble for Ronald Meek in writing his pioneer study *Social Science and the Ignoble Savage*.[15] For Goguet, and also for Gibbon, the shepherd stage is not a crucial break with the hunter-gatherer condition, but rather a prolongation of its savagery. The effect, or more properly the cause, is that for them there are not four stages in the history of society but two: the one vagrant and the other sedentary. Goguet, whose work is illustrated with handsome drawings of heavy ploughs, insists that only as individuals became capable of intensive cultivation and so of appropriating fixed points on the earth's surface, did vagrant savagery begin giving way to sedentary civilization. Once farming began, there was a social space, defined by the points which humans had made their own; and across the space which separated and therefore joined these points, social messages and transactions began to pass back and forth, with infinitely greater sophistication than had been possible between migrant groups of hunters and herdsmen. It was the stationary life that made civilization feasible, and there was no essential difference between the farmland and the township. Interchange of both material goods and social functions began to be possible, and as a result there could be interchange of ideas and elaborations of language. Some of the most interesting passages in Goguet, and others like him, are devoted to the relations between poetry and law. The earliest songs, he thinks, were dooms, the chants of lawgivers giving cadence, metre and assonance to law as a series of mnemonic

---

[14] An Australian term for the grassy borders of motor highways.   [15] Meek, 1976.

devices; and from this it follows that, as Goguet's title asserts, there must be laws, verbalized rules for the regulation of social exchange, before there can be arts and sciences, the expressions of the social relations which exchange creates. It is the ploughlands which make all this possible, because they create stationary and durable human groups between whom communication can be continuous and self-elaborating; and from this hypothesis develops the argument which later fermented into the debate over the poems ascribed to Ossian – could complex messages be preserved through social time by oral transmission alone, or was it absolutely necessary that there should exist some means of writing? Gibbon takes a strongly (and I think consciously) anti-Ossianic line when he asserts that because the ancient Germans lacked money and letters, the two essential media of human communication, they could not be other than 'a herd of savages',[16] deficient in both law and historic memory. His predecessor, the Jacobite historian Thomas Carte, had, however, already studied Welsh bardic poetry and reported that it contained a code of assonance and alliteration so complex that it could serve as a mnemonic and transmit information from one generation to another in stable and durable forms.[17] The great methodological debate between text and tradition had begun.

Money and letters. We are looking at a theory of society which telescopes and equates agriculture and commerce, because arable exploitation stabilizes and creates the social space across which relation, transaction and exchange become possible. The invention of durable media of communication and exchange is the next step, and the advent of money, though of far-reaching importance, is not a conceptual break with what has gone before. Distribution and exchange are more distinctively human even than production, and it will be linguistically proper to call this a bourgeois theory of society, so long as we keep in mind that the term *bourgeoisie* meant 'citizenship', the condition of having rights of membership in an incorporated and law-governed human group, such as it was the function of agriculture and the plough to create in schemes like Goguet's. The plough was essential to this process, because it alone could create stable and durable families occupying the same acreage and replenishing the earth with manure and the society with culture. To think of pre-arable horti-culture was to think of slash-and-burn, of transient human groups making clearings in the forest and scratching the ground with hoes for a while before moving on. They had not escaped from the vagrant condition, and

---

[16] Womersley, 1994, vol. I, pp. 234–7.   [17] Carte, 1747, vol. I, pp. 33–4.

were no further from savagery – the hunter-gatherer condition – than transhumant swineherds or grassland nomads were. When Goguet and Carte thought of Phoenicians and Romans landing in primitive Britain,[18] they drew the analogy with Europeans colonizing the tidewaters of forest America and inducing the *selvaggi* (or *tangata whenua*) to come out of the bush and settle on the margins of their plantations. So long as there was plenty of uncleared forest, thought Carte, the natives could go walkabout, and resume the hunter-gatherer existence, whenever they wanted to.

The presumptions of primeval individualism were still at work. The savage was the pre-sedentary human, hampered by an incapacity for either production or exchange from developing the laws, arts and sciences which were the codified expressions of social relations, themselves essentially commercial. Agriculture was the precondition of commerce, and commerce of civilization. A consequence was the polarization of what Meek taught us to think of as four stages of human history into two, with the hunter and shepherd relegated to vagrancy, the ploughman and merchant to sedentary civilization. Goguet supplied Gibbon with an account of the production of culture, and in his chapter on the Germans Gibbon went beyond Goguet in analysing the relations between culture and personality, psyche and even libido. The forest Germans are savages, but not in a simply negative definition. This is because they are herdsmen as well as hunters, possessed of large flocks of beasts with whom they move from pasture to pasture, and so are capable of mobilizing themselves in formidable armed migrations. They understand war, therefore, but because they are not ploughmen understand nothing else, and this imposes limits on their understanding of themselves. They do not appropriate because they do not labour, and their energies are consequently underemployed.

The care of the house and family, the management of the land and cattle, were delegated to the old and the infirm, to women and slaves. The lazy warrior, destitute of every art that might employ his leisure hours, consumed his days and nights in the animal gratifications of sleep and food ... The languid soul, oppressed with its own weight, anxiously required some new and powerful sensation; and war and danger were the only amusements adequate to its fierce temper. The sound that summoned the German to arms was grateful to his ear. It roused him from his uncomfortable lethargy, gave him an active pursuit, and by strong exercise of the body, and violent emotions of the mind, restored him to a more lively sense of his existence.[19]

[18] Goguet, 1758, vol. I, pp. 59–61; Carte, 1747, vol. I, pp. 25–6.
[19] Womersley, 1994, vol. I, pp. 237–8.

In this culture, bardic poetry is no longer the chanting of laws which extend and moderate the social space, but 'the military song', exciting the heroic appetites that save the berserker from his boredom. It is a much more sophisticated and introspective account than Hobbes's of the inherent violence of the state of nature. Fear pushed Hobbes's primitives to acquire power and collide with one another; the savage, midway between hunter and herdsman, is impelled to heroic and frenzied action by a deficient sense of self, and this deficiency is accounted for by his imperfect capacity for appropriation. If he had ploughed the land he would have acquired property and other proprietors for neighbours. Relations would have sprung up between them, laws and morality to regulate those relations, rational and symbolic sign-systems to express the meanings of law and morality, and he would have come to know himself as a being involved in and defined by all the modes of his own socialization. As civilized man, the individual acquired a much richer and more diverse sense of his own identity, because there were infinitely more schemes of relationship in which it could be expressed, articulated, elaborated and discussed. But it had to be acknowledged at the same time – as Gibbon does in discussing the difference between bardic and modern poetry[20] – that the primitive sense of self, precisely because it was deficient, was far more intense and immediate, on those berserk occasions when it found expression, than the civilized sense of self could ever be. The progress of society was from the hot to the cool medium; civilization consisted in the production of more and more ways of being and knowing one's self, so that in the end one was left aware that whatever self one was asserting at a particular moment was other than the self one might assert at some other moment. The enrichment of the self was the diminution of its identity. It is very much the problem of Rousseau, and it is also the problem of gender as the eighteenth century commonly formulated it. Women were perceived as the sub-heroic mediators of complex and civilized society, constantly engaged in softening and refining the passions of man: this gave them a positive role in the progress of civilization, but at the same time helps explain why civilized men so gravely feared becoming 'effeminate'. The civilizing process might of its nature be carried too far.

I want now to generalize from what I have been saying, and move towards its implications for a situation in which *pakeha* and *tangata whenua* find themselves in confrontation and may need dialogue. I shall be considering

<hr>

[20] Womersley, 1994, vol. I, p. 247.

these two categories somewhat abstractly and theoretically, without giving the immediate practical situation the direct consideration which of course it needs. The justification for doing so is that theoretical analysis may bring information and clarification to the practical situation, which the latter may not reveal to itself. It is of course the discourse of the *pakeha* which I have been considering all along, because it is this discourse which I have made a career of studying. I am emphasizing what there is in *pakeha* discourse which has tended to exclude the *tangata whenua* from getting a hearing; the danger here is that I may slip into representing *tangata whenua* discourse as simply that which *pakeha* discourse excludes, which would be inadequate, even though it is important to see why the latter excludes it. Obviously, the *tangata whenua* are both free and necessitated to articulate their own discourse; and fortunately for us all, they are eloquent and outgoing in doing so. I have two aims: the first to show what there has been in *pakeha* discourse which has tended to exclude them, while at the same time enquiring where in that discourse doors may be found which might be pushed wider open; the second is to say some things about how the two discourses may look to one another, and even about what they may have to say to one another. In this, I shall be rejecting the now fashionable premiss that every discourse is sealed against every other, because irretrievably it is the possession of those whose power has shaped it. It has been said that language possesses 'an infinite capacity for being appropriated'; and if that capacity is infinite, no language can completely predetermine how it is to be appropriated, or by whom. A dialogue between discourses, therefore, may be infinitely difficult in practice, but may not be impossible in principle.

I have been examining *pakeha* discourse as it was in the Enlightened eighteenth century, when the *tangata whenua* were theorized as 'savages', and denied any relation with the *whenua* on the grounds that they had not appropriated it through the arable techniques of agriculture. This was how it came about that, from Ulster in the seventeenth century to Canterbury in the nineteenth – to say nothing of contemporary Amazonia where the process is still going on – successive *tangata whenua* found themselves expropriated on the grounds that they had not appropriated, separated from the land on the grounds that they did not occupy it, and even denied the capacity to become ploughmen, proprietors and litigants, on those occasions when they tried to assert that they possessed it. All over the world they are still extremely angry about this, as they should be. But I have also been saying that though the ideology of agriculture and savagery was formed to justify this expropriation, it also articulated things which the *pakeha* – otherwise known as 'Western man' – very deeply believed about themselves, and have come to believe in the course of their own history; things which emerged from debates and contestations conducted at the heart of *pakeha* culture. It follows, therefore, that though the *pakeha* were expropriating the *tangata whenua* and this was the only thing which the *tangata whenua* had occasion to notice about them, it was not the only thing which the *pakeha* knew about themselves. They were not only expropriators, and this made it easier for them to deny that expropriation was what they were doing; and when we bring expropriation back to the centre of the picture where it belongs, we have to avoid the reductionism of supposing that it is the only thing in the picture or explains the presence of everything else which is there. The *pakeha* debate with themselves about themselves; they appropriate and expropriate, but they have debated for centuries about how they shape themselves and create problems for themselves in doing so. Even when they debate their actions in expropriating the *tangata whenua*, they are more often than not debating what they have been doing to themselves in the process, rather than to the *tangata whenua*. This is why *tangata whenua* intellectuals often find *pakeha* intellectuals extremely irritating people, and it may seem at this point as if I were after all describing a closed system of discourse. If the *tangata whenua* want to debate the *pakeha* at all, they will have to find ways of breaking into this discourse and modifying the ways in which *pakeha* – even *pakeha* intellectuals – conduct it; and this is going to mean that the *tangata whenua* accept some of it for themselves. The premises on which it is conducted are often most unfair, and we have to look for ways of rendering them less so. This is why, in this part of the essay, I am looking for doors which may be pushed a bit wider open.

The *pakeha* discourse was fundamentally individualist, but this did not necessarily mean that it was crudely, philistinely or even accumulatively individualist. It presumed that individuals logically preceded societies and systems of sociability, and that history was a process by which the individual rendered himself increasingly a sociable being by entering into a denser texture of social relationships formed through appropriation and exchange. Most of the attributes of humanity – including those of humanity in its relation with God – were attributes of sociability; history was a process of humanization through socialization. This was how the *tangata whenua*, characterized as 'savages', came to be unjustly identified with individuals not yet humanized through socialization, and so neither fully individual nor fully social. All through the sixteenth into the eighteenth centuries and on into the nineteenth, we find records of *pakeha* debating, often very seriously, whether the non-*pakeha* with whom they were dealing were in this sense primitive, pre-human, or so far short of a capacity to conduct their own relationships that they could be governed only despotically.[21] It was not the case, however, that the *pakeha* concerned took themselves to be free and autonomous individuals and nothing more; they believed themselves to be individuals who had mastered the process of self-socialization to the point where they could submit to law and remain free at the same time. The freedom and autonomy of the savage meant that he was not yet social or fully human; the slavish oriental was capable of submitting to law only in the form of despotism which denied his freedom and humanity.

The process of history as the *pakeha* understood it could begin only when individuals appeared who were capable of conducting their own socialization, and this could occur only when appropriation was the precondition of civilization. The individual must establish his own relationship with the *whenua* – let us put it this way so as to remind ourselves that it was a patriarchal relationship – in order to be a person and embark on the voyage towards law, freedom and exchange. Gibbon's lazy and bipolar warriors are examples of what the individual is like before he does this; and the culture-specific assumptions of an economy based on agriculture and jurisdiction meant that *pakeha* ideologies were very nearly incapable of imagining that property, which was their name for relationship, could be vested in any tenants other than the individual heads of patriarchal families. The idea that it could reside in a tribe, a kin-group, a *hapu, iwi* or any other such term it may be convenient to employ, was extraordinarily difficult for *pakeha* jurists to accept, unless the kin-group could be represented as a corporation, which is to say a group of individuals supposed by metaphor and fiction to act as a single individual. [This the Ngai Tahu have subsequently become.] Their jurisprudence, and their political philosophy, presupposed that the basic human community consisted of individual proprietors, whose disputes with one another were capable of being resolved by the adversarial procedures of law. This community could be preceded only by an anarchy of vagrant individuals, not yet humanized by property, whose disputes must take the form of the Hobbesian war of all against all. When they described *tangata whenua* as savages, they quite incorrectly declared that this was their social condition.

It has to be remembered that in thus stigmatizing the *tangata whenua*, the *pakeha* believed that they were describing their own origins. They did

---

[21] E.g. the Spanish debate over the rationality of American Indians, and the English debate over despotism and servility at the time of the Bengal land settlement.

not in the least mind conceding that they had been savages once, or even that they had carried a basic individualism from the vagrant into the sedentary condition. When Chief Seattle, in a famous if fictitious oration on another Pacific sea-coast,[22] accused his *pakeha* of being wanderers who left their dead behind them in the earth, he was telling them nothing about themselves which they did not know already. They believed that they were journeying through the progress of individuality and leaving Seattle and his people behind them in a vagrant and savage condition. If the chief was trying to tell them that his *iwi* lived in a state of communion with the earth and the dead ancestors, they were simply unable to listen to him.[23] They invincibly believed that Seattle's people were impoverished, both materially and spiritually, by their condition of undeveloped and unsocialized individuality, and that their own civilized condition had enriched them socially, culturally and spiritually, as well as materially. The premise of individualism did not motivate them consciously to destroy such conditions of community as I have imagined Seattle describing; rather, it made them incapable of comprehending that such conditions might exist. Even when, in the early nineteenth century, anthropologists formulated the concept of the Indo-Germanic agnatic community occupying the ground as a kindred, the *pakeha* response was to characterize this mode of occupancy as a 'cake of custom', which must be broken up in the 'progress from status to contract'.[24] The implication was that the agnatic community was less a primeval condition of humanity than a false start, an evolutionary dead end.

The term *tangata whenua* is nowadays employed to put forward those assertions of community within the human group and between that group and the earth, which I mentioned a moment ago. These associations were of course utterly precluded by the Enlightened anthropology I have been describing. The human individual it was capable of supposing could develop a sense of community, even of self, only after he began to appropriate and cultivate, to produce and exchange; he could not even have imagined the intimate associations with kin and earth which the *tangata whenua* imagination does in fact proclaim. The Enlightenment mind had begun to grow aware of the animist perception which locates an *atua* in every rock and at every bend a *taniwha*,[25] but dismissed it as superstition, a

---

[22] Quoted in Sharp, 1990, 1997, p. 66. The version of this speech now engraved on monuments in the city of Seattle is understood to be apocryphal.

[23] Unless, indeed, Seattle's oration should be the work of a *pakeha* criticizing his own culture.

[24] Burrow, 1966. 'The cake of custom' is Walter Bagehot's phrase (Bagehot, 1869), 'from status to contract', Sir Henry Maine's (Maine, 1861).

[25] A Maori dragon or water-spirit.

product of the fear and guilt of Vico's solitary giant surprised by thunder in the act of copulation. It knew of complex religious systems, which imagined spirit and matter emerging together out of some undifferentiated primary substance, but dismissed these as mysticisms, constructed by ancient oriental sages seeking to co-ordinate primitive animisms into unitary metaphysics. The Enlightened mind was bent on the separation of spirit from matter, of the appropriator from the substance appropriated. Paradoxically, it may have been in his philosophic materialism, which made spirit and matter one again, that Diderot got closest to the mentality of the Tahitians he otherwise made use of without understanding.

His *Supplément à la Voyage de Bougainville* is of course evidence that there was in the Enlightened mind an impulse to rebel against its own perception of history as the progressive diversification (which often looked like the regressive fragmentation) of the individual personality and to travel back against the stream of history, in search of some primeval state of undistracted and undifferentiated being. But it was extremely hard to do this within the paradigm of primeval individualism. If the Tahitian or the Huron or the Highlander were simply a noble savage, he would be nothing more than a hero whose passions were simply expressed and not yet corrupted by civilization. Rousseau was as forward as any *philosophe* in pointing out that the hero was the product of some measure of social progress, and that the quest for the noble savage might end with the discovery of the pre-human giant. The tragic paradox in Rousseau's view was that the first step away from prehumanity towards humanity was also the first step towards the corruption of a humanity not yet achieved. History was a self-defeating process, an attempt to do the impossible, a confrontation between Polyphemus the savage and Odysseus the liar, in which any relatively uncorrupt condition could only be a transitory moment. The union between *tangata* and *whenua*, and the sacred time-lessness in which that union is often said to repeat itself, could only be such a moment in history.

I am now positing a *pakeha* imagination in which history is the departure from the *whenua*, and starts from the breaking of the circle, the confusion of tongues, the expulsion from the garden; something which happened very long ago and goes on happening all the time, so that history is the normal condition of the human species. This is to invite the opposition between history and dreamtime, in which to assert the existence of a *tangata whenua* is to affirm that there exists, or has existed, a human community living in a non-historical condition, a sacred and self-relegated communion with the earth; an affirmation which may be made by *tangata whenua* because that really is how they live or used to live, or made by *pakeha* in a state of rebellion against being *pakeha* and living in history. Once it is made, we are obliged to see history itself as an ideological construct, an instrument of *pakeha* ideology, just as to some radical feminists it will appear a male ideology and to some radical environmentalists a human ideology, formed for the use of *homo sapiens* the destroyer of the ecological order. All these charges, of course, can be seen as part of a thoroughly Western discourse of self-accusation, in which Adam and Eve clutch at their fig leaves and dream angrily of a way back to the garden; so that there are times when modern *tangata whenua*, expounding their vision of a sacred order in the middle of the post-industrial city, sound depressingly like counter-culture intellectuals out of the 1960s. Of course it is important not to believe this (except when it is true) and to bear in mind that the *tangata whenua* discourse articulates a state of affairs which did exist and in some ways exists still. But once we posit the dreamtime, we have to believe that the damage has been done, the circle has been broken, and the *tangata whenua* have been expelled into history, carrying the dreamtime with them and necessitated to articulate it as history.[26] Like the dispossessed worshippers in the Hasidic fable, they cannot light the fire, they cannot speak the prayer, they do not know the place; but they can tell the tale of how it was done,[27] and they find *pakeha* discourse in a condition vulnerable, if not always responsive, to hearing the tale told. Once the *pakeha* stop seeing their first ancestors as heroic barbarians and see them as dispossessed exiles from paradise instead, dialogue with the *tangata whenua* becomes possible. The question is whether either group will retain a discourse of liberty, or merely one of self-pity.

Let us return to the contemporary situation. I have reached the point of presenting the dialogue between *te iwi Maori* and *te iwi Pakeha* as a dialogue between two histories or, more precisely, between two peoples in history, who find that history itself is heavily biased in favour of one *iwi* but is capable – in part for reasons inherent in its character as a *pakeha* construct – of being subverted and partly rewritten so as to give voice to the *tangata whenua* and substantiate their claims. I have been trying to show that the *pakeha* articulation of their history is complex and resourceful, to

---

[26] [It should be remembered that 'dreamtime' is an Aboriginal, not a Maori, concept; but for a philosophical consideration of the point here made, see Tau, 2001a and b.]

[27] Quoted and restored to historical discourse by Joseph Levinson at the end of vol. III of Levinson, 1965.

the point where it is full of means of self-criticism, but that even this tends to reinforce its capacity to maintain itself. It arises from debates of great antiquity within Greek and Latin, Christian and Enlightenment civilization, over matters of which the drive to subjugate exterior peoples and the global environment is only one aspect, however great its importance. It is therefore a very tough discourse to tackle and may even take you captive when you try to subvert it. You cannot subvert it beyond a certain point without demanding of the *pakeha* that they give up and cease trying to represent themselves as an *iwi* of any kind. There have been uncompromising nationalists among the *tangata whenua* recently who came close to making this demand; and since *pakeha* self-expression has always been full of self-division and self-repudiation, there are always *pakeha* intellectuals who sound as if they were conceding it. I am suggesting, however, that it is most unsafe to believe them: what sounds like self-rejection may turn out to be self-reinforcement and concealed backlash.

The history of the Ngai Tahu claim,[28] however – and, one would want to add, the history of all discourse based on the Treaty of Waitangi – has not been the history of an encounter between two mutually exclusive discourses, but that of an attempt to persuade *pakeha* jurisprudence to modify its premisses and render itself capable of admitting claims based on the *tangata whenua* perception of history and of justice as arising out of history.[29] To a very real extent, the Ngai Tahu have been claiming compensation for what *pakeha* history has done to them, and alleging *tangata whenua* history as a basis of right. This is to propose a bi-cultural perception of both history and justice, and of social personality as arising out of both. It is an ambitious if a necessary programme, and there are those who do not believe it can succeed. It is a question of the possibility of dialogue between those, employing different discourses, who seek a political relationship. This is certainly a negotiation of power, but one may hold power to be negotiable and the negotiation a possible foundation for relationship. The dangers of negotiation are obvious; one party may entrap the other, or both may entrap themselves, in some pattern of discourse whose hegemonic potential they do not know how to resist. One should listen carefully to those who warn that this may happen; but those who deliver their warnings as indictments have predetermined the outcome.

[28] [This meeting of the New Zealand Historical Association was focussed on the recent history of this claim before the Waitangi Tribunal (Sharp, 1990, 1997).]

[29] [I am basing this statement on Sharp, 1990, 1997, and Kawharu, 1989. See also Sharp and McHugh, 2001.]

Let us revert to the problems of a bi-historical discourse. The term *tangata whenua* carries with it two claims: one to priority of occupation, the other to a certain community between *tangata* and *whenua*, which forms the basis of a claim of right. Translated into the Enlightened discourse of anthropology and jurisprudence which this essay has explored, the latter claim challenges the *pakeha* assumption that only appropriation by individual patriarchs tilling with the plough can create property, right and social personality. It makes a claim in a deeply important language of myth; it avers that a community may dream or imagine itself into being by imagining a collective relationship with the earth, and that this poetic or mythopoeic act constitutes an act of appropriation as effective as any carried out by arable individualism. The claim challenges the *pakeha* understanding of the modes of appropriation, not the concepts of appropriation and property themselves. 'Property' has always been a *pakeha* term for the relation between human and environment, between *tangata* and *whenua*. The *pakeha* eye instinctively translates *rangatiratanga*[30] as 'property', and the *tangata whenua* question the adequacy of the translation; the Ngai Tahu claimants are asking the *pakeha* to reconstruct their notion of property, not to deconstruct it. The question it is proper to ask is whether the *pakeha* are capable of doing this, or whether both *pakeha* and *tangata whenua* in New Zealand/Aotearoa are irrevocably committed to situating property in a process leading from the plough to the computer, from the appropriation of land to the commodification of everything. That is the Rousseauist and post-Marxist criticism of their present enterprise, and it will have to receive serious attention.

The aim of the present essay, however, is to look into the past of *pakeha* jurisprudence (which is very much a living past) and enquire whether the obstacles to recognizing *tangata whenua* claims that have been identified there may be overcome. Here it seems relevant to consider the language of Lord Glenelg, in a memorandum of 1837 which is thought to supply a basis for the recognition of *rangatiratanga* in the Treaty three years later. Glenelg spoke with the voice of Enlightened anthropology when he wrote: 'The chiefs and people of New Zealand ... are not savages living by the chase, but tribes who have apportioned the country between them, having fixed abodes, with an acknowledged property in the soil',[31] which property may have been the basis of *rangatiratanga* as the crown understood it and was certainly the basis of the tribes' recognized capacity to enter into a treaty.

---

[30] A word literally translatable as 'chieftainship', but better by the Latin *dominium*.
[31] Quoted by P. G. McHugh in Kawharu, 1989, p. 31.

Unless Glenelg supposed the *iwi* to be agriculturalists appropriating through the plough, he must have recognized some other process through which they could 'apportion' the land, take up 'abodes', and acquire 'property'. No doubt he was entirely vague about what this might be, but his language opens up a range of possibilities which the Ngai Tahu claimants are inducing the Tribunal and the courts to consider. English common law is no longer so medieval that it is committed to the plough; we are, rather, afraid that it may have left the plough too far behind; but there is some reason to believe it capable of recognizing a variety of claims to property and *rangatiratanga*. Forty years after Glenelg, Chief Justice Prendergast pronounced that only a people whose social system was capable of generating sovereignty could enter into treaty relationships, and that therefore a treaty between *kawanatanga*[32] and *rangatiratanga* was without force or meaning. We are now being reminded that Prendergast was employing a positivist and ultra-modernist mode of jurisprudence and that a better understanding of the issues of both 1840 and today may be obtained by reverting from the positivism of the nineteenth century to the 'natural' jurisprudence of the Enlightenment, in the hope of finding that the gulf between sovereign and non-sovereign social systems was then less unbridgeable.[33] This is to urge the *pakeha* to explore their own tradition and history, as one in which positions are contested and debated; another 'liberal' programme. If they go back far enough, they may even come upon Sir John Fortescue in 1471, discussing the customs which give a people its distinctive identity and observing that 'all that is loved transfers the lover into its own nature by usage, wherefore, said Aristotle, use becomes another nature'.[34] Lying deep in the *pakeha* past, we find language that affirms a large part of what *tangata whenua* have to say about themselves and their claims to recognition; but it is a long time since English common law found customary communities at the base of its own practice.

Since *tangata whenua* typically employ a language of myth rather than usage, they are liable to find themselves affirming a dreamtime, a condition of sacred relationships with the *whenua* from which the expulsion into history is as the expulsion from the garden. If we premise that this expulsion has occurred and is irreversible, it will seem that they are in need of a perception or philosophy of history in which the dreamtime is seen as a phase or episode of the past, a species of Hawaiki.[35] Here it may be

---

[32] A quasi-Maori neologism, rendering into Maori phonetics the English word 'government'.
[33] See in particular Hackshaw, 1989.   [34] Chrimes, 1949, p. 17.
[35] A mythical homeland or point of origin.

suggested that the situation of the *tangata whenua* of Aotearoa is unlike that of the Aboriginals of Australia, from whom the term 'dreamtime' is derived. These enormously ancient communities perceive a past which can only be described in 'dreamtime' terms, both because no 'history' exists as an alternative to it, and because they have been what Glenelg and the Enlightenment misdescribed as 'savages living by the chase': food-gathering groups moving across an unappropriated land surface, to which they relate themselves as *tangata* to *whenua*, through song, dream, ritual and other forms of mythopoeic appropriation which may be hardly possessive at all. Such are both aboriginal myth and the myth of the aborigine; but in these islands not in narrow seas the dreamtime is less supported by antiquity. We are a very recent human colony, perhaps one thousand years old; we could treble or quadruple that figure, and remain recent in ethnological time. The effect of this is not to eliminate the dreamtime, but to change its status.

It is perhaps a still utilizable strength of the old *pakeha* historical anthropology that it began with the confusion of tongues, with a dispersion and diffusion of human groups to populate the planet; if we hold human history to have begun from some particular and localized genetic mutation, we still believe something like that. Now in such a vision it is obvious, as it always was, that there never were any *tangata whenua* in the crude sense of people generated by or in the particular area they happened to inhabit; the *whenua* must be considered as the totality of the global surface over which human groups have been moving on the long road from the Olduvai Gorge to the Rakaia.[36] The migratory condition turns out not at all inconsistent with the claims which *tangata whenua* make for themselves; but it does tell us that we have been a species much given to adapting ourselves to various environments, and the relation with the earth of which *tangata whenua* speak was not given or natural or inborn, but had to be achieved through the exercise of human capacities. This is the point at which the organic implications of the word *whenua* turn out to be less literal than metaphorical; they describe a relation with the earth which was not until it was imagined, until it was constructed by humans exercising their poetic and linguistic capabilities. If we call it a dreamtime, we should remember that somebody had to do the dreaming; it was created in the course of history.

The *tangata whenua* thus become actors in history, who have created the dreamtime but cannot use it as a refuge. A consequence for self-understanding is that we were all *tangata waka* (if I may coin the term)

---

[36] A Canterbury river, like the Waimakariri (above, p. 42, n. 29).

before any of us became *tangata whenua*; we came here by sea and set about making ways of living on the land. In terms of modern secondary-world fiction, we are not of Middle Earth, but of Earthsea.[37] Those who very justly pre-empt the title of *tangata whenua* were not here from the beginning; they made a beginning, and in their historic memory as well as in the *pakeha*'s, human occupation is historically specific and remembered. Nor did they leave the sacred earth undisturbed. If I could speak with the spirit voice of the great moa in the Canterbury Museum,[38] there might be several things I had to say to the *tangata*, of every *whenua* and every *waka*. The big-brained bipeds modify the environment drastically wherever they go, and the difference here between *tangata whenua* and *pakeha* is only one of very great degree. The first human explorers of this island must have found themselves in a terrain unimaginably different from any they had seen before, and when I think of them penetrating the high-country sources of Te Wai Pounamu[39] – even the gorge of the sacred Arahura itself – I wonder whether they saw all that bush and snow and shingle and water as a womb or *whenua*, or whether they saw things much more like what Samuel Butler and Arawata Bill[40] saw.[41] Poetic appropriation, dreaming or imagining one's way into a relationship with the environment, is a high and precarious human achievement, particularly when one has to do with the waiting hills and the encircling seas, and it is a poor compliment to the *tangata whenua* who achieved it to think about what they did uncritically, just as it is a mistake to think about the *pakeha* hypercritically, as if they never achieved it at all. Here, of course, I am speaking ideologically; I am affirming that the *pakeha* have a *whenua* in their own transitory way, and I am thinking of the Canterbury poets of my younger days, who set about poetic appropriation on the clear understanding that no dreamtime was available. I hold this to be something which the South Island has to say.

[The remainder of this essay, in its previously printed form, consisted of discussion of some points raised by Tipene O'Regan in his Beaglehole

---

[37] The allusion, if it needs explication, is to the trilogy of J. R. R. Tolkien and the two trilogies of Ursula K. Le Guin. [This essay was written before Middle Earth was filmed in Earthsea, and the latter's imagery became that of the former.]

[38] An articulated skeleton still on display; the title of a poem by Allen Curnow (1939; *Early Days Yet*, p. 220).

[39] 'The Greenstone Rivers', a term sometimes applied to the South Island as a whole. The Arahura is the most *tapu* of the rivers where greenstone was found.

[40] William O'Leary, a prospector who spent his life in the Southern Alps without finding gold; the central figure of a poem-cycle by Denis Glover (Glover, 1953).

[41] See nevertheless such lines in Glover's *Arawata Bill* as: 'What metal lies / Between those granite thighs, / What parturition of earth / Yields the golden miraculous birth?' ('To the Coast', III, lines 10–14). The point is that there isn't any.

Lecture for 1991, delivered on the same occasion and printed with it.[42] He considered the relations between legal and historical evidence, common law and indigenous discourse, and the problems of verification raised by the latter. The issues, of sovereignty and jurisprudence, law and history, which arose, are pursued, in greater detail than I then attempted, in the next essay in this volume.]

[42] O'Regan, 1992.

CHAPTER 13

Law, sovereignty and history in a divided culture: the case of New Zealand and the Treaty of Waitangi

(1)

The aim of this essay[1] is to introduce a series of explorations of the relations between law and history, considered as activities of the human mind in various states of society. Viewed in such a perspective, 'history' is perhaps better renamed 'historiography': the writing of history and the consciousness of it as a thing made by human activity, and in the end the making of history and the suffering of it as the consequences of human actions and the processes they have set in motion and cannot always control. Law, I think, can very often be seen in the same way: as the making of judgements, coupled with the attempt to determine how far we can live with the judgements we have made in the past; and this is one reason that law has been so powerful a contributor to the formation of the historical consciousness which characterizes our civilization.[2] Historiography has been, on the one hand, the narrative of human actions, and on the other, the archaeology of human practices seen as constituting the contexts in which the actions have been performed. The codes of law and the records of

---

[1] Pocock, 1998b; originally delivered and printed at Lancaster University as the 1992 Iredell Memorial Lecture (Pocock, 1992c). It was the first of a series of essays on the transformation of politics and historiography in New Zealand by the Treaty of Waitangi; see further Pocock, 2000e, 2001b, 2002a. The attached glossary may assist readers unfamiliar with Maori.
 Aotearoa: New Zealand
 hapu: sub-tribe
 iwi: tribe
 kawanatanga: government
 mana: prestige, authority, charisma
 manawhenua: authority over land inherent in *mana*
 marae: a meeting ground
 pakeha: New Zealander of European descent
 rangatiratanga: chieftainship, lordship
 tangata whenua: people of the land, indigenous, aboriginal
 turangawaewae: a place to stand
 waka: canoe, ship; lineage tracing descent from a given canoe
[2] Kelley, 1990.

courts have constituted perhaps the greatest series of archives in which these practices have been conserved, while the practice of jurisprudence itself has furnished a great part of the methods and mentality with which we interpret the actions of the past and connect them with the conditions of the present. There can be no doubt of the intimate connections between jurisprudence and historiography since the two began to assume their modern forms about five hundred years ago.

Yet there are differences between the lawyer and historian in their reasons for approaching the past and in their practices when dealing with it, and among these differences is one which separates the relations between practice and theory in the two disciplines. Lawyers go to the past in search of authority more or less directly applicable in present actions; historians in search of information which they know full well can be converted into authority and which may well be applied to present actions, but which they are capable of treating in alternative manners – such as the study of the past for its own sake. It is a consequence that lawyers regularly study jurisprudence and even the philosophy of law, whereas historians seldom engage in the study of historiography, less still the philosophy of history.

The difference is that lawyers well know that their activity is a practical one, with immediate and drastic effects on the human beings who appear in the courts for judgement, and that there are strong practical reasons why they should use theory to heighten their awareness of what they are doing and allow the consequences of theory to flow back into practice and affect it. But historians are engaged in no such immediate practice, and do not have the same practical reasons for engaging in theory. It is therefore easier for them to believe that the way to write history is to practise the activity, and that no theory of historiography and no philosophy of history exist which can be applied to that activity as theory to practice. They are clearly right for the most part in believing this, not because they are immediate practical actors but because they are not. The importance of the history of historiography and the philosophy of history is to be sought elsewhere. What historians write has consequences for other human beings because it helps to shape the assumptions and structures, the ideologies, mentalities and discourses by which social groups define themselves, others and the world, and act in the relations between the entities so defined; who they think they are and what they think has been going on can easily have consequences for themselves and others, and these consequences can easily be disastrous. Thus there are very strong practical reasons for exhorting historians to heighten their consciousness of what they are doing in the world, and what assumptions about the world they are putting into effect; but the relations between reflection and action to which we are exhorting them will be relations less of theory to practice than of criticism to ideology.

This is why there are so many situations in which juristic and historiographic activity are intermingled and imperfectly distinct; in which lawyers are making history and historians contributing to the making of law; and why it is both philosophically interesting and humanly important to study these situations and note in what a variety of ways history is being made in them. I have a case of the kind to examine: one in which the affairs of my own country of New Zealand have become interesting to the lawyer[3] and the historian, the political philosopher and the historian of political thought, in ways which, I have to confess, in my younger days I never thought they would be. New Zealanders, somewhat against their inclinations, have come upon interesting times; it is to be hoped they will survive them.

(II)

In a number of societies created by British and European settlement in the seventeenth through twentieth centuries – New Zealand and Australia, Canada and the United States – there is a political resurgence of the peoples called indigenous because their ancestors lived there before European settlement began, and usually because these ancestors remain of immediate importance to them. In the societies I have mentioned, where language, law and values are in significant measure English in their derivation, these resurgent peoples state their claims in the language and law of the majority culture. They claim right, justice and compensation; they rely on principles of common law and *jus gentium* (a term I shall prefer to 'international law'); but at the same time they allege their aboriginality, their status as cultures with an existence antedating European settlement, both as entitling them to make claims which the majority law is bound by its own rules to respect, and as a source of cultural values and usages which must continue to guide them and which the majority law must acknowledge as authoritative even when these are not contained within its structure or its spirit. In a sense, then, they claim to be living by a law of their own, which is separate from the majority law and to which the latter must

---

[3] [Paul McHugh, a figure far more important to the making of this volume than his appearance in its footnotes has suggested, is studying the history of common law in the light of its encounters with indigenous claims to title. See McHugh, 1991, and a handlist of his writings in Sharp 1990, 1997, p. 329; McHugh, 2005, reached me too late for profit from its study.]

accommodate itself. However, they commonly do not refer to their own cultural codes by the name of 'law'; sometimes because they look on 'law' itself as the instrument by which the majority has been dispossessing them of their land, culture and identity; sometimes because the codes, assumptions and vocabulary of Anglo-European jurisprudence are too culturally and economically specific to be appropriate to the aboriginal codes which they recall, rediscover, or re-invent; sometimes because they are making use of the vocabulary of Western radical dissent, which suits their needs because it presents law itself as an instrument of hegemony in the hands of some race, class, gender or mode of production.

On the one hand, then, a vocabulary which is not that of the majority's law is addressing itself to the courts and legislatures of the majority in search of legal redress, and in some measure accepting the discourse and procedure of majority law by doing so. On the other hand, that vocabulary is being used to claim autonomy from that law and offering itself as an alternative cultural code with the same authority as law, whether it styles itself by that name or not. In the language of European jurisprudence – which our cultural conditioning obliges most of us to accept – the problem which the claims of indigenous peoples present moves between the theatres of common law and *jus gentium*. These peoples are claiming the status of *gentes* or nations – in the early modern or pre-modern sense in which *jus gentium* uses the latter term – and thereby raising the question of what degree of sovereignty – again in the pre-modern sense known to the classics of *jus gentium* – they possessed at the time of European settlement and may be said to possess now.

This is not merely a question framed by the needs of late twentieth-century debate: it can be found, asked and answered – and has served as the foundation of legal and political arrangements – in the past history of European settlement; so that to ask it is not to re-invent the history of that settlement so much as to review and re-state it as it was constructed by the actors themselves. From the time of the Spanish conquests in Mesoamerica, European settlement was conducted by agents living in a universe of *jus gentium* and endeavouring to avail themselves of its rules.[4] It can of course be said that this branch of law took shape largely in response to the needs imposed by the encounter with non-European peoples, and it must be said with great frequency that the ways in which it took shape were often skewed in favour of the invading settlers and directed towards the

---

[4] There is an extensive literature on the Spanish debate. See most recently, Pagden, 1982; Muldoon, 1994.

dispossession of the indigenous peoples. Even that language is suspiciously mild when applied to many of the stories which this history contains. But the invading Europeans did make use of a code of *jus gentium*, even if it was only to legitimate their own behaviour. Their use of that code ensured that in a great many cases treaties were entered into with indigenous people, who were therefore treated as competent actors, and indeed capable, as possessors of sovereignty, to enter into such treaties as the kind of contracting parties whom that law envisaged. In many instances, these treaties were subsequently disregarded; in many more, they were interpreted as a kind of legal self-annihilation or suicide on the part of the indigenous contractor, so that to enter into a treaty was to lose the right to enforce it and consequently all rights under it. But enough of these treaties have survived – in the sense that there are still peoples defined by them and living under them – to make it a common strategy in the politics of indigenous resurgence to appeal to them, claiming not only rights under them but the measure of sovereignty which their status as treaties affirms to have existed then and to be claimable now.

Such appeals and claims necessarily generate debates in the interpretation of history, occasioned in the first instance by the decision to treat an action in the past as possessing authority in the present; a decision taken by lawyers or persons acting as lawyers, which raises questions to be answered by historians or persons acting as historians, but over which lawyer and historian must in the end diverge and go separate ways. The history of how a treaty was drawn up and entered into must be rehearsed in the light of the always contestable question of how it was intended and understood by the original parties, of whom it may be presumed that one was and the other was not European and already familiar with the language of European law. An attempt must be made to reconstruct the mentality of an indigenous society already distant in time; but it must be added that persons in the present, affirming themselves the descendants, representatives or continuators of that society, will be interpreting the acts and intentions of their supposed ancestors, imposing pattern on the past, authority on the present, and interpretations of history on the events and processes between. The heirs of the original European signatories will be doing the same, and their situation will be complicated by the circumstance that they possessed then and probably possess now the upper hand in imposing the categories of European jurisprudence, but now consent to have their position questioned and evaluated, both by the categories of their own law and by the injection into the argument of cultural codes which are not European, but must be reconstructed in a largely (but challengeably) Europeanized present. Two points must sooner or later be reached. At one it will be recognized that alternative histories are contesting for authority; not simply alternative accounts of the same events, but alternative cultural codes which give conflicting accounts of what authority is, how it is generated in and transmitted through time, and how time and history are themselves structured by the authoritative systems set up by humans existing in them. At the other, the historian will have made an appearance, declaring that the enterprise of reconstituting events and processes, mentalities and authority structures, existing or ongoing in the past, has developed beyond the point at which it serves the jurist's need to find authority there which is applicable in the present. This historian will be operating in bihistorical and bicultural terms, recognizing that all parties to the debate are trying to live in two histories simultaneously penetrating one another.

During the establishment of European settlement, many treaties were entered into with tribes – if that is the appropriate term[5] for societies operating a complex kinship structure rather than a state, identifying themselves by means of shared genealogies and mythologies, and living by hunting and gathering and planting rather than by arable cultivation. These tribes were recognized by treaty and *jus gentium* as 'nations' or *gentes*, and endowed with the capacity to exert rights and hold property – often, of course, to no other end than that they should be deemed capable of parting with it or selling it. Many fictions were thereby imposed on peoples who did not always understand them, but had their own ways of understanding themselves and what they were doing when they entered into what the Europeans called treaties – hence of course the European conviction that all men by nature possessed the legal capacity for possession and alienation, compact and confederation.

But it is evident to our historic sensibility that any such treaty was a compact between two discourses, two means of understanding and operating what it was, and the modern indigenous nation has access both to European means of interpreting a treaty and to the modernized form (whatever it may be) of the indigenous discourse by which the treaty may have been understood then and is understood now. If the dominant European culture has remained ethnocentric to the point where it does not understand the indigenous discourse and cannot operate it, that culture

---

[5] In New Zealand it has been found appropriate to use the Maori word *iwi*, and leave its meanings to emerge through bicultural discourse. [The word, however, has a history in both Maori and *pakeha* usage, which leaves it at some points open to challenge (Ballara, 1998). There are points in this essay where I might have done better to use *hapu* for *iwi*.]

does not have access to the bilingual resources open to the otherwise repressed indigenous culture. The latter can therefore: (1) claim to be the 'nation', sovereign to the point of ceding some things and retaining others, which the original treaty presumed it to be; (2) operate its indigenous discourse to affirm its customary, traditional, genealogical and mythic identity, and employ this identity in affirming its legal personality under the treaty and claiming rights, or compensation for lost rights, in both treaty and traditional terms. If the dominant culture does not have access to the indigenous discourse – what in New Zealand is called *te reo Maori* – it must choose between allowing that discourse to be used against it, and facing the charge that it is seeking to annihilate the indigenous discourse and the nation that employs it. Often, of course, the dominant culture has been seeking to do exactly that; but we have reached the point of encountering the politics of bilingualism and biculturalism, and of recognizing how an indigenously affirmed identity may be both the grounds and the means of conducting a claim simultaneously *in* the discourse of European law and *against* that discourse and law. The appellant comes before the court partly to challenge its jurisdiction, and in so doing alleges indigenous history against the history of the law and the treaty. Yet there remains the paradox – which operated for Europeans at the time of settlement – that it is hard in law to indict an opposed authority without at the same time legitimating it.

Treaties under *jus gentium* are entered into by nations, and nations possess both sovereignty at the time of making the treaty and a self-defining history antecedent to its making. This provides the double force behind such words as 'indigenous', 'aboriginal', the Maori *tangata whenua* and so on. It is crucial to the indigenous group that it should be able to define itself as a 'nation', possessed of both history and legal or rights-bearing personality both before and since the making of the treaty; and in so doing it lays claim to sovereignty – if that term be used to denote the possession of rights and the capacity to alienate and resume them – in both the pre-treaty past and the post-treaty past and present. To the extent that the indigenous group is part of a larger sovereign state, it has now reached the point of affirming that the state's sovereignty is based on the treaty and is shared among sovereign contracting partners. State and sovereignty rest on the exercise of what Locke called the federative power, the power to form treaties, whether or not the state in question is a confederation. It is evident to our minds that this is an extremely risky assertion; it is less evident that it entails both pre-modern and post-modern thinking.

Australia is largely an exception to the pattern I have begun to describe, since there it was not typical to enter into treaties with aboriginal groups, which were often too small and mobile to render treaties of much use and could easily be dismissed as in a 'savage' condition that rendered them incapable of treaty-making. The United States and Canada are perhaps the most typical, in that they possess political structures which are federal or confederal for reasons of their own, and were not formed by processes in which treaties with indigenous nations played a central part. They can thus recognize the forming of federal covenants with such nations and not feel the exercise of their own federal structure to be threatened. The Sioux or the Mohawk can claim to be sovereign nations in a special treaty relation with the United States; but as the Canadian confederal structure has been laid open to redefinition, there has emerged a 'Conference of First Nations' whose adherents claim 'inherent rights' – i.e. rights inherent in their structure as nations and antecedent to any Canadian nationality or sovereignty – which entitle them to be consulted and give their consent before any new relations between provinces reconstituting Canada assume a final form.

New Zealand is exceptional for the reason that it is not a confederation but a unitary and sovereign state, whose sovereignty seems to rest upon a treaty – the Treaty or *te Tiriti* of Waitangi – which preceded and can be said to condition the declaration of the crown's sovereignty in 1840. Alone among the cases I have been considering, then, the political sovereignty which affirms and defines the national identity can be considered contingent, or dependent, on the performance or non-performance of a treaty between two cultures or discourses, whose meaning and history can be debated in two languages entailing two understandings of law, culture, sovereignty and their existence in time. It is potentially a very exciting debate and a very dangerous one; the more so as it comes at a time when New Zealand's identity, sovereignty and national continuity are already exposed to a variety of challenges. The fact that these challenges are so posed that they cannot be met without using the term 'sovereignty' on more than one level of meaning lends complexity, both political and historical, to the issues to be discussed.

(III)

As part of the process of establishing the crown's sovereignty over New Zealand in 1840, a treaty was drawn up and signed by the crown's representative, Captain Hobson, and the chiefs of a number of independent *iwi* ('tribes') at Waitangi in the north of the North Island. It was subsequently proffered to the chiefs of other *iwi*, and accepted by most if not all of them, in both islands. It was not a treaty with the Maori people as a whole, and that people did not then or subsequently form a single unit or confederation for purposes of legal or political action; the word 'Maori' was only just coming into general use to distinguish the indigenous Polynesians from the European settlers, and the tribe, *hapu* or *iwi* remains for most the group of identification. However, since nearly all *iwi* have entered into the treaty relationship, it is reasonable to see its provisions as underlying the relations of Maori to the crown wherever they can be found.

It can be debated just what role the Treaty has in the establishment of crown sovereignty in New Zealand. A claim could be made on the grounds of prior discovery, which gave Britain a right not shared with any European nation to pre-empt land from the indigenous inhabitants, and this right of pre-emption has been exercised, in ways often hard to reconcile with the language of the Treaty, to purchase and sometimes confiscate land or dispose of it by legislative or executive action. The crown's sovereignty can be defined as an exclusive right to acquire land and to dispose of the title to it by sale or grant, and this right is claimed exclusively of other nations on the grounds of discovery. But a series of proclamations, instructions to royal officials and private memoranda belonging to the period make it quite clear that the crown had no intention of proclaiming sovereignty without the consent of the inhabitants, and give us a number of clues as to how this consent was to be granted. In written statements by the Prime Minister, Lord John Russell, and the Colonial Secretary, Lord Glenelg, it is confirmed that the inhabitants of New Zealand are not 'savages living by the chase' (i.e. not hunter-gatherers with no relation to the soil, which is to assign them a fairly advanced place in the scheme of history worked out in the recent Enlightenment), but that they are capable of occupying the land and apportioning it between them.[6] It would be interesting to know whether Russell and Glenelg had been informed, by missionaries or others, that the Maori were turning to agriculture and beginning to plant and harvest cereals, as some of them were; whether they recognized in them some other capacity for occupation and apportionment, such as is claimed and conceded today; or whether the crown's intent was to attribute to them a capacity for property as a preliminary to a capacity for alienation. This intention was shared by the agents of several

---

[6] Charles Grant, Lord Glenelg, memorandum, 15 December 1837; CO 209/21/21409; Kawharu, 1989, p. 31.

commercial enterprises, including the New Zealand Company, who were making land purchases from Maori and desired to legitimate them.

These documents further state that though the tribes or *iwi* do not constitute a sovereign state, in the sense that there is no supreme authority which rules them all and can speak on their behalf, they nevertheless possess a 'sovereignty' (the word used) which cannot be subordinated to another without their consent; and this appears to state the juridical basis on which the meetings occurred at Waitangi and on which the Treaty was drawn up and signed. A good deal could certainly be said about the motives of the British ministers in using this language. They were trying to establish a negotiating position in advance of the French (always a prudent thing to do); and if we take the view that their intention already was – as it soon afterwards became – that of investing the crown with a title to New Zealand land which it might dispose of in parcels to settlers, we can add with much plausibility that their purpose in attributing sovereignty to the *iwi* was to invest them with the capacity to transfer it to the crown. Nevertheless their language did attribute to the indigenous people a capacity to enter into treaties and to possess land and rights before they began to negotiate; and we must add that this attributed to them a history, a previous and inherent existence, a past, a present and a future. The language of European jurisprudence had that effect, and it further attributed to the Treaty itself the status of a historical document, a document performing an authoritative act in history, to which reference could be made in the future by actors who saw it as exerting authority in their present arising from their past. Much of the subsequent history of the Treaty recounts the attempts of *pakeha* jurisprudence to deprive it of that status, and the counter-attempts of contemporary bicultural jurisprudence to restore it.

It would be reasonable to give a Lockean reading to the language used by Russell and Glenelg. A dispersed sovereignty is being attributed to the *iwi*; having occupied their lands, they possess a right in them, and this right extends to the authority to do, by the law of nature, what is necessary in virtue of their occupancy. They may, for example, make war upon one another – as was certainly their practice at the time – in defence or furtherance of their claims. What is missing from the discourse is the further Lockean principle that one acquires property in land only by mixing one's labour with it; the *iwi* are distinguished from hunter-gatherers by their capacity for occupancy, but how far that capacity depends upon one for labour in the form of cultivation is not made clear, and this was to be a source of philosophical difficulty when a Maori perception of occupancy which did not depend upon cultivation and exploitation collided with a *pakeha* perception which did. However, that was not the issue in the approach to Waitangi. Russell and Glenelg were saying that the *iwi* possessed sovereignty dispersed among themselves, but had not yet found it necessary – and, they may have silently added, had not yet developed the capacity – to transfer that sovereignty to a civil government capable of exercising authority over and on behalf of them all. The language of the British ministers made it plain that this transfer should not occur without the consent of the *iwi* freely given; but at Waitangi they invited the chiefs there assembled to give that consent. There was, as it happened, in the islands composing New Zealand, no one like Kamehameha in Hawaii, Cakombau in Fiji, or Tubou in Tonga, capable of conquering and establishing a territorial hegemony which Europeans might consider a kingdom, doing so from within indigenous history and using it to act in the new history imposed by European contact. The programme of establishing a central sovereign authority arose out of the activities of the British and French governments, missionary and settler enterprises; and this origin rendered more problematic the business of explaining the programme at Waitangi in inter-cultural terms – that is, of speaking out of a European discourse to a Polynesian discourse when the two were framed in discontinuous cultural worlds and had different immediate agenda. The chiefs were not to know the whole of the British reasons for wanting a sovereign government in New Zealand; they had not evolved, or expressed in their own discourse, reasons of their own for conceptualizing or wanting one. Nor would the British officers, missionaries, speculators and settlers have been able to see far into the Maori mental world, even if they had desired to do so.

Where the minds of the two cultures came close enough to meeting at Waitangi to engender misunderstandings – divergent interpretations of the same events or utterances – was over the conceptualization of title to land. The British desired sovereignty not just in the form of a protectorate defending control over New Zealand against external or foreign competitors, but in the form of a civil government with authority to effect and regulate the transfer of lands from indigenous occupants to immigrant or settler owners. The *iwi* so far involved in this process knew that they were effecting such transfers, but did not expect to be dispossessed as a result of doing so; and such language is inadequate in so far as it is too European to express the Maori perception of what the occupancy of land was. The *iwi* for their part had difficulty in grasping that the crown was proposing to acquire a preemptive sovereignty, a sovereign role for itself in acquiring title to land from indigenous occupants and transferring it to settler owners.

What was at issue was not merely the creation of a Lockean sovereignty with authority to regulate the transfer of lands, but that of a pre-emptive sovereignty with authority to make itself the source of legal title to land. The nature of both possession and sovereignty was being developed along lines well known to the civil law; transitions from *usus* to *dominium* and from *dominium* to *imperium* were being invoked and brought into the process. The Maori participants were not to know this, since it was not their language; but they had a highly developed language of their own for talking about the occupation of land, the claiming of land, and the passage of land from one control to another. Whether means of translation from one discourse to another were found, whether they could have been found in good faith, and whether they were indeed pursued in good faith, are issues in the historical interpretation of the Treaty of Waitangi.

The Treaty (or *te Tiriti*) was bilingually conducted and texts were drawn up for signature in both English and Maori. Literacy was developing among Maori and the texts had been orally debated; the issue is not therefore that the chiefs did not know what they were signing, but that no satisfactorily final text existed or ever has.[7] The redactors of the Maori text were themselves *pakeha* – a term I shall use from now on when speaking of Europeans in the New Zealand bicultural setting – missionaries, with interests of their own not identical with those of the Maori or necessarily of the crown. They employed what is known as 'missionary Maori', a vocabulary which contains Maori terms adapted or created to express *pakeha* legal, political and religious concepts. More than one Maori text of *te Tiriti* exists, and was presented to various *iwi* for signature after the gathering at Waitangi; these texts are not identical with one another, and philologically exact English translations of them do not always reinforce the official English text recorded by the officers of the crown. It is therefore possible to understand both the extreme Maori view that *te Tiriti* is a fraudulent document, and the extreme *pakeha* view that the Treaty has no binding or legal force. In circumstances I shall presently describe, however, it has attained the status of a fundamental text, possessing authority and open to interpretation; and both lawyer and historian will recognize the problems in reconstituting a past and assessing its authority in the present which must next arise. Law is being made in a context of disputed authority and disputed interpretation; that is how law is made and history is written. It is less common, though not unknown, for this to happen in a context of bilingual documents and bicultural interpretation.

---

[7] Kawharu, 1989.

The crucial area in the several texts has come to be one in which something is ceded to the crown, which in the Maori text is termed *kawanatanga* and in the English 'sovereignty', and something is retained by the chiefs and *iwi*, which in Maori is termed *rangatiratanga* and in English 'full, exclusive and undisturbed possession of their lands and estates'. The passage obviously – at least to European minds – raises the classic issue of the relation of sovereignty to property, but behind that lies the fundamental issue of the crown's adoption of a pre-emptive title. What looked like a guarantee of possession to the *iwi* has in practice meant to them the imposition of a greater capacity for alienation than they desired. The crown has in the past used its *kawanatanga* to determine who the possessors of *rangatiratanga* in fact are, to individualize tribal tenure in order to facilitate the sale of land, and to take into possession and dispose of lands which the *iwi* understood to be theirs by the kind of title which *rangatiratanga* connotes and which, though undefined in 1840, the crown implicitly recognized them as capable of exercising. Now that the crown's title to have done these things is being disputed in terms of a retrospective and retroactive reading of the Treaty, it is important to discuss what was, and what has been, conceded under the name *kawanatanga* and retained under the name *rangatiratanga*.

Kawanatanga is missionary Maori, an attempt at a rendering of the English word 'government'; similarly, and rather potently, the Treaty itself is sometimes called a *kawanata* or 'covenant'. The English text renders *kawanatanga* as 'sovereignty', by which the Maori signatories may have understood in the first instance something like a 'protectorate', though they would also have understood that the Crown intended, and was being empowered, to maintain this exclusively of other Europeans or Americans who might seek it. What is less clear is how far they understood the extensions of the English word 'sovereignty' into the powers of civil government. Was it understood as keeping the peace among the *iwi* and *hapu* (tribes and sub-tribes) or as adjudicating disputes over land between them? It is perfectly clear, however, that they did not think they were conceding to the crown any ultimate authority over or title to the lands of the two major islands; it is the question of crown title which has in the end become crucial. On the other hand, the distinction between *kawanatanga* and *rangatiratanga* itself makes quite clear that they were intent on retaining some ultimate authority over land, and were aware of the dichotomy between something which they were retaining and something which they were conceding. One of them is on record as saying 'the shadow goes to the Queen, the substance stays with us', but later declaring that he had been wrong and the saying should be reversed; I regret that I am unable to comment on the Maori words he used or their significances.

The crucial term in Maori understanding of *te Tiriti* both was and has become *rangatiratanga*; in full *te tino rangatiratanga*. This is much nearer being an authentic Maori term, though it was already capable of missionary usage; significantly, it was being employed as a Christian sacred term, in translating the words 'thy kingdom come' in the Lord's Prayer. *Rangatira* was the word for a chief, and the suffix *tanga* gives to English-speakers the word 'chieftainship', which by no means inappropriately suggests that the signatories intended to retain authority as well as possession, *dominium* as well as *usus*. *Rangatiratanga* connotes not only 'possession of the land', but 'possession according to Maori ways, according to the structures of author-ity and value inherent in *iwi* society'. The chiefs had no intention that they or their peoples should become mere subjects of the crown, whose posses-sion of the land was protected by crown law indeed, but only by the kind of law the crown was accustomed to administer. *Rangatiratanga* connoted their own authority as *rangatira*, and at least one of them announced that he would never sign the Treaty for fear of finding himself subject to a power not his own. For these reasons, modern Maori interpretation reads into *rangatiratanga* the Treaty's recognition of a right to possession, not of lands, forests and fisheries alone, but of the norms and values, the social structure and culture, inherent in the occupancy of land as the *iwi* then recognized themselves as occupying it; in other words, the possession of themselves, their identity as a people. They claim to have been dispossessed of this identity, contrary to the provisions of *te Tiriti*; and they claim that the dispossession was unjust, and that the Treaty entitles them to reposses-sion of both land and cultural identity (which are inseparable) where repossession is possible, and to compensation and resources to use in building a new identity where it is not. A new problem instantly arises. Claims under a treaty, or under a common law, are in principle negotiable; claims to a unique and all-inclusive cultural or spiritual identity easily become non-negotiable. In the terms being used in this essay, the question becomes whether the Maori and the *pakeha* occupy a single history of interaction, or two histories incompatible with one another; and this problem is occasioned by the fact that *kawanatanga* and *rangatiratanga* are each translatable as 'sovereignty', when the word is used on its two levels of Lockean meaning. 'Sovereignty' begins to denote the power to consti-tute one's own history, on the level of conceptualization and possession and on that authority and action. Even to write history may entail a claim to make it; but to what or whom can that claim be addressed?

We encounter here the crucial significance of the term *whenua*. Its primary meaning is land or an area of land, inhabited by *tangata*, or people, constituting a *hapu* or *iwi*; but it further and simultaneously means placenta, and alludes to the custom of burying the afterbirth in the land as a symbol or vehicle of unity with the ancestors. Consequently, *tangata whenua* – a term by which modern Maori distinguish themselves – means both 'people of the land' and 'people of the birthplace'; it asserts both priority of occupation and a physico-spiritual unity with ancestors and with the land, through one another, which constitutes the identity of the *iwi*; and the last word now denotes both particular tribes and the Maori people or nation – *te iwi Maori* – as a whole. These are modern usages, and I do not know how far the phrase *tangata whenua* was used in the debates at Waitangi in 1840; but the word *whenua* was certainly present, and carried with it the load of meanings I have been describing, which would pervade the meaning of the treaty term *rangatiratanga* to an extent which the missionary draughtsmen may not have understood and which would overflow the distinctions between sovereignty and property present in the minds of the crown's representatives. The crown was already in the position of having the chiefs transfer sovereignty in one sense to it, while having the chiefs retain sovereignty in another for themselves. This verbal ambiguity mattered only in English, but the transaction was vastly complicated by the unacknowledged circumstance that *rangatiratanga* – sovereignty in the second sense – carried with it the psychic and mythic loads of the term *whenua*.

There was a Maori term – there is little reason to consider it a post-contact invention – for the authority with which an *iwi* could claim occupancy of an area, thus exercising that capacity for appropriation which in European eyes distinguished Maori from savages. This term was and is *manawhenua*, an extension of the word *mana*, with which we are somewhat familiar as denoting prestige, authority, and traditional and charismatic force of personality; we have many words of our own for it. An *iwi* in the person of its chief or *rangatira* – though chief and people were not so far distinguished from one another as to require a conscious fiction of representation – might – to the extent that the ancestors were in the *whenua* as placenta – assert that the *iwi* derived its physical and spiritual identity (of which *mana* was the dynamism) from the *whenua* as land. When one *iwi* subjugated another and appropriated its *mana* and *whenua*, it absorbed the defeated into its own substance, occasionally and for specific reasons by methods too direct to be described. The ancient community of a people with its lands and ancestors was not always an idyll; the point is that it all stood, and to some degree still stands, in Maori eyes as the mode by which they possess not merely land but themselves, and are what they are. The mystifying thing about Western capitalist society is that we believe property to be an extension of the self, yet believe that it can constantly be in a state of transference from one self to another; and it was this mystery that the crown was about to impose on the *iwi* at Waitangi. It is a large part of what we mean by the term 'history'.

It has been suggested by more than one modern Maori author that if it was the crown's intention to acquire sovereign authority in the sense of a title to land, a sovereign capacity to act in all transfers of property in land from one possessor to another, the term *kawanatanga* as used in the Treaty concealed the reality that what the chiefs were being induced to concede to the crown was *manawhenua*. Moreover, this reality had to be concealed, not merely because they would never have agreed to the proposal, but because it would have been an unthinkably deep affront even to ask it of them. The chief who exploded into rage saying he would never sign the Treaty and the chief who hoped for the moment that they were giving up the shadow and retaining the substance may have sensed that something of the kind was afoot. But to suppose that they were being deliberately deceived, we must suppose that the British officers and missionaries knew what *manawhenua* was, and knew that they dared not ask the *rangatira* and the *iwi* to give the crown not merely control over transactions, but *mana* over the physical and spiritual substance of themselves. They may not have understood this, and the guarantee of *rangatiratanga* may have meant in good faith that the *iwi* would be able to sell land and accept the crown's jurisdiction over sales, without giving up the essential *dominium* over it; but the implicit concession that the Maori were not savages does not necessarily mean that the *pakeha* recognized in them any kind of sovereignty they were going to keep. Extinctions of title, it was believed, could be justly arranged under the *kawanatanga–rangatiratanga* relationship.

The modern Maori claim is twofold, or rather is being made on two levels. On the one hand, it is being asserted that many dispossessions of Maori have occurred which must be judged unjust in terms of the agreed meanings of the language used in the Treaty. On the other, it is being asserted that the surface meaning of that language is itself inadequate, and can be rendered just only when we recognize the implication that the *rangatiratanga* reserved to the *iwi* both conceals and contains all that is meant by a multitude of Maori terms from which I have selected *manawhenua* as the most informative. The Treaty and *te Tiriti* are therefore unsatisfactory and even fraudulent on one level, justifiable only by interpretation on another, and this judicial procedure is a means of recognizing and rectifying much that has passed in New Zealand history since 1840.

We are to recognize here a judicial and historiographical situation of a familiar type. A document from the past which exercises authority in the present is being interpreted and the thrust of its authority re-assessed, in the light of perceptions exercised in the present. At the same time it is being asserted that these are perceptions of the historic reality of what occurred in the past and has gone on occurring into the present, and we are not yet at the point where lawyer and historian must go separate ways and arrive at positions adopted for separate reasons. It is worth noting also that historical criticisms which reveal shortcomings and perhaps dishonesties in the language and conduct of the Treaty are not being used to subvert it and dismiss its authority, but rather to reinforce it. By this blend of historical criticism and judicial interpretation, we offer to render the Treaty a better instrument for assessing what has happened in the past and rectifying the past's consequences in the present. The historian will add – and the lawyer need not deny – that this is both a way of heightening our understanding of history and a means of enhancing our capacity to act in it.

(IV)

To say these things is to utter a series of relatively reassuring statements in the familiar discourse of the ancient constitution; that is to say, English legal reasoning, which has long understood the similarities and differences, the complex but not antagonistic relations between judicial interpretation and historical criticism. The situation becomes much more complex, and perhaps a good deal less reassuring, when we recognize that the claim made on behalf of the *tangata whenua* entails the statement that *te Tiriti* both conceals and fails to recognize, and implicitly contains and does recognize, a complex system of property, sovereignty and culture – of *whenua*, *mana* and *tangata* – which is discontinuous with that system built into the historical structure of English common law and European *jus gentium*. It means among other things that those inhabiting the system inhabit a history which is differently conceptualized, differently based and maintained by different modes of action, from the history presupposed by English and European jurisprudence. This recognition is thrust upon us once we acknowledge that the claims of *manawhenua* entail, or once did entail, or may be said to have once entailed, the occupancy of the earth by ancestral communities, linked with their ancestors through the earth, and maintaining their identity, sovereignty and *mana* through this continuity. To live in such a continuity is to live in a different history from that of the *pakeha*. The claim that the Treaty guarantees *rangatiratanga* now becomes the claim that *te iwi Maori* possess a treaty right to their own history, have been unjustly dispossessed of their history, and may now justly repossess it or make claims to compensation where this is not possible. Bicultural is bihistorical; the language thus stated implicitly concedes that the Maori have been partly forced out of their history into *pakeha* history, but at the same time calls on the *pakeha* to recognize and restore Maori history, living in relation to it where they cannot live within it themselves. Bicultural jurisprudence becomes a mediation between radically dissimilar perceptions and experiences of history.

It is a premiss of this essay that sovereignty, legislative and political, is among other things a mode by which a human community seeks to command its own history; to take actions which shape its policies in the present, and even – since a great deal of history has in fact been written in this way – to declare the shape of the historic past and process out of which it deems itself to be issuing. Neither of these modes of self-determination ever has been or will be in the absolute power of any sovereign community; but this does not prevent us asking what may become of a community's capacity either to make or to write its own history if its political sovereignty should be surrendered to forces from without or radically challenged by forces from within. With respect to the latter possibility, what has happened in recent New Zealand politics may be described as follows. Maori people, in part if paradoxically because they were becoming increasingly urbanized, found it proper to emphasize their status as *tangata whenua* in claiming either restitution of their relation to the land or compensation for its loss. Though now a moderate-sized minority of the population, they were able to get attention for their claims, and adopted the strategy of making these claims under the Treaty of Waitangi. There has come into being the Waitangi Tribunal, a body judicial in character and even authority, empowered to hear claims by Maori arising out of performance or non-performance of the Treaty's provisions. Though its proceedings are judicial in character and distinguished judges – several of them Maori learned in the law – have sat on and presided over it, its findings are not binding at law, but rather take the form of recommendations of such authority – one might say *mana* – that courts and parliament do well to give them attention. This authority derives from the circumstance that the Treaty which the Tribunal interprets states the preconditions under which the sovereignty of the crown, and therefore of courts and parliament, came to be established and New Zealand came into existence and later became a sovereign nation. The Tribunal therefore does more than hear cases against the crown; it investigates whether the crown has or has not been discharging conditional obligations subject to which sovereignty was transferred to it in the first place. This is why its recommendations cannot be binding at law, but are such that the law is well advised to give them attention; it has, in the last analysis, a real if limited capacity to query the legitimacy of the sovereign's jurisdiction. Clearly, this is a capacity to be exercised at discretion. In demanding restitution from a sovereign, it is a poor strategy to suggest that the sovereign lacks the authority to make such restitution. This was one route by which the kingdom of England fell into civil war and dissolution of government in the seventeenth century.

Issues brought before the Tribunal may in principle turn upon the relations of *kawanatanga* to *rangatiratanga* in the language of the Treaty; that is, upon the questions of how sovereignty was conveyed to the crown, of whether the crown has been discharging the conditions under which sovereignty was conveyed to it, and of whether sovereignty, while conveyed to the crown in one sense (*kawanatanga*), was retained by the *iwi* in another sense (*rangatiratanga*), thus constituting a fundamental condition under which the crown legitimately exercises its sovereignty. To anyone with an elementary knowledge of English and European history, these are momentous and rather frightening questions. The Treaty of Waitangi has become New Zealand's ancient constitution, its Magna Carta, its fundamental law, its original contract; and all these historical analogies should serve as reminders of how easily a challenge to sovereignty in the name of any of them can become a dissolution of government, an appeal to heaven, and a lapse into civil war and the state of nature. Moreover, not even Magna Carta and the original contract were presented in the form of treaties between equal sovereign partners, between whom, *jus gentium* informs us, there must be either the state of treaty or the state of war; and the fundamental law of New Zealand was being presented in the form of a treaty. Finally, the effect of the Treaty was, however you look at it, to transfer title to land into the jurisdiction of the crown, and all real property in New Zealand, *pakeha* and for the most part Maori, is now held under a title conferred by the crown. To press contractual doctrine so far that the crown's sovereignty ceased to be legitimate would mean that no proprietor was certain of the title under which he held; and what the *pakeha* of 1628 and 1688 did in the like circumstances is a warning against letting them recur. During 1988 I found myself reminding New Zealand students that all classical *pakeha* political philosophy was about land rights and sovereignty, and all of it was a remedy for civil war. In 1998, the prospect of New Zealand's repudiating the crown and establishing a republic appears remote.[8]

Happily, in the view of most of us, none of these dire consequences ever looked likely to recur. The Treaty was not represented as a negotiation between equal sovereigns, but as a Lockean process whereby sovereignty in its dispersed form was conditionally converted into sovereignty in a centralized form; so that to remind sovereignty of the conditions under which it has been granted remained a claim against it, and did not become the 'appeal to heaven' which is issued when sovereignty is declared forfeit or delegitimized. Nevertheless, the original contract remained as a treaty between two nations, with the difference that one was then possessed of sovereignty only in its dispersed form, while the other possessed it in its centralized form. The Maori were able to contend that their treaty was with the crown direct, with the consequence that only Maori may bring complaints before the Tribunal, and individual *pakeha* are debarred from doing so on the grounds that their relations with the sovereign are conducted through other channels. There has also occurred a significant retreat from the position laid down in 1877 by Chief Justice Prendergast in *Wi Parata* v. *Bishop of Wellington*,[9] to the effect that the Treaty was of no legal force because only nations already possessed of legislative sovereignty possessed the federative capacity to enter into binding treaties. What is noteworthy here is that Prendergast's judgement is now seen as resting upon a strongly positivist jurisprudence, which made so much of full political sovereignty as to relegate to the condition of savagery any social form not possessed of it. New Zealand's newly bicultural jurisprudence is now withdrawing from these nineteenth-century presuppositions towards those of the more naturalist *jus gentium* of the sixteenth through eighteenth centuries, which conceived of the acquisition of property, rights and sovereignty as taking place by stages in the process of history as then conceived. It has to do so if it is to make sense of the Treaty at all; we have seen that this was specifically based on the presumption that the Maori were not savages and were sufficiently possessed of sovereignty to be capable of transferring it to the

---

[8] [The authority of the crown has passed to the parliament and people of New Zealand. The Maori have a treaty with the crown, contracted before either existed, and have successfully prevailed on parliament and people to acknowledge that the crown's obligations have passed to them with its authority. In the event of a republic, the Maori would be compelled to renegotiate the Treaty with a parliamentary and electoral majority that had just carried out a dissolution of the government and a reversion of power to the people. There are few, if any, Maori republicans.]

[9] Kawharu, 1989, pp. 110–13.

crown. Whether this means that the Treaty can check the sovereign parliament in its legislative course is a question it may be wise to leave unanswered.

The jurisprudence of the Waitangi Tribunal – which is *prudentia juris* even more than *ratio legis* – thus enjoins the *pakeha* to explore the history of their law retrospectively, moving back in time in search of a perspective in which they can understand the *tangata whenua* and their own attitudes towards them. The *pakeha* may thus discover how deeply rooted in their history is their perception of property and sovereignty, with the self-propelled activity of the individual at its centre. However far back one goes in the past of feudal and Roman jurisprudence, one never comes upon the community linked with its ancestors in the *whenua* as the primary tenant of land; that was left behind in an antiquity so remote that no Western myth declares it plainly. Travelling back through the past of the common law, one may indeed come upon a time when statute was rooted in custom and second nature, which may assist in understanding what the *tangata whenua* have to say about themselves; but one may end convinced that, since their Hebraic and Hellenic beginnings, the *pakeha* have been travelling away from the *whenua* towards the individualization of tenure and the conversion of land into commodity and commodity into information, which governs our history today even if Karl Marx said it was going to. In the history of that process, the full and absolute sovereignty which the later *jus gentium* predicted and the positivists like Chief Justice Prendergast imposed upon history seems to have become an incident. In reverting to a pre-positivist jurisprudence, one reverts to a phase before the absolutism of sovereignty; it is necessary to do so in order to cope with a situation in which sovereignty rests on a treaty and may be contingent upon its fulfilment. But we all live in a world in which it is becoming rapidly contingent upon many more things than that, and is everywhere being subjected to the requirements of the international market; even when confederations break up and sovereignty is claimed by their constituent republics or tribes, that is the effect aimed at or achieved. It is an ideological consequence that the individual finds an identity less and less in membership of any sovereign community, state, nation or *iwi*; more and more, the individual is commanded by a convergence of forces to think of identity as contingent in itself, to be negotiated in an allegedly free market of interacting possibilities. Since modern indigenous peoples do not live on reservations which shield them from these constant displacements of personality, one must ask what they are achieving by their characteristic strategies. In what history will they find themselves living, when they claim to be living in the *whenua*?

(v)

We have simplified (and perhaps radicalized) the Maori claim to rights under *te Tiriti* by saying that they claim the guarantee of *rangatiratanga* to have been a guarantee of *manawhenua*; that is, a tribe's occupancy of the land furnishes it with a spiritual substance or continuity (*mana*), which in turn is extended as power over that land (*whenua*) and becomes a mode of appropriating it and constituting personality on its foundation (the Maori term for this is *turangawaewae*, the place where one stands). The personality thus constituted is that of a group whose communion with the ancestors and the land is constantly being renewed, and there is notoriously little room in this image for those creative conflicts between revolutionary groups and individuals which furnish history as the *pakeha* understand it. There are potent ancestor figures, but one must go back to the demigod Maui to find the Polynesian Prometheus. In the nineteenth century it used to be held that only the European masters of the planet possessed a history in the sense of autonomy, self-determination, progress and revolution, and that this was one reason why they were its destined masters. Today the *whenua* in one form or another is being used to challenge this view of history, and is finding much favourable response from a post-industrial civilization increasingly tired of its own history. Perhaps conservation is better than revolution; it may not be conservatism to say so. But if jurisprudence is a main source of our sense of history, the use of the *whenua* in jurisprudence brings up the problem that the *whenua*'s extension in time may be not history but the dreamtime – to use the invaluable Australian term for the communion with ancestors that may be experienced but is not to be narrated or criticized. What is to happen when the dreamtime is used as a basis for claims at law?

The term *tangata whenua*, like its homonyms 'indigenous' and 'aboriginal', implies two kinds of claim. One is simply a claim to priority of occupation, and need not entail more than a linear sense of time; the other is a claim to the kind of occupancy of space and time implicit in the concept *whenua*, and entails a relationship with the cosmos so close and exclusive as to contain both space and time within itself. The *iwi*, the ancestors and the *whenua* are all, as it were, contained within one another in the self-repetitive scheme whose items reduplicate one another; Adam has not stepped out of paradise into a world he must make and change by his own labour. The dreamtime may thus be contrasted with history, and may contrast itself to its own advantage with the latter's universe of ends and means, effort and frustration, self-realization and self-rejection.

The tribunal and the courtroom, whether ethnocentrically Western like Prendergast's or conscientiously bicultural like the Waitangi Tribunal, are necessarily acting in the world of history; they may respect the dreamtime but cannot submit to it. Their business is with the contestable, and there is no contesting with the dreamtime; this is painfully apparent when the latter is appealed to, not simply to discomfit the world of the *pakeha* in the name of the *tangata whenua*, but to assert contestable claims disputed among the *tangata whenua* themselves. Sir Tipene O'Regan, a Ngai Tahu activist from the South Island who shrewdly understands both law and history, has distinguished two types of situation in which *iwi* contest for primacy.[10] In one, both contestants allege genealogy and tradition, surviving in both oral and written forms; dispute is possible between them, each attaches truth-status to the statements it puts forward as history, and the courts are free to decide what kinds of evidence outweigh others. Courts of common law have of course been dealing with this type of situation since time whereof the memory of man runneth not to the contrary, and in most cases of this kind they are required to determine only what complainant has last been unjustly dispossessed in a plea of novel disseisin. However the professional historian may evaluate the claims of oral history, the courts are in search only of rules and evidence and testimony acceptable to both parties, and there are times when the historian is out of place in the courtroom; O'Regan warns him how easily the expert witness becomes a hired advocate without knowing it. The *prudentia juris* governs the situation; nevertheless it is important to remember that the contestant *iwi* may be not merely staking out claims but affirming their deepest sense of identity. The *whenua* is not just the tribe's lawful possession; it is the tribe itself.

This is where the second type of situation may arise out of the first. Litigants may appear claiming to represent, or constitute, an *iwi* more ancient than any other, *tangata whenua* in the literally aboriginal sense. When asked to substantiate their claims with evidence, they may reply that they have no need to; the voices of their ancestors speak to them in the rocks and trees, and speak to them as they speak to no others. I do not have to remind a readership including lawyers how any court or tribunal is likely to respond to that. It is entirely possible that such claims are fraudulent and

---

[10] O'Regan, 1992.

put forward in no good faith. Any tribunal will be strongly inclined to think so, since the representation of evidence which cannot be assessed will look like an attempt to mislead the court or derail its jurisdiction. Yet the evidence presented by litigants in the first and more manageable type of situation will contain accounts of times when the ancestors spoke directly to the occupants of the *whenua*, and the second set of litigants is only expanding and exploiting the kind of testimony offered by the first. Courts may be obliged to deconstruct *whenua* and dreamtimes in order to render them justiciable (in a sense, that is what has been happening ever since 1840), but the Waitangi Tribunal has been charged with rectifying, if not reversing, this process. In the universe of jurisdiction statements may be either true or false; it is not so in dreamtime, which is the universe of myth. History, the breakdown of the dreamtime, may be the precondition of judgement, and a dreamtime which comes to court for judgement may destroy itself, win or lose.

The problem before such courts is to treat dreamtimes with respect while regarding them as incidents in contingent reality; the law has faced such problems before, encountering or inventing a 'time beyond memory'. Here the *tangata whenua* of New Zealand present a problem less daunting to the *pakeha* philosopher than that of the Aboriginals of Australia. The latter, an inconceivably ancient people, arrived so long ago that no mythic or historic record preserves the memory of the journey from the there to the here; all Aboriginal myth is cosmic myth and the only time known to it is the dreamtime. This may well be connected with the fact that at the time of British settlement they were the hunter-gatherers whom Lord Glenelg described as 'savages living by the chase' and unable to apportion land as did the *iwi* of New Zealand. They moved long distances across a land surface they did not much cultivate, relating themselves to it as *whenua* by dreams and songs and sand paintings. Myth or not – and there is now a myth of the Aborigine in the Australian imagination – they present the image of a dreamtime so perfectly realized that there was nothing else; and how this is converted into a legal claim to rights must be a fascinating and complex story, perhaps yet to take place.

But Aotearoa – a modern Maori and *pakeha* term extended to the whole of New Zealand – is a very young *whenua* in terms of human occupancy, settled no more than a thousand years ago, in comparison with the minimally forty thousand of Australia. The *iwi* and *hapu* can name the *waka* or canoes in which their ancestors arrived, and locate in genealogical and chronological time the names of ancestors who came from other islands to Aotearoa, or from one part of Aotearoa to another. The ability to do so is part of the affirmation of *manawhenua*; one's name, one's mountain, one's river, one's ancestor and one's tribe – and so one's *turangawaewae*. The individuals named may be mythical; yet there is an important sense in which those who can name them are living in history rather than myth, and can take their *manawhenua* with them to court with less fear of losing it. Those who have resorted to the ineffable voices of their ancestors are justly suspect if they cannot name them. How the ancient Australians set about the process of naming is another story, and I would not even dream of suggesting that they did not do it; but I am suggesting that those they named were located in a different sort of time.

From this point it is possible to re-inspect the discourse which divides the inhabitants of New Zealand-Aotearoa into *tangata whenua* and *pakeha*, indigenous minority and settler majority. For one thing, the latter is becoming diversified by new waves of immigration – Europeans who are not *pakeha*, Polynesians who are not Maori, Asians who are not either – to the point where the old term *pakeha*, with its British and Irish connotations, may cease to be comprehensive, and may be replaced (none too satisfactorily) by the new *tau iwi* (for immigrants in general). But to confine ourselves to the two older terms, it is possible in the perspective I have presented to suggest that Maori and *pakeha* are not simply indigenous and immigrant, but that both may be characterized as *tangata waka* – peoples of the ship, who have ocean voyages and the discovery of islands in their memory, their language and their history. This argument may well be mistrusted as tending to deprive the *tangata whenua* of their priority and aboriginality, but I do not see that it would do that. It would firmly assert that their ancestors were the first human settlers, with a right of priority in that sense unequivocal. As for the wider and more intimate connotations of *whenua*, *mana* and *rangatiratanga*, it would affirm the extraordinary achievements of the ancient *tangata waka*, who arrived from beyond seas at islands very unlike those they had previously known and set about establishing, by myth, dream, genealogy and all their practices of occupancy and culture, the sort of relations with the environment that made them *tangata whenua*. The *whenua* and the dreamtime would thus be situated in history, made the achievements of human beings acting in human time to invent mythic time; it would be like the reduction of custom to statute, of the ancient constitution to historic changes in the patterns of land tenure, proposed to the common law in the increasing historical sophistication of the seventeenth century. *Whenua* and dreamtime would indeed be deprivileged to the extent that they lost any status so sacred that it could not even be discussed, and instead became contestable and negotiable before the tribunals and the courts; but contests for *mana-whenua* between separate *iwi*, or groups replacing *iwi*, have ensured that result already, and both Maori *marae* (or meeting-places) and *pakeha* law courts are already equipped with complex speech-patterns designed to assign priority between claims to ancient standing. The court can respect the dreamtime, though it cannot abdicate before it.

There seems to be no reason in principle – though there are plenty of alarming difficulties in practice – why the procedures being set up should not be capable of dealing with disputes arising since the Treaty, under the Treaty and even before the Treaty. The parameters of common law are capable of being expanded to the point where they can recognize and decide to respect the parameters of *manawhenua*. I see this process as having begun and, if it can be continued, as one of the things being done well and going well in contemporary New Zealand. Even the debate over the ultimate location of sovereignty, implicit and explicit in the appeal to the Treaty, can lead to the definition and renegotiation of sovereignty. But these are propositions about law, constitutional law and *jus gentium*; and this paper is concerned with the interrelations of law and history. It should not be difficult, and I hope I have not made it more difficult, to see how legal argument, conceived as appeal to past practices and the preconditions of authority, leads to reconstruction and reconstitution of history, conceived as the history of practice and authority, and even to juridical debate between such reconstitutions. To this point we are in the world of the lawyer, guided by the purposes of jurisprudence. But once we begin to debate questions of human identity and selfhood, questions of property and personality, *whenua* and *mana*, the scene changes; both lawyer and litigant find themselves faced with the preconditions of legal behaviour, the preconditions of who and what they are, and with history as the process of creation and change in those preconditions. If this sounds like an idealist conception of history, I shall reply that we are sometimes necessitated to conceive of history in that way.

I have tried to show that the differences between Anglo-European law and Maori-Polynesian *manawhenua* are such as to lead to very different conceptions of how human beings live in society and social time, and to that extent in history. By expanding – somewhat beyond the practical necessities of the contemporary New Zealand situation – the mythic and cosmic implications of the term *whenua*, I have tried to show how the concept of history itself can become the antithesis of another way of conceptualizing the continuity of human existence, for which I have used the term dreamtime. It can of course follow that the concept of history is itself a tool of cultural imperialism, and my proposal that there should be two *tangata waka* is quite frankly a programme for bringing the *whenua* and the dreamtime into the domain of human history and subjecting them to contingency, contestability and the sovereignty of human judgement.

I see the entire Treaty debate as a negotiation of the term under which that sovereignty is to be exercised. If it is said that this is to give the *pakeha* the advantage, by subjecting the *tangata whenua* to history which is a *pakeha* construct, I shall reply that the *pakeha* has, since his first beginnings as he remembers them, been necessitated to live in history and not in paradise or the dreamtime; Adam, Cain and Nimrod, Cadmus, Odysseus and Orestes, saw to that at the beginnings of our mythology. Second, I shall reply that the modern *tangata whenua* are living in history when they remind us of what we so much want to hear, that there is an alternative to history. They are not so much living in the time of the ancestors, as reminding us that they were recently and unjustly expelled from it by history, and using the law's capacity to recognize injustice as a mode of making claims against history and those who have profited by it. They both submit *manawhenua* to the courts, and use *manawhenua* as a challenge to the courts. This is unsurprising to the traditions of common law, as well as to the tradition of the Maori *marae*, a meeting ground where challenge and acceptance are very closely related. It is therefore possible to take a sanguine view, and speak of a contestation with law within the law, and with history within history.

But such sanguine views can themselves be challenged; denounced, for example, as 'liberal' by those to the left of liberalism who use 'liberal' as a term of opprobrium. The root of this criticism is undeniably strong and deep.[11] It reduces to the assertion that the *pakeha* history which both common law and *jus gentium* help define has been from the beginning, and still is, irreversibly set towards individualization of tenure, towards the conveyance and commodification of lands, towards the dissolution of property into credit – of the *whenua* into the cash flow – and beyond history as the *pakeha* have conceived it into that unchecked reign of the world market in which some have rather prematurely (but still not imperceptively) discerned 'the end of history'. Such criticism urgently warns the Maori against having anything to do with the law of the *pakeha*, on the grounds that it is an instrument designed to dissolve any claim to *manawhenua* the *iwi* might make, and would even dissolve such a claim in

---

[11] Kelsey, 1994, p. 131. 'Liberal' as a term of opprobrium is of course now overwhelmingly a tactic of the right.

the act of seeming to concede it. This, it is said, is precisely what the Treaty of Waitangi itself was designed to achieve, and what New Zealand history has been achieving ever since. The issue raised in reply by the whole story I have been discussing is whether the current Maori resurgence is capable of exploiting the law in the name of *manawhenua* and persuading it to certain reversals of the course its history has been taking.

The criticism here outlined has a good deal of substance; it is put forward by surviving Marxists among others. As Marxism recedes into the past as either a system or a programme, we may pick its bones and find there some important critical perceptions. Let me conclude by examining some of its predictions as they may affect the *pakeha*, rather than the *tangata whenua*, in the historical context shared by both. We are living in a time when sovereignty is being devolved, debated, deprivileged and consolidated. It is being claimed by some who have not had it before, as political confederations break up, and it is being given away by others whose history has been shaped by it, as new economic communities are formed and acquire governing authority. As a New Zealander, I find it significant that the debate over the Treaty of Waitangi, an investigation and redefinition of the foundations of national sovereignty, was initiated under the fourth Labour government of 1984–90, which will be remembered in the national history – if the nation survives to have one – as a unique blend of the creative and the radically destructive. I use the adverb to give emphasis to the latter adjective because the other politics initiated by that government are reducible to the rapid and often the forced sale of national assets – those owned by the state to begin with, and then more and more of those which might constitute a national economy – into hands so widely dispersed that their sale amounted to a radical (and not yet a profitable) abdication by the state to a market international or extra-national in character. It is no accident that the Waitangi Tribunal owes much of its authority to an appeal to the Treaty against a decision to transfer lands acquired by the crown to state-owned enterprises over which the market was to have an authority which the crown has abdicated; or that it could be asked what meaning there would be to Maori re-acquisition of ancestral *mana* over off-shore fishing grounds if all that could be done with it was to negotiate the sale of fishing rights to operations based in Korea and Taiwan.[12] The *iwi* found themselves in a world where sovereignty might mean mostly the right to dispose of sovereignty, the re-acquisition of

---

[12] *New Zealand Maori Council* v. *Solicitor-General* [1987] 1 N.Z.L.R. 641; *Muriwhenua Fishing Report* (1988); Sharp, 1990, 1997, pp. 80–5.

rangatiratanga and the renewed abdication of *kawanatanga*; precisely where they had been one hundred and fifty years before. This time the *pakeha* – or quite a number of them – shared the same predicament.

(VI)

I would like to conclude by emphasizing the concepts of property and sovereignty in relation to history, as they have stood since they were first formulated in European and English thinking. Property – the capacity to call something one's own – denoted the link between personal and social identity and the material world; sovereignty denoted the capacity to employ membership in a self-governing community to affirm personal and communal self-determination in the taking of political acts which determined national and international history. Hence, of course, the disastrous German idealist conviction that the state (even the state at war) was the highest expression of freedom of the personality. The link between property and sovereignty was long attacked by socialists on the grounds that it led too rapidly towards the commodification of both property and personality; it is now attacked by free-market theorists on the opposite grounds that it impedes what looks remarkably like the same process. Instead of living in political communities where we were – supposedly – members as individuals of the sovereign which determined its role in history, we are to live in economic communities where our role as self-enacting individuals has yet to be defined as other than that of the consumer. And it is hard to say that consumers determine their own destiny. We may all have to go and live where the market most has need of us – as consumers, by the way, more than as producers. I have heard Sir Tipene O'Regan observe that the problem before both *tangata waka* is how to avoid becoming boat people.

   The history of New Zealand, since and including the Treaty of Waitangi, can easily enough be brought under this paradigm. I have been using terminology both Maori and *pakeha* in examining an enterprise in renegotiating sovereignty, items which require both *te iwi Maori* and *te iwi pakeha* to recognize their identities as historically contingent; to do this can stimulate one's capacity to rethink and regroup. But negotiability and contingency are dangerous grounds. It is no accident that the decay of the sovereign state has been accompanied by a criticism, which at times amounts to an assault, on the notion of personal identity, which we are enjoined to see as perpetually renegotiated under conditions which can never be other than contingent. To be forever renegotiating one's identity, inhabiting the other's contingent universe as well as one's own, is politically stimulating and morally educative, so long as one retains a self to negotiate with and some allies in negotiation. It is an altogether destructive experience once one lies under the imperative to surrender one's achieved identity to the first comer with a stronger accusation of guilt or greater purchasing power. One of the shrewdest of New Zealand political theorists, Andrew Sharp, has warned against mistaking his conclusion about the irreducibility of Maori and *pakeha* conceptions of justice for a post-modernist manifesto.[13] We cannot always be foxes, he says, negotiating our selves all the time; we must be lions sometimes if we mean to act, hedgehogs sometimes if we mean to think, and the political conclusions are not always irenic.

To put a similar point in my own way, I confess myself tired of being deconstructed, and in search of *turangawaewae*, not so much a place to stand as a means of standing somewhere. As an expatriate from a world of vast seas and small islands, I know about the special significance of making landfalls and setting foot ashore; and the archetype I admire is Odysseus, that man of many wiles who has seen many cities and been captured by none of them, not even Ithaca his home. Odysseus therefore lives in history and not in the *whenua*; if he has a *whenua* he can leave it and return; but at the end of the poem, he and his son are left remarking that as they have just killed most of the political élite of Ithaca, it is not clear what is to happen next, and we do not quite know what peace Athena makes for them. Political community therefore matters, and so does sovereignty. In the case I have been reviewing, Maori and *pakeha* have been renegotiating sovereignty even as it is being sold out from under them, and I can imagine conditions in which they both want their *rangatiratanga* and *turangawaewae* back again, and have to begin by deciding whether they are still there to demand them.

[13] Sharp, 1992, p. 27.

PART V

Britain, Europe and Post-Modern History

CHAPTER 14

Sovereignty and history in the late twentieth century*

(1)

An aim pursued in the preceding section was that of showing it possible for a sovereign state, a self-governing community, to open its sovereignty to debate, to render that debate open-ended and ongoing, to debate the history in and on which it has been founded, and to proceed to a confrontation and negotiation between two concepts of sovereignty and of history; all this without dissolving the state or abolishing its sovereignty. It follows that a debated sovereignty is still a sovereignty, and a debate over sovereignty an exercise of sovereignty. It follows also that sovereignty entails a making of history, and may rewrite a past in the act of making a future; though it is equally true that the past which the state has partly made in the act of making itself is resistant to rewriting, for the reason that it has in some measure happened, and its preconditions and consequences do not simply go away. All these propositions suppose that the debate imagined does not end in secession, stalemate or violence, but reaches some measure of agreement; either a decision to terminate or transform the debate and its history, or an agreement to continue it into a future, in which the differing concepts of sovereignty and history continue a dialogue that changes them even while they persist. This is to suppose a great deal, but not an impossibility; we live, however, in times ideologically unfriendly to the exercise of sovereignty in history, and there are pressures on us to assume that to debate a sovereignty and acknowledge that it is problematic is thereby to terminate its history. These essays contain an argument that this is not necessarily the case.

The United Kingdom is a far more complex entity than New Zealand, and is situated in a history much older as well as more complex. In the thirty years since these essays began to take shape in New Zealand, as a response to

*[Written for this volume in 2003.]

the United Kingdom's pursuit of membership in the union of Europe, both entities have endured a complex history, in each of which their sovereignty and its history has been challenged.[1] The present writer has no intention of relating either history in depth, for the reason that he has not lived in them; he has watched them take shape from the standpoint of an expatriate living in the United States, and claims only that there are things that can be said from that distance, and with the godwit's degree of detachment. While New Zealand has been engaged in redescribing its sovereignty and its history as consequences of a treaty between two peoples, it has also been exposed to forces of globalization which render it more doubtful than ever whether it exercises sovereignty over its own resources or in its own economy. Since it has always been a dependent economy, however, these doubts are not new in its history; and it has not been faced, as the United Kingdom has, with an immediately adjacent union of states demanding that it progressively surrender its sovereignty to an association in which the concept of sovereignty is itself doubtful, and that it rewrite its history to meet the demands made by absorption into such an association. Such has been the historic experience the United Kingdom has faced, and is still living through, in the thirty years of this volume's formation. Since the term 'Europe' implied a role for Britain in whose future New Zealanders expected no place, and from whose past history they might find themselves written out, it seemed desirable to stake our own claim to a part in that history by rewriting it ourselves; to do so, however, was to raise the question whether the 'British history' thus rewritten might not continue, rather than disappear.

This has been the importance – in so far as it has been important – of the original proposal that 'British history' should be conceived as the convergence of a number of histories, and the formation of a single state, nation or history be considered problematic; it being borne in mind that problems are questions to which the answer may not yet be known. From the antipodean viewpoint the primary consideration was that the 'Commonwealth', as an association of British nations acting together as a world power, was being eroded in consequence of a loss of 'empire' in several senses, and of a British decision to join 'Europe' – an association of recently defeated states compensating for their loss of extra-European empire by constructing a shared and highly globalized economy, in which sovereignty became problematic. There was a consequent demand that 'British history' should be rewritten, as in future it should be enacted, in terms set by such an association; though what this 'European' history

---

[1] For an earlier treatment, see Pocock, 1992d.

would be was unclear, since it had not yet been written and entailed the unmaking of much history that had been; it would apparently replace 'European history' hitherto written as a history of states. What was clear was that it would be a history not imperial, not oceanic, and above all not in any way American; these being histories that 'Europe' was being constructed to displace. Not much time went by before it became clear that it would also not be a history of sovereignty, since 'Europe' entailed a surrender of sovereignty, the precondition of so much of the history that had been written hitherto. There arose an invective which proclaimed that 'nation state' and 'sovereign state' were obsolescent, and the histories written in them an imprisonment within false and dying identities; though more has so far been written with the intention of dissolving these histories than of replacing them. It is not yet clear what kind of history 'Europe' requires or whether it wants one at all; its perception of human action in social time may be both post-modern and post-historic.

Together with this invective – almost but never quite as part of it – arose another, which proclaimed the 'breakup of Britain' and sought to use the proposal to write 'British history' as the convergence of a number of histories as a means of bringing that convergence to an end.[2] This was in some measure conceived on the left, or what had been the left, where enmity to the alliance between capitalism and the state produced a willingness to see the state abolished. It should have been evident that capitalism would survive this abolition and might even welcome it; 'Europe' might well be seen as a merger of states no longer sovereign in a globalized economy whose directors were responsible to no state (and no people) at all. What was remarkable about this programme, as it affected British history, was that an ideology of nationalism – Scottish, Welsh and at a distance Irish – was being used to project the breakup of a multinational state by ideologues who claimed that the nation-state was obsolete. It might well follow that the target of this invective was the state, with the nation and its unmaking alike means to the state's abolition; a scenario in which the nations used to break up the state would then find themselves not states at all. There were proposals for a Europe of 'regions', which were to enjoy economic rationality and cultural exchange – very real benefits – but would not exercise any sovereignty, or government of the self, or perhaps any self at all. Nationalism might be a mere prelude to a consumerism which would swallow it entire.

The intended deconstruction of the United Kingdom becomes, in a rather interesting way, an intended deconstruction of the English as

---

[2] Nairn, 1977, 2000; Pocock, 2000c.

a nation, or as the language now in fashion goes an 'identity'.[3] We have seen that the Kingdom of Great Britain, the First and Second Unions, and the 'first British empire' in colonial America, were all extensions of the 'empire' of the English over themselves. The 'breakup of Britain' is proposed on the grounds that the English are no longer capable of this extended empire – or, it would seem to follow and the gravediggers of sovereignty would have it, of empire over themselves. There occurs at this point a complaint against them for refusing to develop an English 'nationalism' under the flag of St George, which would conduce to the breakup of the United Kingdom; instead, they stubbornly persist in seeing themselves as an imperial people, governing themselves in unity with 'Britain'. Their alleged incapacity for empire in the island or the archipelago, however, is explained by this school of thought as the consequence of the termination of the Second British Empire; that is, of empire in the modern sense of rule over peoples not European by culture. Lacking this empire, and the global power that went with it, the argument continues, they no longer need, nor have they the power to maintain, the United Kingdom constructed at the outset of the eighteenth century as an instrument of power in Europe and empire beyond it. They are no longer capable of empire in any sense, even over themselves – or they would have developed the quasi-nationalism suggested by the scenario of breakup – and have no future outside a regional Europe in which their 'identity' is by no means assured, since they refuse to adopt any alternative history to that of empire. To enlarge the apophthegm attributed to Dean Acheson, they have lost an empire and are failing to find a role, or even engage in the negation of one.

There now arises a rhetoric of 'Europe' as either an alternative identity or an alternative to identity; concepts to be considered later in this concluding section. Before examining them, it is important to reiterate that the account of 'British history' proposed in these essays draws lines between 'empire' in the archipelago and 'empire' beyond it. It may not be a sufficient truth that the Union of 1707 was constructed merely as a means to power in Europe and commercial and colonial empire beyond it. The history of civil and religious war in both British kingdoms and between them may suggest that 'empire' in the Tudor sense had a history of its own, and the commercial and polite civil society which Enlightenment offered as a remedy for such wars may have set up interactions between the two nations which persist independently of 'empire' in the modern sense.

---

[3] The literature of 'identity' in recent years would fill a voluminous bibliography. A representative item is Kumar 2003, the subject of some but not all of the reflections in this paragraph.

And if economic and cultural globalization are rendering political autonomy unnecessary, why are the Scots encouraged to pursue it? As against such arguments, however, it is a certain truth that the failure of global empire and power is one of three forces – the failures of industrialism and socialism being the others – which have produced in the English and the British (supposing there to be such a people) what is known as a 'crisis of identity', in which they doubt who they are and what they have done and should be doing in the world – the Acheson formula being once more applicable – and Scottish nationalism can be perceived as a response to an English failure of nerve. In these circumstances, an abandonment of history and sovereignty, and an acceptance of a mass culture as much global as European, might well seem attractive alternatives; even self-contempt may be a means of escape.

But it is a noteworthy circumstance – which the schematization of British history in these pages serves to highlight – that the last decades of the twentieth century, during which post-imperial and post-historical ideologies were at their height, were also the period of the Irish Troubles: a second phase of the warfare between semi-insurgency and counter-insurgency which the Second Union had done so much to give to the world. The advocates of the breakup of Britain and the end of sovereignty have used this ongoing crisis as another instance of the devolution which they see as bringing the United Kingdom (of Great Britain and Northern Ireland) to an end; but what this semi-visible thirty years war has in fact illustrated is the truth that 'empire' – in the primary sense of the distribution of sovereignty within the Atlantic archipelago – has not ceased to be a problem in statecraft with the emergence of the Irish republic as a sovereign state. Two stable sovereignties, the kingdom and the republic, each legitimated by its own history, are now allied – one could almost say confederated – by the need to inform a border province that can never belong fully to either of them that it no longer has the power to disturb the legitimacy of authority in either state, and that these have the power to compel its factions to remain face to face until they can reach some accommodation. This policy depends upon the willpower of the two sovereigns, and its success is not guaranteed; but it is a clear case of the exercise of *imperium* by the two states that have found themselves obliged to partition the second island of the archipelago between them.

Faced with subversion or terror, the sovereign state comes back – however clumsily – to life; a problem in empire, even when it calls for a solution in mixed sovereignty, is not to be dealt with by renouncing it. Writings from time to time appear which suggest that the problem of

Northern Ireland would disappear if the kingdom and republic were not sovereign states but regions of a European Union. To the present writer, it is evident that they are handling their problem by the exercise of sovereignty, where the clash between sovereignties is at the heart of it. Europe, whose recent record in such matters is less than impressive, wisely steers clear of the dangerous politics of Northern Ireland, but contributes to a possible solution by providing the republic with a prosperity – the first in Ireland's long history – that the northern mini-state desires to share. It is for sovereignty to arrange the politics under which this may be possible.

Where there is sovereignty, there is also history. I have written elsewhere[4] of the impressive evidence that the Irish Republic – long noted for the obsessiveness of its historical memory – is coming to realize that, precisely because its sovereignty is legitimated by an agreed reading of history, it can afford to entertain alternatives to that reading and admit that the reading of history never comes to an end. It will be a long time before two histories can stand face to face in the North, but sovereignty entails an ability to face history, not to face away from it. This is why the history of Britain in Europe requires careful consideration; it is not to be a literature of self-annihilation.

(11)

In the first of the two following essays – they were written ten years apart – I examine the concept of 'Europe' as it appears in the perspective adopted in this volume. As an Antipodean and a neo-Briton I have no cause to love the concept of European union; it does not offer me inclusion, and tends to exclude me from an association and a history to which I thought I belonged. This, however, is a quarrel I have with the now European British; other subspecies of European do not know or care that I exist. Furthermore, the experience of marginalization is neither unknown nor unmanageable in the antipodean and expatriate terms in which I am accustomed to encounter history. There are other reasons for the attitude I adopt towards Europe and the European project: an attitude that may be termed 'Eurosceptical', in the proper sense that it is sceptical about 'Europe'. A reason for this is the apparent inability of 'Europe's' apologists to confront scepticism, exemplified in the vulgar use of the word 'Eurosceptics' to indicate those caught up in an atavistic and undiscriminating opposition to the project in its entirety.

---

[4] Pocock, 2001b, pp. 94–5.

I see this as (of course) a rhetorical tactic, but more intimately as a part of what has been termed Europe's 'democratic deficit', itself a consequence of a deep-rooted conviction that democratic electorates will not readily consent to a renunciation of their sovereignty, and must be lured into doing this by stages. They are induced to take limited steps in that direction, and are then told that these steps are irreversible and oblige them to more of the same kind; democratic legitimation can come only late in the story and can indicate only acceptance of what has been done without their understanding it. I have many times heard, as a main argument for further steps towards union, that 'we' – whoever is speaking at the moment – have no choice but to take them; a very bad reason for doing anything, since it ensures that 'we' will do it unwillingly and badly – assuming that 'we' continue to exist, as perhaps it is intended that we shall not.

The 'democratic deficit' may therefore be deliberately imposed. A more immediate consequence is that the nature of the decision being taken may be rhetorically justified but cannot be critically explained, so that 'Europe' is the less able to explain itself or respond to the questionings of others. In these essays and others accompanying them, I have explored the indeterminacy of 'Europe' as a concept or a reality, and its consequent tendency to define itself in uncriticizable terms. This indeterminacy is partly geographical; 'Europe' has no natural frontiers on its eastward side, and the claim that 'Europe is a continent' is as imprecise as the claim that 'England is an island'. The indeterminacy now becomes cultural as well as geographical; a culture formed within an open space is now seeking to define it. 'Europe' – a term originally denoting the lands we call the Balkan peninsula – has come to denote the civilization, and the history, that took shape in the Latin-speaking western provinces of the former Roman empire. This civilization, while undergoing the complex processes which still dominate our understanding of 'history', expanded eastward, into the peninsulas of western Eurasia, and westward, into the oceans of the world, where it colonized the two American continents and established transitory but important empires in the rest of the planet. Having lost control of its former colonies and empires – I set the 'neo-Britains' somewhat apart from these categories – 'Europe' now retreats into itself and, at least in the case of Britain, requires its former imperial powers to proclaim that the history internal to neo-Latin Europe is the only history they have.

I have been interested in the indeterminacy of 'Europe' on its eastern side; the extension of the European Union beyond, first, the frontier established by a disintegrating Soviet power; second, the open marches, as they might be called, where neo-Latin history – Catholic, Protestant,

Enlightened – merges uneasily with a history formerly Greek Orthodox and Ottoman Islamic (a history, it should be kept in mind, that has produced less of the intensive and reconstructive self-examination which has made 'Western' history so dominant a science). On this frontier the European Union and its American quasi-partner fought a damagingly unsuccessful police action in the former Yugoslavia, and now confront new indeterminate frontiers with a post-imperial Russia and a radically incoherent Islam. (Turkish historians are invited to comment.) This volume, however, has been concerned with a westward expansion and a westward openness and indeterminacy: archipelagic and Gaelic, Atlantic and American, oceanic and antipodean; and with contending that in these processes – to which a neo-Iberian dimension has not been but should be added – histories have taken place which those of 'Europe' cannot ignore or abolish.

To say this, however, is to ask how, or whether, histories written as distinct from one another can subsequently be connected and even integrated. There instantly arises a further series of questions: those of how histories have come into being of which the former question can be asked, and whether they will continue in being. These prove to be questions in political history, in the political history of historiography, in which the concept of the sovereign – miscalled the 'national' – state proves central and problematic. It is not really the case that the history of 'Europe', or of a globally distributed Euro-American 'West', has been or should be written simply as a series of 'national' histories; but it has been written as a process in which the formation and problematic survival of self-determining human communities has been centrally important, and most of the histories formerly written and presently scrutinized have been constructed in, and in various senses by, such communities, as narratives of their origin and experience, the problems they have encountered, and their internal contestations as to the form they will take as human associations and structures of power. These narratives have been political constructs, have performed all manner of political intentions, and have been involved in all manner of political processes; but to the extent to which the politics in which they have been formed have been open politics, they have been self-contestatory and open to criticism, and can be read as records of societies' arguments with Self and Other, as to what manner of human association the historic communities shall have been and shall be. The ability to relate such histories does something to make a 'state' a 'nation', distinct from its linguistic, ethnic or cultural base. For this reason the word 'nationalism' has been deliberately exiled from these pages, and I shall consider the term 'identity' only in the last essay of the volume, when its relations with 'alterity' and 'history' may be taken up.

But we have next to consider the possibility that 'Europe' may be part of a process intended to ensure that there will no longer be autonomous human communities writing histories that narrate the problem of autonomy. Since the European project has from the start been based on the surrender of their sovereignty by states, nations and peoples, and its transference to agencies which are not those of any known form of political association – the 'democratic deficit' forbids 'Europe' to define itself – the possibility exists that it aims at terminating the phenomenon of politically autonomous communities, and that of history, lived as well as written, as the continuous life of an always-precarious autonomy. If this were so, political life, considered as the association of individuals to form societies and conduct their histories, would be targeted for extinction. There was from the outset a case for regarding 'Europe' as a project with such aims: not neo-Latin but global, not modern but post-modern, professing an ideology of post-modernism which presents all human experience as immediately fictitious, and thus serves the needs of a global economy and information technology always desirous – in a way that recalls Marx's 'revolutionary bourgeoisie' – to destabilize existing human relations in order to commodify new fictions, themselves targeted for early obsolescence.

In 'Deconstructing Europe', the next essay in this volume, I imagined a 'Europe' in which this process should have been carried out, and 'history' would be reduced from a series of problems in which 'we' had been and still were living, to a series of images encountered in a tourism of the mind. This was an apocalypse or dystopia, and I did not present it as more than a set of possibilities that needed to be considered. There was already a possible scenario of *Jihad* v. *McWorld*,[5] in which tourists might be killed, as they were later in Luxor and Bali, for their cultural aggression against those who could not afford to be tourists; and I was writing in 1991, ten years before the increase of tensions (always present) between Europe and a deeply disturbed United States, between British, French and Germans as to the structure of Europe and its relations with America, or between Europe and America on the one hand and a deeply disturbed Islam on the other. There were forces here that could lead to revival of sovereignty, empire and even national autonomy, whose dialogue or dialectic with globalization might not be at an end.

[5] Barber, 1995.

To this angry and confused 'conversation of mankind' I ventured to contribute the suggestion that there were relationships between the existence of autonomous communities, the capacity to write history, and the government, and even the presence, of the collective or the individual self. What I am calling post-modernism for short reduces all these to fictions, as indeed they often are – historians have known this for a long time – but we need means of criticizing these fictions, including those arising in immediate response to experience, if experience itself is to survive (as some suggest it will not). I see these means of interpretation as requiring the continued existence of social and political communities, which shape themselves as they interpret themselves and their encounters with the world, and command the time in which to do this. How these communities are to exist, and the narratives they construct are to be justified, in a global condition of instant information and multiple identities is a problem to be confronted, in face of an existing rhetoric which enjoins their immediate surrender. I find myself at this point saying that we must have selves if we are to govern them, and that histories are ways of having selves in communities of autonomy. This is not going to be easy.

In 'The politics of the new British history' – originally a lecture written before but delivered after the events of September 11, 2001, which have yet to be re-experienced, re-imagined and interpreted – I went over much of the ground covered by the essays in this volume, and considered the effects of writing such history in its insular and archipelagic, and therefore its European, settings. I was implicitly contending that a history of either Britain, or at another level of generality Europe, must consider, before it can transcend, the extent to which it has been the creation of national and multinational states, and that this is particularly applicable to the history of the archipelago enacted and written since Irish independence. I was also concerned with the relations between sovereignty, autonomy and historiography, a subject on whose theory I had begun to write,[6] and with the proposition that any autonomous entity requires both a history of what it has been to itself and a history of what it has been to others. Given a degree of political autonomy, these two histories may criticize each other, but neither can reduce the other to falsity or non-entity. To say this, however, one must deal with problems of alterity, self and other. The last essay in this volume will consider the politics of identity and historiography.

---

[6] Pocock, 1997d, 1998a.

CHAPTER 15

Deconstructing Europe

History is about process and movement; yet up to now it has taken as given the perspectives furnished by relatively stable geographical communities, of whose pasts, and the processes leading to their presents, history is supposed to consist. All that may be changing, with the advent of the global village, in which no one's home is their own; with the advent, too, of a universally imposed alienation, in which one's identity is predefined either as some other's aggression against one, or as one's own aggression against someone else, and in either case scheduled for deconstruction. Yet the owl of Minerva may continue to fly, as long as there is an ark left to fly from; and the historian, who must today move between points in time, must recollect voyages, and may still recollect voyages between known points with known pasts, recalling how the pasts changed as the presents shifted.

Two voyages, then, furnished the prelude to this essay in historical reflection:[1] one beyond what is known as 'Europe', the other within it. The former was the later, and is therefore the nearer in time; it is therefore remembered first. It was a voyage in May 1991 to New Zealand, which is this historian's home culture; he is aware that few of his readers know that there is a culture there, or can readily believe it stands at the centre of anyone's historical consciousness. It was in that month a culture very deeply in crisis and threatened with possible discontinuation: more than for most reasons because the Europeanization of Great Britain had deprived it of its economic (and, like it or not, its previous spiritual) *raison d'être*, and it had not yet found another. Not having yet found – wherever the fault might lie – new markets of outlet, it had resorted to policies of privatization which amounted to the forced sale of national assets in the hope of attracting new investment capital, a subjection of national sovereignty to international market forces such as the European

---

[1] Pocock, 1991b, 1992a, 1993a, 1994a, 1997c (the text here followed). For other essays on the same subject, see 1993b, 1993c, 1997a, 2002b.

Community – only in this case there was no community – is supposed to stand for. This had reached the point where it was being seriously proposed to sell New Zealand public schools to their own boards of trustees, and the trustees were making it known that they had no money to buy them with. In the midst of this scene of understandable demoralization, relations between the largest minority and majority ethnic groups – Maori and *pakeha*, Polynesian and Anglo-European – were giving rise to a complex, serious and conceptually sophisticated debate over the legal, moral and historical foundation of the national identity. The owl had taken flight, but the dusk could be felt approaching. In history nothing is as certain as night and day; but it was a measurable possibility, if not an inevitability, that the history being intelligently debated might simply be terminated because the international economy had no further need of the community whose memory and identity it was.[2]

An effect this had upon a historian who had lived for twenty-five years in the Northern Hemisphere, while remaining a product of the Southern, was sharply to jolt his awareness of 'Europe'. The historic process he saw before his eyes in New Zealand had begun with the British entry into the European Community, and had not been alleviated by that Community's economic policies. This is to say nothing of the moral policies of some of its member nations: the sinking of the *Rainbow Warrior* has not been forgotten in New Zealand, and there is a deep conviction that the French do not care, and cannot understand that anybody else does. In New Zealand – as when resident in the United States of America – he found himself in a culture governed by 'Western' values and given shape by their historic (and imperial) expansion: yet it seemed that there was a mystique of 'Europe' which laid claim to these values while excluding others from the community which claimed to base itself upon them. And the same mystique seemed to proclaim the subjection of national sovereignty to international market forces without making more than sporadic progress towards the creation of any new kind of political community governed by its citizens, to replace that whose obsolescence it so readily proclaimed. New Zealand, only yesterday a viable social democracy with policies and a government of its own, looked like an extreme, because extra-marginal, case of where the post-sovereignty process might lead.

The response might be a retreat into militant and even violent local populism – the Third World, to which New Zealand was threatened with relegation, was full of examples of the kind. But New Zealanders had

---

[2] [That was then; this is now.]

been and still were a non-impoverished, civilized and international people, used to travel, to join the world and its history – distant though they found them – and to look at history through looking at others' way of seeing it.

An owl departing from the South Island of New Zealand must define the region in which its flight has navigational meaning. Until half a century ago, New Zealand's national existence was situated less in the Pacific ocean than in a global area defined by British naval and imperial power, running from Britain and Flanders through the Mediterranean and India to Australia, Singapore and beyond. This imperial area possessed a consciously preserved history which was less that of empire or imperialism than that of British culture, political, religious, social and historical. Of this, New Zealanders – and, subject to their own more Irish mythology, Australians – saw themselves as part; it was believed to be the history of a culture with a global capacity for creating and associating new nations. Even now, when it has survived the power that once held it together, this history is part of their perception that they inhabit 'Western civilization', though they do not inhabit 'Europe'. The accession of the United Kingdom to the European Community entailed a rejection by that kingdom's peoples of the former global capacity of their culture; it was a confession of defeat, and at the same time a rejection of the other nations of that culture, which seemed to entail a decision that there was no longer a British history in which New Zealand's past or future possessed a meaning. The South Pacific owl of Minerva, finding its environment endangered, faced the task of rewriting New Zealand's British history, while taking part in the revision of all British history in which the historians of the United Kingdom have engaged in the post-imperial and quasi-European era now going on.

An assertion by means of which the owl defined its flight path and air space was therefore the assertion that 'Western civilization' extended beyond 'Europe' into those oceanic and continental spaces irreversibly Westernized by navigation and settlement in the seventeenth through nineteenth centuries. Europeans are often anti-American enough, and the United Kingdom British hostile enough to their imperial past, to deny and wish to sever this relation to the world: but the inhabitants of the world thus created are under a necessity of keeping its history alive, and an obsessive 'Europeanness' can appear to them a device aimed at excluding them from visibility. As part of the assertion that 'the West' extends beyond 'Europe', therefore, there are owls of Minerva who define themselves as navigating in the continental spaces of North America and Australia, or – and this is the case of the sub-species under examination – the enormous oceanic spaces of the austral Pacific ocean, which Polynesian and European navigators have lodged in their memory and tradition. Take a globe in your hands, one not mounted on a spindle which preserves the intellectual dictatorship of Gerardus Mercator; rotate it until the islands of New Zealand are at the centre of the hemisphere you face. You will be looking at one facet of the New Zealand historical imagination, and you will be able to see Australia and Antarctica, but nothing worth mentioning of Indo-Malaysia, Asia or the Americas. There is a history which has to be created in this space, and when it is not a history looking back up the lines along which culture has travelled – towards what Maori called *Hawaiki-paa-mamao*, the spirit land high up and distant – it has to be the history of small communities in an ocean of planetary size. Writing Pacific history is a challenge to the imagination: it both is and is not a history of 'the West', and it certainly is not a history of 'Europe', even when a history of 'Europeans'.[3]

These are spaces by which the antipodean historian defines his relation to the world, and the need to see the planet as if the Southern Hemisphere contained its centre makes him aware of others. There is the Indonesian or Indo-Malaysian space from which he is separated by the mountains of New Guinea and the deserts of Australia; there is the northern ocean defined by the 'Pacific rim' and the movements of Japanese, American and neo-Confucian capital; there are the spaces defined by the major civilizations of Asia, and west of them the extensive and at present disastrously incoherent domains of Islam. There is the enormous space of northern Eurasia, formerly co-extensive with the Soviet Union, which may be glimpsed from cruising altitude on a flight from Tokyo to London. These offer the imagination a post-colonial route towards Europe, and towards the memory of the second voyage by which this essay is dominated.

This is the memory of a seven-month sojourn in Europe during 1989, moving through Calabria, Sicily, Tuscany, the Alpine region, south-west Germany and the Netherlands. The revolutions of Eastern Europe were beginning, and it would have been possible to set out by *ferrovia* or *autostrada* and watch the border crumble: but there was work to be done, and in any case a lingering feeling that history is for its immediate participants and not a spectacle for tourists. One was close enough, at all events, to experience a sensation that we were witnessing the end of a

---

[3] [In the *Journal of Pacific Studies* issue in which Pocock, 1997d, appeared, the possibility was canvassed that 'Pacific history' should be defined as that of central Polynesia, exclusive of Hawaii and New Zealand, seen as involved in histories other than that so defined.]

European era forty years long, and of a definition of 'Europe' predicated on the partition collapsing before one's eyes. The term 'Europe' had come to be often used co-terminously with 'the European Community', an association of former imperial states having in common the experience of defeat – Germany of defeat and partition, France, Italy and the Low Countries of defeat and occupation, Britain of exhaustion following victory – and the loss of colonial empires (in all cases except the first after 1940) which had recovered enough to form a powerful combination based on the pooling of some sovereign powers and the removal of obstacles to the movement across their frontiers of international economic forces and some of the ways of living immediately dependent on them: this was the process intended to reach a culminating point in 1992.

The formation of this Community had been accompanied by an ideology of 'Europeanness', which sometimes affirmed that the culture possessed in common by these national communities, and the history of this common culture, was of greater moral and ideological significance than their several distinct national sovereignties or than the history shaped and written – as in the classical age of European historiography it had been – by their several existences as sovereign nation-states claiming to exercise control over their several histories. Politically as well as historiographically, there had been problems attending this fecund and exciting enterprise: it was not asserted, for example, that there existed or should exist a 'European people' or a 'European state', using these terms in the singular; and consequently – following the logic of political historiography – the 'European history' which was developing was (rightly enough) a plural history of divergences and convergences, in which a cultural commonality interacted with a diversity (often a warlike and destructive diversity) of political sovereignties and national histories.

In this, European historiography continued in its classical patterns, the history of the state retaining its primacy even after giving up its claim to be a moral absolute. In partitioned Germany, and in an Italy still plagued by consequences of the forced unification of the Piedmontese and Neapolitan kingdoms in 1861, there continued to be debate whether the national state had been a historical necessity or could have taken some other path. There was less sign that the French were inclined to regard 'France' as a contingency or accident of history; but even in Britain – which came to 'Europe' late, reluctantly, and with many signs of self-contempt – there was an enterprise of considering 'British history' as existing distinctly from the history of 'England' and of asking whether the extension of English sovereignty had created a 'British' nation with a history of its own. The historian writing this essay and remembering these voyages could claim some role in furthering this enterprise, and since the questions which it posed could be answered in the affirmative or the negative, it might either reinforce or subvert the existence of 'British history' as a distinct and intelligible field of study.

In ways such as these, the process of 'Europeanization' stimulated the classical historiography based on the conception of the state: it became more exciting, and yielded richer information, when the state and the nation were perceived as precarious, contingent and ambivalent rather than as moral absolutes and historical necessities. At the same time, however, the experience after 1945 of Western Europe, and the planet's advanced cultures in general, was conducive to post-modernism and alienation – meaning by these overworked terms that there were many competing memberships, allegiances, values and involvements, of which none was altogether satisfactory and each might be seen as competing with the others for mastery of the individual subjectivity which they had formed among them without rendering it satisfactory to itself. This was a problem at least as old as the European Enlightenment, and long antedated the temporary settlement of 1945. Under these conditions, however, it greatly encouraged an ideology, historiography and sub-culture of alienation in which every historic formation bearing on the individual consciousness became a candidate for deconstruction and rejection by that consciousness, which was in turn forced by the logic of historicism to deconstruct and reject any self or identity it might seem to possess. Since 'Europe' was the classic locus of this kind of consciousness, the deconstructive attitude became part of the ideology of 'Europeanness', and 'Europe' was thus well placed to deconstruct its competitors, while retaining for itself an essential lack of identity, of much tactical advantage in the assertion of hegemony: the Great Boyg won by refusing to name himself.

It was of course open to anyone to give him a name. When one saw praise of *la cultura europea* in graffiti on south Italian university walls in 1989, one was given to understand that some conservative Catholic programme was using these words in a code of its own; 'Europe' meant different things to different people, and they were busy deconstructing one another's meanings. All this, however, was ideologically and historiographically normal: a 'Europe' which incessantly challenged and debated its own identity was part of the civilization to which as a 'Westerner' one belonged, and 'America' in its own way did the same thing. What left the closed or open character of 'Europe' in greater doubt was its geopolitical situation. Demarcated down to 1989 by a military, political and ideological barrier running through central Germany and Europe, the European Community could look like a neo-Carolingian construct: a regrouping of Neustria, Franconia, Burgundy and Lombardy in the area defined by the Treaty of Verdun in the ninth century, modified by one major exclusion and one inclusion of lands not so defined. The exclusion was that of eastern Germany, the inclusion that of the British islands; both areas had been historically dominated by differing forms of Protestantism.

In the latter case, standing nearer to the concerns of the owl of Minerva, the entity's insular situation had separated it in some degree from two of the major historical experiences undergone in western Eurasia. Through military weakness, it had avoided involvement in the Wars of Religion fought down to 1648 (though some argued that it was by that date caught up in a war of religion of its own insular kind); through naval, mercantile and industrial power, it had escaped conquest and liberation in the Wars of Revolution after 1789, and again after 1939, and had succeeded in playing a dominant role from an external situation. From the time of their consolidation at the end of the seventeenth century, the British kingdoms had been able to exercise power in Europe while maintaining their distance from it. Only the loss of that capacity since 1914 was obliging the United Kingdom to seek membership in the European Community, and however strongly the step could be justified it could not altogether lose the character of a historic defeat and an enforced separation from a past by which the British had previously known themselves. It was this step which had left the British nations of the Pacific ocean denied a role in 'European' history and in 'British' history considered as part of it: oceanically situated in the face of the economic power exerted by Japan and the Lesser Dragons, and liable to be told that as neither 'European' nor 'American' (nor 'British'?) they belonged to no 'Western' community acting together to maintain itself (should it need to).

These were the circumstances in which the ideology of 'Europeanness' could appear closed, exclusive and deconstructive. It is, in fact, not the case that the European Community had developed an accredited historiography of its own; there have been tentative ventures in that direction, which down to 1989 would have led towards a neo-Carolingian synthesis addressing itself to Germans on the loss of the east, Italians on the miseries of the south and British on the loss of detachment from the adjacent continent. What took a much more visible shape was an ideology of 'Europeanness' which enjoined the rejection of previously distinct national histories without proposing a synthetic or universal history to take their place. When the British are enjoined to consider themselves 'European', it is usually with the implication that they should not consider their history as in any way distinctive; and though this injunction has not been notably effective, it has strengthened the tendency towards the kind of post-modernism in which any *Lebensform* is presupposed an act of hegemony, an imposition to be deconstructed. 'Europe' could therefore become the ideology of a post-historical culture, in which varyingly affluent and varyingly alienated masses – there is an alienation of the consumer as well as an alienation of the deprived – float from one environment to another with no awareness of moving from one past, and one commitment to it, to another. It would be a problem in historicity to determine whether this freedom from commitment were an illusory or a real condition; either seems possible.

The mystique of 'Europe', which has often made it possible to use the word as an incantation with which there can be no argument, may have been the product of a turn towards a post-historic consumer culture, but it has also been a product of the Community's singular success in creating a common economy, elements of a common culture, and some institutions of a shared administrative – it seems too soon to call it 'civic' – political structure. All these were the connotations of the word 'Europe' as it was being used down to 1989, and as it was still used as it looked toward 1992.

In the former of these years, however, the collapse of the Wall, the Curtain, and much more besides, deprived 'Europe' of its partition along the militarized and policed frontier which had defined its identity, as opposed to the presumed alternative culture of late Leninism. It turned out that this alternative was not merely a failure, but had for a long time been no more than a pretence; mass action and mass sentiment rejected it, because for many years nobody had believed in it enough to make it work; and the liberal-democratic capitalism of the Community was faced with the task, not of transforming a counter-culture, but of filling a vacuum and tidying up a gigantic mess. The collapse extended beyond the Central and Eastern Europe occupied in 1944–5, deep into the Soviet Union itself and the heartlands of northern Eurasia, where what collapsed in 1991 was not only an economic and political order but a system of states historically included in an empire: so that the ideological transformation of the continent instantly took on a geopolitical dimension. 'Europe', used both as a term of mystique and as a synonym for the European Community, came face to face with a Central Europe, an Eastern Europe, and a Eurasia extending through Siberia, which had not been integrated into its post-modern culture and did not belong with any simplicity to its history. The Community proved to be a regrouping of the lands of west Latin culture, as modified by Enlightenment, revolution, and the wars of Germany with France and Britain, uncertain in its relations with the historic consequences of Protestantism, and now obliged by the re-unification of Germany to recall how far the twentieth-century wars had been a consequence of German–Russian encounters in the environment formed by Eastern Europe. Beyond a Slavonic Europe of largely Catholic culture could be discerned a wide cultural zone whose history was Orthodox and Ottoman beyond the point of belonging to the history of Latin Christianity and its secularization.[4]

The region was ethnically diverse and politically indeterminate. Among the disturbing consequences of the liberations of 1989–91 – the tunnels at the end of the light, as someone put it – was the discovery that forty-five to seventy-five years of revolutionary totalitarianism, long credited with a capacity to wash brains and rebuild minds, had eliminated none of the ethnic and sub-national antagonisms of western Eurasia. (It did not help to add that two centuries of West European imperialism had enjoyed no better success in Africa and southern Asia.) The collapse of socialism proved to be a collapse of empire, the only if inadequate force which had attempted the subjugation of these hostile identities; and the Russian-dominated federation of the Soviet Union, the Serbian-dominated federation of Yugoslavia, began a disintegration which continued through the revolution of August 1991 and the war in Bosnia. Both European and United States policy-makers faced a choice between encouraging the devolution of sovereignty as a means of creating larger market economies, and maintaining existing centralizations of sovereignty as a means of preventing endemic inter-ethnic warfare – war having become a means less of asserting the interests of states than of posing ethnic challenges to their authority. The European Community faced this problem in respect of Yugoslavia, the United States of Iraq, both of the Soviet Union; and there were uncomfortable parallels in Canadian North America. This problem has many aspects. It raises the conceptual question – now extended from west to east – whether sovereignty can be re-arranged without re-arranging the pasts of which sovereignty makes human communities aware, and whether sovereignty can be treated as a contingent convenience or inconvenience without history itself becoming similarly contingent and manipulable.

---

[4] [I edit these words in 2004 as these regions are at the point of being drawn into the European Union. It is in the logic of my argument that this should call for massive rewriting of history, but that this may not happen.]

This is a familiar problem in Central and Eastern Europe, where the distinction between 'historic' and 'non-historic' peoples was invented as a debating device in the Austro-Hungarian Empire and turned against it – but by no means eliminated – by the policy-makers of Versailles and Trianon. A New Zealander has some reason to know what it may be like to belong to a people which thought it had a history and is now instructed by others that it has none. These are devices in the discourse of empires and the unmaking of empires. The next discovery is that 'Europe' may be at the point of becoming an empire uncertain of the frontiers of its own discourse, as it faces the question of how far to intervene in the ethnic strife of Croats and Serbs, and as differences between the policies of its major nations emerge over the admission of central and eastern states to the Community. The greatest single truth to declare itself in the wake of 1989 is that the frontiers of 'Europe' towards the east are everywhere open and indeterminate. 'Europe', it can now be seen, is not a continent – as in the ancient geographers' dream – but a sub-continent: a peninsula of the Eurasian land-mass, like India in being inhabited by a highly distinctive chain of interacting cultures, but unlike it in lacking a clearly marked geophysical frontier. Instead of Afghanistan and the Himalayas, there are vast level areas through which conventional 'Europe' shades into conventional 'Asia', and few would recognize the Ural mountains if they ever reached them. In these regions the states and cultures of Latin, Catholic–Protestant and Enlightened 'Europe' both merge and do not merge with others, of Orthodox, Islamic, Russian and Turkish provenance, as what we call 'Europe' is ambiguously continuous with what we had better learn to call 'Eurasia'.[5]

This is an essay in and on historiography, a meditation for owls of Minerva watching history change behind them under changing global light-conditions in which it is monocentric any longer to speak of 'gathering dusk', since dusk to one culture may be dawn to another; though again, it has to be remembered that we claim to be diversifying the world's cultures precisely when, and because, we are in fact homogenizing them. The debate over multicultural education has to be read in that complex of lights and shadows. At the outset of this essay it was premissed that historiography was the study of change and memory, which is why it lies both behind and before the owls flying against the time-stream: the study of the processes of change in which we are all involved, counterpointed by the maintenance in the present of identity as members of coherent

---

[5] [A paragraph is omitted here, as too far removed from the circumstances of 2004.]

communities possessing coherent and recollectable pasts. Since it has been regularly assumed that these communities in the present are relatively autonomous political entities – it is less than a century since 'history' could be defined as 'present politics' and 'the memory of the state' – these definitions of historiography have a political dimension. They presuppose that one of the aims of the state is to exercise some control over its own history, defining its past and seeking to determine its future; that the liberal state associates individuals with it in this enterprise, that of seeking the freedom – thus history used to be defined as 'the history of freedom' – to act as citizens in the determination of their own historicized identities; that political sovereignty was so far the state's means of prescribing its historic past and future that it was doubtful whether the individual could be accounted free, in history as in politics, unless a citizen of an autonomous and sovereign political community.

There is consequently an association between sovereignty and historiography; a community writes its own history when it has the autonomous political structure needed if it is to command its own present, and typically the history it writes will be the history of that structure. Such a history need not, though it very often will, be written uncritically; it may be written in ways that reveal its existence within a historical context larger than itself, its contingency upon many historical processes which it does not command. There are other kinds of history which can and should be written, and a historian or person of historical sensibility is at liberty to decide that these kinds possess priority over political history and history of the state. A class, gender or ethnic group which has been excluded or repressed by the political community must write its own history and that of the state in terms of this experience, though whether such a history can be written in exclusively negative and eristic terms is another question. A national community which has existed by assimilating diverse ethnic groups to an ethnically specific culture – the United States is a major example – must decide how to measure the history of the assimilating culture against that of the cultures undergoing an assimilation which may be incomplete or false. There is nothing sacrosanct, or privileged, about the history endangered by sovereignty: and yet the history of historiography as we know it obliges us to ask whether it would exist without history of this kind, whether historiography would exist without the state. One reason for this is that sovereignty and historiography, a voice in controlling one's present and a voice in controlling one's past, have been and may still be necessary means by which a community asserts its identity and offers an identity to the individuals composing it. Certainly, it can and must be asked whether it can pursue this enterprise, and maintain the means of doing so, without making war against other communities or denying an identity, a politics and a history to subjugated communities within its hegemony. But if the abandonment and the redistribution of sovereignty are to become general practices recommended to or imposed upon states, or communities of states, which were formerly sovereign and wrote their national histories as histories of their autonomous politics, one must also ask: if the sovereignty is to disappear, what is to happen to the historiography? If the historiography is to disappear, what is to happen to the identity? If the autonomous political community is to disappear, what is to happen to the political identity and autonomy of the individual?

These questions appear to be intimately linked, and one can imagine an 'Austro-Hungarian' set of answers, in which the surrender of sovereignty to a common set of institutions is found to have privileged some communities, but not others, to claim certain kinds of hegemony as 'historic peoples', while failing to provide the governing structure itself with a history which is that of a community or provided anyone with an identity. There was in the Austrian case an 'imperial' mystique, as there is now a 'European' mystique, which claimed to have a history but on the whole failed to make good that claim; and to this it may be added that empires commonly claim to be communities and to possess histories, but often fail in a diversity of ways to satisfy the communities they incorporate that their claim is good.

At this point new sets of questions may be asked. Is the supranational community we look at in the double perspective of this essay – the European Community, since no Pacific community is in process of formation – a species of empire, in which ultimate political control belongs to some institutions rather than others, to some national communities rather than others? The problems placed before the Community by the changes taking place in Central and Eastern Europe seem to make this a reasonable question; there are certainly differing German, French and British policy preferences regarding the future of the states of Eastern Europe. If we answer the question in the affirmative, we return 'Europe' to the domain of reason of state. 'Empire' and 'confederation' are not mutually exclusive terms, but are ranged along a spectrum of meanings: it may be said, however, that if there is to be a 'Europe' commanding its political present, there must be a political structure capable of defining its own past and writing its own history. On the other hand, the 'mystique of Europe' that has taken shape does not seem to offer a political history, which as far as can be seen would have to be that of a plurality of states acting in their own history and never yet confederated or incorporated in a lasting imperial structure. This opens the way to the reply that the question has been wrongly posed, and that the community being shaped is not a political community in the sense of a redistribution of the sovereignty possessed by states, but a set of arrangements for ensuring the surrender by states of their power to control the movement of economic forces, which exercise the ultimate authority in human affairs. The institutions jointly operated, and/ or obeyed, by member states would then be not political institutions bringing about a redistribution of sovereignty, but administrative or entre-preneurial institutions designed to ensure that no sovereign authority can interfere with the omnipotence of a market exercising 'sovereignty' in a metaphorical because non-political sense. There would be an 'empire' of the market which would not be an empire as the term is used in the vocabulary of politics, because that vocabulary would itself have lost its hegemony.

One might emerge with an uneasy hybrid, an 'empire' of the market in which residual political authority was unequally distributed between the political entities subject to its supra-political authority; or with a more benign, at least a more familiar, scenario in which confederated nations successfully operated shared institutions designed to allow market forces that freedom of operation which it had been agreed should belong to them. The problem of empire would not have disappeared, since it would be possible to find former national communities which had been denied their sovereignty and their history, or simply abolished as viable human communities, either by inclusion within or by exclusion from supranational common markets of the sort being imagined. It will be remembered that this essay is being written in part from a New Zealand point of view. In the East European and Eurasian settings – perhaps also in the North American as regarded from Quebec – member states of hegemonic confederations are to be seen claiming an independent sovereignty, very possibly with a view to joining common markets to which sovereignty must be given up as soon as asserted; the pooling of sovereignty in some regions and the fragmentation of sovereignty in others may be two sides of the same medal; but there may be yet other regions in which market forces simply reign without bothering to exact common institutions from the communities they rule, make and unmake. There have been informal empires as well as formal.

This essay is designed to ask questions about the voice of politics and history in what Michael Oakeshott termed 'the conversation of mankind'. What happens to the sometime citizens of a formerly autonomous community when it is enjoined to give up its political sovereignty and the capacity to write its own history? To the United Kingdom British when they are enjoined to cease claiming a history of their own and accept that they have no history except that of a Europe which has not been written yet? To the New Zealand British when they are ejected from Anglo-European history and enjoined to consider themselves part of a Pacific world which has no common history and may never acquire one? The craft of historiography suggests some responses to these predicaments. The United Kingdom British have the option of writing the history of Europe on the assumption that the history of the British peoples does indeed form part of it and radically modifies the ways in which it must be understood once this is admitted. The far more isolated and differently threatened New Zealanders, to whom others rather deny than extend options, may easily recognize that they are made up of voyaging peoples, Polynesian, European and latterly Asian; they may write their own history as shaped by voyaging, and voyage themselves in search of other histories to which oceanic distances connect them by the very radicalness of separation. Owls of Minerva may send back messages from other points in what is only planetary space.

But this is to presuppose that the voice of self-defining political and national historiography will survive. There have been political and social preconditions of its existence, and these may be in process of supersession. Let us imagine a state of affairs in which political communities had been effectively reduced to insignificance, and humans could identify themselves only as existing in market communities, engaged in no other self-defining activities than the manufacture, distribution and consumption of goods, images and the information (if that is the right word) relating thereto. It would in principle be possible to write the histories of such communities, and these histories might be full of unexpected and intriguing information about their conduct and the character of human life as shaped by them. The proposition that life in the non-political community is as historically informative as life in the political is as old as the New History, which has cropped up at intervals since Voltaire published the *Essai sur les Mœurs*; but New Historians have usually been political actors, with political motives for de-emphasizing the political. If we imagine a dystopia or eutopia in which market communities exercised complete hegemony, we may ask whether the ruling élites of such communities would have much interest in seeing their official histories written, or whether the individual as consumer would have the same interest as the individual as citizen, or as social actor interacting with the political, in seeing himself or herself as a critical actor modifying rule by his or her responses to it, and wishing to see the history of such modifications written.

The preconditions of historiography would not be met if the market communities had acquired an unlimited power of changing the produced and distributed images of what they were and what human needs they were designed to satisfy, if there were no alternative to responding to the images presented by the system that distributed them, and if the communities were incessantly and therefore uncritically engaged in this transformation of their self-images. There could then be no critical histories of images, but only images of history. To imagine this is, of course, to imagine the dystopia of *Brave New World* or *1984*, in which rulers as well as ruled are totally assimilated to the systems they operate. It may be replied that market communities do not deprive the individual of agency to the dystopian extent, while leaving open the question whether they will, under post-political conditions, contain individuals with enough sense of agency to require histories, as we know them, to be written. The problem will become more acute if we imagine market communities as lacking temporal stability, as constantly dissolved, transplanted and transformed by the market's insatiable demand for new human needs to satisfy; or if we imagine communities marginalized by the market, mere pools of unwanted labour with little or no purchasing power. Such fluctuating or frozen human masses would have little history and less need or will to write it; perhaps there are prerequisites for having a history at all. For the purposes of the present essay it is not necessary to predict the prevalence of such non-communities; but it is not mere fantasy to imagine them.

It is nearer description than imagination to say that we already have the makings of the historical or post-historical ideology which might take the place of historiography in such communities and non-communities as we have been supposing. This is the ideology of post-modernism, which – to simplify matters – may also be called the ideology of alienation, and a great deal of post-political historiography is already being written according to its specifications. It presupposes that all history is invention, and that all invention is alien and an imposition; any context in which the self might find meaning is imposed on the self by some other, and any specification of the self is similarly imposed, with the consequence that the self is always false, an imposition of, or imposture against, its own unrealizable existence. History is the study of constructs, and its aim is invariably their deconstruction. It used to be argued that this knowledge was the escape into freedom, until it was discovered that there remained no subject to be free, and it can still be argued, within limits, that it teaches a critical skill very useful to selves constantly threatened with identities imposed by others, and constantly obliged by the nature of history to be on the move between contexts in which identity must be varyingly realized and asserted. As a strategy, it is a good one for living and fighting back in the world of uncriticized market forces which incessantly impose new and non-referential images of who one is and what one wants: but as ideology it is the instrument of that world and operates to reinforce it. The marketers of images instruct us that we have no selves other than those they choose to impose upon us; the deconstructionist intellectuals, if they are not willing to stop somewhere and make a stand, tell us exactly the same thing. In all too many cases they have become anti-humanist enough to get no nearer making a stand than casting us either as oppressed – which is not so bad – or more commonly as oppressors of some other, to whose alienated consciousness they then enjoin us to submit our own. Their motives in doing so should be scrutinized and may be conjectured.

It is easy enough to see how this could become the ideology of a post-political, post-industrialist and post-modernist Europe or America. The affluent populations wander as tourists – which is to say consumers of images – from one former historical culture to another, delightfully free from the need to commit themselves to any, and free to criticize while determining for themselves the extent of their responsibility. How far this is a freedom to make their own history, how far a freedom from any need to make it, may be debated. Meanwhile the non-affluent form underclasses, pools of labour ebbing from one area of underemployment to another. The ideology of alienation, a luxury to the affluent, is a necessity to them, and as long as the state, feeling little need of a highly educated workforce, chooses to underpay its teachers, public education will be a means of perpetuating the underclass's pseudo-revolutionary discourse, which will double as the means of promotion into the educated bureaucracy. It will produce quite an intelligent, articulate and disenchanted populace, offered by history no means of associating themselves in politically active communities, but only in self-congratulatory yet self-accusatory sects and counter-cultures of the apparently or really alienated, capable at best of the special-issue activisms which constitute populism but not democracy. Thus the post-historical and post-political culture one can imagine taking shape in Western Europe if not North America; more isolated communities might be more deeply threatened.

   These are regions of continental and oceanic proportions beyond the common markets in which post-modernism can flourish. Early in 1991, Tatyana Tolstaya drew attention to such a region in western Eurasia not far beyond Europe: 'in the West the sense of history has weakened or completely vanished; the West does not live in history, it lives in civilization (by which I mean the self-awareness of transnational technological culture as opposed to the subconscious, unquestioned stream of history). But in Russia there is practically no civilization, and history lies in deep, untouched layers over the villages, over the small towns that have reverted to near wilderness, over the large, uncivilized cities, in those places where they try not to let foreigners in, or where foreigners themselves don't go.'[6] In using 'civilization' and 'history' as antithetical terms, Tolstaya is engaging in a dramatic departure from conventional Western language. By 'history' she means the experience and memory of the past unprocessed, in the nature of raw sewage: unmediated, uninterpreted, uncriticized and (incidentally if not centrally) unsanitized, present but not controlled, unimpeded in its capacity to drive humans to do unspeakable things. There are many areas of the settled earth (some of them in great Western cities, as the United States knows to its cost) where 'history' is like this. But when Tolstaya says that 'history' dies where there is 'civilization', she departs deliberately from Western discourse, since there we still believe that 'civilized' societies can write and debate their history, interpret it, argue over it, succeed or fail in coming to terms with it, even regard it as 'the nightmare from which one struggles to awake', and be the more 'civilized' for this ability to criticize it and reduce it to process. Even the loss of sovereign autonomy can stimulate the owl to take flight and map the territory of the past in greater detail and new perspectives: this happened in Edinburgh and Glasgow during the Scottish Enlightenment, and has been happening in both British and New Zealand historiography in response to Europeanization.

To us it does not follow that history disappears when it is interpreted,[7] but Tolstaya may be reminding us that this state of affairs cannot be relied on to last. The privatizing state may be ending its alliance with the clerical and intellectual élites who were its accredited interpreters and critics; it would rather its universities were vocational schools – if that – than centres of inquiry; and as we look through Europe into Eurasia, where the intelligentsias have been devastated by the life and death of the Party, we may be looking into a world where the post-modern which is indifferent to history lies side by side with the pre-modern which cannot rule history and is ruled by it. Along this faultline between tectonic plates, we wish

---

[6] Tolstaya, 1991.   [7] See, however, Plumb, 1970, and Lowenthal, 1985.

to say, unspeakable things will continue to happen, and the historian – that spokesperson for excluded modernity – may find something useful to do: but if there is no political domain in which historical understanding seeks an opportunity to act, is there anything that can be done?

Tolstaya's very striking language reminds us of a sense in which the 'end of history', prematurely announced a little while ago, might theoretically happen. Francis Fukuyama was (perhaps) imagining that the growth of the state and the processes of revolution might cease to be effective makers of history, given the universal triumph of a global market which took no account of frontiers; that the politics culminating in state and revolution were the means by which human beings attempted to control their history; that 'history' was the name for that process when under human control; and that henceforth humans would not make their history by their own thought and action, but the forces of the market would make it for them. Tolstaya is envisaging a not wholly different state of affairs, in which 'civilization' resolves and abolishes history and only barbarism retains it. Given these premises, the post-modern historian – when not living, as many still do, in a fantasy world in which linguistic criticism secures and continues the Leninist supremacy of the inquisitorial intelligentsia – will attempt to discover 'history' in the micro- or macro-experiences of humans in the global market and its culture. Those who maintain the modernist, or at any rate the pre-post-modernist, perspective will maintain that politics does not disappear with the Bismarckian or the Stalinist state, that humans continue to set up political structures to control their own history and contest for the power which comes from the attempt to control it, and that politics and history remain among the active forces which shape human lives and give them meanings. But the new world disorder coming after 1989 calls in question the premises of this debate, by calling in question the bipolarity of Tolstaya's (to say nothing of Fukuyama's) projection. The boundaries between 'civilization' and its opposite, barbarism, between history assimilated and history uncontrolled, have been broken open, and there is a zone to which politics and history are once more relevant. Europe is again an empire concerned for the security of its *limites*, and we may cautiously recall Gibbon's projection, in which the inhabitants of the civilized provinces have 'sunk into the languid indifference of private life' and history is being made for them by the encounters of soldiers and barbarians along the frontiers – the new barbarians being those populations who have not achieved the sophistication without which the global market has little for them and less need of them.

It is time to stop projecting and fantasizing:[8] but in late 1991 it seems apparent that 'Europe' – both with and without the North America whose addition turns it from 'Europe' into 'Western civilization' – is once again an empire in the sense of a civilized and stabilized zone which must decide whether to extend or refuse its political power over violent and unstable cultures along its borders but not yet within its system: Serbs and Croats if one chances to be Austrian, Kurds and Iraqis if Turkey is admitted to be part of 'Europe'. These are not decisions to be taken by the market, but decisions of the state; and they are revealing clearly enough that 'Europe' is still a composite of states, whose historically formed interests give them non-identical attitudes towards the problems of 'Europe' and its border-lands. Classically state-centred historiography returns to relevance, and even salience, once the crises of historic Russia and Yugoslavia present themselves before a Europe in which Germany has once again become united. There is still something for history to do – this is not put forward as a cheering prospect – whether written about the past or enacted in the present; the end is not yet. One may of course perform an act of faith, professing that these phenomena are all transitory and that sooner or later the global market will have exterminated politics and history all around the globe. When that happens, the end of history will have arrived; but to celebrate 1992 as if 'Europe' were a secure and self-regarding 'homeland', intent only on its post-modern and post-historical self, might be to look rather like the emperor Philip the Arab, celebrating the Secular Games at one of Gibbon's great ironic moments.

This essay has been written with a certain disrespect for the post-modernist intelligentsias, whose arrogance and provincialism at the moment expose them to their share of derision. But the post-modern phenomenon itself is entitled to respect: there really are senses in which the political community is losing its place at the centre of our allegiance (and allegiance itself any centre in consequence), and the non-political structures – or alternatively, those structures which enlarge the meaning of the 'political' until it has no boundaries – surrounding our existence are acquiring histories, or non-histories, of their own. Therefore the current 'new history' or anti-history is entitled to its place. The thrust of this essay is towards suggesting that it is not entitled to more than a place, and will not be enabled to claim a monopoly or an allegiance. Politics, the state, and various kinds of war, will continue to command our attention; Tolstaya's confrontation between 'civilization' and 'history' will continue to generate a history in which both

---

[8] [I did not fantasize the Islam of 2001–4.]

are involved; and even within, as well as outside, the global consumer culture generated by the all-conquering market, communities will continue to assert their politics in order to have a voice in determining their history. It is reasonable therefore to predict, and even to recommend, a continuing dialogue, or family quarrel, between the political and the post-political, the modern and the post-modern, the historical and the post-historical, history in older and in newer senses. It is perhaps in eastern, not western, Eurasia that it will finally be seen whether 'history' has come to an 'end' or not.

'Europeans', in this prediction, would write their history in ways which both privileged and deprivileged the centrality of states, admitting that they cast long and sometimes dark shadows in a present which may transcend the past but cannot abolish it; the pretence that there can be invented some uncomplicatedly 'European' history which both includes and excludes the histories of all the nations would be given up. The British would write their history into that of 'Europe', rewrite the latter's history as modified by their presence in it, and continue on occasion to write the former as seen in perspectives which are less continental than insular, archipelagic, oceanic and imperial. They would probably not be the only European national society to do so. As for that culture with which this essay began – New Zealand, cut adrift from its 'British' history by the advent of 'Europe', and for some purposes to be renamed 'Aotearoa' – it may already have lost both political and economic control of its present and future: but if it survives at all, its historians will have learnt (as they are learning) many new perspectives. They are learning rather rapidly to write their history as that of two cultures in stubborn interaction, and this reinforces rather than diminishes their sense of its autonomy; engrossed by the processes of settlement, they are already writing micro-histories of local experience and discourse, at their own distances from the history of politics and the state. If (again) they survive, their owls of Minerva will send out messages before as well as behind them on their flight, and they will address both Pacific history – which is that of small intense communities formed, separated and connected by voyagings over oceanic distances – and the history of 'Europe', 'Britain' and other northern land-mass cultures from which they are derived and which they need to see in their own way. They will inform 'Britain' that it has a planetary history it will not be able to forget, and 'Europe' that, as there is a Eurasian world into which it shades without fixed borders, so there is an oceanic (and likewise an American) world which it created and which enlarges it into 'the West'. Barriers between empires went down in 1989, and the intercontingency of the world increased. What do they know of Europe who only Europe know?

CHAPTER 16

The politics of the new British history

I have been asked to give this lecture[1] in several places to audiences interested in the concept, perhaps also in the programme, known as 'the new British history'; a name I hope it will soon shake off, now it is becoming accepted as a programme worth discussing and, more importantly, practising. The lecture is being delivered to audiences Irish, Scottish and English, all situated, as I am myself, outside that south-east region of the British island where the English kingdom and state took shape and learned to help fashion an English and British identity. Since this new history was originally offered as a replacement for a history which was that of the English state and the provinces of its empire, we now need to get past a stage in which it is that of the latter peoples with the English left out; I shall be arguing that British history of the English is something which we need and have difficulty in providing. British history is an archipelagic and oceanic rather than a merely English history; but it is not a history of a group of offshore islands doomed to re-absorption in a sub-continental hegemony from which they have been contingently and temporarily separated.

I have just uttered an ideological and therefore a political statement; to say anything about the history of a political association – in these cases an association of state and nation – is to say something about its politics; and to say something about what its history has been or may be is both to say something about its politics and to express a political judgement. So I have entitled this lecture, 'The politics of the new British history', and I should now like to pursue what that title implies in two directions. In the first place I shall say something about the political situations in which this 'new history' was conceived and to which it has been addressed, and something about what

---

[1] Originally delivered at University College, Dublin (particular thanks to Maurice Bric), King's College, University of Aberdeen (particular thanks to Jane Ohlmeyer) and the University of Liverpool (particular thanks to Anne McLaren), during October 2001. At Liverpool it became the David Beers Quinn Lecture, the last delivered in Professor Quinn's lifetime. It is here published for the first time.

it may signify as a discourse in and upon these situations. In the second place, I shall enter into the domain of political theory, in which I was once trained, and try to say something about what it may mean for a political society to have a history, and what sorts of political action are performed when such a history is constructed, interpreted, criticized or overthrown. It will turn out that the history of a political society is not unconnected with its sovereignty, and the pursuit of this history is very far from unconnected with the present and future distribution of sovereignty within these islands and outside them.

Let me remind you, then – following up my first set of intentions – that the 'new British history' was proposed to a meeting of the New Zealand Historical Association in Christchurch in the year 1973. New Zealand's history was formed in a relationship with the United Kingdom during the latter's imperial period and entailed a mythos according to which that kingdom and the several neo-Britains formed an association with a good deal of equality about it. 1973 was a moment in the process of British entry into Europe, and it was already apparent that this process was requiring the British to adopt a new view of their history, in which they were no longer, and as far as possible had never been, an imperial or oceanic people at all, but something called European instead; and whatever that meant it entailed the negation of our historic existence as neo-Britains, and of any account of British history in which we had part. Clearly, something would have to be done about this situation, and a variety of strategies presented themselves. One was to set about writing the history of New Zealand in ways that made it as autonomous as possible, stressed the ways in which it had been made there and nowhere else, and presented elements of Britishness and connection with Britain in an exterior and alien perspective. In the ordinary processes of settler nationalism, this kind of historiography was already well in place in 1973. It has gone on developing ever since, and has shed enormous amounts of light in many unexpected places; in particular, it has facilitated the writing of a history of the encounter between the settler and the indigenous peoples, between *pakeha* and Maori, in which the imperial crown has not ceased to be a presence. But there are limits to the extent to which it can be denied that New Zealanders have been a British and neo-British people. Even when they deny that they are, they are admitting the importance of that thesis in their minds; and there are moments when settler nationalism looks like some kind of British radicalism in transplanted form. They can deal with this by continuing to write their history as that of an argument with themselves and with others, which is of course the only way in which the history of a self-conscious association can be written at all; but this is a point at which it becomes desirable to have an alternative strategy to that which I have described so far.

In retrospect, the 1973 proposal for a new British history looks like the search for such an alternative. If one version of that history – let us call it the Anglo-imperial one – was at the end of its utility, at least one other must be found; and if the Brits (as we now learned to call them) were indeed proposing to rewrite their history in ways that left us out, it was clearly in our interest to rewrite it ourselves, in ways that both made sense of us to ourselves and reminded them that we and they were parts of one another's history. The proposal to diversify the history of the Atlantic archipelago, and present it as a problematic system of empire, was put forward in an archipelago on the other face of the planet, which needed to define its own place in this increasingly problematic history, and for which must be claimed a right to take part in interpreting it as a means to its own self-determination.

It is important to notice the central, conscious and deliberate ambivalence of this 'new history' towards the concept of empire. It was a response to the winding-up of empire, but it was never a call to idealize that empire in the past or continue it into the future, for the reason that the winding-up of empire struck us as an act of empire in its most objectionable form. The Brits – and this does mean particularly the English – were behaving as if we were items in their patrimony, and they were entitled to pension us off and dismiss us when it suited them; we were replying – in language once used by Scots to Charles I and the English parliament – that we had part in David the King as well as they. (I find in much contemporary literature that Scottish nationalism increased in proportion as it appeared that the English did not know what to do with themselves, and were therefore behaving as if nobody else existed.) But to assert, as the 'new history' did, that empire, meaning a history shared by an association of peoples, had never belonged exclusively to the Brits – in the Anglocentric sense of the word – and was therefore not theirs to wind up as they chose, was necessarily to assert also that this empire and history belonged exclusively to no one, and therefore to render problematic the extent to which it was an empire at all. 'British history' is therefore the history of a problematic; it renders problematic the extent to which it has been unified, the extent to which it can be called 'British history', the extent to which there exists or has existed a 'British' people or community of peoples who say it is their history. But to problematize is not to deconstruct; the questions I have just asked are questions, meaning that we do not know the answers, that there may be answers, that there may be more than one answer, that we may have to choose between them or to combine them. Implanted in our minds, we suddenly realize, is the malignant assumption that to question a human construct is to prepare its disappearance; but human institutions disappear, not because they are questioned, but because they have run out of answers. To ask a question is to take this risk, since we ask it because we do not know the answer; but human associations may be thought of as devices for finding the answers to questions, even for reframing the questions so that they can be answered; and to suppose a 'British history' which constantly asks itself what it is, and whether that is the right question, may be to suppose that it will continue to ask these questions and find answers to them, and so to exist. All this may be built on the single point that 'British history' is among other things the history of an empire, which problematizes that empire's history. It does not ensure that this history will continue, but it entertains the possibility that it may.

Clearly, British history faces problems, because its business is to problematize itself. I shall leave undiscussed, as to be settled only in the future, the central problem of how far there has been, or will continue to be, a 'British' national or multinational community which has a history and possesses the political means of continuing it into a future. The politics of this historiography are directed more towards asking this question than to giving answers to it – though to those who already have an answer, the proposal to leave it unanswered will look like giving an answer other than their own. I want to turn to a historiographical problem that underlies even this central question. The 'new British history' was offered as a replacement for an older view of that subject, in which it was presented as that of an English state enlarged into a British kingdom, and of a predominantly English political community underlying it, so that histories other than English were presented as peripheral, to be recounted and indeed noticed only when they were capable of modifying a history which hardly sprang from them. Let me remind you that this proposal was put forward in New Zealand, whose highly interesting history is never noticed by anyone, on much the same grounds. It followed, however, that the term 'British' could be used as the equivalent of this Anglocentred history it was proposed to replace, and both Scottish and Irish historians were heard to wonder whether it would not perpetuate this history instead of replacing it. The original proposal, I think, was to use the term 'British' in a rather different way: to denote a context which the several histories both shared and contested among themselves; and because there was no unified history – no history to be finally written as that of a self-defining inclusive history – available or predictable for this context, 'British history' was from the start intended to be self-problematizing in the way that it has been. There remained, nevertheless, an important problem in nomenclature: should the adjective 'British' be used comprehensively, as it is for example when the islands of this archipelago are collectively referred to as 'the British Isles'? These terms 'British' and 'Britain' are not politically neutral; their history in Scotland is unlike that they have in England, and both these are unlike that they have in Ireland, where there are good reasons in the republic for rejecting them altogether. I was from the start willing to use the term 'the Atlantic archipelago', but this has failed to catch on: partly for the rather interesting reason that you cannot form a generic adjective from it, partly for contrary reasons having to do, as I see it, with a general invective against naming or defining or having any identity at all, which is part of the politics of post-modernism.

Problematization again lies at the heart of this matter, but it is both possible and necessary to look beyond it. The Irish entity has steadfastly and with much success refused inclusion in a British political community or its history; there is obviously a strong case for saying that Irish history is not part of British history and demands to be considered apart from it. In reply, however, there is a strong case for saying that the rebellion against inclusion in British history is a very large part of Irish history and has done much to shape the national identity of which it is the history; and there is also a case for saying that 'British history', in any sense in which it can be defined, has been deeply shaped by the Irish rebellion against it. This applies certainly to the history of state formation in these islands, and also to that of the formation and existence of self-defining communities; and all these histories would seem to be still going on, and to defy both immediate resolution and prospective liquidation. We need to go on writing them, as we need to go on enacting them. The rejections of 'British history' in one sense are part of it in another; and in projecting a periodization of 'British history', I have found myself organizing it both around successive attempts at a 'British' union – 1603, 1707, 1801 – and around the concept of two massive secessions, American in 1776, Irish in 1921, which both modify the course of this history and are themselves modified by what they are seceding from. This both problematizes 'British history' and juxtaposes it with histories to be distinguished from it; but problematization does not cause it to disappear.

The case of Ireland raises another set of questions, which I should like to look at in ways that may lead us back to the problem of the conjunction of the words 'British' and 'English'. To use the term 'Ireland' is to imply, very truthfully, that there may be supposed to exist a community known by that name, with which and with whose history individuals may identify, to the point where there exists a state formed by, affirming and continuing that history; that there are areas where the boundaries of this identity are violently contested only underlines its existence. Where such entities exist – and there are several of them going to make up 'British history', if not to exhaust its meanings – each of them requires and constructs a history of itself, designed to make sense of itself to itself, and to record how the people composing it have come to be what they are and to have interacted among themselves so as to construct it as it is and themselves as part of it. Histories on this, let us call it 'national', scale are both ideologically inevitable – since without them the pronoun 'we' cannot be used at a political-historical level – and politically and historiographically justifiable, since it is possible to write them in ways both complex and self-critical, encouraging a similarly sophisticated awareness among 'us' of who 'we' are and what 'we' have been doing. There will be those among us who press for alternative histories, and there will be those who object strenuously to the presentation of history in any form that admits an alternative; but it is in the nature of politics that we should confront these problems, and in a properly working politics there will be means of dealing with them. It is true, however, that a historiography, sophisticated and self-critical about the relations between those perceived as included in the society whose history is being written, may be a good deal less so about those not perceived as included. These latter may be found within the society itself – the enormous and universal problem of the history of women here arises – or they may be found outside it, or ambiguously situated on its borders. Here we meet the famous Others, and we are familiar with a rhetoric that seems to suggest that the Self cannot be constructed without the distorted image of an Other, and is itself distorted by the falsity of the relation in which it defines itself. Now this is all too often all too true; but I want to say that ways exist of moderating this situation, and that when we meet with histories that seem to recount the formation of Selves in no other way than by the invention of Others, we should remember to mistrust those for whom the deconstruction of identities and communities seem to have become a programme; they may not know who they are working for, but I think I do. We need to work towards a state of things in which the self may criticize itself in its relationships with others – accepting by the way the fact of its historical contingency and non-final determinacy – while maintaining the political and historical continuity of its association with those with whom it is associated. I have no great difficulty in envisaging a historiography quite good at maintaining this complex and multiple kind of awareness, and I am interested in the 'new British history' as that of a number of entities, converging and diverging in ways that render them contingent upon one another, while retaining the ability to recount their several histories in so far as these continue to make sense to those who find them to do so.

It is a premiss, then, that any long-standing political community – nations rather predominantly included – needs two histories, recounted in narratives which should be perpetually confronted but are distinct. One is the narrative of how its members have interacted with each other in order to produce it and conduct its affairs; the other that of how they and it have interacted, or failed to do so, with those internal and external who are not included in it. These two histories shade into one another; there are vast gray areas where they do so; frontier disputes between them can have real and bloody political meaning. Before passing on, let us note the fallacy of supposing that the second history necessarily discredits or deconstructs the first. It supplies a context to it, and gives it new and uncomfortable meanings; but the fallacy I have mentioned is part of a conspiracy against the democratic state. It is because political histories have this dual character that a multinational history like the British has its problematic character; and it is for this reason that 'new British history' can be regarded as politically suspect from every point on the spectrum. If Scottish and Irish historians have suspected it of a design to deprive their national histories of autonomy by including them in a wider narrative, Anglo-British historians may as well suspect it of dissolving that narrative into its national components; and what becomes of any autonomous history when it is contextualized by association with others? There are those who have tried to use the new British history – and there are those who distrust it because it cannot be used – as part of a design to deprive all its components of their sovereignty in their history, and reduce them to autonomous regions of an acephalous empire known by the name of 'Europe'. To those who may want to say that 'Europe' is not designed to be such an empire, I should reply that they have an interest in resisting such a design whenever it shows itself. The politics of regional nationalism in an era of globalization are complex, ambivalent and potentially treacherous; and this is part of the politics of historiography.

Let me revert to the historiographical problems that arise when 'British history' is written as the convergence and divergence of a number of histories, many of them defining peoples, nations or sub-nations who may be thought of as contributing either to the making of British history or perhaps to its unmaking. There are at least three national histories visible as parts of this mixture, and at least one of them must be thought of as both national and imperial. Some national and sub-national formations antedate the attempted formation of a 'British' state; others are shaped in the course of the latter formation or in reaction against it. Scottish nationalism, for example, rests on the history of a state which existed before its entry into the British union and now desires to redefine its position and its identity; Irish, on the other hand, has been far more directly confronted by the problem of what kind of state and what kind of nation were to be formed by the resistance to Anglo-British and Scottish domination. There is the question of how far both 'Scotland' and 'Northern Ireland' are the products of a Norman-Anglian kingdom's offensives against maritime Gaeldom. David Quinn raised the problem of how far these, and the much larger English offensive against Ireland generally, carried over into the colonization of Atlantic America. 'British history' observes that this colonization was largely but by no means wholly an English affair, and as such played its part in British history until these colonies associated themselves in a federal union – an act deeply un-English and un-British – and engaged in a conquest and colonization of the North American continent.

'American history' at this point departs from 'British history' more decisively, I wish to suggest, than 'Irish history' succeeds in doing. There is a paradox here: American history is decisively shaped by Protestant sectarianism – English, Scottish, Irish and German – and is therefore culturally akin to Anglo-British history, whereas Irish history can be contextualized within a history of Catholicism which 'British history' excludes as its Other. Here perhaps is the central problem of writing an Irish history. But American history becomes that of a continental and global civilization, while Irish history remains committed to the problem of distributing sovereignty within these islands. There is a certain question which Kingdom and Republic are having to address together and cannot give away with their sovereignty to 'Europe'; they must retain sovereignty if they are going to deal with it.

Not all component peoples of 'British history' are nations or desire to be states; and the term 'Britain' designates a state which may have been simply an empire and may not have consolidated a nation (I use those verbs and moods to ask a question, not to suggest that the answer is known). It is when 'state' and 'nation', politics and history, begin to designate one another that there arises that need of a double history of which I have been speaking; and the function of 'British history' here is not only to supply each Self with its Others, but to furnish as many as possible of those Others with histories of their own as Selves, and the means of speaking and acting back at the primary Self – who is, as often as not, the English. The political function of contextualization, to put it in other terms, is not to disarm history, but to re-arm histories. Let me remark, in parenthesis, that the enterprise in New Zealand historiography with which I have had most to do is that of redesigning it as a relationship between *pakeha* history and Maori history.

Clearly, there are risks being run in taking up such enterprises. There are so many forces operating at present to take 'our' history from 'us' and deconstruct 'us' as historical beings – there is even something to be said for such forces and I may be addressing hearers who want them to succeed – that to employ contextualization as a means to the strengthening of histories is to play cards that may be turned against one. But if politics is the art of being ruled while one is ruling, there should be no objection to histories which empower Others to act upon one while one acts upon them. This is the case for British history as problematic, the history of several nations and sub-nations which may or may not have shared a political association. But there is a central problem here about which I should say something in the last part of this lecture.

This is the problem of the English: of fitting them, and of seeing how they may fit themselves, into this 'new British history'. Because it has been presented as an alternative to an older scheme in which it was the history of an English state and the latter's occasionally visible provinces, it has necessarily counter-privileged histories written from the point of view of these provinces, no longer seen as such; and these histories have been in the usual measure self-regarding, designed to explain the Welsh or the Scots to themselves, with the English as external if omnipresent actors. But they, the English, have their history, which has acted in the history of others. T. M. Devine's *The Scottish Nation*[2] is a wonderful book, from which I have learned a great deal I ought to have known long ago; but there are moments in reading it when I say to myself, 'Where were the English all this time?', meaning the English, not just the Westminster politicians. Many Scots went to live in England – there is a tradition of English comment on this – and it seems that some English went to live in Scotland. Professor Devine mentions that they did, but though he tells us in some detail what became of the Lithuanians, the Jews, the Irish, the Italians and the Asians in Scotland, he does not pursue the fortunes of the English there. Perhaps there were not enough of them to merit treatment; but on the larger scale of British history, I should like to know more about how these cultures interacted and helped to shape one another, conceivably into Britishness. That Scottish culture was in danger of Anglicization would seem to be an important feature of the story, but not the only reason for telling it. We have to get beyond relations of inequality if we are to get beyond them.

I am saying that the new history has to get beyond the unmaking of an Anglo-British paradigm, the aim with which it began; after which that paradigm can be re-admitted to the story and seen to act within it. This is

---

[2] Devine, 1999. [See now Watson, 2003.]

not easy, both because of a past of Anglo-British domination and because the histories of distinct communities cannot altogether cease being written in terms of Self and Other; but once this is admitted, we can see that the new history has made very considerable progress in overcoming these difficulties. This is even true of the historiography written by the English, to which I now want to turn. The predicament of the English is that it is peculiarly hard for them to separate English from British history and use the latter to contextualize the former, for the reason that the history of how they have governed themselves is hard to separate from the history of how they have governed others. (This, by the way, contains the explanation of the famous 'empire in absence of mind'; more than most imperial peoples, they have been intent on governing themselves and have failed to pay equal attention to their governance of others, or their partners in that rule.) During what I propose as the early modern period of British history – say from 1530 to 1830 – the central problem was the often insecure maintenance of empire as defined in the English Act in Restraint of Appeals (1533): that is, the empire of English authority over the English realm, exercised through royal and parliamentary sovereignty in both kingdom and church. For reasons either essential or accidental, it had to be decided, and the decision either imposed or negotiated, how far this 'empire', and the forms of church and kingdom it implied, were to be extended to other realms subject to the wearer of the English crown; and in Scotland, Ireland and English America, we meet with profoundly different histories stemming from this question. If we take the English Reformation and the Church of England as one tap-root of British history, it will follow that Norman Davies was not talking absolute nonsense when he identified their foundation as the fatal moment when British history became separated from that of 'Europe' and succumbed to the illusion of its own existence.[3] The histories I have identified take place in an empire formed by the multiple sovereignties of the British crown; they do not take place in, though they interact with, the relations between that crown and the adjacent sovereignties of the west European peninsula. That being so, you are welcome to call them 'European' if you can attach some stable meaning to the word; I dare say there are several.

For these and some further sets of reasons, it may never be possible for the English to see their history as other than that of an imperial people; one

---

[3] Davies, 1999, p. 512. To be Anglican was to be neither Catholic, Lutheran, nor Calvinist; and these, being European, pass the test of reality. For Davies's view of Pocock, 1974, see pp. 1025–7; I of course see it as less deconstructive in its intention, and less ineffective in its reception, than he does.

possessing extremely distinctive institutions, memories and culture of its own which have nevertheless incessantly involved them with others who do not share them or have put them to purposes of their shaping. This does not mean that the English are imbued with a relentless need to dominate others; it does mean that sovereignty and empire are hard to separate in the histories they remember of themselves, so that with the ending of Anglo-British empire in the association of the archipelago, they are finding it exceptionally hard to furnish themselves with a new history, of the sort which we might call British. A 'British history' of the English is much to be desired; it should be constructed by the English themselves; but it would be unwise to hold one's breath.

Let us explore some further reasons for this. The successive failures of imperialism, socialism and industrialism – a triple hammer of blows hard for any people to endure – fell upon the British and upon the English, the Scots and the Welsh in so far as they were and might remain engaged upon the British enterprise. Unlike the Scots, and more doubtfully the Welsh, the English did not have open to them the recourse of nationalism as an ideological and emotional replacement for their former history. Unlike the flag of St Andrew, the flag of St George – and it is of interest that one sees this displayed – indicated no alternative politics and no alternative history. It is a cardinal problem of the new British history that the Scots, and incomparably more the Irish, are able (and obliged) to recount it from the outside, retelling the imperial narrative in the voices of people to whom it was done, and who had histories of their own that interacted with it; whereas, the more one insists that the old British history was at bottom the history of England, the clearer it becomes that the history of England is not to be separated from the old British history, the empire of the English over themselves from the history of their empire over others. The only alternative offered them to the nation-centered histories available to the other peoples of the archipelago has so far been the fine old radical history of a people perpetually in rebellion against the empire of their masters – a historiography which may be traced back to William Cobbett, author of the first anti-history of England,[4] in which he decided that the root of all evil lay in the Dissolution of the Monasteries; a conclusion not only Tory and crypto-papist, but deeply and unalterably English, as if English history could only be unmade from within.

I think I am saying that the 'new British history' of the English will have to be the 'old British history' retold: the ironies of a history in which sovereignty over themselves was inseparable from sovereignty over others,

---

[4] Cobbett, 1824.

an empire they didn't much want but couldn't help exercising and, of course, at times enjoying. The future of 'Britishness' depends on the prospects of remaking their relationship with the relevant others in new forms which they will share with them, and I am reasonably cheerful about these prospects. A 'new history of England' is in fact developing at breathtaking speed, on levels both populist and academic, but it will feed into the perception of a 'new British history' in ways which the inescapably imperial character of English history of the past will make unlike the 'British histories' taking shape outside England. It will consist of re-interpretations of the ways in which the English have interacted with their empire, and these re-interpretations are already taking shape.

If this were to happen in the sort of future predicted and preferred by the 'new British history', it would occur in a world of mixed, conditional and shared sovereignties. That history is rather far from forming part of the rhetoric of abdication. It supposes that there are political, sometimes national, entities possessing histories which they are able to criticize, re-interpret and see as both affecting and affected by the histories of others; so that the identity formed in a history, and the political will to continue forming it, are contingent and contextualized. To recognize one's identity as historically contingent is the best way of maintaining it in a universe of histories; to recognize it as contingent upon the identities of others the best way of maintaining it in a political universe. There is a correlation between the political community's ability to recount its history critically, and its ability to continue that history into the future; I call that ability sovereignty, and I am prepared to assert that there can be no sovereignty without a history. I see identity, history, sovereignty and politics as under attack, on a front probably global and certainly European, and I oppose the project of a multipolitical history to the project of absorbing states and their histories into a global culture of commodification enforced by its attendant bureaucracies. The present state of archipelagic history interests me because just as the latter project is at the height of its demands, the Kingdom and Republic find themselves obliged to deploy their sovereignties on an imperial scale, hoping thereby to bring about a redistribution of sovereignty in a province which can finally belong to neither of them. Their shared history seems likely to be prolonged into an indefinite future; and so may that of the English and even the British. The future history of the peoples of New Zealand will no doubt recount itself.

CHAPTER 17

*Conclusion: history, sovereignty, identity**

(1)

The title of this essay is adapted from 'Conclusion: contingency, identity, sovereignty', an address delivered to the 1994 Conference of Anglo-American Historians and subsequently published in the volume recording the proceedings on that occasion.[1] I confessed myself, in my opening remarks, tempted to adopt the role of old Simeon in the Gospel and cry *Nunc dimittis*; after twenty years of misleadingly apparent neglect, the subject I had proposed in Christchurch at a conference in 1973 had recently and rapidly acquired a literature and become the subject of the conference at which I was speaking. I said I would reject that temptation, however, since I did not wish to vanish into the history I had proposed, and there was still a good deal to be said about it. Ten more years have passed, and I find myself presenting a selection from what has been said and a synthesis of what may remain sayable.

In this volume I have laid emphasis on the antipodean perspective. Situated as it is at the ends of voyages, it presents societies and their histories, and even the autonomy needed to create such histories, as inventions (not to say creations) of fairly recent date. New Zealand, where human habitation may be less than a millennium old, encourages this vision in one way; Australia, where European settlement just as recent confronts an Aboriginal presence so ancient as to be paleolithic and recoverable only by carbon-dating and cosmic myth, in quite another. In these lands of settlement the *lieux de la mémoire* are either recent or almost irrecoverable; they cannot be documented and renarrated over two to three millennia in the ways that permit European and Mediterranean cultures to regard themselves

*[Written for this volume in 2004.]

[1] Pocock, 1995b.

as old and lands of settlement (including of course the American) as rather contemptibly new. Settler cultures, where memory and history are either new or transplantations of the old, must renarrate history in ways that pay attention to the voyage; but the forces that threaten the *lieux de la mémoire* with commodification or oblivion are the same in the new worlds and in the old. Tourism at Luxor or Stonehenge is much the same as tourism at Ayers Rock (renamed Uluru[2]) or Waitangi; it may be possible to re-educate it as an awareness of history, but the obstacles are evident and formidable.

These essays have been much concerned with sovereignty, and with a supposed relation between sovereignty and history, of which more must be said in conclusion. They lead to a present, and look towards a future, in which the continued existence of sovereignty is questionable but may persist. In that future the neo-Britains will pursue the problems of sovereignty, imposed upon Canada since the beginnings of its history, but self-imposed upon New Zealand by a recent decision to open sovereignty to debate and treaty. These are internal problems, independent of any relationship with Great Britain, but entailed by the history of crown in parliament as sovereignty's principal constituent. These nations, or combinations of nations, will continue to exercise some kind of sovereignty and make, write and interpret some kind of history. It is of the United Kingdom that this statement cannot be made without incurring some kind of challenge.

The rewriting of British history, as proposed and practised in these essays, has been an exercise in multinationality. Without abandoning the premiss that the 'empire' or government of the English nation over itself has been enlarged into an 'empire' of Britain included in a state predominantly English, it has proposed the histories of two other nations, of which one – Scotland – remains within Britain while challenging and possibly terminating its structure as a state, while the other – Ireland – has become independent through a revolutionary process, while remaining linked with Britain by a shared economy and the problems of a self-disputed border province. This has been a history of states, and of the nations formed around these states: Scotland possessing a nation-state structure antedating the union of Britain and now seeking greater autonomy outwith[3] it, Ireland presenting a history in which state, church, nationality, and it may be

---

[2] There are now programmes of restoring indigenous place-names, with or without the abolition of those conferred by settlers.
[3] I defer to the practice of using Scottish words, as here instead of the English 'without', when endeavouring to give voice to Scottish thinking.

added identity, had to be hammered disputatiously into being in the process of resisting English/British rule. If Welsh history has received less attention than it should have been given, it is because the absence from earlier history of a Welsh state structure has excluded the Welsh people from the history of states and the formation of nations around them which was long the mainstream of Euro-American historiography, and of which this 'new' British history is so manifestly a specimen. It has presented a problem within mainstream historiography, in so far as it has left problematic the question whether a durable British state has consolidated around itself a durable 'British' nation whose history may be written. We live in a time, however, when any question about the duration or identity of a state or nation seems framed to expect a negative answer. We need to ask why this should be.

Two sets of answers have presented themselves. In the first place, a post-industrial global economy has produced patterns of human interaction which disregard – the fashionable word is 'transgress' – existing boundaries between states, nations and the civil societies formed around them, with the result that many humans no longer feel themselves to be living in such associations, participating in their politics or belonging to their transmitted or inherited cultures. The communication of culture has become a good deal more electronic than behavioural or social, and the patterns in which humans live have become fluid to the point where they are images in the mass mind, instantly transmitted and rapidly replaced. In such circumstances it is difficult to have a history at all, or to live in a state or society whose history is the record of its continuity. In the second place – it may be only a distinctive aspect of these conditions – humans now live in the midst of an information explosion, in which they are intensely aware of the instantaneous and fictitious character of most of the information conveyed to them, but are immersed in it to such an extent that information and fiction appear to constitute the only social universe available. The barriers between information and entertainment are thus eroded, with highly specific consequences for both politics, which become comedy, and history, which becomes fiction. There has always been much truth in both these visions, but vision now becomes substituted for truth.

New power groupings, and their ideologies, arise. The executive class – it looks like a class – directing the global economy demands, not only that states and national cultures shall get out of the way of the flow of commodities and information, but that the sovereignty of the state and the distinctiveness of the culture shall be modified, eroded, obsoleted and abolished, to the extent necessary to the economy's supremacy. This is bad news for the retention and study of history, up to and beyond the very considerable extent to which histories have so far been written in, for and by autonomous communities, as records of their formation, development and internal or external crises and resolutions; written narrations and interpretations of the history they claim to have made and suffered. These histories have always been in considerable measure selective, authoritative, rhetorical, biassed and fictitious; but the internal contestations characteristic of political societies will have produced discourses capable of challenging all these attributes, and a developed political society will claim the ability to criticize and renarrate its own history even as it invents it. At the point, however, at which criticism becomes what we term post-modern, criticism and invention are alike swallowed up in fiction. Employing such phrases as 'the invention of tradition' – traditions, of course, are at various speeds invented – a discourse will take shape which depicts all history, past and present, not only as invented but as instantly invented, by actors as few and in circumstances as transitory as the narrative can be made to bear; a view of history produced by and reinforcing the conditions of an information explosion, in which all information is fiction recently produced and instantly to be replaced. This discourse is the work of a new class, in which the entrepreneurs of culture (including politics and history) as entertainment are joined by allegedly subversive critics who, pretending to warn us that all information is fiction, perpetuate the condition in which it can be nothing else; they will attack with peculiar vehemence any body of information – such as history as historians use the word – which offers to criticize, and so conditionally to validate, itself. This is a generalization, to which counter-generalizations may be offered, but it depicts a state of affairs recognizable enough.

(11)

A political society may be expected to have a history – remembered, discussed, written and interpreted, in ways that approach the meanings of the term 'historiography' – which affirms its origins, the source and continuity of its authority and legitimacy, and significant events and processes constituting the narrative it relates to itself. The function of this history is of course ideological, in the sense that it maintains the society's authority rather than subverting it, and much of its content will be mythical in several senses of the word; it will be difficult to question it, and one may be discouraged from, or persecuted for, doing so. On the assumption that the intellect is always opposed to authority, therefore, one may see a society's publicly received history as necessarily opposed to criticism: a structure of myth and ideology which the intellect cannot but subvert. Yet the history of the term ἱστορια itself suggests that historians have always asked questions about history, and that the word suggests both authority and enquiry; nor need we leap to the conclusion that the history of historiography is reducible to the collision between the two. Politics is a contestatory activity, and the history of a political society will be a history of contestation. It is not a long step to the further conclusion that the history such a society constructs of itself will be both contested and contestable; there will be contested accounts of what has occurred in history, contested accounts of what political authority has been and should be – it is at this point that political theory and philosophy appear – and contested accounts of how history has been, may be and should be written, in the ongoing context of a society's debate with itself as to what it is, has been and ought to be. This will not be enough to ensure that the debate will be conducted under liberal, open or tolerant conditions; but it will ensure that the debate is present and seen to be present. We may therefore think of a political society as one that constructs a history of itself that is contestable and contested.

It is not necessarily true, then, that history is always written by the winning side; the relations between winners and losers are complicated, and most histories of the Caesars were written by defeated senators who wrote the history of their defeat without expecting to change it. It is nearer the truth to say that histories are written by those with enough power and voice to take part in the political contest, and that those excluded from that contest to the point where they were never even losers will find it hard to write history or have it written of them. The silence of the subaltern presents itself. Any political society excludes two classes of persons: those interior to the society but denied political voice within it – this definition has very often included women – and those exterior to it, organized or not organized into political societies of a comparable kind, who must be accounted strangers and may be accounted enemies. These two classes contain most of those currently termed 'the Other' – that strange and flattening term so much employed as a means of undermining the authority of the Self. What is immediately to be noticed is that the history a political society constructs will be a history of its self; it will be written by and for those engaged in its self-contestatory activity, and will be contestable in the sense that it is a narrative of contests already known to be going on. It will not be news to the citizens – if we may employ that term – that they live under a contested authority structure, or that they have neighbours whose authority structures (and histories?) differ from their own; knowing these things is part of what makes them citizens. They will possess a history of contests among themselves over the distribution, justification and character of authority, and will believe that these contests may be continued, if they cannot be resolved, without bringing their history to a final disruption. As Machiavelli observed, the point about the Secession of the Plebs is that the plebs did not secede.

The political structure which enables a society to contain its self-contestations and continue its history may be described in terms which combine and offer to reconcile the notions of authority and liberty. *Ex imperio libertas*, in the words of an ancient Roman; we are free because we possess authority, exercised over ourselves and over others, which we use to determine what we are and shall be – at which point arises the problem of those included in our *imperium* but not in our *libertas*. There has been an empire over ourselves, as well as an empire over others; our history empowers us to continue contestation among ourselves, and may or may not meet the challenge to it arising when those excluded from it claim a voice in contesting it. But so far as 'we' are concerned – 'we' being the members of any society free and sovereign enough to use the word – 'our' sovereignty, 'our' liberty, and (to introduce the word) 'our' identity, depend upon 'our' having a history which we are able to continue. It helps, to say the least, if 'we' are in a position to go on recounting it. We know it to be contested and self-contestatory; we have installed among us a set of beings called historians, whose task is not only to record the contests, but to record the conditions and pre-conditions under which these have been conducted; we have empowered them both to reach conclusions irrespective of their immediate impact on the contestations currently going on, and to point out that the conditions under which society exists and conducts its contests are historically contingent and may not endure. These are the terms on which sovereignty and history exist together, and 'we' exist within them. If 'we' should cease to have the authority to say what we have been or to decide what we shall be – a decision which sovereigns take in acting upon a world of infinite contingency they cannot command – 'we' should not exist at all. 'You' and 'they', not included in 'us', may challenge 'our' authority over them, and recount the histories that entitle them to this challenge; but 'we' must have both history and sovereignty sufficient to reply to it.

These essays in British history have deliberately multiplied the sovereignties engaged in it, and consequently the histories of which it may be seen to consist. They have emphasized the contestability of all these sovereignties and histories: the extent to which they are contestable within the societies they provide with histories, in their exterior relationships with one another, and under the historical conditions whose contingency they do not deny. At the conclusion of the narrative in which these essays are combined, 'British history' and perhaps 'history' as so far conceived encounter the conditions here termed 'post-modern' (a use of that term which does not extend to every use to which it may be put): a set of conditions under which human identity is so far absorbed into a global economy and culture that the formation of political societies employing sovereignty to determine their histories appears obsolete, impossible or dangerous. These essays do not conclude with an apocalyptic vision in which this has already happened or is bound to happen; but to say that it may not happen betrays a willingness to suggest that perhaps it should not. Certainly, to supply a history of sovereignty that emphasizes its complexity and contestability is to lean towards suggesting that perhaps it will, or should, continue into the future. This concluding chapter will itself conclude by examining some rhetoric aimed against the continuation of sovereignty, and enquiring what these suggestions may imply.

(III)

'But don't the *pakeha* have a terrible identity problem?' said a New Zealand television interviewer to an Auckland colleague. No, he replied; they know perfectly well who they are, and if they have problems deciding what they are, they know they are the people who have these problems. In the same way, but with reference to a time three centuries ago, an excellent work entitled *The People with No Name*[4] envisages Scottish settlers in Ulster at the point of a further emigration to North America, where – but interestingly not in Ulster – they would become known as 'the Scots-Irish'. At that point, the author suggests, they knew they were neither Scots nor Irish, if only because they might be considered either, but defined themselves by that predicament; 'the people with no name' was not a self-description that would have frightened them. Here's to the selves they would never, never be! Certainly, their subsequent conduct, on both sides of the Atlantic, does not suggest any great lack of self-confidence, nor can their recurrent ferocity be ascribed to an identity crisis – though it may have something to do with the establishment of identity among others. The immediate point of these anecdotes is that it may be more important to have a history

---

[4] Griffin, 2001.

than to have an identity. To have a history, and know what it is, is to know that it may be contestable; if it supplies you with an 'identity' that is contestable, it may empower you to live in that contestation and know yourself as its outcome, in which case you establish your identity by continuing to contest it and to allow others to contest it with you. If you end by conceding that your identity will always be contingent and imperfectly resolved, that may be a sign of adulthood and the ability to live in history; the eye will be more or less satisfied with seeing, and may find that condition stimulating. It is an implied pre-requisite, however, that your history is one in which you have not quite lost a voice in determining your identity. The condition called post-colonial is the condition of having lacked any power to contest an identity imposed upon you, which is why it is never quite the condition of former colonists, such as the Scots-Irish and the *pakeha*.

It is implicit in the first anecdote, however, that you should initially mistrust those who ask, or offer to tell you, about your identity, because the term has been annexed by those who use it with an intention of weakening it; from which it may follow that you should think carefully before embarking on a search for it, since the search may have been framed to ensure its failure. Identities are human creations, and the creation takes place in history; but much of the contemporary literature on this subject makes use of a post-modern idiom, employing such terms as 'invention', 'making' and so on to present the process as fragile, instantaneous and dependent on an immediate context, so that the 'making' of an 'identity' is often designed to lead as quickly as possible to its unmaking. The possibility that identities may come into being over time, may be 'invented' and assented to by humans involved in complex processes, or that they may be reinforced by their survival in changing circumstances, is not to be counted on but is too easily left out of account. So is the possibility of a history of changing and contested identity, of which we may see ourselves as the self-conscious products; our 'identities' as roles we choose to adopt, knowing that they have been shaped for us over time and that history has filled them with ambivalences we knowingly accept as we take them on. It is more important to have a history, and to know what it is, than to ransack it in search of a moment at which we acquired an identity we may not have any longer.[5]

It is of interest that in the British and even the English cases, the self-destructive search for identity has become associated with the concept of

---

[5] I think this is a possible criticism of Kumar, 2003.

empire. Britishness, we are told, comes into being and goes out of it with the success – so described as to point direct to subsequent failure – of English empire in the Atlantic archipelago and British beyond. These essays have endeavoured to supply a more complex narrative, in which empire within the archipelago is distinguished from, and related to, empire in the global oceans, and the empire of the English over others from the empire – the sovereignty – of the English over themselves. We are told, however, that because the English lack any identity apart from their empire over others, and have generated no nationalism separable from that empire, their post-imperial identity crisis is more severe than that of those in the post-colonial condition, and peculiarly likely to lead to their being melted down into Europe; though at the same time it is blamed for their resistance to that euthanasia. These essays have asked whether empire, meaning the exercise of sovereignty within the archipelago, has in fact disappeared with the emergence of the Irish republic as a second sovereign state. As to Britishness, they might also have asked whether the Unions have or have not set up a shared history in which the nations of the larger island will find it convenient or necessary to continue living.

Logically at least, the thesis that the English can imagine themselves only when they are ruling others is akin to the doctrine that the Self can be defined only in relation to an Other, either dominating or dominated as in the relation of master and slave. There is substance to this; it has been convincingly argued that the eighteenth-century British were invented in antagonism to the French, and even that the French of that era achieved national identity only by hating the English.[6] To add examples from the field of the present volume, the Declaration of Independence invents a 'British people' – who had yet to invent themselves – so that an 'American people' may be invented by separating themselves from the former. 'Europe' certainly defines the United States as its Other, but has not attempted the invention of a European 'people'; it would be too political and democratic to do so. Australian nationalism a century ago was built upon pretending to hate the English[7] and really hating the Chinese; and there are New Zealand literary intellectuals so far unable to imagine themselves in any way but as the result of 'decolonization' that each age cohort in turn dates their emancipation from English cultural models at a

---

[6] For the French as necessary Other to the British, see Colley, 1992; for the English as necessary Other to the French, Bell, 2001; a fearful symmetry. For a different approach to the formation of identity in the eighteenth century, see Kidd, 1999.

[7] Not all Australians were Irish.

time more recent than did their predecessors, thus perpetuating what they pretend to escape. The phenomena of alterity are very real, but there is the danger that they may be over-simplified. The world is full of Others; they are a heterogeneous lot, and our relationships with them are diverse (where they exist at all). We do not have to select any one of them – though it is true that we often do – for the paranoid and sadomasochist relation between inventions that the Other is used to designate; and the contention that the Self cannot exist without positing an Other of this kind is clearly intended to deconstruct the Self, which must be as false and fictitious as the Other it has defined itself by inventing. To warn us is one thing; to convict us, in advance of the act, is another.

There is reason to suspect that the ideological offensive against political associations capable of making, remembering, interpreting and questioning their own histories has reached the point where the individual as well as the collective self is targeted for demolition, and the concept of 'identity' is being used to deconstruct itself. There are forces in our world that do not wish us to say 'we' or act on that basis – since to do so might impede their selling us a new 'identity' tomorrow – and since saying 'we' and saying 'I' are intimately linked, they discourage the Self from believing it can manage its own experience, just as they discourage the society from believing it can manage its own history. These forces have succeeded in creating a world in which it is indeed difficult to act or reflect in the ways discouraged by their ideology, and we may have to experiment with new kinds of association and new kinds of history if we are to retain the autonomy which politics and history stimulate by challenging. Meanwhile, we had better mobilize all the resources we have and can retain, for seeing, remembering, criticizing and continuing the histories we may have had. These essays have endeavoured a strategy of conservation – to use a good word where 'conservatism' is accounted a bad – for the protection of history as an endangered environment; but they suppose its ecology to be as full of active forces, both creative and destructive, as it ever was. History in danger may be dangerously capable of continuing itself.

Bibliographies

A. PUBLICATIONS BY THE PRESENT AUTHOR, 1974–2004, IN FIELDS CONSTITUTING BRITISH HISTORY

Note: Footnote references have been by author and date. Works marked (B) in footnotes will be found in Bibliography B.

1974: 'British history: a plea for a new subject', *New Zealand Journal of History*, 8, 1, pp. 3–21 (Chapter 2 in present volume).

1975: Reprinted, with comments and a reply, *Journal of Modern History*, 47, 4, pp. 601–24.

1980: 'Hume and the American Revolution: dying thoughts of a North Briton', in David Fate Norton, Nicholas Capaldi and W. L. Robison (eds.), *McGill Hume Studies* (San Diego: Austin Hills Press), pp. 325–43.

1982: 'The limits and division of British history: in search of the unknown subject', *American Historical Review*, 87, 2, pp. 311–36.

1983a: 'Josiah Tucker on Burke, Locke and Price: a study in the varieties of eighteenth-century conservatism', in Marie Peters and others (eds.), *Essays Presented to Professor N. C. Phillips* (Christchurch: University of Canterbury), pp. 5–47.

1983b: 'Outgrowing the hucksters: review of Keith Sinclair, *A History of the University of Auckland*', *New Zealand Journal of History*, 17, 2, pp. 185–91.

1985: *Virtue, Commerce and History: essays on political thought and history, chiefly in the eighteenth century* (Cambridge: Cambridge University Press). (Items 1980 and 1983a reprinted.)

1987: 'States, republics and empires: the American Founding in early-modern perspective', *Social Science Quarterly*, 67, 4, pp. 703–23.

1988a: Reprinted in Terence Ball and J. G. A. Pocock (eds.), *Conceptual Change and the Constitution* (Lawrence, KS: University Press of Kansas), pp. 55–77.

1988b: 'The fourth English Civil War: dissolution, desertion and alternative histories in the Glorious Revolution', *Government and Society*, 23, 2, pp. 151–66.

1988c: *The Politics of Extent and the Problems of Freedom* (Colorado College Studies 25, Colorado Springs).

1991a: 'The significance of 1688: some reflections on Whig history', in Robert Beddard (ed.), *The Revolutions of 1688: the Andrew Browning Lectures, 1988* (Oxford: the Clarendon Press), pp. 271–92. (Chapter 8 in present volume.)

1991b: 'Deconstructing Europe', *London Review of Books*, 13, 19 December, pp. 6–10. (Chapter 15 in present volume.)

1991c: 'Sicilian origins of Homer's Odyssey: Samuel Butler and Lewis Greville Pocock: the discovery of islands' (*The Press*, Christchurch, 20 July 1991).

1992a: 'Die Dekonstruction Europas', *Lettre Internationale*, 16, pp. 15–21.

1992b: 'Tangata whenua and Enlightenment anthropology', *New Zealand Journal of History*, 26, 1, pp. 28–53. (Chapter 12 in present volume.)

1992c: *Law, Sovereignty and History in a Divided Culture: the case of New Zealand and the Treaty of Waitangi* (University of Lancaster; the Iredell Memorial Lecture). (Chapter 13 in present volume.)

1992d: 'History and sovereignty: the historiographic response to Europeanisation in two British cultures', *Journal of British Studies*, 31, 4, pp. 358–89.

1993a: 'La déconstruction de l'Europe', *Lettre Internationale*, 37, pp. 11–16.

1993b: 'Notes of an Occidental Tourist I, II', *Common Knowledge*, 2, 2, pp. 1–5, 8–18.

1993c: 'Vous autres européens – or inventing Europe', *Filozofski Vestnik/Acta Philosophica*, 14, 2 (Ljubljana: Slovenska Akademija Znanosti in Umetnosti), pp. 141–58.

1993d: 'Political thought in the English-speaking Atlantic, 1760–1790. Part I: the imperial crisis. Part II: Empire, revolution and an end of early modernity', in Pocock, 1993, pp. 246–320[B].

1994a: 'Deconstructing Europe', reprinted in *History of European Ideas*, 18, 3, pp. 329–46.

1994b: 'Two kingdoms and three histories? Political thought in British contexts', in Roger A. Mason (ed.), *Scots and Britons: Scottish political thought and the union of 1603* (Cambridge: Cambridge University Press), pp. 293–312. (Chapter 4 in present volume.)

1995a: 'Empire, state and confederation: the War of American Independence as a crisis in multiple monarchy', in John Robertson (ed.), *A Union for Empire: political thought and the union of 1707* (Cambridge: Cambridge University Press), pp. 318–48. (Chapter 9 in present volume.)

1995b: 'Conclusion: contingency, identity, sovereignty', in Alexander Grant and Keith J. Stringer (eds.), *Uniting the Kingdom? The making of British history* (London: Routledge), pp. 292–302. (Title source for Chapter 17 in present volume.)

1996a: 'Standing army and public credit: the institutions of Leviathan', in Dale Hoak and Mordechai Feingold (eds.), *The World of William and Mary: Anglo-Dutch perspectives on the Revolution of 1688–89* (Stanford, CA: Stanford University Press), pp. 87–103.

1996b: 'The Atlantic Archipelago and the War of the Three Kingdoms', in Brendan Bradshaw and John Morrill (eds.), *The British Problem, c. 1534–1707: state formation in the Atlantic Archipelago* (London: Macmillan), pp. 172–91. (Chapter 5 in present volume.)

1996c: *La Ricostruzione di un Impero: sovranità britannica e federalismo americano.* (Trans. Sergio Luzzatto. Macerata: Biblioteca del Laboratorio di Storia Costituzionale Antoine Barnave; Manduria, Bari, Roma: Piero Lacaita Editore.)

1996d: 'The making of new kinds of history', *New Zealand Books*, 6, 4, 25, pp. 15–17.

1997a: 'What do we mean by Europe?', *Wilson Quarterly*, winter 1997, pp. 12–29.

1997b: 'Removal from the wings', *London Review of Books*, 19, 6, pp. 12–13.

1997c: 'Deconstructing Europe', reprinted in Peter Gowan and Perry Anderson (eds.), *The Question of Europe* (London: Verso), pp. 297–317.

1997d: 'The historian as political actor in polity, society and academy', *Journal of Pacific Studies*, 20, pp. 89–112.

1997e: 'The making of new kinds of history', reprinted in Lauris Edmond, Harry Ricketts and Bill Sewell (eds.), *Under Review: a selection from New Zealand Books, 1991–97* (Lincoln, NZ: Lincoln University Press), pp. 158–63.

1998a: 'The politics of history: the subaltern and the subversive', *Journal of Political Philosophy*, 6, 3, 219–34.

1998b: 'Law, sovereignty and history in a divided culture: the case of New Zealand and the Treaty of Waitangi', reprinted in *McGill Law Journal*, 43, 3, pp. 481–506.

1999a: 'The Four Seas and the Four Oceans', in *Cool Britannia? What Britishness means to me* (Lurgan: Ulster Society Publications), pp. 158–63.

1999b: 'Nature and history, self and other: European perceptions of world history in the age of encounter', in Alex Calder, Jonathan Lamb and Bridget Orr (eds.), *Voyages and Beaches: Pacific Encounters, 1769–1840* (Honolulu: University of Hawai'i Press), pp. 25–44.

1999c: 'The New British History in Atlantic perspective: an Antipodean commentary', *American Historical Review*, 104, 2, pp. 490–500.

1999d: 'British history: the pursuit of the expanding subject', in Wilfred Prest (ed.), *British Studies into the 21st Century: perspectives and practices* (Melbourne: Australian Scholarly Publishing), pp. 58–72.

1999e: 'Thomas May and the narrative of civil war', in Derek Hirst and Richard Strier (eds.), *Writing and Political Engagement in Seventeenth-Century England* (Cambridge: Cambridge University Press), pp. 112–44.

2000a: 'The Third Kingdom in its history: an afterword', in Jane H. Ohlmeyer (ed.), *Political Thought in Seventeenth-Century Ireland* (Cambridge: Cambridge University Press), pp. 271–80. (Chapter 6 in present volume.)

2000b: 'Protestant Ireland: the view from a distance', in S. J. Connolly (ed.), *Political Ideas in Eighteenth-Century Ireland* (Dublin: the Four Courts Press), pp. 221–30.

2000c: 'Gaberlunzie's Return', *New Left Review*, 5, pp. 41–52.

2000d: 'The Union in British history', *Transactions of the Royal Historical Society*, 6th Series, 10, pp. 181–96. (Chapter 10 in the present volume.)

2000e: 'Waitangi as mystery of state: consequences of the ascription of federative capacity to the Maori', in Duncan Ivison, Paul Patton and Will Sanders (eds.), *Political Theory and the Rights of Indigenous Peoples* (Cambridge: Cambridge University Press), pp. 25–35.

2001a: 'Tangata whenua and Enlightenment anthropology', reprinted in Judith Binney (ed.), *The Shaping of History: essays from the New Zealand Journal of History* (Wellington: Bridget Williams Books), pp. 38–61.

2001b: 'The treaty between histories', in Andrew Sharp and Paul McHugh (eds.), *Histories, Power and Loss: uses of the past – a New Zealand commentary* (Wellington: Bridget Williams Books), pp. 75–96.

2002a: 'The uniqueness of Aotearoa', *Proceedings of the American Philosophical Society*, 145, 4, pp. 482–87.

2002b: 'Some Europes in their history', in Anthony Pagden (ed.), *The Idea of Europe: from antiquity to the European Union* (Cambridge: Cambridge University Press), pp. 55–71.

B. WORKS CITED OR REFERRED TO IN THE TEXT
AND FOOTNOTES

Armitage, David, 2000: *The Ideological Origins of the British Empire* (Cambridge: Cambridge University Press.)

    2004: *Greater Britain, 1516–1776: essays in Atlantic history* (Aldershot, UK, and Burlington, Vermont: Ashgate Variorum).

Armitage, David, Ohlmeyer, Jane, Landsman, Ned C., Gould, Eliga H., and Pocock, J. G. A., 1999: 'AHR Forum: the new British history in Atlantic perspective', *American Historical Review*, 104, 2, pp. 426–500.

Asch, Ronald G., 1993: (ed.) *Three Nations – A Common History? England, Scotland, Ireland and British History, c. 1600–1900* (Bochum: Brockmeyer).

Ashworth, M. G., 1974: *The Life and Fortunes of John Pocock of Cape Town, 1814–1876* (Cape Town: College Tutorial Press).

Bagehot, Walter, 1869: *Physics and Politics* (London).

Ballara, Angela, 1998: *Iwi: the dynamics of Maori tribal organisation from c. 1769 to c. 1945* (Wellington: Victoria University Press).

Barber, Benjamin, 1995: *Jihad v. McWorld* (New York: Times Books).

Bartlett, Robert, 1993: *The Making of Europe: conquest, colonization and cultural change, 950–1350* (Princeton: Princeton University Press).

Basho, Matsuo, 1966: *The Narrow Road to the Deep North and Other Travel Sketches* (trans. and ed. Nobuyuki Yuasa: Harmondsworth: Penguin Classics).

Bayly, C. A., 1989: *Imperial Meridian: the British Empire and the World, 1780–1880* (London: Longmans).

Beaglehole, J. C., 1937: *The University of New Zealand: a historical study* (Auckland and London: Whitcombe and Tombs and the Oxford University Press).

    1954: *The New Zealand Scholar* (Christchurch: Canterbury University College).

    1974: *The Life of Captain James Cook* (London and Stanford, CA: A. C. Black and Stanford University Press).

Beckett, J. C., 1966: *The Making of Modern Ireland* (New York: Knopf).

Beddard, R. A., 1991: (ed.) *The Revolutions of 1688: the Andrew Browning Lectures, 1988* (Oxford: the Clarendon Press).

Belich, James, 1996: *Making Peoples: a history of the New Zealanders from Polynesian settlement to the end of the nineteenth century* (Auckland: Penguin Books NZ).

2001: *Paradise Reforged: a history of the New Zealanders from the 1880s to the year 2000* (Auckland: Penguin Books NZ).

Bell, David A., 2001: *The Cult of the Nation in France: inventing nationalism, 1680–1800* (Cambridge, MA: Harvard University Press).

Bennett, Martyn, 1997: *The Civil Wars in Britain and Ireland, 1638–1651* (Oxford: Blackwell).

Berthoff, Rowland T., 1953: *British Immigrants in Industrial America* (Cambridge, MA: Harvard University Press).

Bindoff, S. T., 1950: *Tudor England* (Harmondsworth: Penguin Books).

Binney, Judith, 1995: *Redemption Songs: a life of Te Kooti Arikirangi Te Turuki* (Auckland and Wellington: Auckland University Press and Bridget Williams Books).

Binney, Judith, and Sorrenson, M. P. K., 1987: (eds.) *Essays in Honour of Sir Keith Sinclair: The New Zealand Journal of History*, 21, 2.

Bonnard, Georges A., 1969: (ed.) *Edward Gibbon: memoirs of my life* (New York: Funk and Wagnalls).

Bonwick, Colin, 1977: *English Radicals and the American Revolution* (Chapel Hill: University of North Carolina Press).

Bornholdt, Jenny, O'Brien, Gregory, and Williams, Mark, 1997: (eds.) *An Anthology of New Zealand Poetry in English* (Auckland: Oxford University Press).

Bradley, James E., 2001: 'The religious origins of radical politics in England, Scotland and Wales, 1662–1800', in Bradley and Van Kley, 2001, pp. 187–253.

Bradley, James E., and Van Kley, Dale K., 2001: (eds.) *Religion and Politics in Enlightenment Europe* (Notre Dame, IN: University of Notre Dame Press).

Bradshaw, Brendan, 1979: *The Irish Constitutional Revolution of the Sixteenth Century* (Cambridge: Cambridge University Press).

1996: 'The Tudor reformation and revolution in Wales and Ireland: the origin of the British problem', in Bradshaw and Morrill, 1996, pp. 39–65.

1998: 'The English Reformation and identity formation in England and Wales', in Bradshaw and Roberts, 1998, ch. 2.

Bradshaw, Brendan, and Morrill, John, 1996: (eds.) *The British Problem, c. 1634–1707: state formation in the Atlantic Archipelago* (London: Macmillan).

Bradshaw, Brendan, and Roberts, Peter, 1998: (eds.) *British Consciousness and Identity: the making of Britain, 1533–1707* (Cambridge: Cambridge University Press).

Brasch, Charles, 1948: *Disputed Ground: poems, 1939–1945* (Christchurch: the Caxton Press).

Brewer, John, 1989: *The Sinews of Power: war, money, and the English state, 1688–1783* (New York: Knopf).

Brockliss, Laurence, and Eastwood, David, 1997: (eds.) *A Union of Multiple Identities: the British Isles, c. 1750–c. 1850* (Manchester and New York: Manchester University Press and St. Martin's Press).

Brown, Keith, 1993: 'British history: a sceptical comment', in Asch, 1993, pp. 117–27.

Brown, Stewart J., 1997: (ed.) *William Robertson and the Expansion of Empire* (Cambridge: Cambridge University Press).

Buchanan, George, 1827: *The History of Scotland* (trans. James Aikman: Glasgow: University of Glasgow Press).

Burgess, Glenn, 1992: *The Politics of the Ancient Constitution: an introduction to English political thought, 1603–1642* (London: Macmillan).

  1996: *Absolute Monarchy and the Stuart Constitution* (New Haven: Yale University Press).

  1999: (ed.) *The New British History: founding a modern state, 1603–1715* (London: I. B. Tauris).

Burns, J. H., 1993: 'George Buchanan and the anti-monarchomachs', in Phillipson and Skinner, 1993, pp. 3–22.

  1996: *The True Law of Kingship: concepts of monarchy in early-modern Scotland* (Oxford: the Clarendon Press).

Burrow, John, 1966: *Evolution and Society: a study in Victorian social theory* (Cambridge: Cambridge University Press).

Butler, Samuel, 1923: *The Shrewsbury Edition of the Works of Samuel Butler* (London).

Butterfield, Herbert, 1949: *George III, Lord North and the People* (London: G. Bell and Son).

Campbell, James, 1995: 'The United Kingdom of England: the Anglo-Saxon achievement', in Grant and Stringer, 1995, ch. 3.

Canny, Nicholas, 2001: *Making Ireland British, 1580–1650* (Oxford: Oxford University Press).

Carte, Thomas, 1747: *A General History of England* (London).

Chrimes, S. B., 1949: (ed. and trans.) *Sir John Fortescue: De laudibus legum Anglie* (Cambridge: Cambridge University Press).

Claeys, Gregory, 1989: *Thomas Paine: social and political thought* (Boston, MA: Unwin Hyman).

Clark, J. C. D., 1985: *English Society, 1688–1832: ideology, social structure and political practice under the ancien régime* (Cambridge: Cambridge University Press).

  1993: *The Language of Liberty: political discourse and social dynamics in the Anglo-American world* (Cambridge: Cambridge University Press).

  2000: *English Society, 1660–1832: religion, ideology and politics under the ancien régime*. Second edition (Cambridge: Cambridge University Press).

Claydon, Tony, and McBride, Ian, 1998: (eds.) *Protestantism and National Identity: Britain and Ireland, c. 1650–c. 1850* (Cambridge: Cambridge University Press).

Cobbett, William, 1824: *The History of the Protestant Reformation in England and Ireland* (London).

Colley, Linda, 1982: *In Defiance of Oligarchy: the Tory party, 1714–1760* (Cambridge: Cambridge University Press).

  1992: *Britons: forging the nation, 1707–1837* (New Haven: Yale University Press).

Connolly, S. J., 1992: *Religion, Law and Power: the making of Protestant Ireland* (Oxford: Oxford University Press).

1999: (ed.) *Kingdoms United? Great Britain and Ireland since 1500: integration and diversity* (Dublin: the Four Courts Press).

2000: (ed.) *Political Ideas in Eighteenth-Century Ireland* (Dublin: the Four Courts Press).

Constable, Archibald, 1892: (ed. and trans.) *A History of Greater Britain as well England as Scotland, compiled from the ancient authorities of John Major, by name indeed a Scot, but by profession a theologian* (Edinburgh: Scottish History Society).

1982: *The Friends of Peace: anti-war liberalism in England, 1793–1815* (Cambridge: Cambridge University Press).

Cookson, J. E., 1997: *The British Armed Nation, 1793–1815* (Oxford: the Clarendon Press).

Cookson, John, and Dunstall, Graeme, 2000: (eds.) *Southern Capital: Christchurch: towards a biography* (Christchurch: University of Canterbury Press).

Cowan, Edward J., 1994: 'The political ideas of a covenanting leader: Archibald Campbell, marquis of Argyll, 1607–1661', in Mason, 1994, pp. 241–61.

Cowan, Ian B., 1991: 'Church and state reformed? the Revolution of 1688–89 in Scotland', in Israel, 1991, pp. 163–84.

Cruickshanks, Evelyn, 1982: (ed.) *Ideology and Conspiracy: aspects of Jacobitism, 1689–1759* (Edinburgh: John Donald).

Curnow, Allen, 1939: *Not in Narrow Seas* (Christchurch: the Caxton Press).

1941: *Island and Time* (Christchurch: the Caxton Press).

1943: *Sailing or Drowning* (Wellington: the Progressive Publishing Society).

1962: *A Small Room with Large Windows* (Auckland: Oxford University Press).

[anon., 1967]: *Whim Wham Land* (Auckland: Blackwood and Janet Paul).

1997: *Early Days Yet: new and collected poems, 1941–1997* (Auckland and London: Auckland University Press and Carcanet Press).

Daiches, David, 1964: *The Paradox of Scottish Culture* (London: Oxford University Press).

Davies, Norman, 1999: *The Isles* (London: Macmillan, and New York: Oxford University Press).

Davies, R. R., 2000: *The First English Empire: power and identities in the British Isles, 1093–1343* (Oxford: Oxford University Press).

Dawson, Jane, 1998: 'The Gaidhealtacht and the emergence of the Scottish Highlands', in Bradshaw and Roberts, 1998, pp. 259–300.

Devine, T. M., 1999: *The Scottish Nation* (London: Allen Lane, the Penguin Press).

Douglas, D. C., 1943: *English Scholars* (London: Jonathan Cape).

Dunn, John, 1990: (ed.) *The Economic Limits to Modern Politics* (Cambridge: Cambridge University Press).

Ellis, Steven G., and Barber, Sarah, 1995: *Conquest and Union: fashioning a British state, 1485–1725* (Harlow and New York: Longmans).

Fairburn, A. R. D., 1938: *Dominion* (Christchurch: the Caxton Press).

1966: *Collected Poems* (Christchurch: the Pegasus Press).

Ferguson, Arthur B., 1965: *The Articulate Citizen and the English Renaissance* (Durham: Duke University Press).

　　1979: *Clio Unbound: perception of the social and cultural past in Renaissance England* (Durham: Duke University Press).

Fideler, Paul A., and Mayer, T. F., 1992: (eds.) *Political Thought and the Tudor Commonwealth: deep structure, discourse and disguise* (London and New York: Routledge).

Fitzpatrick, Brendan, 1988: *Seventeenth-Century Ireland: the wars of religion* (Dublin and London: Gill and Macmillan).

Flanagan, Eugene, 1999: 'The anatomy of Jacobean Ireland: Captain Barnaby Rich, Sir John Davies, and the failure of reform', in Morgan, 1999, pp. 158–80.

Fletcher, Anthony, 1981: *The Outbreak of the English Civil War* (New York: New York University Press).

Ford, Alan, 1998: 'James Ussher and the creation of an Irish Protestant identity', in Bradshaw and Roberts, 1998, pp. 185–212.

　　1999: 'James Ussher and the Godly Prince in seventeenth-century Ireland', in Morgan, 1999, pp. 203–28.

Francis, Mark, 1992: *Governors and Settlers: images of authority in the British colonies, 1820–1860* (Cambridge: Cambridge University Press).

Fruchtman, Jack, 1994: *Thomas Paine: apostle of freedom* (New York: Four Walls Eight Windows).

Galloway, Bruce, 1986: *The Union of England and Scotland, 1603–1608* (Edinburgh: John Donald).

Gentles, Ian, 1992: *The New Model Army in England, Ireland and Scotland, 1645–1663* (Oxford: Blackwell).

Gibbons, Peter, 2003: 'The far side of the search for identity: reconsidering New Zealand history', *New Zealand Journal of History*, 37, 1, pp. 38–49.

Gillingham, John, 1995: 'Foundations of a disunited kingdom', in Grant and Stringer, 1995, ch. 4.

Glover, Denis, 1953: *Arawata Bill: a sequence of poems* (Christchurch: the Pegasus Press).

Goguet, Antoine-Yves, 1758: *De l'Origine des Loix, des Arts et des Sciences* (Paris).

Goodall, Jane, 1990: *Through a Window: my thirty years among the chimpanzees of Gombe* (Boston: Houghton Mifflin).

Gould, Eliga H., 1991: 'To strengthen the King's hands: dynastic legitimacy, militia reform and ideas of national unity in England, 1745–1760', *Historical Journal*, 34, 2, pp. 329–48.

　　1992: 'War, empire and the language of state formation: British political culture in the age of the American Revolution', Ph.D. dissertation, Johns Hopkins University.

　　2000: *The Persistence of Empire: British political culture in the age of the American Revolution* (Chapel Hill: University of North Carolina Press).

Grant, Alexander, and Stringer, Keith J., 1995: (eds.) *Uniting the Kingdom? The making of British history* (London and New York: Routledge).

Greenberg, Janelle, 2001: *The Radical Face of the Ancient Constitution: St. Edward's laws in early modern political thought* (Cambridge: Cambridge University Press).

Greene, Jack P., 1986, 1990: *Peripheries and Center: constitutional development in the extended polities of the British empire and the United States* (Athens, GA, and New York: University of Georgia Press and W. W. Norton).

Greig, J. Y. T., 1932: (ed.) *The Letters of David Hume* (Oxford: Oxford University Press).

Griffin, Patrick, 2001: *The People with No Name: Ireland's Ulster Scots, America's Scots-Irish, and the creation of a British Atlantic world, 1689–1764* (Princeton: Princeton University Press).

Griffith, Arthur, 1904: *The Resurrection of Hungary* (Dublin: Whelan and Son, repub. 1918).

Gunn, J. A. W., 1971: *Factions No More: attitudes to party and government in eighteenth-century England: extracts from contemporary sources* (London: Frank Cass).

Guy, J. A., 1993: 'The Henrician Age', in Pocock, 1993, pp. 13–46.

2004: *Queen of Scots: the true life of Mary Stuart* (Boston: Houghton Mifflin).

Haakonssen, Knud, 1996: (ed.) *Enlightenment and Religion: rational dissent in eighteenth-century Britain* (Cambridge: Cambridge University Press).

Hackshaw, Frederika, 1989: 'Nineteenth-century notions of aboriginal title and their influence on the interpretation of the Treaty of Waitangi', in Kawharu, 1989, pp. 92–120.

Hanham, H. J., 1969: *Scottish Nationalism* (London: Faber).

Harlow, Vincent T., 1952, 1964: *The Founding of the Second British Empire, 1763–1793.* Two volumes (London: Longmans).

Harris, Tim, 1997: 'Reluctant Revolutionaries? The Scots and the Revolution of 1688–89', in Nenner, 1997, pp. 97–120.

Head, Lyndsay, 2001: 'The pursuit of modernity in Maori society: the conceptual bases of citizenship in the early colonial period', in Sharp and McHugh, 2001, pp. 97–122.

Helgerson, Richard, 1992: *Forms of Nationhood: the Elizabethan writing of England* (Chicago: University of Chicago Press).

Hendrickson, David C., 2003: *Peace Pact: the lost world of the American founding* (Lawrence, KS: University of Kansas Press).

Henry, Robert, 1771–93: *The History of Great Britain ... written on a new plan* (London).

Hickford, Mark, 1999: 'Making "territorial rights of the natives": Britain and New Zealand', D.Phil. dissertation, Oxford University.

Hill, Jacqueline, 1995: 'Ireland without Union: Molyneux and his legacy', in Robertson, 1995, pp. 271–96.

Hoak, Dale, and Feingold, Mordechai, 1996: (eds.) *The World of William and Mary: Anglo-Dutch perspectives on the Revolution of 1688–89* (Stanford, CA: Stanford University Press).

Holcroft, M. A., 1940, 1946: *The Deepening Stream* (Christchurch: the Caxton Press).

1943: *The Waiting Hills* (Wellington: Progressive Publishing Society).

1946: *Encircling Seas* (Christchurch: the Caxton Press).

Holder, Marjorie, and Gee, Christina, 1980: (eds.) *John Thomas Pocock: the diary of a London schoolboy* (London: Camden History Society).

Holmes, Geoffrey, 1967: *British Politics in the Age of Anne* (London: Macmillan).

Hont, Istvan, 1990: 'Free trade and the economic limits to national politics: neo-Machiavellian political economy reconsidered', in Dunn, 1990, pp. 41–120.

1993: 'The rhapsody of public debt: David Hume and voluntary state bankruptcy', in Phillipson and Skinner, 1993, pp. 321–48.

Howe, K. R., 2003: *The Quest for Origins: who first discovered and settled New Zealand and the Pacific islands?* (Auckland: Penguin Books, NZ).

Hughes, Robert, 1993: *The Culture of Complaint: the fraying of America* (New York: Oxford University Press).

Hume, David, 1754–62: *The History of Great Britain* (in later volumes *England*: London).

Hutton, Ronald, 1985: *The Restoration: a political and religious history of England and Wales, 1658–1667* (Oxford: Oxford University Press).

Israel, Jonathan I., 1991: (ed.) *The Anglo-Dutch Moment: essays on the Glorious Revolution and its world impact* (Cambridge: Cambridge University Press).

1995: *The Dutch Republic: its rise, greatness and fall, 1477–1806* (Oxford: the Clarendon Press).

Jackson, Clare, 2003: *Restoration Scotland, 1660–1690: royalist politics, religion and ideas* (Woodbridge: the Boydell Press).

James, Mervyn, 1974: *Family, Lineage and Civil Society: a study of society, politics and mentality in the Durham region, 1500–1640* (Oxford: Oxford University Press).

1986: *Society, Politics and Culture: studies in early modern England* (Cambridge: Cambridge University Press).

Johnson, Robert C., *et al.*, 1997–78: *Commons Debates 1628*. Four volumes (New Haven: Yale University Press).

Jones, J. R., 1972: *The Revolution of 1688 in England* (New York: W. W. Norton).

1978: *Country and Court: England, 1658–1714* (Cambridge, MA: Harvard University Press).

Jones, Lawrence, 2003: *Picking up the Traces: the making of a New Zealand literary culture, 1932–1945* (Wellington: Victoria University Press).

Judson, Margaret, 1980: *From Tradition to Political Reality: a study of the ideas set forth in support of the Commonwealth government in England* (Hamden, CT: Archon Books).

Kantorowicz, E. H., 1957: *The King's Two Bodies: a study in medieval political theology* (Princeton: Princeton University Press).

Kawharu, I. H., 1989: *Waitangi: Maori and Pakeha perspectives on the Treaty of Waitangi* (Auckland: Oxford University Press).

Kearney, Hugh, 1989: *The British Isles: a history of four nations* (Cambridge: Cambridge University Press).

Kelley, Donald R., 1990: *The Human Measure: social thought in the western legal tradition* (Cambridge, MA: Harvard University Press).

Kelsey, Jane, 1994: 'Judicialisation of the Treaty of Waitangi: a subtle cultural repositioning', in *Australian Journal of Law and Society*, 10, pp. 131–63.

Kenyon, J. P., 1997: *Revolution Principles: the politics of party, 1688–1720* (Cambridge: Cambridge University Press).

Kenyon, J. P., and Ohlmeyer, Jane, 1998: (eds.) *The Civil Wars: a military history of England, Scotland and Ireland, 1638–1660* (Oxford: Oxford University Press).

Kidd, Colin, 1993: *Subverting Scotland's Past: Scottish Whig historians and the creation of an Anglo-British identity* (Cambridge: Cambridge University Press).

   1999: *British Identities before Nationalism: ethnicity and nationhood in the Atlantic world, 1600–1800* (Cambridge: Cambridge University Press).

Koebner, Richard, 1961: *Empire* (Cambridge: Cambridge University Press).

Kumar, Krishan, 2003: *The Making of English National Identity* (Cambridge: Cambridge University Press).

Laing, D., 1841–42: (ed.) *The Letters and Journal of Dr. Robert Baillie* (Edinburgh: the Bannatyne Club).

Landsman, Ned C., 1995: 'The legacy of British union for the North American colonies: provincial elites and the problem of imperial union', in Robertson, 1995, pp. 247–317.

Lawson, Philip, 1989: *The Imperial Challenge: Quebec and Britain in the age of the American Revolution* (Kingston and Montreal: the McGill-Queen's University Press).

Lenman, Bruce P., 1992: 'The poverty of political theory in the Scottish Revolution of 1688–90', in Schwoerer, 1992, pp. 244–59.

Levack, Brian P., 1987: *The Formation of the British State: England, Scotland and the Union, 1603–1707* (Oxford: the Clarendon Press).

Levinson, Joseph, 1965: *Confucian China and its Modern Fate*. Three volumes (Berkeley and Los Angeles: University of California Press).

Lewis, C. S., 1954: *English Literature in the Sixteenth Century excluding Drama* (Oxford: Oxford University Press).

Lieberman, David, 1990: *The Province of Legislation Determined* (Cambridge: Cambridge University Press).

Litchfield, R. Burr, 1989: (trans.) *Franco Venturi: the end of the old regime in Europe (1768–1776): the first crisis* (Princeton: Princeton University Press).

   1991: (trans.) *Franco Venturi: the end of the old regime in Europe (1776–1789)*. (2 volumes, Princeton: Princeton University Press).

Lowenthal, David, 1985: *The Past is a Foreign Country* (Cambridge: Cambridge University Press).

Macaulay, Thomas B., 1901: *Critical and Historical Essays* (Boston: Houghton Mifflin).

MacCraith, Mícheál, 1995: 'The Gaelic reaction to the Reformation', in Ellis and Barber, 1995, pp. 139–61.

Macfarlane, Alan, 1979: *The Origins of English Individualism* (Cambridge: Cambridge University Press).

MacInnes, Allan, 1995: 'Gaelic culture in seventeenth-century Scotland', in Ohlmeyer, 2000, pp. 191–200.

Mackay, Jessie, 1909: *Land of the Morning* (Christchurch: Whitcombe and Tombs).

Macpherson, C. B., 1967: *The Political Theory of Possessive Individualism* (Oxford: Oxford University Press).

Maine, Sir Henry, 1861: *Ancient Law* (London).

Mansergh, Nicholas, 1969: *The Commonwealth Experience* (Toronto: Toronto University Press).

Marshall, P. J., 1998: (ed.) *The Oxford History of the British Empire: the eighteenth century* (Oxford: Oxford University Press).

Mason, Roger A., 1994: (ed.) *Scots and Britons: Scottish political thought and the Union of 1603* (Cambridge: Cambridge University Press).

  1998: *Kingship and the Common Weal: political thought in Renaissance and Reformation Scotland* (East Linton: the Tuckwell Press).

Mathew, David, 1933: *The Celtic Peoples and Renaissance Europe* (London: Sheed and Ward).

McBride, Ian R., 1998: *Scripture Politics: Ulster Presbyterians and Irish radicalism in the late eighteenth century* (Oxford: Oxford University Press).

McGinnis, Paul J., and Williamson, Arthur H., 1995: (eds.) *George Buchanan: the political poetry* (Edinburgh: Scottish Historical Society).

  2002: (eds.) *The British Union: a critical edition and translation of David Hume of Godscroft's De Unione Insulae Britannicae* (London: Ashgate).

McHugh, Paul G., 1991: *The Maori Magna Carta: New Zealand law and the Treaty of Waitangi* (Auckland: Oxford University Press).

  2005: *Aboriginal Societies and the Common Law: a history of sovereignty, status and self-determination* (Oxford: Oxford University Press).

McLaren, A. N., 1999: *Political Culture in the Reign of Elizabeth I: queen and commonwealth, 1558–1585* (Cambridge: Cambridge University Press).

McNaught, Kenneth, 1969: *The Pelican History of Canada* (Harmondsworth: Penguin Books).

Meek, Ronald, 1976: *Social Science and the Ignoble Savage* (Cambridge: Cambridge University Press).

Mendle, Michael, 2001: (ed.) *The Putney Debates of 1647: the army, the Levellers and the English state* (Cambridge: Cambridge University Press).

Millar, John, 1787–1803: *A Historical View of the English Constitution* (London).

Miller, Eugene F., 1985: (ed.) *David Hume: essays moral, political and literary* (Indianapolis: Liberty Classics).

Minuti, Rolando, 1978: 'Proprietà della terra e despotismo orientale. Aspetti di un dibattito sull'India nella seconda metà del Settecento', *Materiali per una storia della cultura giuridica*, pp. 29–176.

Moloney, Pat, 2001: 'Savagery and civilisation: early Victorian notions', *New Zealand Journal of History*, 25, 2, pp. 153–76.

Molyneux, William, 1698: *The Case of Ireland being Bound by Acts of Parliament in England* (Dublin).

Monod, Paul, 1989: *Jacobitism and the English People, 1688–1788* (Cambridge: Cambridge University Press).

Morgan, Hiram, 1991: 'Mid-Atlantic Blues', *Irish Review*, winter 1991, pp. 50–5.

1993: *Tyrone's Rebellion: the outbreak of the Nine Years War in Tudor Ireland* (Woodbridge: the Boydell Press).

1999: (ed.) *Political Ideology in Ireland, 1541–1641* (Dublin: the Four Courts Press).

Morrill, John, 1993: *The Nature of the English Revolution* (London: Longmans).

1996: 'The British problem, c. 1534–1707', in Bradshaw and Morrill, 1996, pp. 1–38.

Muldoon, James, 1994: *The Americas in the Spanish World Order: the justification for conquest in the seventeenth century* (Philadelphia: University of Pennsylvania Press).

Murdoch, Alexander, 1998: *British History, 1660–1833: national identity and local cultures* (Houndmills and New York: Macmillan and St. Martin's Press).

Murray, Stuart, 1998: *Never a Soul at Home: New Zealand literary nationalism and the 1930s* (Wellington: Victoria University Press).

Muthu, Sankar, 2003: *Enlightenment against Empire* (Princeton: Princeton University Press).

Nairn, Tom, 1977: *The Breakup of Britain* (London: Verso).

1998: *After Britain: New Labour and the return of Scotland* (London: Granta).

Nenner, Howard, 1997: (ed.) *Politics and the Political Imagination in Later Stuart Britain: essays presented to Lois Green Schwoerer* (Rochester: University of Rochester Press).

Nicholls, Mark, 1999: *A History of the Modern British Isles, 1529–1603: the Two Kingdoms* (Oxford: Blackwell).

Ogilvie, Gordon, 1999: *Denis Glover: his life* (Auckland: Godwit Books, Random House NZ).

Ohlmeyer, Jane H., 1993: *Civil War and Restoration in the Three Stuart Kingdoms: the career of Randal MacDonnell, marquis of Antrim, 1609–1683* (Cambridge: Cambridge University Press).

1995: (ed.) *Ireland from Independence to Occupation, 1641–1666* (Cambridge: Cambridge University Press).

2000: (ed.) *Political Thought in Seventeenth-Century Ireland: kingdom or colony* (Cambridge: Cambridge University Press).

Ohmori, Yuhtaro, 1988: 'The artillery of Mr. Locke: the uses of Locke's Second Treatise in pre-revolutionary America', Ph.D. dissertation, Johns Hopkins University.

Oliver, W. H., 2002: *Looking for the Phoenix: a memoir* (Wellington: Bridget Williams Books).

Onuf, Peter S., 1983: *The Origins of the Federal Republic: jurisdictional controversies in the United States, 1775–1787* (Philadelphia: University of Pennsylvania Press).

O'Regan, Tipene, 1992: 'Old myths and new politics: some contemporary uses of traditional history', *New Zealand Journal of History*, 26, 1, pp. 5–27.

Owen, J. B., 1957: *The Rise of the Pelhams* (London: Methuen).

Pagden, Anthony, 1982: *The Fall of Natural Man: the American Indian and the origins of comparative ethnology* (Cambridge: Cambridge University Press).

1990: *Spanish Imperialism and the Political Imagination: studies in European and Spanish-American social and political theory, 1513–1830* (New Haven: Yale University Press).

1995: *Lords of All the World: ideologies of empire in Spain, Britain, and France, c. 1500–1800* (New Haven: Yale University Press).

Palumbo, Rina, 2001: 'The boundaries of empire: writing, authority and the feudal imaginary in forging the British Atlantic community, 1580–1670', Ph.D. dissertation, Johns Hopkins University.

Patterson, W. B., 1997: *King James VI and I and the Reunion of Christendom* (Cambridge: Cambridge University Press).

Paul, G. M., 1896–1911: (ed.) *The Diary of Archibald Johnston of Wariston, 1632–39* (Edinburgh: Scottish Historical Society).

Pawlisch, Hans, 1985: *Sir John Davies and the Conquest of Ireland: a study in legal imperialism* (Cambridge: Cambridge University Press).

Peck, Linda Levy, 1991: (ed.) *The Mental World of the Jacobean Court* (Cambridge: Cambridge University Press).

Penovich, Katherine R., 1995: 'From Revolution principles to Union: Defoe's intervention in the Scottish debate', in Robertson, 1995, pp. 228–42.

Peters, Marie C., 1980: *Pitt and Popularity: the patriot minister and London opinion during the Seven Years War* (Oxford: the Clarendon Press).

Phillips, J. E., 1948–9: 'George Buchanan and the Sidney circle', *Huntington Library Quarterly*, 12, pp. 23–55.

Phillips, N. C., 1961: *Yorkshire and English National Politics, 1783–84* (Christchurch: University of Canterbury Publications).

Phillipson, Nicholas, and Skinner, Quentin, 1993: (eds.) *Political Discourse in Early Modern Britain* (Cambridge: Cambridge University Press).

Plumb, J. H., 1967: *The Growth of Political Stability in England, 1675–1725* (London: Macmillan).

1970: *The Death of the Past* (Boston: Houghton Mifflin).

Pocock, J. G. A., 1957, 1987: *The Ancient Constitution and the Feudal Law: a study of English political thought in the seventeenth century* (Cambridge: Cambridge University Press). Reprinted with a retrospect, 1987.

1975, 2003: *The Machiavellian Moment: Florentine political thought and the Atlantic republican tradition* (Princeton: Princeton University Press). New edition with an afterword, 2003.

1985: 'Clergy and commerce: the conservative Enlightenment in England', in R. Ajello and others (eds.), *L'Età dei Lumi: studi storici nel settecento europeo in onore di Franco Venturi* (Naples: Jovene, 1985) I, pp. 523–62.

1988: 'Religious freedom and the desacralization of politics: from the English civil wars to the Virginia Statute', in M. D. Peterson and R. C. Vaughan (eds.), *The Virginia Statute of Religious Freedom: its evolution and consequences in American history* (Cambridge: Cambridge University Press, 1988), pp. 45–73.

1993: (ed., with Gordon J. Schochet and Lois G. Schwoerer) *The Varieties of British Political Thought, 1500–1800* (Cambridge: Cambridge University Press).

1995: 'Within the margins: the definitions of orthodoxy', in Roger D. Lund, (ed.), *The Margins of Orthodoxy: heterodox writing and cultural response* (Cambridge: Cambridge university Press, 1996), pp. 33–53.

1999: *Barbarism and Religion*, vol. I: *The Enlightenments of Edward Gibbon*; vol. II: *Narratives of Civil Government* (Cambridge: Cambridge University Press).

2005: *Barbarism and Religion*: vol. IV: *Barbarians, Savages and Empires* (Cambridge: Cambridge University Press).

Pocock, Tom, 1996: *Travels of a London Schoolboy, 1826–1830* (Chichester: Historical Publications Limited).

Pole, J. R., 1966: *Political Representation in England and the Origins of the American Republic* (London and New York: Macmillan and St. Martin's Press).

Popper, Karl, 1945: *The Open Society and its Enemies* (London: Routledge).

Powell, David, 2002: *Nationhood and Identity: the British state since 1800* (London: I. B. Tauris).

Pownall, Thomas, 1971: *The Administration of the Colonies* (4th edition, London, 1768, reprinted, New York: Da Capo Press).

Reid, John Phillip, 1981: *In Defiance of the Law: the standing army controversy, the two constitutions, and the coming of the American Revolution* (Chapel Hill: University of North Carolina Press).

Robbins, Keith, 1988: *Nineteenth-Century Britain: integration and diversity* (Oxford: Oxford University Press).

1998: *Great Britain: ideas, institutions and the idea of Britishness* (London: Longmans).

Robertson, John, 1986: *The Scottish Enlightenment and the Militia Issue* (Edinburgh: John Donald).

1993: 'Universal monarchy and the liberties of Europe: David Hume's critique of an English Whig doctrine', in Phillipson and Skinner, 1993, pp. 349–73.

1995: (ed.) *A Union for Empire: political thought and the Union of 1707* (Cambridge: Cambridge University Press).

Robertson, William, 1759: *The History of Scotland during the Reigns of Queen Mary and James VI* (London).

1824: *The Works of William Robertson, DD* (Nine volumes (London)).

Romney, Paul, 2000: *Getting It Wrong: how Canadians forgot their past and imperilled confederation* (Toronto: University of Toronto Press).

Rupp, Gordon, 1986: *Religion in England, 1688–1791* (Oxford: Oxford University Press).

Russell, Conrad, 1990: *The Causes of the English Civil War* (Oxford: Oxford University Press).

1991a: *The Fall of the Stuart Monarchies* (Oxford: Oxford University Press).

1991b: *Unrevolutionary England* (London: Hambledon Press).

Sainsbury, John, 1987: *Disaffected Patriots: London supporters of revolutionary America, 1769–1782* (Kingston and Montreal: McGill-Queen's University Press).

Samuel, Raphael, 1998: *Island Stories: unravelling Britain* (London: Verso).

Schwoerer, Lois G., 1981: *The Declaration of Rights, 1689* (Baltimore: Johns Hopkins University Press).

  1992: (ed.) *The Revolution of 1688–89: changing perspectives* (Cambridge: Cambridge University Press).

Scott, Jonathan, 1988: 'Radicalism and Restoration: the shape of the Stuart experience', *Historical Journal*, 31, 2, pp. 463–7.

  1989: *Algernon Sidney and the English Republic, 1623–1677* (Cambridge: Cambridge University Press).

  1991: *Algernon Sidney and the Restoration Crisis, 1677–1683* (Cambridge: Cambridge University Press).

  2000: *England's Troubles: seventeenth-century English political instability in European context* (Cambridge: Cambridge University Press).

Sharp, Andrew, 1990, 1997: *Justice and the Maori: the philosophy and practice of Maori claims in New Zealand since the 1970s* (Auckland: Oxford University Press).

  1992: 'Representing *Justice and the Maori*: or why it ought not to be construed as a post-modernist text', in *Political Theory Newsletter* (Canberra), 6, p. 27.

Sharp, Andrew, and McHugh, Paul, 2001: (eds.) *Histories, Power and Loss: uses of the past – a New Zealand commentary* (Wellington: Bridget Williams Books).

Sher, Richard B., 1985: *Church and University in the Scottish Enlightenment: the moderate literati of Edinburgh* (Princeton: Princeton University Press).

Sher, Richard B. and Smitten, Jeffrey, 1990: (eds.) *Scotland and America in the Age of the Enlightenment* (Princeton: Princeton University Press).

Simms, J. G., 1982: (ed. P. H. Kelly) *William Molyneux of Dublin: a life of the seventeenth-century political writer and scientist* (Blackrock: Irish Academic Press).

Sinclair, Keith, 1961: (ed.) *Distance Looks Our Way: the effects of remoteness on New Zealand* (Auckland: Oxford University Press).

  1986: *A Destiny Apart: New Zealand's search for national identity* (Wellington: Allen and Unwin, Port Nicholson Press).

  1993: *Halfway round the Harbour: an autobiography* (Auckland: Penguin Books NZ).

Smith, David L., 1998: *A History of the Modern British Isles, 1603–1707: the double crown* (Oxford: Blackwell).

Smith, Hilda L., 1998: *Women Writers and the Early Modern British Political Tradition* (Cambridge: Cambridge University Press).

Smyth, Jim, 2001: *The Making of the United Kingdom, 1660–1800* (Harlow and London: Pearson Education Ltd).

Speck, W. A., 1988: *Reluctant Revolutionaries: Englishmen and the Revolution of 1688* (Oxford: Oxford University Press).

Springborg, Patricia M. 1990: *Royal Persons: patriarchal monarchy and the feminine principle* (London: Unwin Hyman).

  1992: *Western Republicanism and the Oriental Prince* (Cambridge: Polity Press).

Spurr, John, 1992: *The Restoration of the Church of England, 1646–1689* (New Haven: Yale University Press).

Stevenson, David, 1980: *Alasdair MacColla and the Highland Problem in the Seventeenth Century* (Edinburgh: John Donald).

Stoyle, Mark, 1994: *Loyalty and Locality: popular allegiance in Devon during the English Civil War* (Exeter: University of Exeter Press).

    1996: 'Pagans or paragons: images of the Cornish during the English Civil War', *English Historical Review*, 111, 1, pp. 307–23.

    1998: 'The Last Refuge of a Scoundrel: Sir Richard Grenville and Cornish particularism, 1644–46', *Historical Research*, 71, 174, pp. 31–51.

Sturm, Terry, 1991: (ed.) *The Oxford History of English Literature* (Auckland: Oxford University Press).

Sullivan, Robert, 1999: *Star Waka* (Auckland: Auckland University Press).

Tau, Te Maire, 2000: 'Ngai Tahu and the Canterbury Landscape – a broad view', in Cookson and Dunstall, 2000, pp. 41–59.

    2001a: '*Matauranga Maori* as an epistemology', in Sharp and McHugh, 2001, pp. 61–74.

    2001b: 'The death of knowledge: ghosts on the plains', *New Zealand Journal of History*, 35, 2, pp. 131–52.

    2003: *Nga Pikituroa o Ngai Tahu/The Oral Traditions of Ngai Tahu* (Dunedin: University of Otago Press).

Taylor, A. J. P., 1946, 1962: *The Course of German History* (repr. New York: Capricorn Press).

    1965: *The Oxford History of England: England 1914–1945* (Oxford: Oxford University Press).

Thomas, W. S. K., 1988: *Stuart Wales* (Llandysul: the Gomer Press).

Thornton, A. P., 1966: *The Habit of Authority* (Toronto: Toronto University Press).

Tolstaya, Tatyana, 1991: 'In cannibalistic times', *New York Review of Books*, 38, 7, pp. 3–5.

Tompson, Richard S., 1986: *The Atlantic Archipelago: a political history of the British Isles* (Lewiston and Queenston: the Edwin Mellon Press).

Trevor-Roper, H. R., 1966: 'George Buchanan and the Ancient Scottish Constitution', *English Historical Review*, supplement 3.

Tuck, Richard, 1980: *Natural Rights Theories: their origin and development* (Cambridge: Cambridge University Press).

Tucker, Josiah, 1781: *A Treatise concerning Civil Government* (London; reprinted, New York, 1967: Augustus M. Kelley).

Tucker, Robert W., and Hendrickson, David C., 1982: *The Fall of the First British Empire: origins of the War of American Independence* (Baltimore: Johns Hopkins University Press).

Tully, James, 1993: *An Approach to Political Philosophy: John Locke in contexts* (Cambridge: Cambridge University Press).

    1995: *Strange Multiplicity: constitutionalism in an age of diversity* (Cambridge: Cambridge University Press).

Venturi, Franco, 1979: *Settecento Riformatore, II: la prima crisi dell'Antico Regime (1768–1776)*. Two volumes (Turin: Einaudi).

1984: *Settecento Riformatore, III: la caduta dell'Antico Regime (1776–1789).* Two volumes (Turin: Einaudi).

Walker, Ranginui, 1990: *Ka Whawhai Tonu Matou/Struggle without End* (Auckland: Penguin Books NZ).

Wallace, John M., 1968: *Destiny His Choice: the loyalism of Andrew Marvell* (Cambridge: Cambridge University Press).

Watson, Murray, 2003: *Being English in Scotland* (Edinburgh: Edinburgh University Press).

Webber, Jeremy, 1997: *Reimagining Canada: language, culture, community and the Canadian constitution* (Kingston and Montreal: McGill-Queen's University Press).

Whelan, Frederick G., 1996: *Edmund Burke and India: political morality and empire* (Pittsburgh: University of Pittsburgh Press).

Williams, Haare, n.d.: *Karanga* (Coromandel, NZ: the Coromandel Press).

Williamson, Arthur H., 1979: *Scottish National Consciousness in the Age of James VI: the apocalypse, the Union, and the shaping of Scotland's public culture* (Edinburgh: John Donald).

1994: 'Number and national consciousness: the Edinburgh mathematicians and Scottish public culture at the union of the crowns', in Mason, 1994, pp. 187–212.

Winks, Robin W., 1999: (ed.) *The Oxford History of the British Empire: historiography* (Oxford: Oxford University Press).

Womersley, David, 1994: (ed.) *Edward Gibbon: The History of the Decline and Fall of the Roman Empire* Three volumes (London: Allen Lane, the Penguin Press).

Wormald, Jenny, 1980: 'Bloodfeud, kindred and government in early modern Scotland', *Past and Present*, 87, pp. 54–97.

1988: *Mary Queen of Scots: a study in failure* (London: Hamlyn).

1992: 'The creation of Britain: multiple kingdoms or core and colonies?', *Transactions of the Royal Historical Society*, 6th series, 2, pp. 175–94.

'James VI, James I and the identity of Britain', in Bradshaw and Morrill, 1996, pp. 148–71.

Young, B. W., 1998: *Religion and Enlightenment in Eighteenth-Century England: theological debate from Locke to Burke* (Oxford: the Clarendon Press).

Zagorin, Perez, 1954: *A History of Political Thought in the English Revolution* (London: Routledge Kegan Paul).

Index